DATE DUE

MY 31 '96			

D0872041

The Aldo Moro Murder Case

Aldo Moro at the peak of his power in the mid-1970s.

The Aldo Moro Murder Case

Richard Drake

Harvard University Press

Cambridge, Massachusetts
London, England
1995

For Rick, my partner

on the fishing waters

of Western Montana

All photographs courtesy of the archive of *La Repubblica*.

Library of Congress Cataloging-in-Publication Data

Drake, Richard, 1942–
    The Aldo Moro murder case / Richard Drake.
       p. cm.
    Includes index.
    ISBN 0-674-01481-2 (alk. paper)
    1. Moro, Aldo, 1916–1978—Assassination. 2. Red Brigades. 3. Red
Brigades Trial, Turin, Italy, 1978. 4. Italy—Politics and
government—1976– 5. Terrorism—Italy. I. Title.
DG579.M63D73 1995
    364.1′524′0945—dc20   95-11343
                        CIP

Contents

Preface   vi

1. Aldo Moro: Symbol for an Age   1

2. The Italian Legal System   36

3. The First Trial: Phase One   43

4. The First Trial: Phase Two   63

5. The Moro Commission Reports   82

6. The P2 Commission Reports   99

7. The Second Trial   116

8. Moro Ter: The First Year   136

9. The *Metropoli* Trial   157

10. Moro Ter: The Second Year   184

11. Moro Quater: To Tangentopoli   206

12. Moro Quater, Tangentopoli, and Giulio Andreotti   224

Conclusion   249

Glossary   265

Notes   271

Acknowledgments   303

Index   307

Illustrations follow p. 115

Preface

Aldo Moro was assassinated more than fifteen years ago, and the murder has been a staple in the Italian news ever since. Given Moro's celebrity status as the country's supreme political figure, and the horrifying circumstances of his death, the case contained irresistible elements for the media, as it did for most Italians. Sensationalism was part of it, but from a deeper level of significance the story raised agonizing issues about the country's manifold and longstanding problems with ideological extremism and political violence. To this day news developments have continued to keep the Aldo Moro murder case in the foreground of Italian civic life.

I cannot hope to end all the controversy about this highly charged and acrimoniously disputed murder case. My goal is more modest: I hope to clarify the case as much as the historical record will allow. I reach conclusions that are firmly anchored in all of the pertinent archival documents and in numerous other primary sources. The various trials and parliamentary inquiries serve as the main framework of the book. Through them we have come to know what in fact we do know about the kidnapping and murder of Aldo Moro.

In discussing the trials I did not settle for an analysis of the final sentences. Instead, I went through all the judicial investigation findings, the courtroom testimony, and the final sentences for each trial, in order to present a full factual account of the case. Such a research effort does not lend itself to facile oversimplifications. My aim is to lead the reader to a consideration of the judicial and political processes engendered by this singularly traumatic event in the history of the Italian Republic. These processes, in their aggregate, afford us the best historical insights into that tragedy.

On the basis of these and related sources I give the cultural and political context of the Moro murder case: the Marxist-Leninist tradition that produced the Red Brigades and various other like-minded groups and sympathizers. That is why all of the trials and parliamentary investigations, even when they ended, as some of them did, in little or no progress toward a resolution of the many mysteries in the Moro case, are important in the historical analysis of its background, particularly for the motives of the perpetrators and their supporters.

Moro's life and career make it clear why these terrorists would have wanted to strike at him. Therefore, I begin with a biographical portrait of Moro. After emerging around 1960 as the dominant figure in his party, the Christian Democrats, he became conspicuous for his willingness to compromise with the left, first with the Socialists and then with the Communists. Gradually, Moro's image evolved as that of the great compromiser in Italian politics, a role that infuriated his many enemies among anticommunists and revolutionary communists alike, both at home and abroad, and ultimately cost him his life.

Because Moro was a leading architect of the Christian Democratic establishment, his story will reveal much about its inner workings. Such information is especially valuable today in understanding why that establishment has disintegrated. For the past two years there has been a public uproar in Italy over the astonishing volume of violations involving the financing of political parties. This took the form of kickbacks for public works projects and spread systematic corruption in the many state companies under the control of politicians. What is happening in scandal-ridden Italy today seemingly confirms the worst that has ever been said and written about the Christian Democrats. Moro himself had presentiments about scandals of this kind, and his comments about them illuminate the country's current predicament.

The Moro case, trailing diverse and still extant conspiracy interpretations of nearly every aspect of the murder, is much more than a parochial matter. It has called into question the role of the United States government, and of other foreign governments, in Italy's domestic affairs. From an analysis of the facts and conjectures much can be learned about the true nature of international influences in Italy, and how the Italians themselves perceive such external involvements in the politics of their nation.

Moreover, terrorism is a worldwide problem. This particular terrorist act reveals, in unmatched detail, the mentality, the tactics, and the strategy of the Red Brigades, an emblematic group of Marxist-Leninist fanatics with ties of sympathy and, in some instances, with logistical ties to similar groups in other countries. Italy may be unique among European countries in the degree to which it has suffered from left-wing terrorism—and, indeed, the Moro murder case sheds light on the drastic and widespread forms that ideological extremism could take, until quite recently, even in an advanced industrial society—but the Red Army Faction, Action Directe, and the Fighting Communist Cells posed threats of the same basic type in Germany, France, and Belgium. The links between such groups, including the Red Brigades, with Middle Eastern terrorists are also part of this book's story. Except in Peru, where the experience of Sendero Luminoso illustrates the continuing appeal of Marxist-Leninist revolution in underdeveloped societies, left-wing terrorism appears to be a rapidly declining threat. Nevertheless, as the phenomenon of resurgent fascism has shown in contemporary Europe, extremist ideologies that we have congratulated ourselves on burying can come back from the dead. A useful function of history is to help us guard against such visitations.

The United States has not been free of left-wing terrorism. The 1960s and 1970s saw the Weather Underground and kindred groups aspire to destroy the capitalist establishment through revolutionary violence. The futility of their efforts makes an almost complete contrast with the long-term destructiveness of the Red Brigades. This particular form of terrorist violence has not been a serious problem for Americans, but some useful historical lessons of a comparative nature can be drawn from an analysis of why Red Brigadism succeeded for as long as it did and why it, too, ultimately failed. The Italian experience, with its deep historic traditions of ideologically motivated violence, will make it clearer why the United States got away very cheaply from its brief and highly atypical encounter with left-wing terrorism.

Americans have been less fortunate with international and domestic right-wing terrorism, as the recent bombings at the World Trade Center in New York City (26 February 1993) and at the Federal Building in Oklahoma City (19 April 1995) demonstrate. Both of these terrible episodes were historic firsts, however, about which it is impossible as yet to generalize or to make even the most tentative and carefully hedged predictions. While more of the facts are known for the first bombing than for the second, speculating about the American prospects of either form of terrorism would be mainly guesswork.

Looking back on the left-wing terrorist violence of the 1960s and 1970s in America—for which the historical record is substantially complete—it is clear that for the fitful momentum it did create, the Weather Underground depended almost entirely on a tragic event in American history, the Vietnam War and, more accurately, the selective service system in force then. With the end of the draft, this momentum came to a full stop and then disappeared. Apart from the war-caused disorientation of a generation, American radicals had a comparatively anemic revolutionary culture to nurture them. In Italy, by contrast, the radicalism of the late 1960s and early 1970s was a product of forces long integral to the country's history. Red Brigadism, unlike the Weather Underground, could count on more than a mere policy of government for its vitality. The Italian terrorists articulated and acted upon revolutionary beliefs that were astonishingly widespread. How many Italians believed in a Marxist-Leninist revolution, and how fervent that faith was, are two of the most striking features of the historical record in the Aldo Moro murder case.

Finally, this case is also the story of a man, his killers, and the government leaders who did not rescue him. We are uneasy today about using the term "great man," but if such a figure, in Jakob Burckhardt's phrase, is the fully reflected image of his age and country, then Moro was one. As such, the poignant universality of his destruction and death through a conflict with overpowering forces is reminiscent of a classical Greek theme about the vulnerability and pathos in the human condition. I seek to tell the story of how the Italian people have come to terms with this tragedy.

1

Aldo Moro

Symbol for an Age

Aldo Moro once told a fellow politician that he had wanted nothing more than the life of a teacher—and some part-time work as a political journalist on the side. His life was just the reverse: politics consumed him almost completely, and teaching, which had been his original vocation, became a sideline, albeit one he always loved. He complained profusely to family and friends about the demands of politics. Although we cannot be sure how much of his complaint was genuine, this shy and intensely private man often looked uncomfortable in public. It certainly seemed that he would have preferred to be closeted with his books away from the hubbub of politics. Italy, as Moro remarked many times, was a badly fragmented and turbulent society, one almost impossible to govern. He often felt frustrated and frequently yielded to moodiness on the subject of politics. Yet he could not have become the foremost political figure in Italy during the 1960s and 1970s without some aptitude and inclination for the job.

Certainly one of Moro's great accomplishments—and many in Italy thought it absolutely his greatest—was the one he prepared to savor on the morning of 16 March 1978. He was then sixty-one years old and president of the Christian Democratic party, a ceremonial post. Behind the scenes, though, he had been the chief architect of a new government with a radically novel feature: Communists would be supporting their traditional enemies, the Christian Democrats. This government was to be presented formally in Parliament at 10 A.M. that day. People did not fully understand what the new arrangement—the "historic compromise"—would mean in practice, or what it would produce. They did know that only Moro, now in full vigor as a political leader, could have secured the necessary assent for this extremely controversial proposal. The Cold War still defined Italian politics. His adversaries in Rome and his critics in Washington viewed the historic compromise as a shocking abjuration of a cardinal dogma in the West's Cold War credo: at all costs to keep Italy's enormous Communist party out of the government. The historic compromise did not provide for that party's immediate entry into the government, but anticommunists at home and abroad accused Moro of working toward that end by becoming a Trojan horse for communism.

At about 9 A.M. Moro set out with his five-man security guard on the short drive to Parliament, traveling in two cars. On their way, they stopped briefly at a church in the prosperous residential neighborhood where he lived, on the outskirts of Rome. Moro carried an assortment of newspapers and student compositions; this was his unusual kind of reading on the morning drive into the city. On this particular morning the normal routine ended abruptly when his driver could not avoid hitting a car in front of him. The accident was nothing more than a bent fender. Moro might have looked up from his reading to see what had gone wrong, but at that instant one of his bodyguards turned around in the front seat and shoved him down hard. He could have seen little of the ensuing barrage of gunfire that struck both vehicles. When the shooting stopped, his five guards were dead or dying. Badly bruised, Moro was lifted out of the back seat and taken to another vehicle. He then disappeared with his kidnappers, never to be seen alive again.

Many years would pass before judicial authorities in Rome could even begin to agree on the circumstances of Moro's kidnapping and murder, but people immediately understood that this act of terror had ended an epoch in Italian politics. As the top man in the ruling Christian Democratic party, Moro embodied Italy's peculiarly religious politics, its values as well as its practices. Both his enemies and his friends perceived him as the highest or perhaps the most complete representative of the Catholic political tradition. Subsequent court testimony revealed that this was also the perception of his revolutionary left-wing kidnappers, the Red Brigades, and the reason he was a target of supreme importance. Moro's death had everything to do with his image as the consummate Christian Democratic politician. The way he came to acquire this image helps to explain what happened to him in 1978 and what has occurred since in the quest for justice in the murder case, which continues seventeen years after his death.

Born on 23 September 1916 in Maglie, Lecce, Moro grew up in a middle-class home. Maglie, a lovely town of about ten thousand people and noted for its furniture craftsmen, lay nestled in an agricultural region that produced wine, oil, and cereals.[1] The Moros had long been a family of teachers, doctors, and magistrates. Aldo's parents had a modest income, and being sober, thrifty, hard-working, cultivated people, they found fulfillment in family, study, professional exertion, and a strong ethical conception of life. On the question of religion there was no family consensus. His school inspector father, Renato, remained indifferent toward the Church, but his mother's religious devotion permeated the Moro family home. Before her marriage, Fida Stinchi had been a kindergarten teacher and, quite remarkably for a woman of that time and place, a writer whose articles had appeared in national magazines and newspapers. She was highly intelligent, well read, curious about the world, ambitious for her five children, and unquestionably the dominant personality of Aldo Moro's youth. Mrs. Moro studied the Bible assiduously, with special attention to the Epistles of Paul, and believed that Christianity meant a life of service to others. This was the kernel of the religious instruction the boy received at home.

Aldo grew to be a handsome, highly intelligent, and studious youth. Unathletic and uninterested in childhood games, he lived for school and Church. Moro passed through adolescence into adulthood without ever having experienced a crisis of conscience or, apparently, even moments of doubt concerning his faith. His fervent religiosity was atypical, because Catholic culture in his native region of Puglie had long been in steep decline.[2] Taranto, where Renato Moro relocated his family in the 1920s, was a particularly depressed area from the Church's viewpoint. By the time Aldo joined the S. Francesco di Assisi Catholic youth group, at age eleven in 1927, the Church was on the lookout, especially in this part of Italy, for bright youngsters who could be trained to lead their peers by example. It did not take long for Moro to be singled out as a boy of exceptional talent and promise. When the family moved to Bari in 1934, he immediately attracted the attention of Archbishop Marcello Mimmi, who later would find him an ideal leader for the local branch of Federazione Universitaria Cattolica Italiana (FUCI), the Italian Catholic University Federation.

Moro arrived at the University of Bari with a profound attachment to the Church and a predisposition toward progressive Catholic thought, attitudes he kept for the rest of his life. The still vibrant traditions of reactionary Catholicism never tempted Moro. Early on he became convinced that the crisis of modern culture could only be overcome by a new understanding of Christianity, not by a return to the outmoded and discredited past. Under the guidance of Raimondo Santoro, the Dominican advisor to FUCI at the University of Bari, Moro deepened his knowledge of Catholic theology and moral teaching. He looked to St. Thomas Aquinas as a spiritual guide for the ages, and even scholastic philosophy, in which backward-looking Catholics could find inspiration for reactionary polemics, Moro interpreted in his usual progressive way.

Growing up devoutly Catholic in Fascist Italy did present some serious challenges to Moro, whose father had run afoul of zealous government officials in 1932 over Fascist policies in the schools. Although Moro had received his entire education during Mussolini's regime, the Church's sporadic opposition to fascism helped to define his politics in high school and at the university. A shared anticommunism bound Catholics and Fascists together, but they feared and mistrusted one another, too. Each group thought of the other as a means toward its own end, and such a relationship was bound to produce tensions.[3] The police always kept a wary eye on the class of Catholic intellectuals to which Moro belonged, because it was obvious that their ultimate loyalty lay with the Church. For the Fascists, this signified antifascism. They aspired to create a totalitarian society, and the Church remained a formidable anomaly, cooperating with the regime most of the time, but always in a position of vexing independence, bent on maintaining its own separate spheres of influence in Italian life. These tensions exploded in 1931, the year Pope Pius XI made a withering critique of the Fascist government in the encyclical letter *Non abbiamo bisogno*. In the brief but verbally lacerating clash between Church and state that followed, the Fascists proscribed Catholic youth groups, including that of the then fifteen-year-old Moro in Taranto. Moderates on both sides argued successfully that fascism and Catholicism needed each other in Italy. Nevertheless, the preceding accusations and castigations underscored the antagonism that always existed beneath the surface, and sometimes on the surface, of Church-state relations in Fascist Italy.

Moro was one of the moderates on these issues and did not suffer from divided loyalties. Like most Catholics, as well as Jews and Protestants in Italy, he sought an accommodation with fascism. To begin with, this was the advice that he received from his spiritual mentors, Mimmi and Santoro. Despite their many misgivings and reservations about fascism, they urged young Catholics to work with the regime, the better to Christianize it. Moreover, some of Mussolini's corporativist policies genuinely appealed to Moro, and in them he saw the basis for mutual understanding and cooperation between fascism and Catholicism. Throughout the decade of the thirties he clung to the hope that the incompatibilities between the Church and the regime would be susceptible to compromise. Moro joined the Gioventù Universitaria Fascista (GUF) and participated actively in the *Littoriali* cultural activities sponsored by the regime for university students. These involvements are especially unsurprising because Moro's mentor at the University of Bari at that time, Biagio Petrocelli, was a dedicated Fascist; moreover, the professor's assistant, Armando Regina, served as the head of the Ufficio Cultura of GUF. Intellectual proclivities and ambition dictated the choices that young Moro made during these years. He continued to view fascism positively, as the best existing social model for the preservation of Christian values. It was a viewpoint typical for a young man of his background who had come to maturity during the middle 1930s, when the regime enjoyed its greatest popularity and consensus.

At no time, however, did Moro imagine that Catholicism and fascism, despite their many points of convergence, were essentially the same thing. Moro understood them as different systems of thought, though amenable to coexistence and even harmony. If he approached fascism respectfully, it was always as a Catholic first and foremost. Such distinctions may seem tortuous today, but in those days there were Catholics who identified enthusiastically with the regime, Catholics who merely cooperated with it, and a very tiny minority of Catholics who opposed it. Great emotional, psychological, and theoretical differences separated these three groups of Catholics, as people at the time understood full well. The distinguishing characteristic of the second group, to which Moro belonged, was the conviction that fascism had to prove its compatibility with the Church, not the other way around.

Moro compiled an outstanding academic record at the University of Bari and from 1939 to 1942 served as the national president of FUCI. He began to teach law at the university, first as a lecturer and then as an untenured professor. Although he was called to military service in 1942, his academic credentials entitled him to a safe and comfortable army assignment as a captain and scarcely altered his scholarly routine. The regime fell apart the next year, and for the final year and a half of the war it could only reconstitute itself in the north under Nazi control. Moro's articles in 1943 and 1944 for *La Rassegna* and *Pensiero e Vita* clearly reveal his abrupt change of mind about fascism. The war was the great eye-opener for Moro as for most Italians; they came out unambiguously and forcefully against fascism only after the collapse of Mussolini's regime was assured. By then Moro saw fascism as the baleful product of Italy's spiritual plight and material inequalities. These roots of fascism would have to be pulled up; otherwise the same rank growth would smother democracy again, he wrote. Arguing that politics was an instrument for the elevation of man in society, he urged that Catholics step forward in rebuilding the nation. In 1944 he participated in the revival of Catholic Action and later served as the national secretary of the movement of Catholic University Graduates, while also becoming active in the newly constituted Christian Democratic party. Already a prominent Catholic leader of the younger generation, Moro almost immediately became a notable figure in local politics. In 1945 he married Eleonora Chiavarelli, also an activist in FUCI; they were to have three daughters and one son.

Moro continued to write for Catholic periodicals and newspapers, making his mark as an intellectual and a social critic before becoming an important politician. He would always benefit politically from this early phase of his career. As Antonio Gramsci once observed, the Italians had an appreciation for men of ideas that verged on reverence. There was a seriousness in Moro's thought that elevated him far above the usual run of politicians, and in the postwar period he firmly established his credentials as a Catholic intellectual. From 1946 to 1948 Moro edited one of the most prestigious Catholic periodicals, *Studium*, an important vehicle for progressive Catholic thought. In passionate and eloquent editorials inspired by the Church's tradition of social justice, from *Rerum novarum* to Pius XII's wartime appeals for Christian mercy, Moro called upon the Italians to be tolerant, loving, and charitable.[4] A great work of reconstruction lay ahead. War, fascism, and greed had smashed the magnetic chain of humanity. The Holy Spirit alone, operating through mankind in mysterious and manifold ways, could repair the damage. Love was the only answer, even for one's enemies; especially for one's enemies.[5] At the deepest level of his being, Moro would always believe in this Christian principle.

Moro's *Studium* editorials chronicled his performance as a Christian Democratic delegate to the Constituent Assembly of the Republic, where he actively defended the cause of a strongly antifascist pluralistic state. Working on the Commission of Seventy-Five, which helped to prepare the agenda for the plenary assembly, Moro voiced his concern for social issues. He called for an interventionist state, one that would actively fight poverty and injustice, not simply create ideal conditions for the enrichment of a few millionaires. The handsome, and sad eyed Moro, at twenty-nine showing a distinctive streak of prematurely grey hair, confirmed his reputation as one of Christian Democracy's most capable young leaders. Despite his austere, phlegmatic, "northern" personality, which clashed at every point with the popular image of the easygoing, good-natured, and gregarious southerner of his native region, Moro had the respect of all who worked with him. He even made a lastingly favorable impression on Palmiro Togliatti, the Communist leader and a major figure at the Constituent Assembly, who thought him intelligent and balanced in judgment.[6]

In his restless search for a Christian synthesis suitable for the modern world, Moro, like many other Italian Catholics of his generation, resolved to look outside the Roman Catholic tradition while remaining faithful to it. These young Catholics, now permanently alienated by fascism, opened a dialogue with the left. As the editor of *Studium*, Moro sought to engage the Socialists and Communists in a respectful dialogue. He praised such left-wing writers as Ignazio Silone and Elio Vittorini for their social conscience.[7] Cesare Pavese, the major Communist novelist of the day, remained one of Moro's favorite authors.

Moro made patent his disagreement with the left about many fundamental principles. His own politics rested on the antirevolutionary conviction that force in the service of justice creates other injustices. He believed that the Christian conception of human nature, with its emphasis on original sin, made Catholics less naive than Marxists, whose theories about human perfectibility under communism had an otherworldly quality about them. Moro did not expect heaven on earth as he believed the Marxists did, for even after all the economic and political reforms had been achieved the problem of evil would remain. Bound up with the essence of human nature itself, the problem of evil went far deeper than sociopolitical realities. Despite all these fundamental disagreements, Moro conceded that Catholics alone could not create the just society in Italy. The diversity of the country and the permanently eclectic character of its political culture made dialogue necessary. This was another principle that Moro would never abandon.

Actively pursuing his academic career at the University of Bari, Moro got his first book published in 1939 and in the decade that followed became a heavily published legal scholar. These scholarly books revealed his principal convictions, chief of which was respect for the dignity of the human person. Reacting to what he called fascist exaggerations about the imperatives of the collective, Moro aspired to present a Christian interpretation of the law. He derived his understanding of the law from a variety of sources, but obviously the great Catholic jurists, especially Francesco Bernardino Cicala from his native Puglie, had a special place in his thought.[8] Expressly taking issue with the fascist claim that the state is an absolute, Moro insisted that in the ethical state authority and liberty exist in a relationship of correlative responsibility. All attempts to monopolize state power he condemned as inherently evil. State power had to be efficacious in certain spheres, but always limited. History repeatedly illustrated the central political lesson in Christian doctrine: man is always an end, never a means. To Moro, the most enchanting dialectic became a prolific source of evil if its realization depended on violence to the human person, and this is why he instinctively recoiled from theoretical Marxism, particularly the Leninist version of it.

Moro's first important synthetic work was *Lezioni di filosofia del diritto*, a compilation of lectures that he gave for two courses at the University of Bari on the law (1944–45) and on the state (1946–47). Before taking up these two subjects, Moro thought it necessary to examine what he called "the problem of life," or moral values.[9] Life had a teleological character, he argued, and then added that purpose and design were apparent in Nature. Life is guided not only by mechanical laws; it moves toward spiritual goals of self-realization through the agency of love. He defined love as the fully conscious energy of God creating man, and of man seeking God. Love in this most exalted sense is the real motor of history.

From that moral premise Moro drew the principles of his Catholic activist political philosophy. He identified himself unreservedly with the fundamental revolution articulated by Christ: all human beings, regardless of background or circumstances, are perfectly equal in the sight of God. Moro held that this was the single most revolutionary assertion in history. For two thousand years the world had struggled in vain to understand it. All other revolutionary programs, he believed, were of trifling significance compared with the message of the Gospel.

Criticizing liberalism and socialism as two incomplete halves of the complete revolution implicit in Christianity, Moro celebrated the Church's basic political teachings. Liberal societies emphasized individual liberty, whereas socialist societies subordinated everything to class terms. Moro argued that individual liberty and social welfare were entirely dependent upon each other. No enclave of prosperity and stability could survive if conditions of misery and violence prevailed outside of it. The state had to promote the ethically inspired Liberty of all, not liberty in the materialistic sense of simply creating a zone of free movement for acquisitive egotists, which Moro thought was simply another name for license.[10] At the same time, socialism discounted the worth of the individual, and this was its fatal error. Man, as the Church always had taught, does not exist solely for social ends; limits had to be imposed on the state's power to control the individual. The state exists exclusively as a tool of man, to help him realize his full humanity. Only such an order of balance and harmony could truly be called free, Moro asserted.

Neither *Lezioni di filosofia del diritto* nor the scholarly studies that preceded and followed it were mere academic exercises; rather, they were passionate expressions of a religious and ethical state of mind, which gave them an unusual quality.[11] In these fervent Catholic discourses, Moro exhorted the Italians to follow a morally uplifting conception of the law.[12] Amidst copious bibliographical references which gave his work a standard scholarly character, the word "spirit" appeared often. To the spirit he unabashedly appealed in its fullest religious sense as the true guide in a world where unaided reason has been found wanting.[13]

Not even Moro's most ardent admirers would claim that these early writings offered a new exposition of Christian doctrine. His ideas were directly in line with established Church teaching. If he tried to interpret Catholicism in the most progressive way possible, there was nothing unprecedented about that. Indeed, similar efforts all over Italy, but particularly in the north, characterized postwar Catholic life. His importance at this time had more to do with where he was writing than with what he was writing. A progressive southern Catholic with ties to like-minded thinkers in the north, who found in him a stalwart ally in a region where allies were few, Moro counted more for his peculiarity than his originality.

Conservatives identified him as one of "the red fish that swam in holy water."[14] This was a reference to Giuseppe Dossetti's left-wing faction in the Christian Democratic party. Dossetti, ascetic and intense, was three years older than Moro, and the two men had been allies at the Constituent Assembly. Their affiliation is a crucial chapter in Moro's biography, although it is important to remember that he brought to this relationship a mind already made up about the central values of life. Prolonged contact with Dossetti confirmed and deepened his thinking, but it also gave him occasion to disagree with a kindred spirit. The only southerner in Dossetti's group, Moro, despite some anomalous character traits, identified strongly with his native region, and always for that reason had a limited relationship with the northern reformers. He was more closely connected with Dossetti in the public mind than in reality, but this *dossettiano* phase would always be an important part of his image.

Like Moro, Dossetti had been a gifted student. A teacher of canon law at the Catholic University of the Sacred Heart in Milan, Dossetti became the animating spirit of a liberal Catholic discussion group that began meeting in the late 1930s. They came together as Catholics devoted to the Church, but anxious about her future. The reforms they had in mind generally resembled those of Jacques Maritain, whose *Humanisme intégral* (1936) served as a book of elementary political principles for progressive Catholics of Moro's generation.[15]

A key issue that put Maritain sharply at odds with conservative Catholics was the role he envisaged for the left as an ally of Christians in creating a just social order. Though regretting Marx's imperious atheism and the horrors that even in 1936 were known to have occurred in the Soviet Union, Maritain professed to see a large element of sincerity in Marxism and in socialism generally. Marx's cruel appeal to class hatred and violence sickened him, but Maritain reacted positively to "the great flash of truth running through his work": namely, that the dynamic of capitalism could only lead to widespread aliena- tion and despair.[16] This part of Marxism at least had been quickened by a moral impulse; indeed, here Marxists had been in the vanguard of the moral attacks against capitalism, a regime of civilization de- scribed in *Humanisme intégral* as "the utilization of all the forces of the world for the fecundity of money."[17] The churches, meanwhile, had allowed themselves to be used and undermined by this regime. For all their intrinsic differences on spiritual matters, Marxists and Chris- tians shared an aversion to the destructive capitalist cult of individual enrichment, denounced by Maritain as the ineluctable consequence of the anthropocentric humanism that he wanted to replace with integral or theocentric humanism. Maritain boldly proposed that a dialogue be held between Christians and those atheists of good faith who, in attacking the moral evils of capitalism, were up to a point objectively furthering God's temporal design for man. Maritain had a crystalline conception of what that design was: "a veritable socio-temporal reali- zation of the Gospel."[18] The obvious first step in this process was the elimination of capitalism, and Christians should look to the secular left for help in taking that step. "He who is not against you is with you," the Gospel wisely counseled.[19]

Maritain's unorthodox ideas served the Catholic left in Italy as a point of departure in their search for an exit from fascism. The *dossettiani*, including Giuseppe Lazzati, Giorgio La Pira, and Amin- tore Fanfani, stood in the vanguard of these searchers. Their common goal notwithstanding, they engaged in robust disputes over how to interpret and implement the "new Christianity." When Moro joined forces with the group, he seconded strongly Maritain's ideas about the necessary connection between political and social democracy and about the fundamental importance of tolerance in political dealings with all adversaries. At the same time, by stressing the necessarily laic nature of politics in a pluralistic democracy, Moro distanced himself from some of the more exalted interpretations of Maritain, particularly that of Dossetti. Although Maritain's ideas made a deeply favorable impression on Moro, he responded to them with his usual caution. He was not by nature disposed to be enthusiastic about theories.

Dossetti was so disposed. Drawing inspiration from Maritain, he expressed a visceral hatred for liberalism. The Depression had convinced him, along with many intellectuals of his generation, that capitalism had entered its final crisis, with communism and fascism as different responses to it. Communism was the misguided but understandable revenge of exploited workers. Fascism was the mechanical anticommunist reaction of threatened elites. To break this tragic cycle, which had begun with a dysfunctional capitalist order, became for him the mission of Catholic political thought. Dossetti, echoing Maritain, claimed that Christ's grace alone had the power to heal a world sick unto death. Moro thought in such images as well, but without Dossetti's fierce refusal to concede any merit to the status quo.

Dossetti's experience in the Resistance moved him steadily closer to the Communists. Maritain's *Humanisme intégral* had been a coaching manual on how to bring about a political alliance between Marxists and Christians, but now Dossetti could supplement his reading with concrete experiences in wartime. The war had provided him with an illuminating example of how Catholics and Marxists could work together. Having joined forces to defeat fascism, they could continue their alliance in the postwar world to create a real democracy. Ideologically, Dossetti, like Moro, was at heart a Christian social democrat, and both men found much to admire in the British Labour party. Much more than Moro, however, Dossetti generously praised Marxism, which he believed had risen above the doctrinal errors of Marx in many practical ways. He enthusiastically agreed with the argument of La Pira's 1947 book, *Il valore della persona umana*, that Marxism had value as a historical and philosophical method of understanding and criticizing capitalism. The year before, in what would become a notorious speech, Dossetti called the USSR a more "vital" society than the United States.[20] America appeared morally bankrupt to him, and he pronounced himself deeply concerned, as a Catholic, to see the Church moving into the American orbit. Dossetti could not peer far enough into the future to predict the destiny of consumerism that awaited the United States, but what little he could discern disturbed him. Even then, at war's end, before the economy could be redesigned to meet peacetime demands, America appeared to be the very image of what Dossetti did not want Italy to become.

That a man with such beliefs could have risen to the vice-secretaryship of the Christian Democratic party in 1945 reveals some essential features of the complexity in Italian postwar political life. Dossetti's prestige as a Resistance leader, especially high because relatively few

Catholics had been involved actively in the struggle, and his renown as the leading Catholic intellectual of the younger generation swiftly carried him to the pinnacles of the party. As vice-secretary, he vowed to make the Christian Democratic party truly Christian and truly democratic; to him this meant, as a necessary preliminary step, a tactical alliance with the other two mass political organizations in Italy, the Socialist and the Communist parties. On this issue the secretary of the party, Alcide De Gasperi, would eventually oppose him, while the most powerful man in the Catholic world, the severely anticommunist Pope Pius XII, opposed him very sharply from the beginning. In the background and increasingly in the foreground as well, an army of American cold warriors, in and out of uniform and with vast sums of money to spend, reinforced the cause of anticommunism in Italy. To the average Italian worried about getting a job that could feed him, Dossetti's earnestly proclaimed theories about creating a society of grace based on Gospel truths made a very untempting contrast with the Marshall Plan, the bounty of which depended on the political choices Italy made in the Cold War. Dossetti was fighting a battle he had no chance of winning, but in the process of losing it his ideas helped to shape the thinking of many future Christian Democratic leaders. One such leader was Aldo Moro.

Despite their differences of tone and even of philosophy on some crucial issues, Moro's encounter with Dossetti had the effect of reinforcing many of his own independently formulated ideas about politics and morality. Certainly during the late 1940s and early 1950s he was identified as one of Dossetti's *dottorini* or *professorini*, young eggheads for short. Moro joined Civitas Humana, a Catholic association of intellectuals that became a national extension of the earlier group Dossetti had led in Milan before the war. *Cronache sociali*, first published in May 1947, became the journal of this group, and Dossetti made prominent mention of Moro as one of the publication's "promoters and contributors."[21] In these pages, the dossettiani carried their fight against the centrist liberalism of De Gasperi. Essentially, they wanted the Christian Democratic party to become something far greater than it was: under De Gasperi the Christian Democrats were little more than an anticommunist force in the pay of the United States, but the dossettiani called for the party to transform itself into an instrument for peace and social justice in the creation of a genuine democracy.

De Gasperi became a problem for them primarily because the party secretary and government leader did not envisage fundamental changes in Italy's internal power relations; he sought to improve existing capitalist structures, not to replace them with anything more ethically advanced. Born in 1881, De Gasperi was a man of vast and unusually varied political experience that included some years as a politician in Vienna when his native Trento was still part of the Austro-Hungarian empire. He had been a leader of the Partito Popolare Italiano after World War I and then had been imprisoned for a time by the Fascists. Because he was the true father of the Christian Democratic party, which began to emerge in 1942–43, Freudian characterizations of the hostile father-son relationship are not out of place in describing the tensions between him and the dossettiani. His conflict with them was partly generational, but mainly intellectual: a liberal democrat, he simply refused to accept that capitalism was in terminal crisis or that Christianity had to be interpreted in a semicommunist way.

Moreover, De Gasperi could never think of politics simply as the elaboration of a thesis but took into account the real forces and fears that made a political situation what it was. He understood from his long experience in the Vatican, where for much of the interwar period he held a position in the library, how great the power of conservatives and reactionaries was and what a strong potential the Church had to take a hard turn to the right, as it had done in 1921–22 and, in fact, during most of the Fascist era. For many in the Church hierarchy, an Italian Franco or Salazar would have been most welcome at this time. Such a prospect became De Gasperi's nightmare and the chief inspiration for his centrism in the absolutely essential undertaking of keeping the Church as an ally for democracy.[22] In contrast, the dossettiani had very little appreciation for these problems.

De Gasperi thought that they had no appreciation at all for the harsh realities of the Cold War. To argue, as the dossettiani did, that NATO was likely to perpetuate the culture of war, might be an interesting thesis for the seminar room, but no responsible leader of postwar Italy would take it seriously for more than a second. De Gasperi could only see the terrible vulnerability of Italy in the face of huge economic, institutional, and diplomatic problems, including the territorial integrity of the state. For all of these problems the United States alone could offer decisive help. To influence American decisions in Italy as best he could and to reassure Washington by his political actions that the country held promise as a democratic capitalist society were the two obvious policies demanded by the situation. De Gasperi fully realized how little room for maneuver Italy had as a defeated nation, and how precarious her situation remained long after war had ended. The dossettiani, in common with the left generally in Italy, could never produce a coherent practical alternative to the American alliance. For De Gasperi, it was a choice of pie in the sky or milk in the pail.

De Gasperi often had to rely on the dossettiani in his struggles with the party's right wing; he actually seems to have liked Dossetti and certainly admired his intellect, but they never did understand each other.[23] De Gasperi once confided to Fanfani that Dossetti, a bachelor, could never be a good government minister, for "he who is without a wife has no contact with the practical problems of life."[24] Moreover, there is little doubt that De Gasperi privately viewed Dossetti's politics of a higher morality with truculent condescension, judging it to be the result of excessive bookishness and conceit. Something of this judgment came out in remarks that he made at the Third Congress of the Christian Democrats, held in Venice from 2 to 5 June 1949. Responding to Dossetti's idealistic criticisms of him, De Gasperi observed somewhat sarcastically how pleasant it would be to have time for meditative studies; however, as the leader of a government engaged in the practical and necessary work of rebuilding the country, he did not have that luxury. De Gasperi conceded that the government needed "a certain stimulus" and even a "sting" from the intellectuals, but in trying to remind them of how imperfectly political action ever corresponded to intellectual ideals he was only returning the favor, of which they truly stood in need.[25]

De Gasperi did not spare Moro either. One of the dossettiani with an important government job during this period, Moro served as the undersecretary for foreign affairs from 22 July 1948 to 12 January 1950. By maintaining a critical attitude toward the Atlantic alliance, he remained at loggerheads with the staunchly pro-American Foreign Minister Carlo Sforza. When Moro missed a crucial vote in Parliament on that issue, citing the birth of his second child as the reason for his absence, he enraged De Gasperi himself. The Prime Minister is said never to have forgiven Moro for this failure to vote and generally regarded him as one of the "meditative" complainers.

De Gasperi's serious problems in the party began with the June 1953 elections, when the Christian Democrats lost more than eight percent of their support from 1948. By this time Dossetti had already given up politics to campaign for a cultural change that would prepare Italy to accept a Christian political program. Eventually, he would take holy orders and found a small religious community near Bologna. At a farewell gathering for his party followers in 1951, Dossetti enjoined them either to imitate his example or to continue working within the party for spiritual objectives. Despairing of politics himself, Dossetti had one regret about this phase of his life: he should have fought against De Gasperi "to the end, whatever the consequences."[26] As Dossetti had become more radical, Moro had not been able to follow him, and it is noteworthy that he never actually contributed an article to *Cronache sociali.* Nevertheless, their personal rapport survived everything, and Moro was among those who chose Dossetti's second option. He joined the Iniziativa Democratica, a progressive political group within the Christian Democratic party, which many former dossettiani also joined. The leader of this group, the man who profited immediately from the party crisis in 1953, was Amintore Fanfani.

Although Fanfani had been a charter member of the dossettiani, he always remained a strongly independent personality. Even less than Moro could he be described as a mere follower of Dossetti's, because Fanfani, born in 1908, was a well-established scholar with a chair in economics at a time when his younger colleague at the Catholic University of the Sacred Heart was just starting out as a professional academic. *Cattolicesimo e protestantesimo nella formazione storica del capitalismo* (1934), in which Fanfani argued that laissez-faire capitalism stood in the sharpest possible contrast to the Church's conceptions of social ethics, became an important book in Italy, much admired by people like Dossetti and others in search of a Catholic synthesis for the modern world.[27] More than any of the other dossettiani, Fanfani expressed some favorable judgments about fascism, specifically its corporativism, which he likened at the time to Catholic economic doctrine. The Fascist bargain—to provide economic security in exchange for political freedom—ended by bringing calamity to Italy during World War II. Only then did Fanfani make haste, in such postwar books as *Persona, bene, società: in una rinnovata civiltà cristiana* (1945), to celebrate the democratic model of the welfare state.

In that same year Dossetti called Fanfani to Rome. The two men shared a *pensione* with other dossettiani and soon found themselves leading the most important left-wing faction in the Christian Democratic party. Fanfani became completely absorbed by politics. He remained a steadfast ally of Dossetti's through the Constituent Assembly, but after 1947 began going his own way. In that year De Gasperi made him minister of labor, inserting a wedge between Fanfani and Dossetti. Only with difficulty could Dossetti persuade him to become associated at all with the antiestablishment *Cronache sociali;* by then Fanfani's rapidly evolving moderation on all the fundamental issues of foreign policy and reform made it difficult to distinguish his stand from that of De Gasperi. Although he retained complete fluency in the language of Christian idealism, which would enable him to keep his standing with the Iniziativa Democratica, his temperateness grew in direct proportion to his proximity to power. De Gasperi thought that he was leaving the party in reliable hands with Fanfani as secretary in 1954. In a much blacker frame of mind, Dossetti came to the same conclusion about his old friend: the Christian Democratic power structure would have nothing to fear from the new secretary.

Fanfani kept control of the party until 1959, continuing to preach idealism while accomplishing few of the agricultural, fiscal, and bureaucratic reforms he had intended. Fanfani's aim in 1954 had been to renew the party, the government, and the country. Little of the kind occurred. At the 1959 party congress in Florence, he admitted that social justice remained a distant goal. "If we have not achieved it yet, we must explain why," Fanfani acknowledged plaintively.[28] The problem lay, as De Gasperi had discovered, in the fragmented condition of the party itself, which became accentuated under Fanfani. Numerous groupings, led by party notables and split along regional, generational, ideological, and tactical lines alternately fought and cooperated with each other as well as with the leaders of other parties in a perpetually shifting balance of power.

During Fanfani's years as party secretary political instability worsened: from 1953 to 1958 six governments fell. His critics compared him unfavorably with De Gasperi, who, after his death in 1954, evoked sentiments of reverence and nostalgia—particularly in Washington, where anxiety began to mount over the Italian problem. For American onlookers, De Gasperi's image now began to acquire a heroic aspect, and Fanfani, an assertive academic with indistinct ideas (except for his long-standing bias against the free market), was not the most reassuring successor to the party secretaryship. Powerful elements in his party also began to worry about him. Fanfani's crude attempt to emulate his predecessor by centralizing party power under his control antagonized an invincible coalition of Christian Democrats, called the *dorotei* because they plotted against him at the convent of the Sisters of Santa Dorotea in Rome. In 1959 they deposed him, as much for his irritatingly authoritarian manner as for his program. The great beneficiary of their action, the next party secretary, was the forty-three-year-old Aldo Moro. His ascent in the party had seemed improbable because of his reticent and shy public demeanor. Yet this very characteristic, in combination with a nimble mind that had ample room for real ideas and original thoughts, lent a certain inevitability to his success, given the fears about a party strongman aroused by Fanfani.

After joining the Iniziativa Democratica, Moro had played a secondary role in party affairs during what remained of the De Gasperi era, contenting himself with the satisfactions of his academic career, but he emerged as one of the ranking Christian Democratic deputies in the new dispensation. Moro combined the gentlemanly qualities of conciliatoriness and cultivation with the aptitudes of a successful politician: astuteness, patience, and, above all, an artfully concealed stubbornness in getting his own way. For nearly thirty years it proved to be an irresistible combination in Italian politics. Appointed leader of the Christian Democratic deputies in Parliament, the quietly ambitious and highly alert Moro used this position as a staging area for swift career advances. In 1955 he became minister of justice and in 1957, of public instruction. Despite these appointments Moro still lacked national visibility, but even that condition worked to his advantage within the party. People habitually underestimated him and did not imagine that the reserved professor might become a serious competitor for supreme power in the party. Moro's unthreatening presence, his image as a reverse Fanfani, appealed to the Christian Democratic hierarchs as they elevated him to the secretaryship. They assumed that in this position Moro, unlike his predecessor, would defer to them.

If these men selected Moro in the confident expectation that things would change only to the slight extent necessary for them to remain fundamentally the same, he did nothing in the beginning to make them lose their illusions. Moro's skill at leading while giving the appearance of only listening, frequently noted in later years, took some time to be developed. As secretary, he moved with the caution of an unpracticed driver who sets out on an unfamiliar road in thick fog. Fresh from observing the crackup of Fanfani's secretaryship, Moro undertook no initiative that might disturb the status quo. To mediate the very serious disputes between the party's conservative and progressive factions he moved from the left to the center; indeed, it was the center-right Christian Democrats who had supported him against Fanfani. A serious risk of party schism always existed in these years, and Moro, with his gift for evasive language and his instinct for knowing what not to say, gradually made himself indispensable as a peacemaker. In effect, here was another *dossettiano* who, even more than Fanfani, had become a *degasperiano* in power.

The issue on which Moro began to develop an independent political identity as party secretary was the much discussed, long delayed, and greatly feared "opening to the left" that Dossetti had said would be the only possible point of ignition for a course of democratic action in Italy. Pressure for a political understanding with the Socialists had been coming in recent years from the new left of Moro's own party, the so-called third generation of Christian Democratic leaders, young men like Giovanni Galloni, who in 1953 had formed the Sinistre di Base and had begun to emerge as an important political force after the 7 June elections of that year. Influenced by *dossettismo* and by the Christian Democratic labor unionism of Giovanni Gronchi, this new faction performed what had become a historic function in the party: to exert fresh pressure from the left as the older progressive Christian Democratic groups had become coopted or faded away. They were not a completely homogeneous faction, any more than the Iniziativa Democratica was or the dossettiani had been, but the "Base," always stronger locally than on the national level, identified itself with the campaign for a Christian Democratic alliance with the Socialists.

Fanfani already had done much to prepare the ground for an opening to the left, but Moro characteristically dithered before identifying himself clearly with this initiative. "Base" arguments, for which his natural sympathies were held in check by conservative forces in the party, had long been in the air, longer than the *basisti* themselves had existed as a faction. The truly new element in the political situation impelling Moro toward a solution associated with the "Base," but not created by it, was the ongoing social revolution in Italy, of which he alone among Christian Democratic politicians appears to have been particularly aware. The Marshall Plan had made possible an economic miracle; in less than a generation it had transformed the still largely agricultural Italy of 1945 into an industrial society, in which consumption at rates unimaginable to previous generations of Italians became the chief visible aim in life. The industrial cities of the north underwent a furious expansion as millions of peasants left the land in the north and south, a process that led to the "anthropological mutation" in Italy noted by the poet and film-maker, Pier Paolo Pasolini.[29]

Uneven development left the south farther behind than ever, but in some ways the changes in the north were the more frightening. The coming of southern immigrants caused ethnic tensions; lack of adequate housing, public services, schools, and hospitals led to social problems, including a rapidly rising crime rate, for which the industrial cities and towns lacked even the most minimal preparations. From 1955 to 1971 more than nine million Italians migrated between regions, but the period of greatest movement overall came in the years 1958 to 1963, precisely when Moro became party secretary.[30] Labor disturbances in the industrial triangle of Milan, Turin, and Genoa grew more numerous and violent during this period, and the worst one of all culminated in days of rioting at Turin's Piazza Statuto in 1962. To many radicals at the time, this strife appeared as an uplifting portent of the revolution they ardently desired.[31]

Against a background of change, disorder, and struggle, Moro reached out to the Socialists. At the party's Eighth Congress in 1962, he spoke for six hours on the theme of Italy's need for a "cautious union" between the Socialists and the Christian Democrats.[32] The party secretary urged that all sincerely democratic forces be invited to join in the daunting task of governing Italy. The Socialists, he felt, had matured into such a force. Since Khrushchev's official unmasking in 1956 of Stalin as the greatest terrorist and mass murderer in history, which instantly led to widespread demoralization and soul-searching on the Italian left, the Socialist party of Pietro Nenni had given up on a revolutionary program. The post–1956 Nenni spoke as an increasingly moderate social democrat whose disgust with the Soviet Union had driven him away from his erstwhile Communist allies. Moro reasoned that now the Socialists had nowhere to go but the center, where the Christian Democrats should be prepared to welcome them as decidedly junior partners in a center–left coalition.

The 1962 Naples Congress ended in a clear personal victory for Moro. Here, for the first time, he fully demonstrated an uncanny power for leading his badly splintered party while only seeming to compose the differences between its factions. Even with this talent, it was no ordinary feat to overcome the regnant political belief of Italian Catholics that socialism suffered from intrinsic defects. For more than one hundred years, beginning with Pius IX's encyclical *Qui pluribus* (1846), the popes implacably had opposed socialism, until John XXIII checked this antisocialist mentality, with his encyclicals *Mater et magistra* (1961) and *Pacem in terris* (1963). Moro gave the new tolerance a practical expression in Italian politics.[33] This was the direction in which all along Moro had wanted the Church to go, and the next pope, Paul VI, a friend of his since FUCI days, helped him to confirm the trend toward ecumenicalism. Conservative churchmen, especially the fiery Cardinal Giuseppe Siri of Genoa, continued to be horrified by Moro's political ideas, on the grounds that Catholics have a fatal antagonism toward even moderate Marxists on the only point worth discussing: God. Fortunately for Moro, John XXIII had insisted that areas of agreement between men of good will, whatever their beliefs, should not be forsaken, and that Catholics should be free to seek effective alliances in creating a just social order. Such was Moro's standard defense of *aperturismo*, as the opening to the left became known, against conservatives in the Church.

If Moro's language was convoluted, his argument was clear: in the Italy of 1962 the party's alternative to the Socialists was the historically discredited right. A frightened conservatism would have been the worst possible choice for the Christian Democrats, Moro warned. This strategy had already been tried two years earlier by the government of Fernando Tambroni with completely negative results, including violent demonstrations and strikes all over Italy that left ten people dead and dozens injured. The tragic Tambroni affair confirmed Moro and other party leaders in their belief that a center–right coalition would disrupt Italy's progress toward democracy while a center–left coalition would facilitate it. Moro argued that to thwart antidemocratic forces in Italy, especially the still dangerous Communist party, all democrats had to work together for real evolutionary change in the country. This logic, with its anticommunist rhetoric, convinced the Kennedy administration as well. Washington offered no objections to aperturismo on the assumption, reassuringly seconded by Moro, that the Communist threat would be reduced as Italian democracy was strengthened.[34]

Events soon deflated these expectations. In the 1963 elections Communist gains and Christian Democratic losses revealed that the center–left opening had not found favor with the voters. Throughout the decade, conservatives would blame Moro for the growing Communist threat. Even in retrospect, however, it is impossible to see any practical alternative to what Moro did. Indeed, the center–left formula would remain the key to Italian politics for the next thirty years. In the 1960s it did not produce the desired political stability because of continuing disunity and schisms among the Socialists, culminating in the creation of the separate left-wing PSIUP (Partito Socialista di Unità Proletaria) in 1964, and Moro's own party's unwillingness or inability to compromise significantly on social and economic issues with its new allies. After surrendering the party secretaryship to Mariano Rumor, Moro was Prime Minister from November 1963 to June 1968. From the beginning, he and Nenni pulled in opposite directions. The Socialist leader vigorously pressed for the reforms that his Christian Democratic partner knew he could not support without destroying his party's unity and frightening Italy's always nervous business community.

Moro also had an eminently justifiable fear of the extreme right in the military, for he knew what the public did not then know about the "Piano Solo" scheme of General Giovanni De Lorenzo and other reactionaries, and their 1964 threatened coup. How many Italian and American leaders might have been involved in or favorably disposed toward this solution for the country's political problems has been a topic of passionate discussion since 1966, when the scandal broke. After becoming aware of De Lorenzo's scheme, Moro always had a weather eye out for right-wing plotters; they, in his judgment, posed the greatest danger of all to the ship of state, precisely because they were on board and in charge of its security and navigation. He became more cautious than ever.

Moro's dossettismo on economic matters became muted as his government caved in to land speculators and building developers.[35] Urban sprawl and some of the worst air and water pollution in Western Europe sullied the once pristine landscape of Italy. It was a heartbreaking spectacle of avarice, philistinism, and pusillanimity. The plight of Naples and Palermo was especially grievous as those magnificent cities were disfigured and, in effect, put to the sack by a new breed of barbarians. Moro did not resist these depredations. His critics on the left have argued that government planning in the socialist manner would have prevented or minimized such blights. The Communists were especially hard on him. Yet Communist administrations proved singularly useless in sparing the environment of Warsaw, of Bratislawa, or of the land long perceived as the flashing beacon of home port for Italian Communists, the former Soviet Union. While the left today is inclined to cite the alternative example of social democratic Sweden, the left-wing circles that dominated Italian university life in the 1960s and that played a paramount role in the whole culture of the time admired China, Algeria, Cuba, and Vietnam. Moro did not play a heroic or even an adequate role in protecting the cultural patrimony and the environment of Italy, but breakneck industrialization has always demanded the kind of price that Italy paid, even in countries acting under the banner of Marx. To single out Moro in a partisan way is, first, to pretend that, for the only time in history, these terrific forces of overnight social change could have been guided with precision, and, second, to ignore the many practical limitations imposed by the country's cumbersome system of coalition government.

On foreign policy, too, Moro's left-wing critics give him failing grades, charging that during the 1960s he served as the chief functionary of America's hegemony in Italy.[36] Such a sweeping judgment, like the similar one made about De Gasperi in the 1940s, ignores the obvious and fundamental aspect of Italy's complex and difficult situation, which, in any case, Moro cannot be said to have controlled: dependence on America was a reality that could be shaped to some extent, but not ignored or rejected. The history of Italy in the Cold War period derives its central meaning from the role that America played in providing the military defense behind which Italy's economic miracle could unfold.[37] No Italian leader from De Gasperi to Moro and beyond could pretend to be unaware of the political implications of such a relationship, of what the historian Roberto Ruffili (killed by Red Brigade terrorists in 1988) called the zone of "effective reality."[38] Reductionist characterizations of the relationship between Rome and Washington completely ignore Italy's considerable room for maneuver in this zone by Moro's day, but the dynamics of the Cold War did tend to have a determining effect on the outcome of issues crucial to the United States. The Cold War explains Moro's fervent declaration that he viewed Washington's problems in Vietnam with "full comprehension."[39] It also explains his response to critics of American policy in Latin America, such as Nenni: "They know not what they do."[40] Here again Moro's dossettismo had been transformed into something like its opposite, but in foreign affairs, even more than at home, he had few political options.

A five-year stalemate developed between the coalition partners. Nenni proposed, but Moro disposed, generally in terms that would result in the least amount of stress for his party. He managed to protect it, but little else. If Moro's reputation as a leader depended on his performance as Prime Minister, he would weigh very lightly in the scales of history. Italo Pietra, a newspaperman and one of Moro's most severe critics, later declared that his record in that office bordered on the pathetic.[41] One could recall from his speeches a litany of movingly expressive phrases and some dramatically conjured visions of Italy, Europe, and the world, but where in this record could it be shown that Moro ever had brought a single major question closer to a solution? In other words, Moro had entertained grand ideas about politics, but when his opportunity for action came, he failed to implement any of them. Pietra's judgment is harsh, but it certainly contains elements of truth.

It would not be difficult to shield Moro from such attacks by pointing to the very real deficiencies of the political system in Italy. Nevertheless, far from rising above the system, as the great leader that Italy truly needed at this time might have done, Moro, with his legendary stalling tactics and obfuscatory rhetoric, became its archetype. The period produced a rich literature of political satire with Moro as the foil. In a characteristic jab, Pier Paolo Pasolini asserted that Moro had invented a new political language designed to misrepresent reality, and that *morologia* had become a special field in Italian politics, calling into existence a veritable cloud of "morologists" with the self-proclaimed power to divine his mysterious meanings.[42] Another classic example of this literature is *Todo modo*, a satirical meditation on the Catholic Church's "splendid past, squalid present, and inevitable end," in which the novelist Leonardo Sciascia lampooned Moro in the character of the minister as the dithering embodiment of the fecklessly corrupt Christian Democrats; a film of the same title, directed by Elio Petri and starring Gian Maria Volonté as the Moro figure, soon followed.[43] The image sprang from anti-Catholic malice, but it was not inaccurate. As Moro himself would later explain, true leadership necessarily requires the capacity to look not only at today, but at tomorrow and the day after tomorrow. His office in Palazzo Chigi was the worst vantage point for a look at tomorrow, much less the day after, as he struggled throughout a tempestuous decade just to keep his party and coalition from exploding. In practice, political survival in Italy meant doing as little as possible.

A passive waiting on events, however, ended in defeat and disaster. The Communists continued to make steady gains at the polls, the very development that the center–left strategy had been designed to prevent. After the 19 May 1968 elections, from which the Socialists emerged as the principal losers, Moro's government fell from power, just as an unprecedented crisis in the factories and the universities threatened to engulf the country in anarchy. The discredited exponent of a failed strategy, Moro suddenly found himself drastically demoted in the party hierarchy. A small faction of Christian Democrats still looked to him for leadership, but he appeared to be a man of yesterday. Nevertheless, it soon became evident that his unique talents and qualities made it impossible to keep him out of the party's limelight. No other Christian Democrat could compare with him as a party mediator, and he possessed an exceptional intellectual presence. Above all, Moro reacted to his mistakes by learning from them. He grew as a leader. His understanding of what was wrong with the country became clearer, his solutions more direct, his defense of them more tenacious and courageous. In the 1970s, as economic recession and political instability worsened, Moro's party would call on him again.

Contemplating the country's accelerating labor unrest, student protest, and political violence, Moro told his colleagues that the unthinkable had become inevitable: the Communist party itself would have to be legitimized as an integral part of Italy's democracy. The original center–left strategy had not been wrong, he thought; it simply had been incomplete. In effect, agreeing for once with the extraparliamentary left, Moro thought that the Communist party had ceased to be Marxist-Leninist. A new generation of Communist leaders, epitomized by Enrico Berlinguer (he became party secretary in 1972) began to follow the reformist path marked out a decade earlier by Pietro Nenni. Moro observed that democracy was the only choice they had now, and he wanted to assist them in making it, with the understandable hope that his own party would remain the pivot around which all Italian politicians had to wheel and maneuver.

On 29 June 1969 he spoke before the Eleventh Congress of the Christian Democrats and urged the party to initiate a "strategy of attention" in the form of a dialogue with the Communists. In one of the most momentous speeches of his career, Moro oscillated between fear and hope. He feared the crisis confronting Italy: "things are being born and are taking the place of things that are dying."[44] He hoped that the party would survive and continue in power, but to do so it would have "to be for the things that are being born, even if they have uncertain aspects; not for the things that are dying, even if they are appealing and apparently useful." Against death and on the side of life were the decisive changes that had taken place in the Communist world. Only an ideologue would insist that communism meant nothing but Stalinism; it could mean many other things, and certainly the Italian Communist party could no longer be regarded as simply an extension of the Kremlin. For example, the party had audibly choked over the Soviet Union's invasion of Czechoslovakia in 1968. "The Italian Communist party says that it wants a free and pluralistic system," Moro remarked with evident sympathy. Now the Christian Democrats would have to discuss this matter with them, he continued, in order to determine how sincere they were. The time had come to explore the possibility of "a new communism [that is] compatible with an advanced industrial economy, a mature democracy, a living and open society."

Moro had come to believe that the enormous and growing strength of the Communists might be coopted in defense of freedom and democracy; it was no longer prudent to quarantine this vital force in Italian political life. The Communists had offered their services at a time when the country's institutional framework was showing signs of buckling under pressure from extremists. The Christian Democrats should not turn down such an offer without a painstaking appraisal of its merits. From the vantage point of the mid 1990s, when the virtual destruction of Communist culture has become an accomplished fact in Italy, resulting in part from political and ideological developments in Eastern Europe, Moro's fears for democracy appear exaggerated. His single-minded concentration on the need for fresh troops in the struggle for democracy is understandable, however, to anyone with his values who lived in Italy and observed at first hand the violent crisis of the country's university system in 1968, the seemingly systemic convulsion of the labor force during the "hot autumn" of 1969, and the Piazza Fontana terror bombing in December of that year. No one could have foreseen then that the protests and rebellions of those days were a swan song for the revolutionary alternative to consumer society. At the time, the "Movement," in which idealists and terrorists had different vested interests, commanded attention. Ironically, Moro and Berlinguer had their own separate doubts about the desirability of consumerism as a value system for society, but both men were absolutely convinced that the violent extremists in Italy had nothing intelligent or even remotely sane to offer in its place.

Moro took the problem of terrorism with the utmost seriousness. He always feared the radical right, which had gained strength, particularly in the south, from the backlash against the events of 1968–69 and from the insidious sympathy and support of factions in the police and military. Moro largely shared the increasingly frantic concern of the left about the danger posed by neofascist intriguers. The terrorist group that came to preoccupy him the most, however, was the Red Brigades. Inspired ideologically by Marxist-Leninism and tactically by the partisans of World War II, the Red Brigades thought that they were continuing the work of revolution corrupted by Stalin in the Soviet Union and by Togliatti in Italy. *Togliattismo* was a term of cutting disdain in the Red Brigadists' vocabulary, and to them it signified the sacrifice of the working class to the machinations of a politician who had lost sight of Marxism's essential meaning: the revolutionary overthrow of capitalism. For these self-styled avengers of Marx and Lenin, revolution was not the main thing; it was the only thing. A handful of radical university students and factory workers, interpreting the generally disturbing close of the 1960s as the establishment's long-awaited crack of doom, founded the Red Brigade organization in the supreme confidence that they represented the communist future made inevitable by the contradictions of capitalism. Their terrorist campaign began in the early 1970s with acts of factory sabotage, then escalated to kidnappings and robberies before culminating in murder. People were deceived at the time by the small number of terrorists involved in this wave of subversion, but the Red Brigades represented the aspirations of a much larger antidemocratic culture on the left that had been spoiling for a fight with the Christian Democratic regime from the beginning. Revolution was a variety of religious experience in Italy, and Moro had presentiments about the Red Brigades as a new generation of true believers.

Numerous other left-wing terrorist groups, as well as neofascist formations, further aggravated the situation. Fringe organizations on both extremes carried on vendettas against the Christian Democratic Italy that had emerged from the defeat of World War II. Terrorism in Italy could not be understood as current events but only as the fulfillment of much deeper forces. The civil war—one that at different levels of consciousness and intention was always implicit in Italy's strongly ideological political culture—became fully explicit at the end of the 1960s as extremists on both sides collided with the status quo, of which Moro had become the strongest personification. If the 1960s was a time of widespread instability, disorder, and violence in cultures where ideological consensus prevailed, it is hardly surprising that this period of general crisis in the West should have produced some especially shocking results in a country like Italy. During the years that followed, Italy acquired the sorry distinction of having the worst problem with terrorism in the industrialized world.

Moro opposed the terrorists of the 1970s, right and left, by working to deprive them of support in society. The most effective antiterrorist strategy entailed prevention, he thought. These enemies of democracy had to be perceived as people with nothing to offer the Italians. If society perceived them otherwise, genuine problems might exist, and the government would be wise to redress them; moreover, the government might be overlooking possible allies and areas of support in the struggle against terrorism. Moro argued that in the Italian case both conclusions were warranted, and from them his politics of dialogue with Communists emerged. Stubbornly clinging to the authentic middle ground, Moro alarmed the right, which feared him as an agent of communism in Italy—an Italian Kerensky—and angered such groups on the left as the Red Brigades, which condemned him for trying to absorb the Communists into a grand antirevolutionary coalition. By bringing upon himself the hatred of opposing groups of fanatics, Moro served as a political lightning rod during the stormiest period in the Republic's history.

The 1970s filled Moro with grave forebodings, and his speeches became increasingly pessimistic about the "great problems and enormous risks" of the decade.[45] The economy had slumped, and the weak, divided government could not effectively address any of the country's serious problems, such as the virtual collapse of the university system. No answers had been found for the student anger and alienation that

Moro had observed at first hand on the University of Rome's continuously agitated campus. Violence on the left had given the forces of reaction an enormous boost, he said on 20 March 1976, because the climate of chaos and terror confirmed the neofascist thesis about democracy's inability to maintain order.[46]

The extremists frightened Moro so much that he vigorously renewed his opening to Berlinguer, himself alarmed by growing signs of mass support for the far right as well as by the violent end of Salvador Allende's left-wing government in Chile.[47] Moro proclaimed that the Christian Democrats and the Communists had worked together before "in the great exodus from the desert of fascism . . . in the long march toward democracy," and they would have to join forces again.[48] Such had been the sense of Dossetti's words twenty-five years earlier, and Moro found himself airing the political principles of his dossettista youth. From long memory he knew the arguments for an opening to the Communists, but only now was it politically feasible to act on them. Differences between the two parties would remain on the vital questions of human nature, social and economic life, and foreign affairs, to be sure. Christians could never accept the materialist values of Marxists, and their relationship would always be a "dialectical" one.[49] Yet realism compelled him to look at the facts. To begin with, the Communists had strong popular roots in Italy. The PCI, the chosen political home for millions of voters, could not be dismissed as just a front organization for deceitful plotters. Moreover, their ranks were growing. Recent election results told the story clearly enough: the PCI had won 25.3 percent of the vote in 1963, 26.9 percent in 1968, 27.2 percent in 1972, 33 percent in the 1975 regional and local elections, and 34.4 percent in 1976.[50] As the PCI gained, the center–left lost. In 1975, the year after a crushing defeat on the referendum that legalized divorce in Italy, Moro's party won only 35 percent of the vote, its weakest performance since 1946. The 1976 elections also ended in a rout for the Socialists, leaving Moro more convinced than ever that the PCI was his only option now. He thought that his party was wasting away, and like a doctor treating a seriously ill patient whose infirmities had been proof against all standard treatment, the Christian Democratic leader resorted to desperate remedies at what he perceived to be a critical moment. Many in Italy and in the United States thought that his cure was worse than the disease.

Moro served as minister of foreign affairs from 1969 to 1974 and twice more as Prime Minister from 1974 to 1976. As foreign minister he became preoccupied by the Middle Eastern problem. During the 1960s he had tried to act as a mediator between his coalition's pro-Arab and pro-Israeli elements. In the 1970s, however, Moro viewed the Palestinians' plight with increasing sympathy. He also thought that the problems in the Middle East threatened the stability of the entire Mediterranean world. American Secretary of State Henry Kissinger once complained that the Italian leader never seemed to be interested in foreign affairs, but in Washington at this time the real problem with Moro may have been that he was too interested and, even worse, too independent. Moro criticized what seemed to him to be America's partisanship in the region and insisted that the dispute called for a compromise, one that would impartially recognize the rights and national aspirations of the Israelis and the Palestinians. Like all great crises, this one had produced obnoxious extremists on both sides, but at the heart of the matter, he thought, was an American-backed Israeli decision to sabotage an equitable solution, using the mistakes and the stupidity of the most fanatical Arabs as an excuse for a policy of intransigence toward the Palestinian people.[51] This policy could only lead to disaster. It was another of his many ideas unpopular in Washington.

In Moro's view, Italy remained a deeply divided country whose fragile political structures might collapse under the assault of foreign and domestic enemies. The careful integration of modern values with existing cultures had been his unfulfilled dream. He knew that Italy, home of the Mafia and of the most active terrorists in the industrialized world, was not a healthy society. The Italian emergency, about which Moro spoke repeatedly in those last years, was real. Political and criminal violence continued to ravage the land, and several terror bombings that caused great loss of life heightened the sense of crisis.

The United States implacably opposed Moro's strategy. Even during the Jimmy Carter years the answer was still "no" to the idea of compromising with the Communists. Democratic president or Republican, a most rigid orthodoxy prevailed in Washington on the subject of Italy's Communist party. The 1975 and 1976 elections, however, had the effect of a political earthquake in Italy. With the PCI on the point of becoming the first party in the land, many other Christian Democratic leaders began to agree with Moro. About this historic compromise, the conservative Giulio Andreotti wrote: "there was no alternative" to it; the arithmetic of Parliament made this kind of agreement inevitable.[52] Moreover, the country needed a political truce, and Moro presented the compromise in just this light. Joined by Fanfani and Andreotti, Moro—then president of the Christian Democrats and through the secretaryship of his ally and friend, Benigno Zaccagnini, fully restored to paramountcy in the party—effected the 1976 historic compromise with Enrico Berlinguer of the PCI. In that year, Berlinguer declared that he did not want to see Italy leave NATO. The very possibility of experimenting with a distinctively Italian method of achieving socialism depended on the protection of American arms; that is, unlike Communist innovators in Budapest and Prague, Berlinguer did not have to worry about Warsaw Pact reprisals. Irony could find no fuller expression than this in Italian politics. The new Communist policy of *non sfiducia* (non no confidence) toward the Christian Democratic government inspired Andreotti to write that "the resources of the Italian vocabulary are infinite."[53] After accepting Communist abstention for nearly two years, the Christian Democrats prepared to lead a national unity government supported by all constitutional parties. The investiture of this government was scheduled to take place on 16 March 1978.

In a 18 February 1978 interview Moro stated the central point in his strategy: "a democracy without effective opposition groups cannot live."[54] Therefore, it was "not at all a good thing that my party should be the essential support of Italian democracy." This role had been thrust upon the Christian Democrats because no practical alternative to them had existed, given the "institutional and international realities" of the Cold War. Moro thought that the country's manifest desire for "real changes" could not and indeed should not be frustrated any longer. He welcomed the prospect of a new era in Italian politics, because if the old order were to continue, his party would inevitably sink deeper into the moral and institutional degeneration produced by one-party rule. Moro fully appreciated the wisdom of Lord Acton's dictum: "power tends to corrupt and absolute power corrupts absolutely."

Moro always stoutly defended his party against the charge that it was nothing but an engine of corruption in Italian life. He called this a monstrous lie, inspired not by a true understanding of Italy's complex postwar history but by a spirit of rank political partisanship often mixed with an ugly anti-Catholic prejudice. Christian Democrats had taken the lead in creating a prosperous republic out of the debris left behind by fascism and in opposition to the plainly ruinous ideas espoused by the Communists during their long Stalinist phase. No epithet could cancel out this historic Christian Democratic achievement. And yet Moro knew that to a worrisome extent the charge of corruption against his party was true. Things could not be otherwise in a de facto single-party state. The so-called Tangentopoli, or kickback, scandal of 1992–1995, which disgraced the Italian political establishment, was the realization of Moro's fears for the party's long-term future. The historic compromise figured in his thinking partly as a way to evade this completely foreseeable outcome of existing political practices in Italy.

Even though he was willing to cooperate with them, Moro claimed to have few illusions about the Communists. For nearly thirty years, the PCI had generated well-founded suspicions about its congenital inability to coexist with other parties in a pluralistic society. The heavy burden of Marxist-Leninist dogma had kept the Communists from playing the kind of role that he now envisaged for them. Through their irresponsibility, they had contributed enormously to the failure of the Italian political system. The more alert Communists seemed to be grasping this point, recognizing that it was in their self-interest to abandon completely the counterproductive radicalism that had resulted in political quarantine. Berlinguer was the party's Moses in reverse, leading the Communists out of Marx's Promised Land while assuring the faithful that he was doing no such thing. The Red Brigades and other Marxist-Leninist revolutionaries knew exactly what he was doing, and they were not in the least deceived by his claims of continuity between the Communist tradition and the new policies of the PCI. To his critics on the left, Berlinguer simply had sold out Marxism—as in fact he had. Moro understood this and sought to take it into his political calculations. He also thought that the regimes of Eastern Europe would soon be faced with the same choice, and on this point, too, the Christian Democratic statesman left his antagonists in Rome and Washington toiling far in the rear. The PCI would have to prove its reliability as a democratic force, and this of necessity would be a long process during which, according to Moro, they could not govern Italy by themselves. He only wanted to call on them now as an "associate" of the country's democratic government.

Moro hoped aloud that Washington would be reassured by this reservation, but his implied characterization of American anticommunism could be equated with Captain Ahab's relentless pursuit of the great white whale. Certainly his policy involved some risk, he conceded, but that was true about any policy. An even greater risk would result from a do-nothing strategy. To persevere in a plodding way with the conventional maneuvers of Italian politics would lead straight to "the undoing of society . . . [and] anarchic revolt." This is about as explicit as his public language ever became on the subject of Italy's internal crisis.

On 28 February 1978 Moro addressed the Assembly of Christian Democratic Senators and Deputies. He spoke about the party's need for an understanding with the PCI that would "respond to the real emergency . . . in our society."[55] There could be no mistaking his meaning: he thought that Italy, "this country of continuous vehemence [*passionalità*] and weak institutions," was on the edge of an abyss. His compromise strategy with the PCI would give the tottering country a chance to pull back from danger. Flaminio Piccoli, one of the most powerful veteran leaders in the Christian Democratic party, later testified that Moro "was full of hope" for the historic compromise.[56] Piccoli remembered a late night visit with him on the eve of that event. During their conversation, Moro "attributed to this choice by the Communist party something that would have changed Italian democracy and made [it] more stable." The dangerous Italian situation called for a strategy of resilience instead of the dogmatic anticommunism that no longer applied to a rapidly changing political scene.

Moro saw the danger in personal terms as well, for himself and his loved ones, as the family members later agreed, but neither the public nor his confidants had any inkling of these fears. Right up until the end he appeared to be what he long had been: an eccentric though far from absent-minded professor who presided as the archetypal man of political power in Italy. On 12 March 1978 just such a portrayal of him came out in the *Corriere della Sera*. In this witty parody Gianfranco Piazzesi made fun of Moro's well-known hypochondria, describing the "portable pharmacy" that he always had with him.[57] The rigor of Moro's wardrobe also came in for some good-natured ribbing. His dark suits, which he wore even in the African jungle on state visits, were a famous Moro trademark. Whenever the stiff, ill-at-ease, and often comically formal Moro essayed the common touch, he looked like a badly rehearsed performer. The discomfort he experienced in crowds is evident in a photograph accompanying Piazzesi's article. There he was, amidst bathers at the seashore on a glorious summer day, wearing a white shirt and silk tie. He even had a dark overcoat with him. His pained expression was the last touch of vintage Moro. From time to time such raillery would give way to suspicion, as on 16 March 1978, when the morning newspapers repeated the long-circulating rumors that Moro might be tainted by the so-called Lockheed scandal, involving bribes and fraud on a vast scale in the selling of American aircraft to the Italians.

The evening newspapers had a very different Moro story to report. The Red Brigades had struck at via Fani, and a hideous nightmare came to life. During the next fifty-five days Moro inhabited a Kafkaesque world in what his captors called the People's Prison. Only long afterwards did the rest of society begin to learn the particular details of his terrible experience, a process of disclosure that is still incomplete. From their first communication, on 17 March, the Red Brigades made it clear why they had kidnapped Moro. After De Gasperi, he was "the most authoritative leader, the undisputed 'theorist' and 'strategist' of that Christian Democratic regime that for thirty years has oppressed the Italian people."[58] He had been "the political godfather and the most faithful executor of the directives given by the imperialist headquarters." Moro, the eternal Christian Democratic powerbroker, was the man of SIM (Stati Imperialisti delle Multinazionali) in Italy. This treacherous and reactionary Christian Democratic regime would now have to answer for its crimes.

The Red Brigadists knew Moro's résumé by heart. They had been accumulating information about him for years and fantasizing about the opportunity now at hand. This "key man of the bourgeoisie" had seen his power steadily grow and sharply accelerate during the years 1974–1978, when he had been the master builder in the structuring of SIM in Italy.[59] Now he would go on trial before the people. The purposes of the People's trial would be to clarify in detail the imperialist and antiproletarian politics of which "the DC [the Christian Democratic party] is the standard-bearer," to individuate "the international structures and the national affiliations of the imperialist counterrevolution," and to ascertain "the direct responsibilities of Aldo Moro for which, with the criteria of PROLETARIAN JUSTICE, he will be judged."[60]

Eventually, the Red Brigades offered to exchange Moro for thirteen imprisoned terrorists. The government and nearly all the party leaders in Italy dismissed this offer on the principle of no negotiations with terrorist murderers. The Socialist leader, Bettino Craxi, did attempt to keep negotiations going with the Red Brigades by promising some kind of prisoner exchange, although even he thought that the thirteen-for-one demand could never be considered. From inside the People's Prison, Moro wrote letters encouraging negotiations and prophesying calamity for his party if they failed to rescue him. To the Christian Democratic secretary, Benigno Zaccagnini, he wrote that his death "would open a terrible spiral with which you would not be able to cope," for his friends and supporters would never accept "this tragedy."[61] In another letter, Moro plainly stated his belief that the Christian Democrats could bring him home safely if they wanted to; and if he were to be killed, that, too, would be a consequence of the party's deepest and truest wishes: "I die, if my party so desires it, in the fullness of my Christian faith and in the immense love for an exemplary family that I adore and hope to watch over from on high in the heavens."[62] The Christian Democratic hierarchy, as well as most other party leaders and the media, maintained that these letters were extracted through drugs or some form of torture, but from the beginning many people accepted Moro's estimate of his situation and accused Andreotti of base motives in his refusal to negotiate with the terrorists.

In the end, on 9 May 1978, the Red Brigades executed Moro by shooting, in circumstances known only to a very restricted circle within the terrorist organization. Under the noses of the police, they then transported his corpse to a spot in Rome midway between the party headquarters of the Christian Democrats and the Communists. The Aldo Moro murder case had begun, along with vituperative polemics about where ultimate responsibility for his death lay.

2

The Italian Legal System

The quest for justice in the Moro case would take place mainly in the courts, and the basic features of the Italian legal system differ significantly from the Anglo-American legal system. Italy practices civil law, whereas, England and the United States have common law. Although the two systems are connected historically, each has developed its own judicial institutions, legal concepts, and courtroom practices.

The first and most important of the historic influences that shaped both the civil law and common law traditions was the sixth-century Code of Justinian. This work of codification, supervised by the great jurist Tribonian, synthesized the heritage of more than one thousand years of Roman law and became the basis, together with the canon law of the Church, of medieval legal study in Italy. From Roman law and canon law emerged Europe's *jus commune*, the basic legal tradition taught in medieval law schools. As in virtually every field of intellectual endeavor during the late Middle Ages and the Renaissance, Italy took the lead also in legal studies. The University of Bologna became and long remained the premier law school in Europe, but the universities at Padua and Pisa also contributed to Italy's unrivaled prestige in the training of Europe's lawyers and legal scholars.

Three styles of interpreting the jus commune emerged during these centuries. The "glossators" developed the gloss as an annotation technique for the interpretation and the modern adaptation of the Roman and canon laws. Then the "commentators" brought to the study of the law a more broadly philosophical viewpoint, informed by scholasticism. Finally, the "legal humanists" made their presence felt in the law schools of Italy by training their students to use sophisticated methods of textual criticism and to revere pure classical Latin as a model for legal writing. These three schools of legal thought produced an immense literature that enriched the intellectual traditions of the jus commune and fortified Italy's international reputation for law studies.

Each national legal system in Europe also perpetuated its own indigenous traditions and practices; in this way local legal institutions merged with the jus commune, making each system distinct. That process gave rise to some peculiar features in England.

England, like all other European countries, absorbed the influences emanating from the law faculties of Italian universities. In the middle of the twelfth century the Italian glossator Vacarius arrived in England to found the law school at Oxford, but the English kings came to view the Roman law as a stalking horse for the Holy Roman Empire. Indeed, the jus commune had been developed by legal scholars who took for granted the political primacy of the Holy Roman Empire. As for England's contentious barons, concerned about protecting their own power, they resisted the Roman law out of fear that it would augment the king's authority. These diverse political considerations contributed to the continuation of the local common law in England, which, though of recent Norman origin, came to be revered as the legitimate English legal tradition. The jus commune only penetrated into limited areas of the English law. Based on the precedent of already settled cases in English law instead of the theoretical expositions of ancient Roman law, and on the jury method of determining the outcome of trials instead of leaving them to the discretion of a judicial authority, the common law tradition developed an ethos and a procedure strongly at variance with those of the civil law tradition on the Continent. The jury system is responsible for most of the differences between the common law and civil law traditions. Over the ensuing centuries, both the English and continental traditions tended to converge in instituting safeguards for individual rights and in many other matters as well, but they remain fundamentally different ways of thinking about and dispensing the law.

Meanwhile, Italian legal scholars continued to be the leading interpreters of the jus commune. Italy dominated the field until the sixteenth century, when the rise of the nation-state weakened the universal appeal of the jus commune. Thereafter, the civil law tradition continued its evolution as a family of related but not identical legal systems. Nevertheless, even after the lead in legal development had passed to France, Italian thinkers remained prominent. Secular natural law theories, arising in the seventeenth century, permeated legal studies in Europe during the French-dominated Enlightenment, but no single work on the law by any eighteenth-century writer could compare in influence or originality with Cesare Beccaria's *On Crimes and Punishments* (1764). A law graduate from the University of Pavia, Beccaria made an eloquent appeal for reason, mercy, and tolerance. His classic book paved the way for a magnificent civilizing advance in the theory and practice of the law. Many of the modern legal standards enshrined in the Declaration of the Rights of Man and Citizen (1789) and systematized in the Napoleonic Codes (1804) were adapted from his formulations.

During the nineteenth century the Napoleonic Codes became the Continent's foremost legal model, and they absorbed the culturally familiar traditions, ideas, and institutions of the jus commune as well as the modernizing spirit and legal ideals of the French Revolution, to which Beccaria had made so signal a contribution. Temporarily discarded by many European governments after Napoleon's fall, his law codes soon returned to favor as an indispensable legal synthesis. That these codes greatly enhanced the power of the central governing authority, in time came to be seen by restoration leaders all over Europe as a compensating good for the regrettable evils of the Old Regime destroyers.

Piedmont, the Italian state responsible for the unification of Italy, employed a legal system heavily influenced by the Napoleonic codes. With the proclamation of a united kingdom in 1861, many of Piedmont's legal norms became Italy's. The Civil Code of 1865 reflected the French-style centralizing tendencies of the new Italian state. Italy's Penal Code of 1889, a model of liberal thinking on crime and punishment and famous for its abolition of the death penalty, was a very cosmopolitan compendium. Its compilers based their work, in significant part, on the positivist and evolutionary theories of Europe's most advanced scientific thinkers, among whom the French still enjoyed eminence.

During the late nineteenth and early twentieth centuries, however, German theories about the law began to command attention in Italy.

The "pandectists," so called because their ideas grew out of researches they undertook in the Digest of Justinian *(Pandekten)*, strongly resembled the medieval glossators in spirit, with the excellent fillip for the age of Darwin of an ultra-scientific consciousness and argot. Because this German legal science, as it came to be known, essentially conformed to and enhanced an honored tradition in the Italian law, the pandectists found many supporters among the best legal minds in Italy. The task of the legal scholar, according to pandectist theory, was to study the Roman codes for their pure legal concepts and, on the basis of these, to arrive at a scientific understanding of the law. What the biologists and the physicists could explain about matter and energy, the pandectists believed that they could do with the law, which to them was a self-contained sphere boasting its own truths and criteria for scientific analysis and verification.

The elaborate theoretical doctrines of German legal science became deeply embedded in the curriculum of Italian law schools and shaped the thinking of the legal scholars who produced the 1942 Code. Despite the date of its adoption, this Code is in none of its essentials a Fascist document. Fascist jurists bitterly complained in the 1930s about the obstructionism of traditional jurists, who in their efforts to hold onto the essentials of Italy's historic legal system were aided by the deep ideological divisions within the regime. Inevitably, the traditional jurists made some significant concessions, but at its core the 1942 Code embodied the country's civil law traditions. The fall of Mussolini initiated the dismantling of fascism. Mussolini's Code was thus revised to conform to the Republican Constitution of 1948 and remains in effect to this day. The related Code of Criminal Procedure (1930) bore a heavier weight of Fascist ideology, but it, too, was adapted to the needs of the postfascist era before being replaced in 1989 by a new code.

The Aldo Moro murder case followed the standard rules of procedure in the three phases of the Italian judicial process for criminal cases, as stipulated in the country's 1930 legal code: pre-investigation, investigation, and trial. In the pre-investigation phase the police must first declare that a crime has occurred, and then produce suspects and accumulate evidence. In the investigation phase, the examining judges analyze all the evidence and ultimately decide whether to proceed with a public trial. This second phase is a wide-ranging investigation in which the examining judges use any evidence that they consider suitable. They not only examine the evidence acquired from the police, but also pursue their own inquiries, principally by interrogating witnesses whose oral testimony is written down by a clerk. The purpose of the investigation phase is to prepare a complete written record of all the pertinent evidence in the case. The investigation ends with a decision for acquittal or a public trial. These first two phases of the Italian judicial process are similar to the grand jury phase of the common law tradition. The grand jury also inquires into alleged violations of the law, in order to ascertain whether the evidence is sufficient to warrant a trial, but here again the emphasis in the civil law tradition on judicial authority sharply differentiates Italy's legal system from that of common law countries.

The trial itself has three phases: preliminaries, courtroom proceedings, and matters subsequent to the trial. The main object of the preliminaries is to ensure that all the parties involved can conduct their cases with proper legal representation. Once the trial begins, witnesses who have spoken only informally with the examining judge appear in court to testify formally under oath and to be questioned. Stated this baldly, the trial might appear to be an anticlimax following the investigation phase, but in fact the questioning in the courtroom can lead to spontaneous developments and disclosures, as in the Moro case.

The president of the court, a career judge, directs the proceedings from the bench. He and the public prosecutor *(pubblico ministero)*, who in the Italian system is also a member of the judiciary, lead in conducting the examination of witnesses. This is another feature of the law in Italy that differs sharply from legal practice in America, where judges do not examine witnesses in criminal trials. One other career judge, called the *giudice a latere* (literally, the judge on the side), also sits on the bench. Six popular judges, selected from citizens aged thirty to sixty-five, who are deemed to be of good moral character and who have at least a secondary education, sit on the bench as well. The popular judges are not to be confused with the jurors in the common law system. The popular judges and the career judges sit as a unitary bench and together decide the outcome of the trial after hearing all the testimony, reviewing all the evidence, and listening to the closing arguments of the prosecutor and of the lawyers. In practice, the career judges elucidate the fine points of the law and procedure, but the lay judges function as their complete equals in the exercise of judicial power. In America, by contrast, judges decide only on matters of law, and it is the jury that must decide the facts of a case. Following the announcement of a verdict, the giudice a latere prepares a document in which the court's legal reasoning is explained and made public. Italian judges take great pride in this part of their legal system, comparing it favorably with the lack of explanation of common law juries on how they arrive at their verdicts.

The appeal process, which is very elaborate in Italy, can concern points of law or fact. In the common law, the jury has the final word on fact, but in Italy an appeal is not a mere review; it takes the form of a new trial. The appeal trial is presided over by another eight-member team of two career and six popular judges. They sift all the evidence again. New testimony may be presented and new legal defenses raised. As in the court of the first instance, the career and popular judges meet as complete equals in the president's chamber to discuss the case, until they render a verdict in full or substantial agreement with the previous act of sentencing or in disagreement with it. The case must then be reviewed for a third and final time by seven career judges in the Corte di Cassazione, the highest court in the judicial system. This court generally limits itself to a review of how the law has been applied in a case, without arguing the merits of the decision. Its chief function is to ensure uniformity in the interpretation of the law.

To this legal system, a product of some twenty-five hundred years of more or less continuous growth and refinement, the Italian people looked for justice in the Aldo Moro murder case. For all of its problems regarding excessive case loads and long delays in bringing trials to a conclusion, the system basically inspired public confidence.[1] The moral and intellectual reputation of the judges as a class of professionals did not raise the kind of questions over venality and fecklessness that generally arose about the country's politicians, a contrast sharply drawn in the recent corruption scandals and anti-Mafia campaigns from which judges have emerged as popular heroes. The Italian judiciary benefited in many ways from its completely autonomous character, as a result of which no other branch or institution of government could in any way influence the recruitment, supervision, and promotion of judges. They recruited, supervised, and promoted themselves. On the other hand, such a system could be faulted as ingrown and arbitrary. In Italy the judiciary has certainly been the target of widespread criticism, particularly for what have been called its high-handed practices in the era of Tangentopoli. Nevertheless, as the first trial got under way, the public could reasonably expect that the endemic political pressures and intrigue for which Italy was infamous would be unavailing in thwarting the quest for justice in the Aldo Moro murder case. The intense public scrutiny of this case guaranteed the best effort of which the legal system was capable, and, indeed, the responsible magistrates were known to be eminently honest, capable, and experienced men.[2]

3

The First Trial

Phase One

Two separate investigation proceedings, "Moro 1" and "Moro bis," preceded the courtroom phase of the first trial. Shortly after Moro's assassination judges Ernesto Cudillo, Achille Gallucci, Francesco Amato, Rosario Priore, Ferdinando Imposimato, and Claudio D'Angelo began the initial investigation. Judge Imposimato also conducted the second investigation. Their voluminous reports became the subject of numerous newspaper articles. By the spring of 1982, as the first trial got under way, reporters were conveying the impression that as a result of the two judicial investigations very few mysteries remained in the case. One reporter assured his readers that the events leading to Moro's death had been reconstructed with "mathematical precision."[1] Another wrote confidently, "of the Moro affair almost everything is known."[2]

Indeed, the investigating magistrates in Moro 1 produced a staggering amount of information. Thirty-two volumes, divided into many dozens of *fascicoli*, or separate booklets, and totaling tens of thousands of pages, detailed the sequence of events from Moro's kidnapping to his death. Included in this great miscellany were all the pertinent messages from the Red Brigades as well as a seemingly exhaustive record of the police investigation. The first volume, "Atti generici," was an 11,000-page-long potpourri of hearsay and evidence from all over the world. One letter, in English, had arrived from Madrid; its author claimed to have proof of a CIA plot against Moro.[3] Diverse extremist groups offered their analyses of the Moro kidnapping, and these, too, became part of the record submitted to the court.[4]

Autopsy reports on the corpses of Moro's bodyguards, with numerous front and back photographs—including close-up shots of their wounds—filled 308 pages of the Atti generici.[5] Raffaele Iozzino had been struck by seventeen bullets, Oreste Leonardi by nine, Domenico Ricci by seven, Giulio Rivera by eight, Francesco Zizzi by three. The bill for each forensic specialist was neatly appended to the autopsy reports. The investigating judges in Moro 1 were nothing if not thorough.

The autopsy report on Moro himself filled four fascicoli in another volume. Unlike his bodyguards, Moro had not been photographed in the nude. The eleven bullet holes in his body had to be pointed out through superimposed arrows or penciled-in circles.[6] Blow-ups of the extracted bullets and the detailed reports of ballistics experts followed. Numerous chemical tests had been conducted in order to determine whether the Red Brigadists had given Moro drugs; they proved negative.[7] Other experts had analyzed sand granules lodged in Moro's clothing, soil samples scraped from his shoes, and tiny fragments of wood, leaves, and other vegetable substances found in the Renault; more blow-ups of all these items, with a detailed description of each, were also included in the autopsy report.[8]

The seven fascicoli of volume two, entitled "The Defendants," ran to more than 1,900 pages and included records of police interrogations. A little longer were the seven fascicoli of volume three, "The Witnesses." Moro 1 also led to the publication of twenty-two fascicoli entitled "Technical Reports" and twenty-nine fascicoli of "Perizi," or "Expert Analysis"; additional reports of both kinds lay scattered throughout other parts of the judicial inquiry as well. Other volumes, often divided into many fascicoli, were devoted to such subjects as "Transcriptions from Tape Recordings," "Translations of Foreign Police Reports," "Other Trials" connected with the Moro case, "The Press"—what newspapers, periodicals, and reviews had to say about the case—"Tapped Telephone Conversations," "Impugnments," "Bank Statements," "Miscellaneous," the "Requisitoria," or "Indictment" of the procuratore generale, and the "Sentenza," or "Sentence." It did not seem that anything further could be said about the Moro case.

The 13 December 1979 *requisitoria* of Guido Guasco, the procurator general, summed up the results of the investigation in close to 200 pages. Thirty-eight defendants stood accused of seventy-six terrorist crimes, the most infamous of which were the Moro kidnapping and murder. These crimes sprang not from passion or greed, but from ideology. Therefore, he devoted many pages of the requisitoria to the historical background of Red Brigade violence in Italy. The country, Guasco argued, had given birth to a virulent revolutionary tradition of which Red Brigadism had been the latest product on the extreme left. If only the Red Brigades had been (and been perceived as) nothing more than a group of maladjusted imbeciles with no connection to anything vital in Italian life, then the country would have been spared the horrible terrorist violence of the 1970s. But Italy had been unlucky in this regard; unlike the relatively feeble left-wing revolutionary groups in other countries, the Red Brigades stood shoulder-to-shoulder with numerous like-minded formations, and together they posed a dire threat to Italian democracy.

Italians have a tradition of ideologically sanctioned violence, and Guasco sought to explain how Red Brigadism had arisen out of that culture. He castigated the large, amorphous Potere Operaio movement and its paramount chiefs: Toni Negri, Franco Piperno, and Lanfranco Pace. They had sought to promote the kind of Marxist-Leninist revolution espoused by the Red Brigades, and for years their dream had been to unite all the country's radical forces into a movement that would bring about "the systematic destruction of capitalist domination and the armed struggle for the conquest of power on the part of the working class by means of the ordering and the organization of the insurrection of the proletarian masses."[9] The Potere Operaio organization had been the home base of Adriana Faranda and Valerio Morucci, two of the most vicious and feared Red Brigadists, as well as of other recruits to that dread terrorist organization. In particular, Negri's career as a subversive while a professor with tenure at the University of Padua revealed a lot about the many soft spots of decay in Italian political and intellectual life, the procurator general admonished.[10] Numerous contacts between Negri, Pace, and Piperno on the one hand and leaders of the Red Brigades on the other had been well established. That for years they all contributed, each in his own way, to the tragedy of Italian terrorism, Guasco did not doubt.

He also sought to establish links between the two groups on specific terrorist crimes, including the Moro kidnapping and murder, which the state would seek to explain in the light of a February 1978 Red Brigade

"Resolution." This document, promulgated on the eve of via Fani, clearly presented the objectives of their "springtime offensive." According to Guasco, the Red Brigades wanted to bring about "the destruction of [the state's] political, economic, and military centers of power by means of a diffuse guerrilla action directed at involving the working class . . . in a real civil war and in a mobilization against democratic institutions."[11] In other words, the taking of Moro would signal the collapse of the Christian Democratic regime, opening the way to a proletarian revolution of which these assorted fanatics long had styled themselves the vanguard. The Moro 1 investigation proceeding culminated in a decision to bring the defendants to trial.

At two volumes and only 672 pages, Moro bis appeared as the briefest of addenda to Moro 1. Judge Imposimato's findings also reinforced the public belief that the courtroom trial would essentially be an anticlimax. He had to concern himself with the entire catalogue of crimes committed by the Rome column of the Red Brigades since 1976, but obviously the Moro kidnapping and murder stood out in high relief. Evidence acquired after the start of Moro 1 had made a second judicial inquiry necessary, and in particular confessions by new *pentiti*, or repentant terrorists, added important information. The "sincerity and genuineness" of these confessions would have to be ascertained.[12] Judge Imposimato wrote that he tended to believe the pentiti, principally because "often those dissociating themselves from the armed struggle have admitted with scrupulous attention to details criminal episodes of which they had not even been accused."[13]

The judge also stressed the importance of ballistics reports as well as conclusions reached by other experts. It had been his experience, though, that eyewitness testimony had rarely been of any serious help in an investigation, partly because of a quite natural human tendency to distort reality in moments of traumatic stress, but mainly because Italy lacked a strong and widely diffused "civic sense," resulting in a depressing public atmosphere where private and individual interests prevailed over the collective good.[14] In short, wherever possible people chose to ignore their public duty, a behavior that had facilitated the cause of terrorism.

Judge Imposimato expressed "disquiet" about one other matter. His investigations revealed that the Italian people had been victimized by "alarming instances of complicity and interference on the part of intelligence agencies and governments."[15] Arms shipments to Italian terrorists from George Habbash's radical Palestinian faction had come to Italy almost certainly with the approval of the Russians.[16] Several pentiti confirmed these connections. Libya, too, had been another country heavily involved in the arming of Italian terrorists.[17] Red Brigade relations with Israeli secret service agents merited an entire section in Judge Imposimato's *sentenza istruttoria.* Numerous pentiti had sworn to the judge that Mossad had offered to help the Red Brigades because it was in Israel's interests to destabilize Italy, so that the Americans would rely on Jerusalem as their only secure ally in the Mediterranean.[18] Judge Imposimato reserved his most scathing remarks for the Italian secret services. It was an outrage that the secret services of Israel and of other countries had attempted to manipulate the Red Brigades for their own ends, but it was a tragedy with farcical overtones that the Italian secret services had been unaware, so far as he could determine, of the terrorist threat in their own country, "involved as they were in affairs completely extraneous to their institutional tasks."[19]

With both judicial investigations complete, the case moved to trial. The first session took place on 14 April 1982 in the gymnasium of Rome's Foro Italico, now transformed into an immense and unlikely looking courtroom. Three thousand men provided security for the proceedings. The whole area around this white stone sports complex, built by the Fascist regime, looked like a military camp as more than a hundred police dog patrol units criss-crossed the grounds outside. Six months earlier authorities had begun to fortify the gymnasium with bullet-proof windows, metal detectors at the entrances, television cameras inside and out, automatic generators to provide electricity in case of emergency, and special alarm systems. A wrought-iron fence protected the perimeter.

Inside, at one end of the oblong-shaped gymnasium, there was a separate section with its own entrance and rows of benches reserved for the public. Many people had arrived early in the freezing rain to make sure of getting a place. At the other end of the facility, behind a long raised bench, sat the president of the court, Severino Santiapichi, a second judge of the robe named Antonio Germano Abbate, and six popular judges who would also help to decide the case. Behind them a row of chairs was reserved for ten supplementary popular judges. The public minister, Nicolò Amato, also took his place near the bench. The judges, aided by two television monitors, could survey the entire assembly. Directly before them were the lawyers' tables, positioned one after the other and extending back nearly to the public section, each one with space for several occupants. Front-left of the judges six white steel cages lined one wall. These held the prisoners, with each cage designated for a certain classification of defendant: *pentiti*, who cooperated completely with the authorities; *dissociati*, who selectively cooperated with them; and *irriducibili*, who did not cooperate at all. Front-right of the judges, long rows of chairs reserved for the journalists lined another wall. Above, to the left and right of the judges, carabinieri and police patrolled on ramps. Additional officers stood guard in front of and inside the prisoner cages, and a small army of 500 men escorted the defendants to and from the courtroom.

That such elaborate security measures were necessary became evident the day before the trial began, when Red Brigade terrorists shot and wounded three carabinieri standing guard outside the courtroom building. The attack was a standard tactic of the Red Brigades. In the past they repeatedly had attempted to obstruct legal proceedings against their imprisoned confederates. Although a rapidly declining military force, Red Brigadism still possessed this kind of disruptive power. No longer perceived as a serious threat to Italy's political institutions, terrorists continued to kill and maim the defenders of those institutions. President Santiapichi later recalled that the atmosphere of the trial was "extremely tense" because of the perpetual fear of terrorist attacks.[20]

The terrorists on trial made a flaunting entrance. Laughing and joking, they loudly greeted their friends and relatives who had come to the Foro Italico. Also present were relatives of the men these terrorists had killed, but no remorse was shown. Inside the cages a festive atmosphere prevailed. The prisoners had the air of normal young people who at worst had gone off on an ill-considered lark. The scene was from the last days of senior year in high school, not from *Crime and Punishment*. In the brief interval between the entrance of the judges and that of the defendants, photographers, journalists, and television reporters mobbed the cages in a frantic contest for the privilege of obtaining interviews. With celebrity comes legitimacy, and the media gave the assassins of Aldo Moro a treatment usually reserved for rock stars and movie queens. One reporter, in extreme embarrassment for his peers, ruefully observed that he had the sensation of being an onlooker at the zoo while an elephant was being born.[21]

The defendants immediately tested the court's president, a judge of vast experience who also had been in charge of the trial for the would-be assassin of Pope John Paul II in 1981, Ali Agca. When President Santiapichi denied a request to return some confiscated materials to them, the hard-core Red Brigadists began to jeer and to insult him. One called him "a buffoon and a clown."[22] Another complained that Santiapichi did not know how to run a trial. He lost no time in ordering his tormentors out of the courtroom. Before leaving, they chanted, "Rosse, rosse, Brigate Rosse," and then Prospero Gallinari, the man accused of executing Moro, led them all in a rendition of the *Internationale.*

The first few sessions of the trial took place in a circus-like atmosphere. The terrorists continued to hector President Santiapichi, claiming that their civil rights had been violated. They did not even bother to appear for the second session on 21 April, and the next day Santiapichi granted their request to leave the courtroom. Their exits were invariably stormy, with the terrorists venting taunts and threats as they went. Soon, however, the novelty of these confrontations began to wear off, and the trial settled into a monotonous legal routine punctuated by moments of high drama. The courtroom became filled for these moments, but average daily attendance by spectators, journalists, and even lawyers began to decline very early in the trial.

As Red Brigade terror lessened in Italy, the organization was left with little to do but talk. Therefore the hard-core terrorists eventually modified their obstructionist tactics in favor of participation in the trial in their own fashion, although disruptive outbursts continued to result in frequent expulsions from the courtroom. They clearly perceived that their more than decade-long war with the Italian Republic had entered a new phase. The terrorists had not succeeded in destroying the state, but they promised to expose its fatal contradictions by producing information about the Moro affair injurious to the governing authorities. Everything would come out in the trial, but first they had to wait for the testimony of the pentiti and the dissociati to be heard.

Sitting in a chair directly before the judges, a tense and pallid Antonio Savasta testified for twenty-seven hours over eight court sessions in late April and early May 1982. At the beginning of each session the short and slightly built Savasta had to endure the curses of the unrepentant terrorists who then exited before his testimony began. During the first session he gave an elaborately detailed sketch of his background in extraparliamentary left and overtly revolutionary groups, down to the time in late 1976 when he joined the Red Brigades. For his generation of extremist left-wing university students it seemed that Italy was then living "in pre-insurrectionary moments," and the appeal of the Red Brigades lay in that organization's unequivocal call for an immediate Marxist-Leninist revolution.[23] Savasta reached these conclusions through what he described as a systematic if not complete reading of Lenin, Marx, and Mao. Applying their theoretical and historical insights to 1975 Italy, he could not improve on the Red Brigade analysis.

Savasta spoke in a monotone with extreme punctiliousness about murders he and other Red Brigadists had committed. The twenty-seven-year-old pentito spoke without regret or any discernible emotion. There was nothing criminal about the Marxist-Leninist project of communist revolution, he explained. It had been a valid cause, although admittedly ill-timed. The Red Brigadists had suffered from subjectivism, Savasta maintained in the left-wing jargon that he employed with the confident authority of a scientist explaining the most self-evident of natural truths. In vain at such moments did an annoyed President Santiapichi enjoin Savasta to speak in a language "accessible to the entire court."[24] On another occasion the judge fumed, "I'm a man who goes after the facts, and I don't like the indirect approach to them *(il can per l'aia non mi piace)*."[25] In short, "political answers" did not interest him at all, but here Savasta energetically rejoined that the court would have to listen to political answers because left-wing Italian terrorism could only be understood in terms of the ideological agenda the terrorists had set for themselves.[26] Cruel and disgusting as their deeds seemed even to him now, Savasta insisted that all the blood had been shed for revolutionary ideals in which the Red Brigadists passionately and uncritically believed. Apart from these ideals the facts of Red Brigade terrorism made no sense.

When asked by Santiapichi about the moral concerns he might have had over taking human life, the voluble Savasta was momentarily disconcerted. Humanitarian concerns did not enter his thinking, he quickly responded. To live the life of a Red Brigadist meant above all else to embrace the conviction that revolutionary violence, as prescribed by Marx and Lenin, was the highest possible good in overthrowing a moribund capitalist order, and this is exactly what Savasta and the others firmly believed they were doing. Therefore, what mattered most to him and to every true revolutionary was the utility of an action in advancing the cause of the proletariat; such was the only morality they recognized. Enemies within the reach of Red Brigade power lived or died according to this measure.

Moro was no exception to the Red Brigades' golden rule, and Savasta freely admitted that in late April 1978 he had cast his vote for the Christian Democratic leader's death, as all the founders of the organization had done.[27] According to Savasta, the Red Brigades had kidnapped Moro because, as the spokesman for Italy in the so-called multinational dominion over the world, he was the key figure in Italian politics. He had completely neutralized the PCI, but this in itself was not the crux of their antagonism toward him. To President Santiapichi's question concerning the Red Brigades' view of Moro's historic compromise with the Communists, Savasta answered that this had no bearing at all on the decision to kidnap him. The PCI had lost its Marxist identity so long ago that the understanding between Moro and Enrico Berlinguer represented nothing fundamentally new as far as the Red Brigades were concerned. At the outset of his trial in the People's Prison Moro was already guilty in their eyes, not so much for any particular act, such as the historic compromise, but because of what he represented: the embodiment of all that was the most intelligent and therefore the most dangerous in the Christian Democratic regime.[28]

In Savasta's view, the trial of Moro in the People's Prison had been a fiasco for the Red Brigades from beginning to end. By interrogating him they hoped "to discover how things really had happened," to unearth all the scandals buried by the corrupt Christian Democratic regime.[29] However, "nothing came of any of these things."[30] It is easy to deduce from Savasta's testimony that the People's Prison trial actually had been a debate, with Moro in effect explaining to his captors that the nature of political power in a modern industrial society was completely different from the clichéd Marxist-Leninist fable of their earnest imagining. This was ground on which the nimble-footed Moro had been tested in a hundred political battles. He knew from experience the matters under discussion, whereas his adversaries had only been exposed to them through books of a singular ideological persuasion. It did not require a fantastic leap of the imagination to envisage the intellectual mismatch that must have occurred at this "trial," although Moro, by nature polite and deferential, was never one to drive his points as far as they could possibly go.

Unfortunately for Moro, the outcome of his kidnapping did not turn on an intelligent and realistic analysis of Italian politics. The Red Brigades conceived the Moro operation as a means of furthering their revolutionary design. Savasta said that in the immediate aftermath of the attack on via Fani applications to join the Red Brigades rose sharply; the leaders wanted to accelerate this momentum, and "a great work of propaganda" was undertaken in the universities, the factories, and in the working-class districts.[31] They sincerely believed that a Marxist-Leninist revolution might be at hand in Italy. All of their communications reflected this belief. Moro was a pawn for them, to be used and discarded as the needs of the revolution dictated.

Savasta added that the Red Brigades used Moro's own prison letters as a means to the organization's strategic end. Moro was allowed to choose his words, but the Red Brigades gave him thematic suggestions. Also, they did not permit all of his letters to be sent: real censorship was always at work. Here Savasta commented on perhaps the single most controversial aspect of the Moro affair: the four-year old debate over the authenticity of the famous prison letters. Savasta's testimony offered support for those who denied their authenticity. One telling detail concerned the 1981 kidnapping of Giuseppe Taliercio, during which Savasta, before finally killing him, had acted as the Red Brigades' censor by reading the prisoner's outgoing letters and suggesting where changes might be made. He could speak from experience about how the Red Brigadist interrogators always undertook to have a political dialogue with their kidnap victims, to clarify what the organization's objectives were. This initial explanation would then be followed by a suggestion that both the organization and their victim faced a problem that they could help each other to solve. The kidnapping could end without tragedy; the victim could get his freedom provided that the organization achieved its political objectives. Such a suggestion unfailingly concentrated the mental powers of the victim along the lines desired by the kidnappers. Therefore, Savasta concluded, all correspondence leaving the People's Prison had to pass through a very effective "political filter."[32]

Savasta told the hushed court that Moro never had a realistic hope of leaving the People's Prison alive. This was another extremely sensitive point in the case. Moro's family, the Socialist party, and the extraparliamentary left had argued—against the government, its allies, and the media—that Moro could have been saved through negotiations

with the Red Brigades; even the "symbolic" release of one prisoner
might have been enough to gain the Christian Democratic leader's
release. Savasta declared, however, that only a complete or at least a
substantial capitulation on the Red Brigades' main demand for an
exchange of thirteen imprisoned terrorists for Moro could have averted
the tragedy.[33] Not even a ransom of billions of lire, which, it was later
learned, Pope Paul VI had offered to raise, would have been sufficient.
From March to May 1978 the Red Brigades sensed the possibility of a
breakthrough to revolution, and Moro's fate depended on their reading
of how best to achieve that goal. They would do whatever made the
government look the most enfeebled militarily and politically. Savasta
testified that they hoped the government would yield on the matter of
the prisoner exchange, thereby increasing the momentum of revolution
in Italy; failing that, Moro had to die, and this had been the decision
all along.

It could not be denied that Savasta had given the state invaluable
military intelligence about the Red Brigades: dozens of terrorists had
been arrested on the basis of testimony he had supplied. Nevertheless,
lawyers and journalists at the trial pointed out that Savasta's testimony
on Moro consisted mainly of secondhand observations, not direct
knowledge. He personally had been involved only in a preliminary
phase of the kidnapping operation, trailing Moro on the University of
Rome campus where the Christian Democratic leader taught law.
Savasta had been impressed by Moro's principal bodyguard, Oreste
Leonardi, and advised his Red Brigade superiors that the University
was not a good place to stage the kidnapping. After that, Savasta had
been relegated to other duties in the organization, and he was neither
a member of the strike force at via Fani nor privy to any phase of
Moro's trial in the People's Prison. He evaded some questions put to
him by President Santiapichi and pleaded ignorance to many others.
His answers to specific questions about the kidnapping, incarceration,
and murder of Moro were usually preceded by such phrases as "It
seems to me" or "Someone told me."

The pentiti who followed Savasta to the witness chair did not shed
any more light on the Moro affair, but the court did learn a great deal
about their motives in joining the Red Brigades. Emilia Lìbera, another
former University of Rome student and once romantically linked with
Savasta, explained that her readings of works by Lenin and Mao led
her to conclude that Red Brigadism was the answer to Italy's social and

political problems. But when President Santiapichi's questioning turned to Moro, she could only repeat what Bruno Seghetti, an irriducibile, had told her. The Brigata Universitaria to which Libèra belonged on the University of Rome campus had a very limited involvement in the Moro kidnapping, and she herself had done nothing more than hand out organization literature—a work of *volantinaggio* was her phrase.[34] Massimo Cianfanelli, a former member of the same Brigata Universitaria who had come to Red Brigadism through the well-traveled path of extraparliamentary left-wing activity and a political education informed by the "classics of Marxist-Leninism," testified for three court sessions in late May 1982 without illuminating the Moro case.[35] Having joined the Red Brigades in late April 1978, when the Moro operation was nearly over, Cianfanelli had to restrict himself to quoting the dissociato Valerio Morucci on what the Red Brigades had done to the Christian Democratic leader.

In Carlo Brogi the court heard a witness who did not come from the turbid world of university radicalism. Far better read than the former university students who preceded him in the witness chair, this part-time Alitalia steward had run weapons for the Red Brigades from the United States. He had drifted from job to job without finding his place in society. From his teenage years on, the one fixed point in Brogi's life had been his passion for the literature of revolution. There could not have been a more ideal social environment for such a passion than the one Italy provided during the early 1970s, when revolution was all that he and his friends ever discussed. Brogi read Lenin, Marx, Trotsky, and Rosa Luxemburg, but they only provided him with a general theoretical foundation. When it came time to apply these theories to contemporary Italy, he turned to the *Quaderni rossi*, the *Quaderni piacentini*, and *Potere operaio*—the classic journals of the extraparliamentary left in the 1960s and 1970s—and to the highly suggestive books by Toni Negri. The University of Padua professor's *Fabbrica della strategia: 33 lezioni su Lenin* and other pamphlets on sabotage rounded out young Brogi's political education.[36] He then felt mentally prepared for the life of political action he undertook after joining the Red Brigades in June 1978, one month after the conclusion of the Moro operation. Brogi could add no new information to the case.

Norma Andriani, Brogi's former girlfriend, spoke with palpable emotion about how her "ideal of communism with a human face" had disintegrated under the impact of the life she had led in the terrorist underground.[37] Communism had been the family tradition, and "therefore I always had this type of idea in mind."[38] As an adolescent she devoured the major books of Marx and Lenin. At the University of Rome Andriani eagerly attended seminars on works of these revered masters. *Das Kapital* gave her a completely satisfying explanation of capitalism's destructive inner workings. In Negri's books Andriani found a brilliant updating of the Marxist-Leninist tradition, and she especially delighted in his theories about the exploitative nature of the multinationals.

From a Marxist-Leninist contemplation of society, Andriani directly progressed to a career of revolutionary action. For years her life revolved around the campus activities of Lotta Continua and Potere Operaio. She attended countless meetings of diverse university collectives, participated in the discussions of this or that revolutionary committee, and marched in protest demonstrations. In such a highly charged atmosphere Red Brigadism appeared to be hardly more than the next natural step in the engagé life she had chosen to lead. The Moro kidnapping thrilled her as a possible signal for the revolution that she and her intersecting circles of radical friends had been preparing themselves to guide. Throughout the period of the kidnapping students on the University of Rome campus talked about how the via Fani events would affect the revolution. Andriani participated in all the discussions, but not yet as a member of the Red Brigades. She did not join the organization until after Moro's death, and only then did the reality of Red Brigadism begin to cast a pall over the revolutionary ideology that had been the irradiating center of her life. Instead of serving as the one necessary means to the noble end of a classless society, Red Brigadism proved to be nothing but "barbarism, continuous violence, and the destruction of every human rapport between people."[39] About the Moro case, however, Andriani had no important information.

Testifying on 1 June 1982, Ave Maria Petricola elucidated the sometimes casual and accidental reasons people became terrorists in Italy. As a teenager she had participated in "the usual assemblies, the collectives . . . and demonstrations" that served as a rite of passage for her generation.[40] Petricola had dropped out of school to take menial jobs in various factories. Unlike Brogi and some of the other Red Brigadists outside the university world, Petricola lacked the interest and the mental discipline necessary to acquire the kind of revolutionary culture that they possessed. At best she had never been more than a passive revolutionary. No, Petricola told the court, she had joined the Red Brigades not for ideology but for love. Her Red Brigadist boyfriend, Giulio Cacciotti, insisted that she join the organization as a necessary condition for continuing their romantic relationship: otherwise "the thing was inconceivable," he had warned.[41] On assurances from him that only "duties of the slightest importance" would be assigned to her, she became a Red Brigadist.[42] During the Moro operation Petricola was working in distant Valmontone, completely unconnected with any of the events in Rome. Even her admonitory boyfriend had been given minor duties to perform during that period, and she said he had never mentioned anything about the kidnapping.

The court learned from the next witness, Teodoro Spadaccini, that the University of Rome Brigade included nonstudents and that it served mainly as a training unit for eventual membership in one of the major brigades. Like Petricola, he was in no sense an intellectual and, in fact, had held only the most subservient jobs. Spadaccini had difficulty finding steady work, and he lived from hand-to-mouth as a house painter and peddler of used clothing. Nevertheless, when he joined the Red Brigades in September 1977, he was assigned, as "a brigadist in formation," to the University of Rome Brigade, engaging in propaganda and proselytizing along with Savasta, Libèra, and Andriani.[43]

From him President Santiapichi hoped to learn something concrete about the Moro operation, because Spadaccini at least had been a member of the organization before the kidnapping. The witness disappointed him, however, explaining that he had been suspended shortly before the via Fani attack because of his disagreements with "the orientation, the strategic line, a little on just about everything that the Red Brigades were doing."[44] The Red Brigades had recruited him because of his role as an activist in Potere Operaio, which they considered to be "a guarantee" of his political reliability.[45] Nevertheless, Spadaccini's persistent idealism caused him to run afoul of his organization's superiors. He had been shocked to discover that the Red Brigades had no interest in the individual; a person "only existed in their view for the organization, for the achievement of this mythical revolution."[46] His enthusiasm for them quickly waned, and he never became a full-fledged member. About Moro he had nothing to say.

With the appearance on 14 June 1982 of Patrizio Peci, who steadfastly had avoided the courtroom until that day, onlookers hoped that the dark corners of the Moro affair would begin to yield their secrets. The press described Peci as the *superpentito* par excellence, the key witness in the state's case against Moro's murderers. President Santiapichi and Judge Abbate later described their highly favorable impression of Peci's "astounding contribution to justice."[47] From him had come information leading to the discovery of Red Brigade hideouts, arms, and ammunition. No one could doubt the importance of Peci's "ample, detailed, and determined declarations."[48] Certainly his ex-colleagues in the Red Brigades, for whom he had become the "infamous one," did not doubt it. For their part the judges found his testimony "completely reliable," because its accuracy had been confirmed by "an incredible series of verifications."[49]

In the witness chair, Peci narrated an ideological itinerary that had led inexorably to the Red Brigades. Growing up in the central region of the Marches, Peci gravitated as a young student to Lotta Continua, "the point of reference" for revolution-minded youths of his generation and locale.[50] Most members of that group were content with nothing more than verbal defiance and ritualistic gestures of protest, but to Peci this was a form of mental onanism that he found increasingly unsatisfying. The young man wanted the real thing, and the Red Brigades alone offered it. Eventually, "the impotence" of that organization, exemplified by its absolute failure to establish even a tenuous relationship with the proletariat, became impossible to ignore. Peci then deserted and told the authorities all that he knew. The results of his confession were catastrophic for the Red Brigades, and they retaliated by murdering his brother, Roberto. To President Santiapichi he explained that this crime had made him more eager than ever to ruin his former confederates: "Now that they've killed a brother [of mine], do you think that I'm going to hide anything?"[51] Peci promised to hold nothing back, and his impassioned statement on 14 June fanned the hope that a breakthrough in the Moro case might be at hand.

As Peci testified during four entire court sessions, it became increasingly evident that he, like Savasta, had no firsthand information to furnish. Although Peci had been a Red Brigadist since 1974 and could give the court hair-raising accounts of numerous assassinations in which he had been involved, none of this testimony shed any light on the Moro case. As a member of the Turin column, he had nothing to do with the Moro operation itself except to participate in the propaganda campaign that followed the kidnapping. Peci was true to his word and answered all the questions about Moro, but on the events in Rome his testimony amounted to little more than what Raffaele Fiore and Rocco Micaletto had told him. The *sentito dire* or "heard tell" syndrome in the trial continued with no relief in sight.

Among the dissociati only Arnaldo Maj testified before the summer recess. The dissociati had distanced themselves from the Red Brigades but refused to tell authorities what they knew about other members of the group. Maj, a twenty-nine-year-old statistician who had come to realize that terrorism was a senseless evasion of political responsibility, willingly responded to President Santiapichi's request to explain why such an obviously intelligent and well-spoken young man would join the Red Brigades: to him Italy in the 1970s appeared to be a country going down the drain, and only the revolutionary terrorists offered the drastic solutions that the situation plainly required. In retrospect, the Red Brigade project might appear to someone outside the movement as nothing but a ridiculous delusion. Maj held, however, that for his generation of Italian radicals, immersed in the culture of revolution, who had spent years in left-wing "assemblies, collectives, and . . . study groups" and at the same time felt themselves caught in a wrenching social crisis, the pamphlets and resolutions appearing under the Red Brigade symbol of the five-pointed star possessed a distinct appeal.[52] For people like him, who believed that the radical evil of the Christian Democratic regime could only be overcome through the necessarily violent struggle of Marxist revolutionaries, Red Brigadism was impossible to ignore and difficult to resist. The paramount chiefs of the Red Brigades, Renato Curcio, Alberto Franceschini, and Mario Moretti had made further equivocation impossible on the central point of revolution: you were either for it or not, and if you were for it, then why would you withhold your support from them? Given the ideas that Maj held at the time, it was impossible for him to think of a single reason, and in September 1978 he joined the organization.

The date was important because it meant that Maj could not have witnessed any of the crucial episodes in the Moro case, having been the type of fence-sitter the Red Brigades had in mind when they took Moro. The witness had entered the army that previous summer, and "a series of personal crises" caused him to give up politics completely.[53] For a long time he did not even discuss the subject. When the kidnapping occurred, however, thoughts of revolution returned to haunt him and became an obsession. By stressing the Red Brigades' image as "a perfectly tuned machine," the media ironically confirmed and reinforced his awe of the revolutionaries.[54] According to Maj, many comrades were taken in by this image, which became a "mortal trap" for the people who also joined the organization at a moment when Red Brigadism appeared to be an unstoppable revolutionary force.[55] In fact, as he would later learn, the Red Brigades were never as efficient as the press made them out to be.

On 19 July Moro's widow, Eleonora, sat in the witness chair. Small, stout, white-haired, she clutched an unusually large purse and spoke in a clear, steady voice about her dead husband. Moro, she said, had lived with terror for years, because his moderate and tolerant views had antagonized men of violence on both extremes of Italian political life and their backers abroad. Not being "one of those gossipy women who wants to know everything and who subjects her husband to a hundred thousand questions," she was unable to provide precise details on these matters.[56] She could only be sure that the threats against her husband had been real and had come "from various sources, groups, and persons," but it was not possible for her to specify names and other details for the court.[57] Certainly many people at home and abroad had resented him deeply because of his opening to the Communist party; that may have been reason enough to eliminate him. This decision, which for her husband was a means of ensuring political stability while Italy completed its modernization, was for others the final insult, and they killed him for it. President Santiapichi and other observers sensed that underlying this testimony was a conviction, often alluded to but never plainly formulated by Mrs. Moro, that behind the murder of her husband, at perhaps a remove or two from the assassins themselves, the United States and, by further implication, its proxies in Italy, could be identified through a fairly elementary process of deduction.[58]

Moro undoubtedly had sensed that his life was in danger. As his widow told the court, he had made it clear to her that terrorism was "a huge problem" in Italy, "a thing of the greatest importance."[59] Toward the end, Moro began to take extra security precautions to an extent that was very far out of character for him. She bitterly recalled how the party had turned a deaf ear to his repeated requests for a bulletproof car. Although he rarely discussed these matters with her, she could not help noticing signs of worry and nervousness in him. More concerned about the family than himself, Moro feared that terrorists might try to kidnap one of his children or his only grand-child, Luca.

Although not every People's Prison document attributed to the prisoner could be accepted at face value, Mrs. Moro had complete confidence in the authenticity of the prison letters actually signed by him. She lashed out at the government for refusing to take these letters seriously. To President Santiapichi's question about whether she thought that her husband could have been saved, Mrs. Moro responded tartly, "At least they might have tried."[60] Moro's colleagues in the party could have negotiated with his captors, as her husband had implored in the prison letters, or conducted a search for him with at least the level of intelligence employed by an ordinary housewife in the running of her home. They did neither, and she would never forgive them for that. It was left to her and the family to make whatever private efforts they could to save him, but the government blocked the Moros at every turn for reasons of state, she acidly observed.

Mrs. Moro's indictment of the party was not new, but it created a sensation anyway. Her appearance in the Foro Italico courtroom was one of those dramatic moments in the trial that the media sensed in advance, and while she spoke the television cameras rolled before a full public gallery and a much larger than usual turnout of journalists. The conspiracy theory—that the Christian Democratic leaders wanted Moro to die in the People's Prison—had never been put to rest, but now it was on page one of the newspapers and was the lead story on television news programs. The government, not the Red Brigade pris-oners, remained on the defensive as other Moro family members testified in a similar vein, deploring the state's failure to save "papa" and alluding to the various threats, both foreign and domestic, to which he had been subjected.

From Maria Agnese Moro the court heard that ever since the Italicus train bombing in 1974 her father had worried about the efforts of both the United States and the Soviet Union to destabilize Italy. He knew, for instance, that individuals in his own party, entirely bought and paid for, had built careers on the basis of how best to serve American interests.[61] Giovanni Moro, who had not testified during the *fase istruttoria* of the trial, described his father's "strong preoccupation" with terrorism and told how he had lately become obsessed with the family's physical security.[62] The family's angry testimony reopened the wound left in Italy's public life by the Moro slaying.

The Christian Democrats defended themselves, although they could not do so immediately at the trial. They and their allies in the so-called *fermezza* (firmness) line at the time of the Moro kidnapping used the press for this purpose. Writing in *Il Popolo*, the official newspaper of the Christian Democrats, Flaminio Piccoli conceded that the Moro family had every right to be appalled and unforgiving over the government's failure to save their loved one. While mistakes had been made by the government, that was all they were: mistakes. The government, this Christian Democratic leader contended, went beyond every reasonable length to return Moro to the bosom of his family. On that point, the central one in the conspiracy theory, Piccoli's conscience was clear. The party had faced a terrible choice: to seek to save their leader, presumably during those fifty-five days of confusion and uncertainty, at the expense of the Republic, or to save the Republic at the expense of their leader. They dreaded making that choice and postponed it as long as possible, but in the end they could not abdicate their responsibility as the governing party of Italy by plunging the country into the certain chaos that would have followed any concessions to the Red Brigades. To imagine that Moro had been the victim of his friends could most charitably be dismissed as an aberration, Piccoli concluded. No evidence could be found for such an indictment, the real aim of which was not to ascertain the truth, but to injure the Christian Democrats.[63]

Piccoli garnered support for this last assertion from the distinguished historian Leo Valiani, who added that, as a point of logic, the government's critics could not have the conspiracy theory both ways. It was one thing to say that certain individuals within the orbit of the government, among the right-wing police and military leaders, were pleased with the outcome of the Moro kidnapping. They delighted in the stilling of his voice for obvious political reasons. It was quite another thing, involving a bizarre leap of the imagination, to include the likes of Giulio Andreotti and Benigno Zaccagnini of the DC and Enrico Berlinguer and Ugo Pecchioli of the PCI—the very people who had supported Moro's opening to the Communists—in a homicidal cabal. The haze surrounding the conspiracy theory lifted the moment the facts were subjected to a serious critical review, although Valiani conceded that conspiracies involving foreign powers could not be ruled out. At this point in the investigation, however, for anyone with a weakness for evidence, the conspiracy theories were gossamer threads floating high above the domain of verifiable facts.[64] To be sure, not everybody in Italy had this weakness.

In the aftermath of the Moro family testimony, numerous lawyers in the case demanded that additional witnesses, including many of the nation's political leaders, be subpoenaed in order to clarify the issues Mrs. Moro and her children had raised. Public Minister Nicolò Amato agreed. He, too, wanted to know exactly what had happened between 16 March and 9 May 1978, no matter how much time and expense it would take to find out. In the early morning hours of 24 July 1982, after an all-night session in the President's chambers, the court decided in favor of new procedures that would necessitate a much longer trial than earlier envisaged.[65] President Santiapiachi then declared that the trial would be reconvened after the summer recess.

4

The First Trial

Phase Two

T he courtroom doors opened again on 20 September 1982, despite legal maneuvers by some of the lawyers to keep the trial suspended until the conclusion of Moro ter, a third judicial investigation in the case. To accommodate the government witnesses next on the court agenda, the trial shifted from the Foro Italico to the Palazzo San Macuto, where a parliamentary inquiry into the Moro affair was also taking place. President Santiapichi announced that Senator Mario Valiante, the head of the parliamentary commission, had forwarded copies of testimony by Giulio Andreotti and Bettino Craxi, as well as by numerous other politicians and head officials of various state agencies.[1] The court, however, did not rest content with this: President Santiapichi wanted to question these people himself. Because of their central roles in the great fermezza-trattativa debate, the most important politicians to testify were Andreotti and Craxi, along with Craxi's vice-secretary at the time of the Moro kidnapping, Claudio Signorile.

Andreotti, the Prime Minister during the fifty-five days, testified on 27 September. A man of enormous political experience and skill, he had followed Moro as the national president of FUCI in the 1940s, and then had become the protégé of Alcide De Gasperi. He went on to hold virtually every major government position at one time or another. Over the years Andreotti developed an international reputation as one of the shrewdest and most politically knowledgeable men in the country; he was perceived as the Richelieu of Italian politics. In many ways his *furbo* image for cunning was exactly the opposite of that of the "good" Moro, described even by people who despised the DC as "the least guilty of them all."[2] To his most severe critics Andreotti embodied all the worst features of the Christian Democratic hegemony, especially the corruption and low ethical standards of the party. Some accused him of offering political protection to the Mafia, others of being the real leader of the subversive P2 Masonic Lodge.

Andreotti now presented himself as a witness before the court. The exceedingly familiar face, inscrutable and bespectacled, had changed little after forty years of public life. A slight hump on his back and two rather large turned-out ears remained the delight and inspiration of political cartoonists, who portrayed him as the eternal Christian Democrat and now the party's supreme living symbol.

In his court demeanor Andreotti was perfectly self-assured.[3] Controlled and in command of the relevant information, he provided no opening for counterattack.[4] Answering the questions of President Santiapichi, Andreotti calmly and thoroughly explained why his government could not submit to Red Brigade demands. Strategic and political realities dictated the *fermezza* course he followed "of not yielding to the blackmail of the so-called prisoner exchange . . . demanded by the terrorists."[5] After 16 March 1978 Andreotti could not be sure what kind of threat the country might be facing, whether via Fani might be "the beginning of a series of criminal terrorist episodes" or an isolated event.[6] In other words, could this horrendous crime set off "an explosion of pararevolutionary phenomena in thirty different parts of Italy"?[7] All the major party leaders in Italy supported his policy in the beginning. Most continued to do so until the end. The only exceptions were some Socialists and the fringe extraparliamentary left. To have abandoned this "substantial compactness" in the contentious world of Italy's coalition politics would have been tragically irresponsible, Andreotti insisted.[8]

He also had to worry about the morale of the police and the carabinieri. Would it have been wise, in the immediate aftermath of the via Fani massacre of Moro's bodyguard, to violate the Italian Constitution by freeing thirteen convicted criminals, or any number of them for that matter, to save the life of a Christian Democratic politician? Andreotti did not think so. That massacre had produced a terrible shock in Italy, the effects of which had to be controlled. Moreover, it might easily be concluded from such a concession that a double standard existed in Italy: supreme sacrifice for policemen in defense of the law, but special dispensation from the law when politicians' lives were in danger. Andreotti had declined to take a chance on lowering morale at a time when police officers were risking their lives in the face of a still enigmatic threat.[9]

Indirectly, without mentioning her name, Andreotti entered into a polemic with Eleonora Moro. He was sufficiently astute to realize that a direct attack would be a public relations disaster, given the impregnable moral position of the Moro family. His polite and deferential manner notwithstanding, Andreotti gave his listeners a version of the fifty-five days sharply different from the one presented by Mrs. Moro and her children, especially regarding the prison letters. In these documents Moro had taken an extremely dim view of Andreotti, calling him, among other things, an unfortunate choice for Prime Minister and a timeserving mediocrity of dubious integrity. Andreotti professed to be completely serene about these attacks, for which, he had no doubt, the Red Brigades and not his friend Moro were responsible. All of these prison papers had to be viewed with the utmost caution, he advised, and some of them could be dismissed as manifest fabrications.[10]

Andreotti vehemently denied the charge that his government had sabotaged the Moro family's private efforts to establish contacts with the terrorists. "What has been said is absolutely false," he asserted, making obvious reference to Mrs. Moro's testimony.[11] When President Santiapichi questioned him further on this matter, he replied, "President, I can say with absolute precision that we did not place a single obstacle before anything that was attempted."[12] He had private doubts about some of these schemes, but had done nothing to impede them. Indeed, his government had tried to facilitate all private efforts to save Moro, and Andreotti could document the variety of ways in which he, sometimes behind the scenes, had assisted the International Red Cross, the UN, and the Pope. Conversely, documentation was the one thing that his adversaries could never quite seem to locate.

Andreotti had been accused of leaving Moro to his fate even before the kidnapping by not providing him with a bulletproof car. As with all the other instances of his supposed neglect of Moro, this charge only appeared to be serious. In the first place, during the long weeks that they had worked together to create the national unity government, Andreotti had never heard Moro complain about his security arrangements or express any concern that he might be in some personal danger. Moro had never asked him for a bulletproof car. Had Moro wanted such a vehicle he could have had Andreotti's, because before 16 March 1978 no one in the government imagined that the Red Brigades or any other terrorist group would dare to strike so high. Andreotti himself did not ride in the bulletproof car that was his by virtue of the office he occupied, and as Prime Minister-designate for the national unity government he was just as exposed as Moro. People simply did not worry about security then the way they did after Moro's abduction. Nobody had ever decided to deprive Moro of a bulletproof car.[13]

These same accusers had wanted to know why a major lead regarding the Red Brigade hideout in via Gradoli had not been followed up properly by the police. In the completely unflappable manner that was his trademark and in a tone of voice that seemed to proclaim his eagerness to help the court in every way, Andreotti testified that the search for Moro was not like looking for the proverbial needle in a haystack, but in a thousand haystacks. If the police had broken down the door of every apartment where Moro was supposedly imprisoned—and they received countless such leads during the course of their investigation—Andreotti would have faced a revolt in Rome. A law-abiding citizen's right to privacy would have collapsed under such a policy. Moreover, this particular lead, about which so much had been made by the DC's habitual enemies, had emerged during a spiritualist session, and "I would not have considered spiritualism a particularly reliable source of information," Andreotti deadpanned.[14]

Some Italians could always be counted on to condemn the DC whatever the issue. For them the real point was not what Andreotti had done or failed to do, but rather Andreotti himself, Christian Democracy itself. One such individual had been Robert Katz, an American author long resident in Rome and a major spokesman for the conspiracy theory in the Moro case. His 1980 book, *Days of Wrath. The Ordeal of Aldo Moro: The Kidnapping, the Execution, the Aftermath,* was cited by a lawyer in the cross-examination of Andreotti.[15] According to Katz, Andreotti adopted the policy of fermezza because otherwise "the state could not have avoided the reaction of the armed right."[16] This was precisely the kind of charge from the extreme left (with which Katz wholly identified himself in *Days of Wrath*) that gave Andreotti intense satisfaction. He retorted, "this sentence, as it is, was never uttered."[17] The truth was simpler and far more believable, because it accurately reflected the full reality of terrorism that Italy faced during the 1970s. In fact, Andreotti continued, his fear then "was multilateral, not of the right or the left," but of both, and for good reason.[18]

Andreotti concluded by saying that he had done his best in a desperate situation. All the evidence pointed toward that conclusion. Wishful thinking on the part of the Christian Democrats' various enemies inclined them toward the conspiracy interpretation of these calamitous events, but Andreotti claimed to be standing on the real historical record.

Testifying the same day as Giulio Andreotti in the Palazzo San Macuto was the PSI's Claudio Signorile, Craxi's second in command in 1978. Signorile attempted to explain what his party's policy had been and how it had differed from the fermezza policy of the DC government and its allies. "We wanted," Signorile began, "an open door and a possibility that I would not call trattativa (negotiation)—I want to be very clear on this—a possibility to create conditions of fact that would leave, I repeat, at least a road open to the possibility of releasing the Honorable Moro."[19] The Socialists called their policy the "humanitarian" line, based as it was on a conviction that the sacredness of human life demanded the most heroic efforts to save any endangered citizen.

President Santiapichi attached the highest significance to Signorile's testimony primarily because of the central role he had played in seeking to establish contacts with the Red Brigades as a preliminary step in negotiating for Moro's release.[20] Santiapichi, in his eagerness to find some "solid ground" (terreno concreto) in this case, wanted to know all about the PSI initiative.[21]

Signorile described how difficult it had been even to take this humanitarian step. It quickly became apparent that "technical consultants" were needed to help the Socialists understand the "environment" of the extraparliamentary left which had spawned the still largely mysterious Red Brigades.[22] The PSI leaders needed someone familiar with what for them, as reform-minded Socialists, had become the dead language of the revolutionary left. On these fine points of ideology, terminology, "debates in progress [and] emerging orientations," Franco Piperno and Lanfranco Pace proved to be very useful.[23] Hailing from the radical Autonomia movement, they were parishioners of a different denomination in the faith of Marxist-Leninist revolution, but at least they and the Red Brigades prayed to the same god. From Piperno and Pace, afraid of the consequences that Moro's killing would have on the Autonomia movement and therefore willing to work with the PSI on this initiative, Signorile wanted only the information necessary for devising an intelligent plan of action. With these consultants and with still others, notably Giannino Guiso, Signorile operated scrupulously within the limits of the law, diligently reporting to Craxi every step of the initiative.[24]

Craxi testified the next day, 28 September 1982. On 6 November 1980 Craxi had given the parliamentary commission a twenty-six-page deposition covering his version of the Moro kidnapping and murder; now the Socialist party chief, whose bald head and fleshy frame called up images of Mussolini in the minds of political cartoonists, discussed the information in that document with the court.[25] He had noted the extreme ambiguity of the situation created by the Red Brigade attack of 16 March. For nearly two weeks afterwards no one knew for sure what the Red Brigades wanted or even if Moro were still alive. Once these doubts had been dispelled, moral considerations compelled Craxi to break with the fermezza line in order to improve Moro's chances of surviving. Furthermore, he responded to Mrs. Moro's urgent pleas to save her husband from the certain consequences of the government's policy of fermezza.[26] Like Signorile, Craxi took exception to the word trattativa, which the media had affixed to his proposals, and instead described them also in terms of a humanitarian initiative corresponding to the PSI's conception of the state. The highest duty of the government, he asserted, was to protect its citizens; lives should not be sacrificed in the name of abstract reasons of state.

Craxi had antagonized many Italians when it became known that the PSI had established contact with the Red Brigades through Giannino Guiso, a PSI member employed as a legal counsel by Renato Curcio and other Red Brigadist convicts. Responding to President Santiapichi's questions, Craxi revealed that Guiso had reported to him his conversations with the imprisoned Curcio. Craxi claimed to have gained valuable information from Guiso. For example, he learned that the Red Brigades had determined in advance not to allow the Moro operation to end as the kidnapping of Judge Mario Sossi had in 1974; in that case the victim went free without concessions by the state. As Guiso reported to Craxi, "Without a counteroffer [by the state] the prisoner would be killed."[27] A second piece of news passed along by Guiso heartened Craxi: Curcio personally declared himself to be against "a bloody solution to this case."[28] The Socialist party secretary then instructed Signorile to continue his efforts to save Moro.

Craxi understood that the terrorist proposal regarding a thirteen-for-one prisoner exchange was "so absurd that no one would have accepted it."[29] Nevertheless, he felt all along, even in 1982, that had the state made a minimal offer of even one terrorist for Moro, "we would have maneuvered them [the terrorists] up against a wall."[30] Indeed, Craxi had proposed the release of a woman terrorist, ill at the time and never guilty of shedding any blood. She stood out as "the most presentable case" the Socialists could find in order to bring the one-for-one prisoner exchange idea to fruition.[31] The Socialists' humanitarian line entailed this "gesture . . . of liberating one prisoner in order to avoid the assassination."[32] But when President Santiapichi asked if the Socialists ever had received any sign from the Red Brigades accepting the one-for-one exchange, Craxi had to admit that "to tell the truth, this was only our idea."[33] When Andreotti told him that the terrorist could not be released because she stood indicted for other crimes for which she was still to be tried, "this virtually ended everything."[34] Andreotti never had liked the prisoner exchange idea anyway, fearing that it would create a situation of great danger in the prisons. To his contention "we risk setting the prisons ablaze," Craxi responded, "then we'll send the fire engines," but legal entanglements ended the debate.[35]

President Santiapichi and lawyers in the courtroom kept coming back to the Guiso connection about which Signorile had not told them very much. Craxi referred to a book that Guiso had written about these events, *La condanna di Aldo Moro: la verità dell'avvocato difensore di Renato Curcio.* Santiapichi then asked one of the lawyers "to produce it for the trial."[36] It proved to be a highly revealing memoir.

In this reverent treatment of the Red Brigades, Guiso portrayed Curcio and Franceschini not as terrorists but as resistance fighters against the political and economic consequences of monopoly capitalism. The capitalist state, wanted to criminalize the proletarian revolution in Italy. For Guiso the real problem was state repression; Red Brigadism was but an outward sign of the political and social tension in the country. To this individual Craxi had entrusted an important role in his humanitarian initiative to break up the fermezza line. Guiso enthusiastically obliged and presented himself in *La condanna di Aldo Moro* as a protagonist in the drama to save the kidnapped Christian Democratic leader.

Guiso's version of the Moro affair was mainly a diatribe against the Christian Democrats for their "logic of annihilation."[37] Because his rapport with the Red Brigades was based on "loyalty and reciprocal respect," Guiso succeeded quickly in conducting serious negotiations, but all his efforts failed because of the "intransigence" of the Christian Democrats.[38] Fatally for Moro, the "human reasoning" of the Red Brigades collided with the "political reasoning" of the government.[39] Moro became a nonperson in the process of being elevated to the status of an icon: his perfectly reasonable prison letters were pronounced the work of a martyr deranged by brainwashing or drugs. Thus it was the Christian Democrats and their allies who stood indicted as the real murderers of Moro. They destroyed the possibility of having a dialogue with the Red Brigades and thereby condemned Moro to the only fate fermezza allowed.

On 6 May 1978, three days before Moro's murder, Guiso met again with Curcio and commented sadly: "But the revolutionary struggles for life, not for death. Why must Aldo Moro die?"[40] His interlocutor answered in Marxist terms: in the historic process through which the masses find their full humanity there must be violence, and "Moro could be one of the dead."[41] Before the force of this revolutionary creed Guiso fell silent. The prisoner then concluded: "Moro can return. If he does not return it means that his friends in the DC and the PCI want him dead."[42]

The Christian Democrats' response to this line of reasoning already had been given in full on 13 November 1980, when Guiso had appeared before Parliament's Commission of Inquiry on Moro. At that time Senator Giovanni Coco of the DC took up the key points made in *La condanna di Aldo Moro*. He brusquely denied that the Red Brigadists or their sympathizers ever had been interested in saving Moro. Their hypocrisy now had a texture of monstrous coarseness. Sympathizers like Guiso and their heroes in the Red Brigades wanted only one thing from 16 March to 9 May 1978, and it was the thing they had always wanted: the destruction of the Christian Democratic establishment as a prelude to the creation of their communist dictatorship. That was the entire Red Brigade truth in its purest form.

Senator Coco thought that the key to the Moro affair could be found in the via Fani massacre itself. The Red Brigades began the Moro operation with an almost totally unnecessary act of bloodshed, for everyone knew that their victim habitually took long walks, sometimes only in the company of Leonardi. The terrorists could have taken him at another time and place. To Coco this fact alone overwhelmed Guiso's claim that throughout the Moro affair the Red Brigades sincerely wanted a political dialogue with the government. What they wanted was blood, terror, and annihilation. All the talk about "human reasoning" colliding with "political reasoning" was complete nonsense. Some good but ignorant souls might believe it; Coco, however, declined to be lumped in with them. Moreover, for the Red Brigades to have killed Moro precisely at the moment when his DC colleague, Amintore Fanfani, was promoting a compromise solution, proved beyond any reasonable doubt that "there was no desire to liberate the honorable Moro at a low price . . . with a minimum of sacrifice."[43] Such humanitarian considerations did not enter the minds of the cruel fanatics whose insane devotion to dialectical materialism subsumed all other values, Coco concluded.

Some lawyers in President Santiapichi's courtroom castigated Craxi and Signorile because of their contacts with Guiso.[44] In their opinion, the Socialist leaders should have been aware that to depend on the likes of Guiso-Curcio on the one hand and Piperno-Pace on the other was to play to the tune of the revolutionary forces intent on attacking Italy's democratic institutions. In other words, the confused humanitarianism of Craxi and Signorile had been an instrument in the hands of revolutionary virtuosos who knew only too well what they were doing.

The testimony of Andreotti, Signorile, and Craxi on 27–28 September 1982 presented to the court a review of the fermezza-trattativa dispute that had left such a troubling legacy in Italian political life. The well-rehearsed disputants had added refinements and flourishes to their arguments, but nothing essentially new about the Moro case came out. Both sides remained hopelessly unreconciled. Doubtless nothing would alter this deadlock, but perhaps, as Public Minister Nicolò Amato had said before the summer recess, "some other shred of truth" might still be forthcoming from the many new witnesses called by the court; if that happened the entire laborious process would be worth the effort.[45] This breakthrough to a deeper level of truth in the Moro affair did not occur, however, during the court sessions held at the Palazzo San Macuto.

Former terrorists returned to the witness chair after September 1982. On 13, 14, and 18 October the court heard Alfredo Buonavita, one of the historic fathers of the Red Brigades but now completely estranged from them. To President Santiapichi's question about his background as a terrorist, Buonavita responded that he had matured since the days when the books of Mao, Che Guevara, and Lenin seemed to him to be repositories of all the political wisdom necessary or possible.[46] Experience had shown that Red Brigadism had been nothing but a tragic pipe dream, and now he accepted the rule of law in the regulation of social conflict.

At first it did not seem that his testimony would be relevant to the Moro murder case itself. In prison at the time of Moro's kidnapping, Buonavita could give the court no new information about what had occurred at via Fani or in the People's Prison. As a fellow inmate of Curcio and Franceschini, however, he was able to explain what the role of the imprisoned leaders of the Red Brigades had been during the fifty-five days. At the same time, Buonavita illuminated many of the hitherto obscure aspects of the PSI-inspired Guiso initiative.

Buonavita began by describing the shock that he, Curcio, and the other Red Brigadists in prison experienced on 16 March 1978. It turned out that the imprisoned Red Brigadists knew nothing or virtually nothing about the planning of via Fani. Even the usually calm and magisterial Curcio yielded completely to the atmosphere of near hysteria in which "the most desperate comments" flew back and forth between the prisoners in their special cell block.[47] When in the midst of this testimony President Santiapichi asked Buonavita if Curcio and Franceschini might have at one time merely suggested the kidnapping of Moro, the answer was: "No, never. This I can exclude in the most absolute way."[48] They were genuinely "stunned" by the news of via Fani. Buonavita asserted categorically that the Moro operation had been the work exclusively of Moretti and the Rome column.

The imprisoned Red Brigadists did become directly involved in the Moro kidnapping once Guiso appeared in his capacity as an emissary of the PSI. In a discussion between Guiso and Curcio at which Buonavita had been present, the lawyer attempted to appeal to the Red Brigade chief's communist idealism. There was an inherent contradiction, Guiso insisted, between Marxist ideals and the killing of prisoners. Curcio conceded this point in theory, but added, "there is a war here, and in war the rules of war prevail."[49] Personally, Curcio might be sorry to see Moro die, "but I cannot reason just as a man; I have to reason as a leader."[50] Obviously, then, either the prisoners named by the Red Brigades would have to be released or Moro would be killed. "This was the essence of the discussion," Buonavita observed, and Curcio dominated it completely.[51]

For President Santiapichi the crucial question at this point in the testimony was whether Craxi's one-for-one proposal or something like it would have been acceptable to the Red Brigades. Buonavita answered: "Once the ultimatum had been posted and the thirteen names chosen, no."[52] Nor would two or three have been enough. If twelve of the thirteen had been liberated, Moro still would have died because the Red Brigades "never took back what they said."[53] It is true, as proponents of the humanitarian line had pointed out, that with the release of one symbolic prisoner the terrorists would have been faced with intense pressure from the rest of the so-called Movement, but Buonavita responded that in fact "the Red Brigades were an organization on its own, with its own frightening principles and subjectivism, with an awareness of itself and its fearful role in history."[54] He thought that pressures exerted by the Movement would not have been decisive. Buonavita simply could not believe that the humanitarian line ever had a realistic chance of success.

Early in November the court heard from the man later described by President Santiapichi as the "most humanly credible" of all the ex-terrorist witnesses.[55] This was Enrico Fenzi, a former professor of literature at the University of Genoa who had now completely rejected his terrorist past. From such a luminary much was expected, and indeed Fenzi did tell what he knew about the Red Brigades. He had been a university radical who wanted to live the revolution, not just to strike a revolutionary pose as so many of his colleagues were content to do. The appeal of the Red Brigades soon became irresistible to him because they, too, were serious about revolution. He entered into contact with the organization sometime in the mid-1970s and then went underground.

Fenzi could tell the court very little about the Moro case. He did say that Moretti had bragged about his outstanding skill as a driver during the via Fani attack and in prison told Fenzi in minute detail how he had caused the accident that brought the two Moro vehicles to a stop that day. Other than that small piece of information, Fenzi claimed to have nothing else to say about Moro. His activities as a terrorist had been confined to Genoa, and he knew very little at first hand about what the Rome column had done in 1978.

President Santiapichi began to lose patience at this point. It seemed improbable to him that an operation of this magnitude would have generated so little discussion among the Red Brigadists. No one in the organization seemed to know anything about it: "What was the point of such an action if no one talked about it?"[56] This observation jogged Fenzi's memory. He recalled that the imprisoned Red Brigade leaders had given "an extremely negative judgment on the kidnapping."[57] It was not that they had any moral scruples about the action; it was just that Moretti simply had no idea about how to guide such an operation successfully. Fenzi concurred, reasoning that the Moro operation had turned into a "great, irreversible crisis for the Red Brigades" and had led to the organization's complete defeat in the armed struggle against the state.[58] After 9 May 1978 the Red Brigades lacked unity and a coherent plan of action, he affirmed.

President Santiapichi was still far from pleased. "I'm forced to say some brutal things to you," he began.[59] The outburst that followed was aimed not only at Fenzi but at all the former terrorists who had testified in the Foro Italico courtroom. "These obstructions, these closed doors, these 'I know and I don't know' [statements]" had angered him.[60] Surely a man of Fenzi's caliber, steeped as he was in literature *(versato nelle lettere)*, was sufficiently alert and culturally enlightened to realize that the Moro kidnapping had an epochal significance. How could he not have made every effort to inform himself about the details of an event on which the outcome of the armed struggle, to say nothing of his own fate, was sure to depend? It did not seem possible to President Santiapichi that a sophisticated individual like Fenzi could be as poorly informed about the Moro case as he wanted the court to believe he was.

Fenzi agreed that President Santiapichi's criticism of him was "brutal," but he promised to respond to it "with great clarity."[61] It was necessary, he began, to be very precise about dates. In 1978 Fenzi was not yet a major figure in the organization and the court would have to understand the policy of rigid compartmentalization that charac-terized relations between the various entities within the Red Brigades. The Rome column had very little assistance from the other columns during this operation. Therefore, when Fenzi and the other witnesses who were not part of the Rome column claimed to be largely ignorant about the Moro operation, they could not be justly accused of conceal-ing information. "I have not had the slightest *(nessunissimo)* loss of memory, in any way" about the Moro case, Fenzi protested; "I just never knew—what more can I say?"[62] This plea convinced President Santiapichi at least, but it left the Moro case as much a mystery as ever.

New details in the case did emerge during the testimony of Corrado Guerzoni, Moro's longtime press officer, who on 10 November 1982 gave an account of the notorious but undocumented 1974 altercation between Henry Kissinger and the Italian leader in Washington. Guerzoni did not actually witness this "extremely bitter conversation," but he claimed that Kissinger tried to coerce Moro to give up his opening to the PCI.[63] Moro told Guerzoni that the American Secretary of State had reasoned as follows: "I am not a Catholic and I don't believe in dogmas; if I were a Catholic I would believe in them. I cannot believe in your political line, and therefore I consider it a strongly negative element."[64] In particular, Kissinger despised what he called Moro's dogmatism on the opening to the Communist left, which the American characterized as a "philocommunist" tactic.[65]

Moro fell ill shortly after this exchange and returned to Italy earlier than planned. Badly shaken by his experience in Washington, Moro thought seriously about abandoning politics, Guerzoni continued. This mood passed quickly, but for the rest of his life Moro believed that the United States government viewed him essentially as an enemy. Right-wing circles in Washington—and on the question of the PCI, no other kind of circles existed there—manipulated the Lockheed scandal in a way that would taint Moro's entire entourage, or so Guerzoni claimed. By insinuating that Moro had been the principal beneficiary of corruption in high places, Italy's leading fifth columnist would be crushed at long last. Guerzoni and Moro were in fact discussing their strategy in the Lockheed case on the eve of the via Fani kidnapping.

Guerzoni's testimony precipitated a polemical uproar in Italy. Kissinger hotly denied that any such exchange had taken place between himself and Moro. Sergio Fenoaltea, Italy's former ambassador to the United States, claimed that Moro had enjoyed "high prestige, trust, esteem, and sympathy" in Washington, especially in the White House.[66] For many in Italy, however, the commentary of *l'Unità* reflected the real value of Guerzoni's testimony; it confirmed what the official organ of the PCI had known all along about "the cynicism with which even the personal lives of uncompliant statesmen are decided and manipulated in Washington."[67] In some minds, it was just a short and irresistible step from this commentary to the even more intriguing idea that the United States somehow and in some way yet to be proved had orchestrated the entire Moro affair. By the time the testifying phase ended in late November 1982, to be followed early the next month by the lawyers' summations of the cases of their clients, the conspiracy theories had yet to be dispelled. If anything, the trial had created the impression that still unexposed sinister forces had been behind the Red Brigades or in a de facto alliance with them.

Lawyers for the aggrieved parties, including the state, spoke first. Enzo Ciardulli, a state lawyer, touched the major points in the case against the defendants. In a three-hour address to the court on 6 December he demanded justice in full measure for the irriducibili and dissociati, but mercy for the pentiti.[68] On the basis of the evidence presented in court, he said, the Red Brigades alone bore responsibility for Moro's death. In the account of that act of terrorism, unlike the others under review by the court, some areas remained unexplained. Nevertheless, the question of guilt had been settled. All the evidence pointed toward the Red Brigade defendants. There was no "country of the East or West, no international terrorist network, no Italian conspiracy, and, above all, no bogeyman (grande vecchio) hidden in the shadows."[69] The state had failed to save Moro, but no proof had been offered to indicate conspiratorial intent on the part of anyone in the government.

On 20 December Public Minister Amato spoke. Also a magistrate but independent of the bench, he began his summation by repeating some of the points made earlier by Ciardulli. Once again a crowd of onlookers filled the courtroom, as always in the trial's moments of high drama. Amato felt the weight of the historic role he had played in Italy's so-called trial of the century. He now solemnly recited to a rapt audience the catalogue of the Rome column's homicides, slowly and clearly pronouncing the names: Moro, Palma, Tartaglione, Bachelet, Minervini, Varisco, and on and on. It had been truly "a long season of crimes," a phrase that would be repeated in the act of sentencing.[70] Amato quoted from the autopsy reports in unsparing detail. He wanted the horror of it to be taken in without euphemisms or concessions to delicate sensibilities.

The entire organization, not just the killers in it, deserved maximum punishment under the law, Amato continued. All the Red Brigadists, high and low, had produced the carnage that had disfigured public life in Italy for a decade. The Red Brigades had done this; no one else. All the theories about long arms reaching into the Red Brigades from Washington or Moscow or the Italian Ministry of Interior satisfied not a single criterion of legal evidence, although obviously they satisfied some deeply felt needs of human nature. It could be said that the state had been abysmally unprepared for terrorism, but to say that the state wanted Moro dead was an article of dogma, not a reasoned judgment based on the facts in the case. Like Ciardulli, Amato demanded severe punishments for the unrepentant, including thirty-four life sentences and more than 1,000 years of jail time, as well as greatly reduced sentences for the pentiti.

The lawyers for the defendants made presentations after the first of the year. In essence, they argued that most of the testimony against their clients had come from the pentiti, themselves terrorists and thus not to be trusted. The trial had not produced complete answers to all the questions about Moro's death, and too many doubts about the case remained for draconian sentences to be justified. For example, it still was not known for certain where Moro had been kept prisoner or where he had been killed. The last word on the Moro case had not been uttered here, and other trials would be necessary before justice could be done.

After ninety-nine courtroom sessions, featuring 244 witnesses and the summations of dozens of lawyers, the judges withdrew to their chamber where they studied 100,000 pages of evidence, reexamined voluminous technical reports, and listened for hours to tape-recorded telephone conversations. The fifty-eight defendants already in jail awaited the judges' word, which came on 24 January 1983. An absolute silence fell on the courtroom when "in the name of the Italian people" President Santiapichi declared the defendants guilty of "trying violently to subvert the economic and social order of the State . . . of promoting an insurrection against the power of the State and of provoking civil war in the territory of the State, of promoting, constituting, organizing, and directing armed bands including one called the Red Brigades."[71] He handed down thirty life sentences together with jail terms totaling 316 years in retribution for the murder of Moro and seventeen other victims of the Red Brigade campaign of terror.

In the main, President Santiapichi granted the requests of Ciardulli and Amato. The irriducibili and the dissociati received no mercy. For the pentiti, leniency prevailed. For example, Savasta, who had been implicated in seven murders, got only sixteen years. Twenty-three of the defendants had to answer for the Moro crime, and eighteen of them got life sentences.

The "Sentenza nel procedimento penale," written by the *giudice a latere* Antonio Germano Abbate in strict collaboration with President Santiapichi, gives a detailed analysis of the sentence. The judges began by observing that the capital error people made about Italian terrorism was to underestimate the seriousness of the violence, to view it essentially as a media phenomenon used to strengthen the establishment, and to conclude that the situation in Italy was not so bad after all. Having now spent many months familiarizing themselves with the facts of Italian terrorism, President Santiapichi and Judge Abbate impatiently rebuked those people whose reflex was always to blame the victims of violence rather than its perpetrators. In fact, terrorism had been devastating Italy, and it raised the most serious questions about the character and health of Italian national life. That this kind of politicized dementia could rage out of control for as long as it did, leaving a trail of corpses and shattered lives in its wake, forced them to sober reflection.

They did not doubt that Red Brigadism could only be interpreted as a product of Italy's potent Marxist-Leninist culture. Obfuscations of every kind had been employed to conceal this crucial point, but there it was. The Red Brigades simply had acted on revolutionary premises that had been around for a long time and had been accepted by many Italians as unassailable truths. This was why Red Brigadism had flourished for so long in Italy: it found "protection in diverse quarters that did not conceal their scandalous 'contiguity'."[72] For these people the revolutionary prescriptions of Marx and Lenin transformed the most bestial acts of inhumanity into thrilling deeds on behalf of the proletariat. To President Santiapichi and Judge Abbate it was unmistakably clear that the revolutionary culture from which Red Brigadism had come was one of the country's paramount misfortunes and a daunting obstacle to a truly civilized polity. Hence they had a low opinion of the PSI advisers whose interest in Moro was only incidental to their campaign for revolution.

The Moro kidnapping and killing occupied President Santiapichi and Judge Abbate for nearly half of the 400 pages in the "Motivi della Decisione." The Red Brigades had taken him because "he was the most authoritative leader, the theorist, the undisputed strategist of that Christian Democratic regime that for thirty years had oppressed the Italian people."[73]

The judges thought that despite all the conflicting testimony in the eyewitness accounts, the trial had revealed the main "dynamic" of the kidnapping on via Fani. They observed that "the high drama of the scene, the emotion, the fear, the different points of observation can have influenced the powers of perception in individual witnesses, producing in some cases imperfect or erroneous impressions and inducing them to fix their attention on certain aspects of events and on specific personal features at the expense of other aspects."[74] The testimony of the pentiti, however, had been invaluable in helping the court to eliminate many contradictions in the case. Here Santiapichi and Abbate concurred completely with the findings of the *istruttoria* judges.

One of the most troubling aspects of the case was the failure of the police to find the victim. The judges commented at length about the fruitlessness of the police manhunt and concluded simply that the Italian police were "psychologically and materially unprepared to confront emergency situations of these dimensions."[75] Nothing like the Moro kidnapping had ever happened before. Everyone involved, from Moro's bodyguard to the police, found himself overmatched. The Red Brigades not only enjoyed the inestimable advantage of complete tactical and psychological surprise but also knew the identity of their enemies, whereas the police groped in the dark. President Santiapichi and Judge Abbate explained the many failures of the Moro manhunt this way: "In a context of that kind, and in the absence of effective coordination, it was inevitable that delays and acts of negligence would occur that contributed not only to the slowing down of a machine already slow and inefficient, but to hindering the task of those functionaries and officials who were engaged in studying the phenomenon and experimenting with new measures to vanquish it."[76] The sorry record of the police in the Moro case was not surprising; surprise would have been in order had they been efficient. They had found Antonio Savasta's analysis convincing: by the time of the successfully resolved General James Lee Dozier kidnapping in 1982 the police knew what they were doing, but in 1978 they lacked the necessary experience.

The Moro trial had produced no evidence at all of any conspiracy, not by the police or by the government. The "interminable series of discussions" about conspiracies was another sign of immaturity in Italian public life.[77] The judges clearly implied that even the most wildly improbable assertions were sure to get a respectful hearing, whereas appeals to reason, evidence, and logic—not the political logic to which the Italians were addicted, but the other, objective kind—were usually met with condescension or contempt. In the Moro case the country had given in to its worst impulses as purveyors of conspiracy theories duped themselves and a gullible public always prepared to believe the worst about their government and its institutions.

What was the basis of these conspiracy theories? Santiapichi and Abbate's answer was straightforward: "Not one piece of evidence, not even circumstantial evidence, not one page of the trial [record] authorize [the conspiracy] hypothesis."[78] As usual in Italy, overheated imaginations had taken a holiday from the world of reality. Santiapichi and Abbate refused to indulge the Italian penchant for this kind of mass entertainment. The judges insisted that the trial had shown conclusively how and why the Red Brigadists killed Moro; it had shown nothing else. People who continued to chatter about conspiracies in the Piazza del Gesù headquarters of the Christian Democrats or elsewhere were either ignorant or malevolent.

On the day of the sentencing some of the hard-core terrorists exploded in a fury against the pentiti. "Bastard," one of the irriducibili cried, "traitor . . . all you need now is to sell your mother."[79] Apart from outbursts such as this, the irriducibili and many of the dissociati had been silent during the trial. Among those not testifying were Mario Moretti, planner of the via Fani attack and Moro's interrogator, Prospero Gallinari, allegedly his killer, and Adriana Faranda and Valerio Morucci, a couple who had broken with the Red Brigades because of the killing. Until these individuals spoke, President Santiapichi would never be able to convince the Italians that the Moro case was closed. Hopes ran high early in 1983 that they would in fact testify at the appeal trial. Even before the act of sentencing, on 24 January 1983, those closest to the proceedings in the Foro Italico courtroom were aware that the appeal trial would be more than routine.

During the *fase istruttoria* of Moro 1 Morucci and Faranda had called themselves "political prisoners" and declared they had no intention of responding to questions, but now they were rumored to be on the verge of talking to the court about their roles in the Moro kidnapping.[80] They did not speak at the first trial, but the repentant tone of a document they submitted on 18 January held the distinct promise of a confession, if only in the highly selective manner of the dissociati. Perhaps Moretti, their chief antagonist within the Red Brigades, might then be induced to speak in rebuttal. Only these convicted assassins truly knew what had happened to Moro between 16 March and 9 May 1978. Despite what President Santiapichi had to say, most people believed that the first trial had demonstrated, through systematic omissions, that the testimony yet to be given was indispensable.

5

The Moro Commission Reports

The appeal in the Moro case did not begin until December 1984, nearly two years after the first trial. In the meantime, beginning in the summer of 1983, the proceedings of the parliamentary Moro Commission were being published. Raw data compiled by the commission had been used by President Santiapichi, but the published majority and minority reports, along with the many thick appendices of supporting documentation, added a huge amount of new material for magistrates to study in the subsequent Moro trials. The commission had begun to gather evidence on 23 May 1980, and by the opening of the first trial in April 1982, leaks to the press had reinforced the widespread belief that the legal proceedings would be mainly a matter of dispensing justice for thoroughly documented crimes. These expectations had been too great, and by the summer of 1984 everyone knew that more investigations would be necessary to get at the truth. Because the main outlines of the commission's work were known long before its publication, people read it not for answers to the large questions but for additional details and examples. Indeed, the Moro Commission reports provided plenty of both and much else besides.

From 23 May 1980 to 19 April 1983 the Moro Commission of senators and deputies, under the direction of Senator Mario Valiante, listened to one hundred witnesses, including party leaders, Moro's friends and family members, widows of slain security agents, and former terrorists who had broken with the Red Brigades. For reasons of security, the commission met secretly in different locations all over Rome. The continued threat of terrorist attacks made such stringent measures necessary, and throughout this period authorities expected a resurgence of Red Brigade activity. A sense of urgency pervaded the commission's deliberations, from which the government and the nation seriously expected genuine results.

As in the first Moro trial, the fermezza-trattativa debate dominated the commission's agenda. Christian Democratic leaders took the lead in explaining why firmness was the only possible response to the Moro kidnapping. The Socialists made the trattativa argument, but the most stirring plea for negotiations with the Red Brigades came from the Moro family. Both sides claimed to speak with authority about how Moro himself viewed the situation in Italy on the eve of the via Fani attack, as if that issue alone would put all the other issues of the case in proper perspective.

Giulio Andreotti spoke before the commission for four hours on 23 May 1980. Insisting that no record could be found of Moro's concern for his security and that the conspiracy theory was complete nonsense, he outlined the points later covered in his courtroom testimony. All the evidence showed that the government had done its best by Moro before and after via Fani. The Red Brigades alone bore the moral and legal responsibility for Moro's death; the government leaders had been fallible in their efforts to save him, but in no way could they be equated with the terrorists or, as some of the more inventive conspiracy theory advocates had it, substituted for them. The Moro case came down to a question of whether evidence mattered.[1]

Francesco Cossiga, the minister of the interior at the time of the Moro kidnapping, appeared before the commission that same afternoon. Closer to Moro than Andreotti had been, Cossiga contended that although his friend had been increasingly worried about the problem of terrorism, he had expressed no fears over his personal safety. Cossiga concurred with Andreotti: taken completely by surprise on 16 March 1978, the disoriented government had done everything it could to save Moro. The witness emphasized the problem of perspective. The government's failure to protect Moro had to be understood in the context of the time. Before the fatal day the government had no idea that the Red Brigades possessed the power and the daring to do what they did at via Fani. It was that massacre and kidnapping that rendered obvious the necessity of maximum precaution, at the highest level of government against terrorist attack. Via Fani altered everybody's perceptions of terrorism, and it was historically misleading to suggest that the government should have possessed a post factum awareness of the problem even before this completely unexpected tragedy occurred. All the conspiracy theories in the Moro case ignored what was known about terrorism before via Fani.[2]

On 9 October 1980 it was the turn of Benigno Zaccagnini, the secretary of the DC in 1978 and a confidant of Moro, to testify. He too had never heard Moro utter a word of concern about his own safety. Zaccagnini's testimony possessed special significance because of his eminent reputation for honesty and his personal closeness to Moro. No one doubted the protestations of friendship by this Moro loyalist. In several prison letters Moro had attempted to get Zaccagnini to break away from the hard party line just for the love of him. His attempt had failed, but Moro had been right in one respect: Zaccagnini did love him. At the price of his peace of mind from that day to this, however, he had supported the government line of fermezza against the "infamous intimidation" of the Red Brigades.[3] The massacre on 16 March convinced him that the government had a war on its hands, in which the Moro kidnapping was not an isolated episode but part of a larger struggle. He told the commission that the government's decisions about Moro had to be viewed in this wider context. In other words, the DC correctly decided to conduct itself in a way that would ensure the final defeat of the Red Brigades while trying to save Moro, but no one in the party councils doubted which goal came first. Zaccagnini's testimony made a deep impression, and he would always be the most humanly credible of all the witnesses for the government.

Moro's wife and children took the lead, as they would do at the Foro Italico trial, in criticizing fermezza as a policy that had doomed their loved one. Eleonora Moro, the party's most implacable critic, testified before the commission on 1 August 1980. She used some striking images. Still in shock over the circumstances of her husband's death, she told the court: "Often I have the impression of being like those persons who are under an oxygen tent: they communicate with those outside, but only up to a certain point."[4] Though she said her brain did not function "too well," in fact Mrs. Moro conducted herself very impressively.

In detailed testimony she portrayed her husband as a man long in the grip of fear for his family. Moro had been threatened repeatedly at home and abroad. Anonymous letters and telephone calls plagued him, and in the summer of 1975, when he had become fully identified with the fiercely controversial opening to the Communists, the threats increased in volume and in rhetorical violence. Extremely reserved, Moro rarely gave her any details about these developments, but she did remember one exception quite well. Without telling her any names, Moro repeated the exact words of a threat that had troubled him deeply: "Look, if you insist on this thing [the opening to the Communists], this thing will bring you troubles. . . . Either you stop doing this thing or you will pay dearly for it."[5] After this Mrs. Moro repeatedly urged her husband to get out of politics.

The widow could not free herself of the suspicion that Moro's assassination had been the capstone of a long campaign against him on several fronts. Certainly, the party had not done its best to protect Moro, and she emphatically contradicted Andreotti and Cossiga about her husband's entreaties for an armorplated car. He had all along wanted such a vehicle and had said so, but the party had a high aptitude for feigning both deafness and forgetfulness, both much in evidence during the fifty-five days of her husband's agony. The party had failed to save Moro; worse, it had done nothing meaningful to try to save him. Mrs. Moro believed, as many other people in Italy did, that the Red Brigades had been "piloted" by a force vastly larger than themselves, and her testimony left wide open the nagging question about the presence of the government itself among those forces. That question would continue to linger throughout the first trial.

Mrs. Moro's children testified in December and January. Anna Maria Moro, pregnant at the time of the kidnapping, remembered her father's growing apprehension about terrorism during the last year of his life; the whole family constantly worried about the threat of violence. Agnese and Giovanni Moro added similar comments, but the most vivid testimony came from Maria Fida, commonly thought to be Moro's favorite child.

Maria Fida explained in disturbing detail what it had been like to live in a house engulfed by "a hundred thousand episodes" of fear and danger.[6] "We spent our lives receiving threats"; from 1969 to 1977 she alone received, on average, one letter a week threatening her father with death. The letters used to arrive at the *Gazzetta del Mezzogiorno* where she worked as a journalist. Then they started coming to the family home. Terrified, she told Moro about them, but he sought to reassure her by saying that all politicians get such letters. Toward the end "great piles" of them came.[7] Sometimes the authors accused Moro of being an agent of American imperialism, sometimes of being a fellow traveler of the PCI. Both extremes wanted him dead.

Maria Fida's testimony before the Moro Commission contained the kernel of an exceptionally revealing account that she wrote about her family's ordeal. *La casa dei cento natali* (1982) is in part an affectionate memoir of her father, whose genuine love for humanity made the Moro family home "the house of a hundred Christmases." She humorously but lovingly portrayed his foibles. So lacking in mechanical skill that opening a can of food presented serious problems, Moro was virtually helpless without his wife. The mechanically apt Eleonora did the family driving and attended to all the practical matters of the household. His dependence on her often reached comical extremes and reflected other eccentricities of his personality. Once, while on a picnic in the open fields surrounding Torrita Tiberina, where the family had a country retreat, he hesitated to drink from a small metal cup because a storm was approaching. "Noretta," he asked gravely, "do you think it is dangerous?"[8] She had to assure him that a lightning bolt would not incinerate the entire family if he drank from the cup. These oddities did not make a favorable impression on the young Maria Fida, who resolved to marry a man as unlike her father as possible.

Only as an adult did Maria Fida fully appreciate her father's unique gifts, especially his immense moral courage. Fumbling, unathletic, and a hypochondriac with a mania for cleanliness, he was, to his growing credit in her eyes, a man of peace opposed to every form of violence, even verbal violence. He unfailingly mediated family disputes. What he did so brilliantly in Italian politics he did with equal success at home. Perfectly sincere and unselfconscious in his Christian faith, Moro lived the Gospel.

Maria Fida grew up hating politics. As a young girl she resented the endless intrusions of Moro's public career into the family's private life. The telephone rang constantly. Visitors came at all hours. Her father pored over bundles of newspapers every day. He read so much that she feared he would go blind one day, "but the Red Brigades liberated me from this anxiety."[9]

As she got older, Maria Fida's resentments deepened. Moro inspired strong love but implacable hatred as well, and his daughter recalled how some of her teachers "who cordially detested my father" made life miserable for her.[10] The family name was always a curse, and she longed for an anonymous existence. A "terrible anguish" afflicted her.[11] She remembered always fearing that something dreadful would happen to her father, and everyone in the family shared this feeling without having to mention it directly. As the oldest child—she was born in 1946—Maria Fida had special responsibilities in the family security system, which included looking after the younger children and reporting any suspicious persons or activity she might observe. These orders were not part of a game, and Maria Fida obeyed them scrupulously. She even learned (from her self-reliant mother, naturally) how to shoot a gun. If the spirit of Christmas once pervaded the Moro household, it was the antithesis of that spirit that came to envelop it.

In the few days just before the kidnapping Maria Fida's fears for her father grew and drove her nearly insane with worry. Suffering from serious back and leg ailments, she alarmed the family with her distracted and compulsive behavior. Against all reason and normal family practice, she was terrified at the thought of leaving her small son Luca with his grandparents during that last week. Then, on 16 March 1978, Maria Fida experienced every feeling save surprise. The kidnapping was the last act of a tragedy that she had seen coming all of her life. When the announcement of Moro's death arrived from her sister Agnese, they spoke of it as if "an ordinary thing were being discussed, as if we were both used to learning that our dear ones had been slain and abandoned in the back of parked cars."[12]

At least there was nothing more to fear. The worst had happened. Her anger remained, however. Maria Fida could not forgive those "friends" of Aldo Moro with their "thousand justifications" for why nothing could be done except what had been done.[13] She still felt outrage over the government's refusal to take Moro's prison letters seriously. A "maleficent circle" had kept him prisoner, formed not only by the Red Brigades, but by their interlocutors in the government as well.[14] She had expected the worst from the Red Brigades, and they had met her expectations. Their action was evil, but it followed quite logically from their hatred. From Moro's self-styled friends she had expected help, and when they withheld it, she found their behavior more infuriating than that of the Red Brigades. For Maria Fida and her family it would never be Christmas again. Moro's dreadful odyssey had ended, but "the refugees of the house of a hundred Christmases" had to continue theirs with bitterness, anger, and an everlasting sense of betrayal in their hearts.

Numerous other witnesses supported the Moro family testimony. The head of Moro's office, Sereno Freato—himself a defendant in an oil scandal trial just as the commission's report became public, and in bad odor with some of the family members because of controversies regarding the defunct Moro Foundation—had testified on 30 September 1980 that his employer long had been concerned about the inadequacy of his security arrangements. Even Freato thought that Moro's concerns were excessive, but then "events legitimized his fears."[15] On the controversial question of an armorplated car, Freato related how the circumspect Moro refused to accept one from concerned friends, looking in vain to the government for adequate protection. Both Maria Ricci and Ileana Leonardi, widows of agents in Moro's bodyguard, claimed that their husbands constantly worried about terrorist attacks. Oreste Leonardi's widow testified that he had repeatedly asked for more and better-trained men. Leonardi never talked openly with his wife about these matters, but she was aware of his mounting fears for Moro. Towards the end Leonardi became "nervous, tense, agitated, preoccupied, and . . . insecure."[16] He was convinced that someone had been following him.

In many of the depositions the commission heard implied and explicit condemnations of Henry Kissinger for his efforts to thwart Moro's opening to the PCI. Mrs. Moro and her children were emphatic about the strong pressure he had received from America, but the exact nature of these threats and warnings could not be determined. Was this simply a heated exchange of political viewpoints between two strong-minded antagonists, or a sinister plot by the United States to destroy Moro? The family had little doubt about the reality of the latter.

On 16 February 1983, however, Moro's interpreter, Carla Lonigro, claimed that she had never seen even the slightest evidence of tension between the two men. Indeed, she could only recall scenes of "maximum cordiality" on Moro's supposedly nerve-wracking 1974 trip to Washington. When asked by a commission member whether Moro could have received a threat from Kissinger unbeknownst to her, Lonigro responded that although his spoken English was poor, he understood the language fairly well. So a private exchange between Kissinger and Moro could have occurred, but she did not believe that it had.[17] The exact nature and even the fact of Kissinger's warning thus remained issues of contention.

The commission's main charge had been to determine why the Moro manhunt had led to "disheartening results," and Francesco Cossiga formulated the point of view that found its way into the majority report. Former Minister Cossiga explained that in 1978 the Italian state was simply unprepared. The police lacked an adequate "policy of security" for a terrorist threat of the magnitude posed by the Red Brigades, while the secret services had ceased to function and were being reorganized.[18] Moreover, it was not known who the Red Brigades were or with what groups or powers they might be allied in Italy or abroad. Indeed, only later would the government understand the full extent of the historic connections between the Red Brigades and other extraparliamentary left action groups—including Autonomia Operaia, Metropoli, and CO.CO.RI. (Comitati Comunisti Rivoluzionari).[19]

The commission majority report addressed this domestic connection in part, but focused more on the role that foreign secret service agencies might have played in the Moro tragedy. The admittedly fragmentary evidence and incomplete testimony revealed no vital connection with any foreign groups: "All the brigadists interrogated were agreed in excluding peremptorily any foreign participants."[20] Red Brigadism was a homegrown plant. Other similarly inclined revolutionary groups, such as the Red Army Faction in Germany and extremist factions of the PLO, might cooperate with the Red Brigades, but at no point did the organization ever lose its completely Italian character.

Not one pentito had confessed to spending any time at a foreign training camp, nor had any of them ever heard of anyone else who had done so. The pentiti Patrizio Peci, Marco Barbone, and Antonio Savasta testified that the Red Brigadists had trained themselves to use automatic weapons. The reasons for their military success were not esoteric. Without exception, they used unsophisticated weapons on missions that entailed a minimum of risk. They prepared each terrorist attack with painstaking care. The Moro kidnapping, for example, had been thoroughly rehearsed, with all the participants carefully groomed for their roles. Above all else, the Red Brigades always enjoyed the advantage of complete surprise against their victims.

Much had been written and said about the Red Brigades as the puppet of the KGB or of other secret service agencies from the Eastern bloc, but the commission found no evidence to support such claims.

Indeed, the one foreign secret service agency singled out in the majority report was Israel's Mossad. The Israeli connection with the Red Brigades had already been described a year earlier in the Foro Italico trial, but the story received added publicity with the publication of the Moro Commission report. Sometime around 1975 Israeli secret service agents had established contact with the Red Brigades, offering them arms and money. This offer, according to the pentiti, had to do with Israel's fear of the PCI's participation in the government, which would certainly move Italy to assume a philo-Arab position. Hence Mossad developed an interest in the destabilizing activities of the Red Brigades, which could ruin the prospects of the historic compromise that Moro had envisaged and, in addition, make the United States increasingly dependent upon the Israelis as its only reliable ally in the Mediterranean. As a gesture of good will, Mossad gave the Red Brigades information about two informers in the terrorist organization, but the offer of money and arms was rejected for reasons of security. The commission decided that the Red Brigades had in fact been an indigenous and independent organization, though it had ties to other terrorist groups, both foreign and domestic. It also had relations with foreign secret service agencies but was not influenced by them.

In its majority report the commission concluded that the government should be faulted for numerous failures and omissions in the Moro case, but there simply was no "secure evidence" that conspiracy had played any role in the outcome of events.[21] The key claim in that report was this: although grave acts of negligence had been documented, which were apparently inexplicable if not motivated either by malice or lack of zeal, there was no "proof" of conspiracy by the government.[22] Such a disclaimer was in itself an extremely serious charge and gave many trattativa critics of the government all the ammunition they needed to continue their offensive against fermezza. On the basis of the evidence, though, the Moro case reeked of "insufficient diligence" by the police but not of calculated betrayal; the upholders of fermezza triumphantly seized upon this distinction. The commission certainly did not spare the sensibilities of Italy's police forces, which, during the fifty-five days of Moro's ordeal, had produced results characterized by "a complex of incapacity, inadequacy and silences," but that was as far as the majority report would go.[23]

The authors of this document also agreed with the government's "more prudent" interpretation of Moro's prison letters, that they en-

abled the Red Brigades "to weaken and to lacerate the political system."[24] The majority report emphatically rejected the trattativa interpretation of "each letter [as] an authentic and original message of the
prisoner."[25] By feeding Moro false information about what the government was doing and saying, the Red Brigades manipulated him to suit
their own purposes, and the letters had to be interpreted in this
context. Authentic only in part, the letters had been exploited from first
to last by the Red Brigades. Lamentably, the prison letters had succeeded in driving a wedge between the Moro family and the government. It was understandable that the family lost "faith in the efficacy
of [government] agencies," but their independent negotiations had
resulted in a most unfortunate division of efforts: "In sum, because of
lack of faith in the action of the police and the magistracy some people
lied, some left things out, some others kept silent, and precious opportunities were lost [in the effort] to ascertain the truth and to get,
perhaps, closer to the prison of Aldo Moro."[26]

Pentito Antonio Savasta's testimony strongly reinforced the majority
report. Of all the ex-terrorists he most forcefully denied the validity of
Moro's prison letters. Any political thoughts Moro expressed had to
have contained "the thought of the Red Brigades," Savasta insisted.[27]
Indeed, only Red Brigade-controlled correspondence would have been
allowed out of the People's Prison. Letters that did not further the Red
Brigade project were held back, and many of them turned up later in
a captured Milan hideout. A kidnapper himself, Savasta spoke with
self-confident authority about the completeness of the Red Brigade
censorship: everything Moro knew about his situation came from them.
He would not have been allowed to read newspapers or watch television or listen to the radio. In this way the organization controlled the
shaping of every argument of Moro's as fully as they controlled his
person.

As he would do in his courtroom testimony, Savasta illustrated this
argument with references to his own experience in the Giuseppe Taliercio kidnapping. Then, as in the Moro case, the Red Brigades had no
intention of allowing their victims to express themselves freely. If they
"freely" expressed themselves in a way that advanced their captors'
designs so much the better, but the main thing was to further the
revolutionary project. With this end in view, the Red Brigades sometimes had to "correct" the letters of the prisoners and to suggest
different "formulations."[28] When differences arose between the writ-

ten expression of the prisoner and what the Red Brigades wanted him to write, a very unequal struggle for artistic control of the final communication ensued. The alternative to compliance with the Red Brigades was well understood. At all times the prisoners remained under total domination and terror.[29]

Given the conditions in the People's Prison, the notion that in his letters Moro had been free to elaborate a thesis consistent with his earlier writings about the theoretical virtues of prisoner exchanges was a delusion. Savasta volunteered that Moro, Taliercio, and the other kidnap victims of the Red Brigades experienced a complete loss of freedom except insofar as they were willing to assist their captors. Such a willingness was not a free choice, however. If Moro had the presence of mind to adjust his thinking to the all-powerful circumstances of his dreadful situation, it could not be argued convincingly that his thoroughly censored correspondence reflected anything but a desperate attempt of a terrified human being to save himself. Moro had the wit to judge the full extent of his danger, and his conduct in the People's Prison, including the writing of those letters, represented the shrewd and experienced leader's best estimate of how he could outrun the fate that overtook him in the end.

In closing, the authors of the majority report resoundingly supported the government for refusing to yield to Red Brigade demands for a prisoner exchange. On 18 April 1978 the Red Brigades had agreed to release Moro if the government would liberate thirteen imprisoned terrorists. From the beginning of Moro's ordeal, however, Prime Minister Andreotti had rejected the possibility that Italy would yield to any form of terrorist blackmail. He and Communist leader Enrico Berlinguer, who in his deposition before the commission declared that, no matter what the cost, the Red Brigades had to be denied every request, led the party of fermezza during the fifty-five days.[30] Both men urged all Italians to unite against what Berlinguer called the "unprecedented gravity" of the threat posed by the Red Brigades.

Andreotti had refused even to consider the offer of a prisoner exchange, the majority report approvingly noted. Most Italian political leaders and opinion makers sanctioned this decision. Only Craxi's Socialists, the Moro family, and the extraparliamentary left encouraged negotiations under the banner of "humanity." A vehement polemic raged between these two groups, and it is still an underlying reality in the currents of Italian politics, rising periodically to the surface and then sinking again, never completely out of the public mind even when out of view. The authors of the majority report, however, never doubted that Craxi's initiative had little chance of success and could only further the political chaos ardently desired by the Red Brigades.

By unambiguously vindicating fermezza, the majority report perpetuated the angry debate within the commission itself. At one point in that body's deliberations the Socialist members—deputies Luigi Covatta and Claudio Martelli and senators Paolo Barsacchi and Libero Della Briotta—resigned, citing "grave and unacceptable" procedures.[31] They believed the commission was guilty of waging "a real political trial" against the "humanitarian" thesis in the Moro case.[32] They eventually came back, but in their minority report complained about numerous attempts to exploit the commission's work for political propaganda. This was their principal criticism of the majority report. The Socialists also criticized the "abstract conception of fermezza." The fermezza policy as applied by the government in the Moro kidnapping was inhuman and untenable; yet the majority report could only repeat the litany of hard-line commonplaces that had resulted in the tragedy of 9 May 1978. The Socialists rejected the report's exoneration of the government's decisions in the Moro case. The troubling circumstances of his death suggested the distinct possibility of criminal behavior on the part of officials charged with the responsibility of rescuing him. The majority report took insufficient notice of these deeper issues, contenting itself with what amounted to absolution for all.

The Socialists balked because they wanted the whole truth; the majority on the Parliamentary Commission, wedded as it was to a defense of failed fermezza policies—including an utterly unconvincing attack on Moro's "lucid," "coherent," and "authentic" prison letters—had failed to find it.[33] The Socialists had looked to Patrizio Peci's testimony for support, but Antonio Savasta, the other leading pentito in the Moro proceedings, contradicted Peci. To Sergio Flamigni's (PCI) question about the authenticity of Moro's letters, Peci replied: "He could write whatever he wanted."[34] Under questioning by Flamigni, however, the witness admitted that "some advice" might have been offered by the Red Brigades.[35] "Some advice?" Flamigni queried. By the time the relentless Flamigni had finished with him, Peci had conceded that Red Brigade kidnapping operations were much as

Savasta had described them. Letters that might have been "damaging" from the Red Brigade point of view were never sent. Other letters were "censured" in one form or another, now that Peci came to think of it. When Peci lauded Moro for his "courageous, dignified" behavior, Flamigni noted that the Red Brigades consistently had lied about their prisoner; for the Communist parliamentarian this constituted further proof of how little faith could be placed in any of the communications issuing from the People's Prison. It was a madhouse in which the one sane person had to humor the insane in his attempt to survive.

Against this powerful argument by a leading exponent of fermezza, the Socialist members of the commission continued to accept the prison letters at face value. Moreover, the PSI parliamentarians refused to give their assent to other assertions of the majority report. They rejected its confident judgment about the "compact universe of left-wing terrorism in Italy" and about the absence of "international sup-port" in the Moro tragedy.[36] Above all, the authors of the PSI minority report contemptuously denied that in the Moro case their party had been motivated by anything but a humanitarian concern for the victim. In particular, Covatta, Martelli, Barsacchi, and Della Briotta resented the commission's attempts to find connections between the PSI and the revolutionary left.

The Neofascist minority report of Deputy Franco Franchi and Senator Michele Marchio also stressed the authenticity of Moro's prison letters, but these members of the Movimento Sociale Italiano-Destra Nazionale (MSI-DN) reached political conclusions sharply opposed to those of the PSI and, naturally, of the majority report. Franchi and Marchio urged every Italian to read the prison letters of Moro: "they certainly are documents of great humanitarian value and of exceptional importance because they contain almost twenty years of Italy's sad history."[37] Moro, the paladin of Christian Democracy, had faced his moment of truth in the People's Prison of the Red Brigades by saying, in effect, "I count and am worth something, not this rag of a state."[38] Moro desperately sought to stave off martyrdom in service to the state he had done so much to create, and his unheroic conduct in the People's Prison eloquently proclaimed the worthlessness of that creation. "Guelph and Mafia oligarchies" controlled everything in it, as Moro knew better than anyone, and as he plainly acknowledged at that moment of truth. These neofascist critics argued that in his prison letters Moro sounded like a man who had been shocked to learn that anyone seriously expected him to die for anything as morally bankrupt as the Italian Republic.

To Franchi and Marchio the Moro affair reflected the "cultural crime" of the Christian Democrats: the Italy this party had created was "a ruined country, the prey of every violence, the ideal land and international crossroads for every felony."[39] The Christian Democratic hegemony had produced a natural habitat for Red Brigadism: the inevitable product of coarse democratic principles mechanically applied. The people did not want the kind of "freedom" offered by the Republic's leaders, and a rising tide of terrorism was a clear symptom of Italy's political neuroses. The pathetic exercise of Christian Democrats' statecraft had to end in the kind of violent anarchy espoused by the Red Brigades. At bottom it had been a poetic irony that caught up with Moro between 16 March and 9 May 1978: "he himself had been the architect of the system that resulted in his death."[40]

Leonardo Sciascia, the left-wing novelist from Sicily, wrote the Radical party's minority report. Noting that political squabbling between the DC and the PCI on the one hand and the PSI on the other had continued throughout the commission's deliberations, Deputy Sciascia asserted that the fundamental question was this: why did the state fail to save Moro?[41] The commission itself never seriously addressed this question. Instead, it wasted time on a repetitious examination of peripheral issues and on political infighting. In Sciascia's opinion the state had been guilty of appalling mismanagement. He could not believe that so many police errors of commission and omission had occurred spontaneously. At best, the official explanation of Moro's kidnapping and murder was a partial one. Even more strenuously than the Socialists, Sciascia insisted that Moro's letters were authentic and deserving of the closest study. The state had dismissed those letters and in so doing had destroyed the best possibility of saving Moro.

Sciascia's bitter castigation of the state scarcely came as a surprise. In 1978 he had written *L'affaire Moro*, the pioneering formulation of the conspiracy theory. Numerous authors on both sides of the Atlantic followed his lead, and today that theory is a central reference point in the debate about Moro.

L'affaire Moro is distinct from the subsequent conspiracy theory books not only because it is first but also because of Sciascia's unique candor. He disliked Moro and said this in his book; not for Sciascia the artificial distinction between the "good" Moro and the "bad" DC, so characteristic of the other books that view his death in the lurid light of a conspiracy by state leaders.[42] Sciascia held quite correctly that Moro, with his archetypal Catholic southerner's world-view, *was* the DC; the two could not be separated. To despise the DC, which Sciascia did with all his heart, meant that Moro had to be remembered for the politician he was: "alert, shrewd, calculating, apparently flexible but actually immovable."[43] Moro fully understood the weaknesses of Italian public life, and he had a genius for adapting his policies to them, as well as for clouding the political atmosphere with patented euphemisms.

In his unsparing portrait Sciascia did make one concession: he gave Moro credit for sincerely believing in Catholicism and trying to live it, which was more than could be said for those churchgoing DC leaders who, behind the masks of Christian piety, were power-hungry opportunists. But given Sciascia's profound distaste for Catholic culture, the strongest emotion he could feel for Moro was one of condescending pity. He cited Bayle ("a republic of good Christians could not last") and Montesquieu ("a republic of good Christians could not exist") and then derisively added, "But a republic of good Catholics can exist and last, à la Christian Democratic Italy."[44] Moro thus loomed as the symbol of an entire age. If, as Pier Paolo Pasolini had said, Moro was "the least implicated of them all," that very element gave him the moral authority to speak for all, to cover the egregious record of the DC with the protective film of one man's relatively honest reputation. According to Sciascia, Moro was the half-hearted exception that proved the rule about the Christian Democrats.

Sciascia had shocked many people in 1978 because of his assertion that he could support neither the state nor the Red Brigades: both repelled him in equal measure. The PCI had been particularly hostile to Sciascia over this sensational remark; to the party he embodied the irresponsibility of the intellectuals at a critical moment in the Republic's history. In *L'affaire Moro* Sciascia examined what had prompted his "neither . . . nor" condemnation, and he insisted that no one had the right to pillory him for being honest about his contempt for the Christian Democratic-run state.

Consider how this state had conducted the search for Moro: an operation which was a fiasco culminating in tragedy. Sciascia interpreted Moro's conduct in the People's Prison as an attempt born of hope to gain time so that the state could find him. Vain hope. Before long, in Sciascia's reconstruction of events, Moro realized fully how misplaced his expectations had been, and this was the real source of his bitter sorrow in the prison letters, which were anything but "delirious." The so-called friends of Moro, who had publicly declared that he was no longer himself, had deceived the public in a "monstrous" way.[45] In fact, the man remained what he had always been, a "subtle politician" who knew his Italians. Every word and gesture was a ploy to help him gain the advantage, but this time his life hung in the balance.

The state failed to comprehend what Moro was trying to do or else comprehended it only too well: in either case Andreotti, Cossiga, and the rest betrayed him. Even Sciascia, a non-Catholic, felt let down by the state's response to Moro. The Radical deputy could only imagine how the victim, a coreligionist and colleague of the men in power, must have felt. Sciascia allowed that, as a sincere Christian, Moro was not afraid to die, but he did not want to die "that" death. He sought with all his cunning and knowledge of human nature to escape such a vile fate, but he needed the succor of his friends, and they withheld it from him. Why did they do that? This is the question that prefaces every conspiracy interpretation of the Moro case.

Sciascia theorized that the state used the Moro kidnapping in a power play for its own ends. There was something grossly inapposite about the policy of fermezza. For thirty years the state "cultivated" corruption and incompetence; for ten years it had put up with "occupied and devastated schools, the violence of the young among themselves and against the teachers," but just at that moment, "before a Moro imprisoned by the Red Brigades, the Italian state raises itself strong and solemn."[46] Sciascia felt it was his right to criticize the dogmatic manner in which the state and the media had reacted to Moro's deadly predicament. Moro himself had said as much and then went further: the party had decided his death sentence; the Red Brigades had served only as a means toward that end. Sciascia merely fleshed this out in L'affaire Moro, ingeniously coupling his own low estimate of the government with Moro's words from the prison letters to produce a scathing indictment. In this way he focused public attention on the DC, not on the Red Brigades, as the real authors of the greatest crime in the history of the Italian Republic.

More succinctly than anyone else among the commission's members, Deputy Egidio Sterpa anticipated the mood of public disappointment that greeted its published reports. In his minority report for the Liberal party (PLI), Sterpa conceded that the commission's members had failed to fulfill the expectations of Parliament and the Italian people. After more than three years of hearings the details of the massacre and of the kidnapping on via Fani were still obscure. The roster of individuals participating in those crimes was still incomplete. The commission never did learn the location of the People's Prison. The incomplete testimony of the two superpentiti, Savasta and Peci—and the disagreements between them—further obstructed the inquiry. An "enormous lacuna" in the evidence badly undermined the commission's work, Sterpa complained.[47] As a result, the commission could only offer the nation "an approximate reconstruction, the fruit in part of indirect testimony, in part of casual stories by spectators [in these] episodes."[48] The only certain element in the tragedy concerned the "great inefficiency" of the police, who had been unable even to hinder the movement of the Red Brigades, let alone find and apprehend them.

Sterpa's brutal criticism echoed the sentiments expressed in the other minority reports. Even the majority report did not make extensive claims for the commission's investigative prowess. Coming so soon after the controversial conclusion of the first trial, the published findings of the commission reinforced the public's confusion about Moro's abduction and death. As usual in such a climate of uncertainty, conspiracy theories gained the upper hand.

6

The P2 Commission Reports

Conspiracy theories received a powerful boost from the Parliamentary Commission of Inquiry investigating the mysterious Propaganda 2 Masonic lodge—an organization that resembles a figment of an espionage novelist's imagination. Ostensibly a recruiting unit for the Grande Oriente d'Italia Masons in 1970, P2 swiftly developed into a powerful secret society dedicated to establishing a more stable Italy and, in particular, to combating communism. These goals were to be achieved through infiltrating the country's institutions. In March 1981 the public learned of the P2 plan and of its author, the enigmatic Licio Gelli. Most disquieting of all, hundreds of carabinieri and other military officers, police officials, politicians, newspapermen, and publishers were known to have supported him. The ensuing scandal brought down the government of Arnaldo Forlani, and Parliament immediately launched an investigation.

The chairwoman of the P2 Commission, Tina Anselmi, publicly declared on 28 May 1983 that the lodge had been implicated in the Moro case.[1] She added little to this tantalizing assertion, only that Gelli had been involved in anti-Moro political activities and that he probably had planned a coup against the state. While there was nothing specific she could say about P2 members' involvement in Moro's ordeal, Anselmi refused to believe it was purely a coincidence that so many lodge members occupied key leadership positions in the police and the military, including in the intelligence services and the office overseeing them. It seemed highly probable to her that a Gelli plot was at the heart of the Aldo Moro murder case.

A vintage Italian polemic followed Anselmi's disclosures. The snappish exchange between Rino Formica of the Socialists and Flaminio Piccoli of the Christian Democrats summed it all up. To Formica, P2 could only be interpreted as a disgraceful consequence of the Christian Democrats' long misrule. Piccoli begged to be spared political preachments from a party that had conceived Benito Mussolini in its unwholesome womb. It was the Christian Democrats who had brought Italy back to life after this "ex-Socialist's malign dictatorship."[2] The Republican party's Giovanni Spadolini tried to tone down this recriminatory hooting and to turn the political discussion away from its deep historical background to the present, for he agreed with Anselmi's assessment of P2 regarding both the Moro case and the lodge's continuing influence in Italy.

After a summer recess, the P2 Commission resumed its investigation of Gelli's lodge. Reports about its work occasionally appeared in the newspapers, and Anselmi continued to draw public attention to the role P2 might have played in the Moro case. The two cases were interwoven, she declared on 20 September 1983. According to Anselmi, the Moro trial and the Moro Commission had left open "some crucial points" that her commission would address in its forthcoming report.[3] On the basis of such assertions, Communist deputies and senators demanded, in the spring of 1984, that Parliament reopen its investigation of the Moro case for the purpose of addressing once and for all "the lacunae, the insufficiencies, the professional incapacities, the acts of unfaithfulness that facilitated the kidnapping of the statesman and that successively impeded his liberation."[4] With this motion, cosponsored by the Radical party, the PCI effectively dissociated itself from the Moro Commission's majority report, which the party had signed the previous year. The Communists now wanted answers to the new questions raised about P2's involvement in the Moro case.

Anselmi presented her commission's majority report on 14 July 1984. The commission had met 147 times, listened to 198 witnesses, and perused many thousands of pages of documents. On the basis of this painstaking investigation Anselmi now hoped to offer a "clear and precise" analysis of Gelli's "polymorphous organization."[5] Essentially, three different versions of P2 emerged from the commission's work. Anselmi authored the majority report, but the Radicals and the neofascists offered strongly dissenting reports of their own. The result was a cloud of confusion about P2 that has never entirely disappeared. No aspect of the uncertainty inspired more acrimony than the possible link of P2 with the murder of Aldo Moro. These three reports, with their very different methodologies and political assumptions, offer a penetrating insight into the conflicting interpretations of key issues in the Moro case.

The majority report began with a biographical portrait of Gelli. He was a long time coming to Masonry. After participating as a youth in the Spanish Civil War on the side against the Republic, Gelli fought in the Second World War and continued to fight for the Republic of Salò after Mussolini's fall from power in Rome. He worked as a liaison officer helping to coordinate relations with the German SS. Soon afterwards Gelli must have realized how the war would end, because he made contact with the partisans and in October 1944 began to work for American military intelligence. He became a notorious informer and spy with no allegiance to anything but himself.

Disrepute clung to him after the war. In 1949 Gelli was convicted of contraband and fraud, but the judge gave him a suspended sentence. Italian intelligence kept a dossier on Gelli because it suspected him of being an agent for the Soviet bloc and of trafficking in arms. Then, in the early 1950s, Gelli himself became an Italian intelligence agent, and his trail suddenly went cold, most probably because the agency placed a protective wall around his activities.

The commission caught up with him again in 1965, when he joined the Grande Oriente d'Italia, the country's largest Masonic lodge. By 1969 Gelli had become a trusted adviser to its Grand Master Giordano Gamberini, and later to Lino Salvini, his successor. It was Salvini who in 1970 gave Gelli permission to create Propaganda 2 in secret, as part of a membership drive. In the beginning P2 concentrated very success-fully on recruiting military men, with carabinieri officers particularly drawn by Gelli's antileftist law-and-order program.

P2 grew rapidly during the early 1970s, and Gelli expanded its membership base to include individuals from all walks of life. But in 1974—a year of widespread violence in Italy, especially notorious for two bloody terror bombings—Gelli's Masonic superiors appeared to distance themselves from P2. It was unclear whether they genuinely felt that he had overstepped his mandate or wanted only to create a smokescreen for his covert schemes. Voting to dismantle P2 in December of 1974, the Masons of Palazzo Giustiniani claimed to be worried about Gelli. They could not be sure that his activities were completely legal. Despite their qualms, they allowed P2 to reconstitute itself in May of 1975, after which the lodge reached it peak of power and influence. Anselmi upheld the smokescreen theory: "We know that in substance the Salvini-Gelli-Gamberini interlacing continued to operate as always, even amidst well-known differences, in the same unchanged direction of support and incentive for the P2 operation."[6] According to her, Masonic attempts to suppress P2 only represented "a more sophisticated form of cover" for Gelli.

On the questions of P2 secrecy and the appeal of the organization to a broad cross-section of the country's elites, the commission had much to say. Gelli conceived P2 as a secret society of the nation's foremost leaders who, in "concentric circles" of influence, would guide Italy toward stable and enduring institutions in politics, culture, and finance.[7] The Italian people could not be trusted to achieve these desirable ends by themselves. Anselmi denied that Gelli alone understood the full scope of P2 activities. The members knew about them and, in the main, had followed the Venerable Master because of them. Some members protested that they had joined only because of pressure from their superiors and in order to advance their careers, but at the higher levels of the organization a "surreptitious" transformation of the Italian Republic inspired the P2 lodge brothers, or *piduisti*.[8]

P2 managed to achieve a "penetrating presence" in the country's public administration, the judiciary, the police and military hierarchies, the political ministries and parties, Parliament, and the centers of finance and publishing. The commission provided detailed information about Gelli's involvement in all of these areas, but of special interest was his close relationship with the financier Michele Sindona, and the banker Roberto Calvi. Both convicted criminals had assisted Gelli. Sindona and Calvi had provided the funds for some of P2's most far-reaching transactions, such as the acquisition of the Rizzoli publishing company and the *Corriere della Sera*. A much fuller analysis of Sindona and Calvi would appear in the commission's minority reports.

The majority report emphasized the importance of Gelli's numerous contacts and protectors abroad, particularly in Latin America and the United States. He was especially well-connected with the Peronists in Argentina and enjoyed the title of "economic counselor" to that country's embassy in Rome. Through his friendship with supporters of Ronald Reagan in the United States, Gelli was invited to attend the

1981 inaugural ceremony. In such conservative circles Gelli was said to have found assent for his plan of rebirth of democracy—in which, according to Anselmi, "one works a lot and discusses little."[9] The plan of democratic rebirth was actually a blueprint for a strong authoritarian society such as the one antiliberal forces at home and in Washington had been demanding for a long while—hence Gelli's strong appeal in these corridors of power.

Anselmi charged that Gelli also had ties to "the complex world of black subversion."[10] Aiming to destroy Italy's existing political institutions, violent neofascists had contributed to his antidemocratic project. He had both "incited" and "encouraged" these fanatics.[11] One of the most securely documented instances of their de facto partnership with Gelli was the coup attempt of 7–8 December 1970, led by Fascist war hero Prince Junio Valerio Borghese. Numerous *piduisti* participated in the plan. Moreover, Gelli himself may have given the order to abort it when national and international support had failed to materialize. In one episode after another of right-wing subversion, Anselmi charged, ringleaders had eluded justice because of protection afforded by members of P2 who occupied key positions in the police, the military, and the judiciary.

As for the neofascist bombings, P2 might not be guilty in "judicial terms," but in "historical-political terms" a case could be made against it for "instigating" and "financing" extraparliamentary right-wing groups.[12] For example, the judges in the case of the Bologna train station massacre, where on 2 August 1980 eighty-five people were killed and two hundred wounded, had declared that P2 possessed the country's "most complete arsenal of real and dangerous instruments of political and moral subversion."[13] Others might have performed the terrorist act itself, but they were "inspired, armed and financed by Masonry."[14] Gelli was still playing his old double game: the self-proclaimed upholder of order sought to undermine Italy's democracy. The Bologna bombing was a typical if exceptionally bloody example of how he fostered all these elements that wanted to topple the state in order to save it. The judges regretted that the "distant instigators" could not be indicted, but the evidence pointed clearly to a confluence of extreme right-wing and P2 elements in the Bologna bombing. Anselmi vigorously concurred with the judges' views.

Taking up less than two pages of the more than 150-page majority report was a section entitled "L'affare Moro." Here Anselmi pointed out "the significance of the presence of numerous piduisti in positions of exalted responsibility during that period."[15] A majority of the ministerial Committee of Coordination—composed of the land's highest police, military, and secret service officers meeting regularly in the Viminale Palace during the Moro crisis—belonged to P2. The commission speculated on the true motives of these individuals during the Moro manhunt. It was not difficult for the investigators to imagine that Gelli and his lodge brothers would have perceived the Moro kidnapping as a godsend. Moro, the friend of the Communist party, was their most hated enemy. The logic of Italy's political situation led the commission to conclude that P2 would have welcomed Moro's death. What might those piduisti generals and other high officials at the Viminale have done or not done to produce the result desired by Gelli in the Moro affair? The official explanation for the failure to find Moro had been "exclusively technical." The Italian authorities were said not to have been prepared for the Red Brigade assault of 16 March 1978 and its aftermath, but the commission bluntly asserted that there might have been "another order of considerations," the hidden agenda of Gelli.[16]

The Anselmi report provoked antagonistic reactions from the Radicals, who claimed that it did not go far enough in the right direction and from the Neofascists, who complained that it went too far in the wrong direction. For the secretary of the Radical party, Marco Pannella, the work of Anselmi was "a P2 report, not a report on P2."[17] Massimo Teodori, the Radical deputy on the P2 Commission, declared that Anselmi was "the last leader of P2."[18] He attempted to document this and other charges in his minority report.

Teodori agreed that P2 had attempted "to ruin democracy" in Italy, but the majority report contained no inkling of Gelli's real motives.[19] In the Radical view of P2, Gelli had been hardly more than a second or third-level functionary: "Now this figurehead was made to be the scapegoat for a political class that with one voice proclaimed, 'I didn't see, I didn't know, I didn't understand.'"[20] Typical of the protestations by Italy's politicians was the remark of Bettino Craxi who claimed to have thought that Gelli was only a businessman, not the leader of a secret society. All of the mainline leaders professed to have been surprised by "unexpected and extraordinary events."[21]

Teodori discounted the sincerity of such claims. Articles on P2 had appeared for years before the scandal erupted in March 1981; there was no excuse for the most politically astute people in the land to have been taken unawares by Gelli's schemes. On the contrary, because "the P2 network is interlaced with the parties of the establishment and with their leaders," it had developed as the consummate expression of the party system, appearing no more threatening to Italian democracy than the usual political practices of the country.[22] Gelli so closely resembled his counterparts among the establishment party secretaries that he blended in perfectly with the natural habitat of Italian politics, speaking their arcane political language and mimicking their pragmatically antidemocratic actions perfectly.

The majority on the P2 Commission did not want to dig deeply for information about unsavory facts, Teodori asserted. The PCI was particularly embarrassed. From 1943 to 1947 Gelli had rendered important services to the Communists. A master of intrigue, he had worked for both sides during World War II and the Cold War, but now the PCI wanted to forget its old involvement with him. Therefore, the majority report of the P2 Commission on the early part of Gelli's career amounted to a compressed and misleading survey of his activities as a Communist agent. He was a "skeleton in the closet" for the PCI.[23]

The other parties in the majority went along with this legerdemain because they, too, wanted to avoid a full disclosure of their dealings with Gelli. The DC, Anselmi's own party, bore the heaviest responsibility for the P2 scandal, and Teodori protested that this crucial fact had been shamelessly suppressed. P2, he said, had been supported from the beginning by right-wing military men and secret service operatives in the government itself, but this history had received only a glancing mention in the commission's findings. Gradually, Gelli's network spread to include more diverse groups and individuals, ranging from violent extraparliamentary right-wing organizations to a motley array of "strong state" forces that were a natural part of the Christian Democratic order.[24]

Teodori singled out Giulio Andreotti as the dark genius of Christian Democracy's political dealings with Italy's labyrinthine criminal underworld. Andreotti had hailed the egregious Sindona as "the savior of the lira."[25] Sindona, as the commission's Neofascist report would attempt to clarify in exhaustive detail, had used his connections with potent financial circles in the United States to assist the Christian Democrats in one economic emergency after another. When disaster threatened to take Sindona down, both Andreotti—described by Teodori as "the Godfather and protector"—and Gelli sought to save him.[26]

Philip Guarino, allegedly tied to the American secret services and to Cosa Nostra, coordinated the Sindona rescue operation in the United States. The CIA and NATO also wanted to keep the truth from coming out, for Gelli's "destabilize in order to stabilize" project coincided with their own plans for Italy. None of these parties and agencies had anything to fear from the bland and superficial Anselmi report, according to Teodori.

With the collapse of Sindona's financial empire, Gelli moved to assume many of the financier's functions for the Christian Democratic establishment. Roberto Calvi, the other principal heir of Sindona's system and head of the Ambrosiano Bank in Milan, was badly hurt by the Sicilian's revelations. When Calvi failed to give Sindona sufficient help during the crisis of 1974, embarrassing disclosures began to appear about improper financial dealings of the Ambrosiano Bank. Calvi, forced to defend himself, was in no position to take advantage of the power vacuum left in Sindona's wake. Gelli was.

P2 grew spectacularly during the mid and late 1970s, just in time to play a crucial role in the Moro affair, according to Teodori. He strongly argued that the presence of piduisti in the Committee of Coordination could only be viewed as part of the problem during the fifty-five days of fruitless searching. True, "certain proof" was missing.[27] It was still too soon to convince a judge that there had been "a deliberate design not to save the honorable Moro and to return him dead rather than alive," but the repeated failures of the police, carabinieri, and intelligence officials pointed toward an "objective opposed to the stated objective."[28] Moro's kidnapping, even more than all the terrorist acts that preceded it, fitted into the P2 design as a "presupposition of exceptional laws, the suspension of constitutional guarantees, the throttling of liberty."[29] Moro's death had to be seen against the deep background of the country's right-wing politics, by then thoroughly penetrated and controlled by P2. Teodori concluded that the party of fermezza, guided by the DC and the PCI and supported by the United States, had done exactly what P2 had wanted. It only remained to be seen whether proof could be found to document a case for conspiracy, but no reasonable person, in Teodori's estimation, could doubt the extreme likelihood of foul play by the P2-contaminated authorities in the Moro manhunt.

The most striking feature of the Neofascist minority report, authored by Senator Giorgio Pisanò, was its heavy reliance on Anglo-American sources. This document, complete with bibliography and footnotes, described the P2 scandal as a particularly gross example of the corruption brought on Italy by the unholy alliance of the United States, the Christian Democrats, and the Vatican. The bibliographic sources included Malachi Martin, *The Final Conclave* (1978), Richard Hammer, *The Vatican Connection* (1982), Larry Gurwin, *The Calvi Affair* (1982), and Luigi Di Fonzo, *St. Peter's Banker* (1983). Pisanò claimed that these books revealed the actual prehistory and history of P2, and he proceeded to summarize their arguments as a rebuttal to what the Movimento Sociale Italiano (MSI) called the left-liberal fables of the majority report.[30]

Pisanò gave dimension and substance to the portraits of Sindona and Calvi, a necessary preliminary, he said, to understanding Gelli and, above all, his connection to the Moro case. That British and American writers had to be used as the source for a serious investigation of these figures revealed how little real freedom existed in Italy, according to him. A review of these often lurid works will not be out of place in establishing how much, at that critical moment, foreign observers conditioned the Moro debate in Italy. Moreover, quite astonishingly in view of the marginal character of Neofascism at the time, they present an image of the Christian Democrats' corruption that has found strong favor today in a large segment of public opinion.

Di Fonzo's *St. Peter's Banker* is a full-length biography of Sindona. It was, in part, a Horatio Alger story. Born in 1920, he grew up poor in Sicily. High intelligence and hard work got the young man a scholarship at the University of Messina, where he studied tax law. The Second World War postponed his career as a tax lawyer, but in 1943 Sindona modestly began his activities as an entrepreneur with the purchase of a secondhand U.S. Army truck that he used to transport lemons to market. His ties to the Mafia date from this early period. It would be a long and profitable association. After the war he returned to the field of his academic training and made a fortune as a tax lawyer; his talent for business also flourished. By 1948 Sicily no longer provided an adequate field of play for his ambition, and he moved to Milan, where still larger fortunes could be made. Sindona realized fabulous profits from real estate and banking coups, and within a decade he had become one of the richest men in Italy.

For this next period in Sindona's life Pisanò relied on *The Final Conclave* and *The Vatican Connection*. From the first one he learned a great deal about the disastrous financial conditions of the Vatican in the 1960s that led Pope Paul VI to make a pact with the devil in the person of Sindona.[31] Connections with high prelates in the Church, particularly Giovanni Battista Montini, had facilitated Sindona's rise in Milan. Archbishop Montini of Milan (later Pope Paul VI) met Sindona in the 1950s shortly after the Sicilian had moved to that northern city. He placed his financial skills, already much in evidence in Milan's booming real estate market, at the service of the Archbishop. Sindona made a lastingly favorable impression on Montini by quickly raising the two million dollars the Church needed for an old people's home in Milan.

Pope Paul VI worried about the Church's mounting financial difficulties. He appointed Father Paul Marcinkus of Chicago as the head of the Vatican Bank, but the American priest lacked investment experience. In 1968 the Pope called on his old friend, Sindona, to reinvest the Church's capital. The following year Sindona signed an agreement that gave him effective control over the Church's vast foreign exchange resources. With the enormous wealth, credit, and prestige of the Church behind him, Sindona became one of the most influential men in the country.

For the details of Sindona's dealings with the Vatican, Pisanò turned to Richard Hammer's *The Vatican Connection*. Hammer set out to document what he called the systematic Sindona-controlled collusion between the Vatican and the Mafia. He based his account on wiretap evidence, on electronic surveillance, and on the recollections of Joseph J. Coffey, Jr., a detective on the New York City police force who had tried to break the case. Through his connections in high finance and the Mafia, Sindona was said to have acted on the instructions of high churchmen in obtaining $950,000,000 million worth of counterfeit securities in large American firms. According to Hammer, the ringleaders—Eugene Cardinal Tisserant, dean of the College of Cardinals and in charge of the Society for the Propagation of the Faith, an unnamed Sicilian archbishop, and Bishop Marcinkus—rationalized the crime as necessary to stave off financial disaster for the Church. They relied on Sindona for advice, and the Vatican poured hundreds of millions of dollars into his international network of companies and banks. In turn, Sindona repeatedly used the Vatican Bank to conceal ill-gotten money and to transfer funds secretly and illegally out of the country. The Church escaped a major scandal only because of its political connections in Washington and control of the Christian Democratic party, but the facts of this sordid case were now out in the open for anyone who could stand to look.[32] Marcinkus's denial of the charges and his claim that the counterfeit bonds story was nothing but anti-Catholic slander failed to persuade Hammer or even to interest Pisanò.

By the early 1960s Sindona had begun to look beyond Italy's borders to the United States market. A 1962 trip to the United States convinced him that his future lay there. "The Americans loved me because of my brains," Di Fonzo quoted him as saying. "They did not treat me like a nigger, the way the Italians treat Sicilians."[33] Always an ardent free-enterprise man, Sindona detested the Italian left. It did not take long for the Republican party to discover in Sindona an Italian expert to its liking, and among his friends he counted David Kennedy and John Connally—future secretaries of the treasury in the Nixon administration—and Nixon himself.

Sindona's outspoken antisocialism endeared him to Licio Gelli as well. Although Sindona would always deny that he even knew Gelli until the mid 1970s, Di Fonzo claimed that the relationship between the two men actually began in 1964.[34] Their politics made them natural bedfellows, and Sindona became a key member of P2. Through his international brokerage firm, Moneyrex, Sindona laundered dirty money for both Gelli and the Mafia, with which he had remained connected since his days as a lemon merchant. In 1957 Sicilian and American *mafiosi* chose him to penetrate legitimate businesses throughout the world by reinvesting drug profits in legal investment channels.[35] Thus it was to the Mafia's banker and Gelli's associate that Paul VI turned as "the one sent by God," and the Pope knew exactly what kind of partner he had selected in Sindona, the hotly anti-Catholic Di Fonzo charged.[36] Pisanò eagerly repeated these charges. From his Neofascist perspective the Church, through its ties to the Christian Democrats, was a negative influence in Italian politics.[37]

With the 1972 purchase of a controlling interest in the Franklin National Bank, Sindona reached the maximum extent of his power and glory. He felt invulnerable now that the resources of the eighteenth largest bank in the United States were his to command in the service of his constantly expanding consortium of international businesses and financial institutions. It was, however, a fleeting and troubled moment that ended in disaster. But Sindona did not fall simply because he overreached himself. True, he suffered from bouts of manic depression, and his general health began to deteriorate under the pressure of his breakneck pace. Moreover, as his empire grew, it became impossible for him to look after his varied interests with the care and thoroughness he had employed when his horizon was bounded by the precincts of Milan. And yet Di Fonzo, who was sternly critical of Sindona in the main, perceived him as a Napoleon of finance whose sheer genius and power of concentration were normally sufficient to contain and eliminate any problem.

Unfortunately for Sindona, his financial empire now rested on an American base, and America remained a country—for all his much-publicized enthusiasm about hamburgers—that he fundamentally did not comprehend. He thought that his high-powered connections in Nixon's Washington would save him in a crisis, but Watergate, which he dismissed as a peccadillo, wrecked his fail-safe plan. Betrayal in Italy at the hands of his renegade associate, Carlo Bordoni, and appalling mismanagement at the Franklin National Bank, particularly in foreign exchange speculation, produced an emergency from which his friends in Washington could not save him while they themselves were being politically destroyed.[38] When the bank collapsed in October 1974, Nixon himself was out of office. After the bank failure investigators discovered many improprieties and crimes, for under Sindona's control the Franklin National Bank had been used illegally as a filter for millions of dollars to his Swiss and Italian banks.

Not mentioned in Pisanò's retelling of *St. Peter's Banker* was Sindona's service to the Nixon administration as a conduit for millions of American dollars to conservative groups in Italy. Sindona continued to support anti-Moro elements in the Christian Democratic party, for, like his associate Gelli and his closest friends in Washington, he wanted to build a political coalition in Italy that would crush the left, not welcome it into the government. Sindona reinforced Washington's belief that Italy's basic problems were neither social nor economic but ideological. In short, the Communists and the left bore exclusive blame for whatever anti-American and anticapitalist feeling existed in Italy. Such a nemesis had to be destroyed; accordingly, Ambassador Graham Martin worked closely with Sindona in earmarking United States funds for pro-American politicians in Italy. This is a story told with powerful understatement in the classic *Pike Report*, whose congressional authors discovered that some of these monies ended up in Neofascist coffers.[39]

The MSI, too, had a Sindona skeleton in its closet, but Pisanò only expressed interest in the Vatican-Christian Democrats aspect of the Sindona-Gelli scandal.

In the wake of the Franklin's failure, Sindona had to face legal proceedings in Italy and in the United States as the greatest swindler of the age. For a time he took refuge in Switzerland and Taiwan, but soon decided to return to the United States, convinced that "America will protect me because I have always protected American interests in Europe."[40] Sindona's American friends continued to believe that he was the victim of a left-wing cabal in Italy, and David Kennedy supported him throughout his campaign to obstruct extradition proceedings. To enhance his image as the victim of some communist conspiracy, Sindona staged his own kidnapping in the summer of 1979, making it look as though a Red Brigade-like group had been responsible.[41] Italian and American authorities saw this for the hoax it was, and Sindona returned to the United States with his credibility irreparably damaged.

Sindona allegedly also asked Gelli and the Mafia for help. Gelli did his best to harness P2 to Sindona's cause. He instructed his lodge brothers in the government and the judicial system to smooth things over for Sindona in Italy. Meanwhile, Giorgio Ambrosoli, a lawyer who headed a team of investigators assigned to review the books and records of Sindona's banks, received threatening telephone calls, some of which he managed to record. The caller spoke with a heavy Sicilian-American accent. When questioned about these threats, Sindona claimed to have no control over what his friends did in their efforts to save him. This continued to be his defense after Ambrosoli was shot to death at the front door of his home on 12 July 1979.

On 27 March 1980 an American court convicted Sindona on sixty-eight counts of fraud, misappropriation of bank funds, and perjury.[42] He attempted suicide two days before the sentencing, but survived to hear the judge condemn him to twenty-five years in prison. Sindona also had to pay a fine of $207,000. In 1981 the Italian government indicted him as the responsible party in the murder of Giorgio Ambrosoli and, on other counts, for heroin trade, illegal possession of arms, fraud, using a false passport, and violating currency regulations. In May 1981 the Italian police raided the home and office of Gelli and discovered secret documents linking him, Sindona, and other piduisti to financial crimes and political conspiracies against the state.

Swamped by this torrent of troubles, Sindona promised to commit suicide "if all else fails."[43]

In Pisanò's account, after the fall of Sindona's empire the Sindona-Marcinkus-Calvi triangle became the Marcinkus-Gelli-Calvi triangle, with Giulio Andreotti still acting as the group's political godfather in the Christian Democratic party.[44] In the new triumvirate Gelli soon became the dominant figure, because the other two were beset by public scandals while he remained virtually unknown. Thanks to continued papal protection, Marcinkus survived his troubles following the Sindona crash, but Calvi's story ended differently. This part of the MSI's minority report rested in the main on Larry Gurwin's *The Calvi Affair: Death of a Banker.*

Of modest middle-class origins, Roberto Calvi battened on Sindona's patronage. Sindona eyed him in the 1960s, when Calvi was only an employee of the Banco Ambrosiano, as a man with unusual banking talents and an "international mentality."[45] Although the two men were exact contemporaries, the forceful Sindona already had become one of the richest and most famous financiers in the country, whereas the shy and taciturn Calvi was an underling and remained subservient to Sindona until the 1974 collapse. Only then did the full extent of Calvi's ambition reveal itself. For more than a decade Sindona's Mafia and Vatican connections had become Calvi's own; he continued to use them after 1974 to transform the Banco Ambrosiano from a small provincial bank into a major financial institution of international standing, operating aggressively in the stock market as well as buying and selling companies.

Sindona also introduced him to Gelli, and Calvi soon possessed a P2 membership card. Calvi firmly believed in "occult power"; that is, that the right telephone call decided the great issues of the day.[46] To survive, one needed contacts and friendships within the secret structure of small groups and individuals who manipulated the government and other institutions. In joining P2—a benevolent organization for "brothers" and a clearinghouse for favors of all kinds—Calvi hoped to reserve for himself a special place among the few who command and decide, that is, close to the "godfather." Indeed, he thought Mario Puzo's *The Godfather* was a masterpiece of world literature because it told the truth about how society really worked.

With Sindona virtually eliminated from the circle of power after the "crack" of October 1974, someone had to take his place. Calvi appeared to be ideally suited as a successor, but Sindona did not go quietly to oblivion. He complained bitterly and in public about Calvi's ungrateful refusal to help him. The Milanese banker sought to fend off Sindona's vituperative attacks, but they left the bank's name besmirched. Fearing that Sindona might ask the Mafia to kill him, Calvi surrounded himself with elaborate security arrangements and became obsessively secretive and suspicious. His dependence on people who could give him political protection grew. He made large contributions to various political parties, but Gelli remained his primary line of defense. In exchange for Gelli's help, Calvi placed the vast resources of the Banco Ambrosiano at the disposal of P2. Through a Banco Ambrosiano loan, P2 came to control the Rizzoli publishing company as part of Gelli's campaign to acquire commanding influence in the media. To protect the Banco Ambrosiano from judicial inquiries, Calvi had to pay bribe money and make questionable loans to P2 brothers.

His own legal problems exacerbated by Sindona's vendetta, Calvi was accused in 1978 of illegally exporting 25 billion lire through the camouflaged subsidiaries of the Banco Ambrosiano. He survived this and other legal problems, and indeed his power and influence actually grew during the next couple of years. The Banco Ambrosiano's 8 billion dollars worth of assets, fortified by Gelli's P2 network, formed a powerful ring of defense. Rumors of wrongdoing, however, continued to haunt Calvi. In June 1980 he was again accused of illegally exporting capital, falsifying bank records, and committing fraud. When the continuing Sindona investigation led to the discovery in 1981 of the soon-to-be-famous P2 membership list, Calvi's legal situation became more precarious than ever.

When Gelli fled, Calvi lost his foremost political protector. He found another one in Francesco Pazienza, who boasted of connections with politicians, intelligence agencies, and the press. Gurwin described him as the new "fixer."[47] Neither Pazienza nor Flavio Carboni, another collector of friends in high places, could protect Calvi from the avalanche of P2 scandals that came crashing down in the spring of 1981. He was arrested on 20 May, the same day that Gelli's list of 962 lodge members was published. The government of Arnaldo Forlani collapsed within days, and the new government of Giovanni Spadolini took office in an atmosphere of moral emergency. Spadolini promised utmost severity for the P2 wrongdoers who had threatened to subvert the state.

The Calvi trial, which began on 10 June 1981, was a key element in the many-sided P2 affair. Like Sindona before him, Calvi threatened to expose his former allies in the Vatican Bank and in the political parties. He told investigating magistrates that in the end he had become little more than a puppet of his protectors, principally Gelli. "I'm in the service of someone else," Calvi confessed.[48] The emotional stress of the trial, followed by the shock and humiliation of prison life, were more than Calvi could bear. On 9 July 1981 he tried to commit suicide, but, again like Sindona, survived to hear a judge pronounce sentence: four years in jail and a $10,000,000 fine.

Pending his appeal, Calvi left prison and returned to work. Despite all the revelations, the bank itself appeared to be unhurt. By the spring of 1982, however, the consequences of loans and investments in support of Gelli's political agenda had driven the Banco Ambrosiano to the brink of bankruptcy. In desperation, Calvi looked to the Vatican Bank for help, but Marcinkus now labored under the watchful eye of a committee of cardinals appointed by John Paul II to reform the Church's financial practices. According to Gurwin this reform had come rather late, considering the central role of the Istituto per le Opere di Religione (IOR) in both the Sindona and Calvi affairs.[49] With the government's banking authorities closing in on him, Calvi lost heart. He fled the country on 10 June 1982, just before the appeal trial was scheduled to get under way.

Unlike Sindona, Calvi never returned to Italy. He made his way to London, the world capital of international finance, and frantically sought to rescue the situation. It was a hopeless mission. The 17 June suicide in Milan of his secretary, Teresa Corrocher, preceded his own death by a matter of hours. His corpse, weighed down by stones, was found hanging from Blackfriars Bridge on the Thames.

Britain's most respected forensic pathologist, Keith Simpson, ruled Calvi's death a suicide, but few people in Italy accepted this judgment. The Italians thought that he had been "suicided," and there was much common sense in such a view. Why, they asked, would a sixty-two-year-old overweight man suffering from vertigo choose to kill himself in a manner that required considerable athletic ability, when he could so easily have taken a pill in his hotel room. Indeed, was it likely that a foreigner who did not know London would wander four miles from his hotel and just happen to find the handy construction apparatus alongside Blackfriars Bridge? No; too many people wanted to silence

Calvi, and the circumstances of his death suggested to many a Masonic ritual. It was much more probable that Gelli ordered the killing. The British coroner might not have been able to find any indication of foul play, but absence of evidence was not a convincing argument to the people who knew the full context of the Calvi affair.[50]

Calvi's bank did not long survive him. The demise of the Banco Ambrosiano on 6 August 1982 caused the most devastating financial crash in the country's postwar history. Overnight, 40,000 investors saw their shares become worthless. New secrets were laid bare as government investigators discovered evidence of dubious bank loans that Calvi had made to his P2 brothers for protection.

The police captured Gelli on 13 September 1982, when he tried to withdraw the $100,000,000 that Calvi had deposited in a Swiss bank account for him. But on 10 August of the following year Gelli escaped from prison, adding new luster to his image as a man who had become a law unto himself. Such a corrupt and corrupting individual would shrink from no enormity, and Gelli stood accused in the forum of public opinion of the country's highest political crimes. His shadow seemed to fall across every subversive attack on Italy's democratic institutions, from right-wing terror bombings to tacit support of the Red Brigades. He was the master conspirator whose evil genius had guided or manipulated the antidemocratic furies of an era. It followed in the public's mind that his pivotal role in deciding Moro's fate could not be doubted.

Neither the majority report nor the minority reports of the P2 Commission put the Gelli case to rest. After three years of parliamentary investigations the parties were deeply divided over the true nature of the Masonic lodge and the role it had played during the Moro kidnapping. The trattativa-fermezza debate continued, but now the fermezza ranks had split. The PCI charged that the policy of fermezza had been sabotaged from within. Berlinguer's position in the Moro case had rested on the assumption of a sincere attempt by the police to liberate the kidnapped Christian Democratic leader, but in the aftermath of the P2 Commission's reports this assumption had been undermined. All of the reports were at odds with each other on every major issue but this: in all probability the search for Moro had been seriously compromised by Gelli's interference. The exact nature of these "piloted inefficiencies" had not yet been determined, but their further clarification would be an important part of the agenda for the second Moro trial, scheduled to begin in early December 1984.

The scene of Moro's kidnapping on via Fani, 16 March 1978.

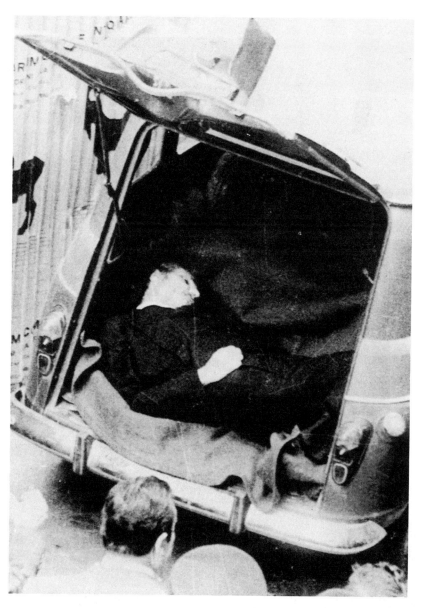

The discovery of Moro's corpse on via Caetani, 9 May 1978.

The Foro Italico courtroom, 14 April 1982: the opening session of the first Moro trial.

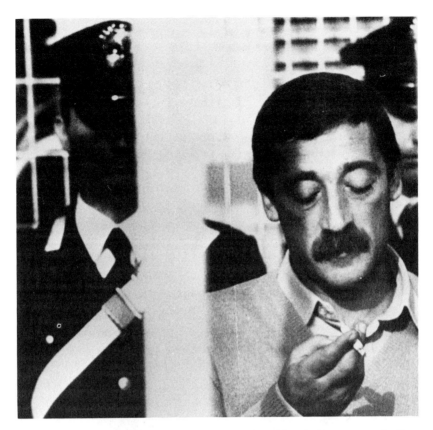

Mario Moretti, the Red Brigade chief in charge of the Moro kidnapping, in the Foro Italico courtroom, 22 April 1982.

Top: Red Brigadists Lauro Azzolini, Franco Bonisoli, Prospero Gallinari, and Vincenzo Guagliardo looking out from the cage of unrepentant terrorists, 22 April 1982. *Bottom:* Red Brigadists Valerio Morucci and Adriana Faranda on the day that she began to testify in the first appeal trial of the Moro case, 4 January 1985.

The widow Eleonora Moro testifying on 19 July 1982.

Giulio Andreotti, the Italian premier during the Moro kidnapping, testifying on 27 September 1982.

Bettino Craxi (right front), the leader of the Socialist party, testifying before President Severino Santiapichi (left front) on 28 September 1982 in the first Moro trial.

7

The Second Trial

Only a few days before the formal presentation of the P2 Commission reports to Parliament, Valerio Morucci and Adriana Faranda began to talk with judges Ferdinando Imposimato and Rosario Priore. The confessions of these dissociati had been long anticipated, but Morucci and Faranda refused to do what the pentiti had done: they would not name names. Even so, the pair supplied hundreds of pages of testimony to the investigating magistrates. Morucci returned to via Fani with the authorities and described in detail what had happened there on 16 March 1978. His lawyer, Tommaso Mancini, claimed that this was "the first time that the Moro event had been reconstructed with historic fidelity."[1]

Few people in Italy agreed with Mancini's claim about the value of his client's testimony. Rival interpretations of the kidnapping and massacre continued to find adherents. Even the most basic facts remained in dispute. For example, Morucci told judges Imposimato and Priore that in the assault only four out of the nine-person terrorist squad had fired weapons, but experts continued to debate how many Red Brigadists were involved in the attack and who did what. Two years after Morucci's testimony one authority would claim that a series of books could be written about the complicated and mysterious Aldo Moro affair, including the kidnapping itself.[2] Morucci's pre-trial assertions did not end speculation even on the matters on which he was willing to comment; for those that he refused to discuss or for which he did not possess firsthand information, such as the address of the People's Prison and the exact circumstances of Moro's murder, opinions varied as before.

As the date for the appeal trial grew closer and newspapers and magazines increased their coverage of Morucci and Faranda, an interview that he gave to Giorgio Bocca created a sensation.[3] Important as a forecast of the testimony that Morucci would give at the appeal trial, one key statement of his had a galvanizing effect: that Moro's cause had been hopeless from the moment of his kidnapping. By putting the Christian Democratic leader on trial, the Red Brigadists hoped to extract a confession from him regarding the nefarious activities of the DC as the Italian subsidiary in capitalism's Washington-run world order, the Stato Imperialista delle Multinazionali (SIM). Moro, they sincerely believed, was the Italian branch manager of this international organization. They expected to learn from him the details of how the CIA, the Pentagon, and the Trilateral Commission laid down the law in Italy through their puppets in the Christian Democratic party. But Moro was able to parry these ideologically infatuated accusations, Morucci admitted. It became clear that the Red Brigades's image of him as the Christian Democratic stooge for American tycoons might need some revision in view of Moro's continuously tense relations with the United States and alleged threats from Washington. The CIA and the Pentagon wanted certain things to be done in Italy, but they did not have absolute power there, Moro explained; the world was complicated and the nature of power ambiguous. In contrast to his interrogators, Moro had the talent and experience to shine in this kind of discussion.

Morucci had not been present in the People's Prison, but as proof of his assertions he offered Bocca a simple observation: after ostentatiously proclaiming that nothing in the Moro trial would be kept hidden, the Red Brigades never said a word about the proceedings. They were uncharacteristically silent because Moro never gave them any information of crucial importance. He caught his captors off guard by proving to be far more equipped to defend his position than they ever imagined possible. This was a discovery about Moro that politicians in Italy had been making for years. His mild manner invited miscalculation by all his political adversaries, because they habitually interpreted it as a sign of weakness. Playing on that image, Moro kept his integrity in the People's Prison by denying the Red Brigades what they dearly wanted: to get the one person who best knew the hated

Christian Democratic order to admit that the historical and political view for which they had risked everything was the truth. If this exchange had been a mere debate, Professor Moro could have gone home after leaving his befuddled captors with some reading suggestions for their political education, but all along the Red Brigades planned to eliminate him.

Morucci's interview with Bocca set off another barrage of polemics between the fermezza and trattativa partisans. Oreste Scalzone, his former colleague in Potere Operaio, complained in a long public letter that Morucci was now completely under the influence of fermezza extremists.[4] From his Parisian exile where he was a leader and spokesman for left-wing Italian émigrés, Scalzone continued to uphold the main trattativa argument, that Moro had been killed primarily because of the state's refusal to enter into negotiations for his life. Moro could have been saved; the Red Brigades would have freed him had there been any movement on the other side. Although it was the Red Brigadists who killed him, the Christian Democratic government did not do what it could have done to prevent that tragic outcome. As with all variations of this interpretation of the Moro affair, Scalzone was here shifting the main burden of blame from the actual agents of the murder to the do-nothing Christian Democratic establishment.

One month later, in November 1984, Mario Moretti broke his long silence and, agreeing with Scalzone, called Morucci's testimony "one of the many convenient versions for the parties and in general for the Italian political system."[5] It was not true that Red Brigade dissension over Moro's execution had wrecked the organization, said Moretti in a December interview with Giorgio Bocca for *L'Espresso*. He defended the Moro operation from beginning to end. Brilliantly devised, the attack on via Fani had been the Red Brigades' deepest penetration into the class enemy's stronghold. It had been perfectly reasonable for them to think that such an attack might destabilize the regime they abhorred. "For at least twenty years [Moro had been] the supreme manager of power in Italy, because he was the demiurge of bourgeois power, [always] present in the moments . . . of decisive choices."[6] Moretti explained that by kidnapping this particular man the Red Brigades hoped to inflame the whole revolutionary left. To Bocca's question, how they could kill a man in cold blood after living with him for fifty-five days, Moretti replied: "You know that we did not kidnap and kill Moro the man, but [rather] his function. We reject the accusation of political homicide." Bocca could not accept this distinction: how could you reduce a human being to his function, he queried. Moretti remained unperturbed. To be a revolutionary required a willingness to commit necessary acts of violence, and "comprehensible or not, this had been our way of thinking and choosing."

Moretti completely rejected Morucci's assertion that the Red Brigades had planned in advance to kill Moro. The Christian Democratic leader's life could have been "saved until the last moment," but "the party of rigor," of fermezza, had made a bloodless outcome impossible. The government would negotiate later for Judge Giovanni D'Urso, but not for Moro. As a result, D'Urso returned home alive; Moro did not. The conclusion for Moretti was obvious: "political obtuseness" characterized the government's handling of the crisis from beginning to end. Even the Pope bungled an opportunity to terminate the impasse; his appeal for the prisoner's release without conditions was "the requiem for Moro." The man died because of fermezza. Although the revolutionary project had become stalled, Moretti continued to find consolation in Lenin: "If now it is necessary to make the classic step backwards in order to go forward again, we will not be frightened to do so."[7]

The appeal trial got under way in the Foro Italico courtroom in early December, nearly two years after the verdict in the first trial. Television cameras recorded the noisy and turbulent scene. The same steel cages again housed the terrorist defendants. Only thirty-eight of the fifty-nine defendants appeared the first day. Missing were many of the pentiti and the irriducibili. President Giuseppe De Nictolis presided over the court, assisted by Judge Giovanni Caso. Six popular judges also sat at the bench. Heavily armed policemen and carabinieri stood guard inside the building and patrolled the grounds outside. Helicopters droned overhead. Terrorism had been in steady decline since 1982, but the authorities behaved as though they believed the many pentiti who warned of a Red Brigade resurgence.

Early during the second session of the trial, on 7 December, Judge Caso began to read the long list of crimes for which the defendants were being tried. He could not finish it. His emotions overwhelmed him as he described these murders: "and under the blows of the Red Brigades magistrates, policemen . . . officers began to fall. . . ."[8] Here his voice trailed off. He turned pale and his eyes reddened and welled up with tears. President De Nictolis granted a half-hour recess so that his colleague could compose himself.

Moretti, newly arrived from a terrorism trial in Milan where he received his second life sentence, appeared in the Foro Italico courtroom for the fourth session, on 10 December. Speaking to reporters through the bars of his cage, the diminutive terrorist claimed that the Red Brigades' war with the state was far from over. "The Red Brigades are alive," he exulted, pointing to the May 1983 wounding of Professor Gino Giugni and the 15 February 1984 assassination of Leamon R. Hunt as proof of the organization's continuing strength.[9] These two attacks exemplified ongoing Red Brigade terrorism, which erupted sporadically as the Aldo Moro trials unfolded.

The Red Brigades selected Giugni for revolutionary justice because of his role as a moderate in the labor negotiations that led to the Statuto dei Lavoratori. He was one of the PSI's leading exponents of unequivocal cooperation with industry, a point of view that was for the Red Brigades the political equivalent of the sin against the Holy Ghost. They condemned him to death as a collaborationist pig of the most degenerate kind, as the authorities learned from a subsequent Red Brigade communication. He was then shot three times on the University of Rome campus by a young woman riding a Vespa driven by her male companion. Although the wounds that he sustained in the knee, thigh, and arm were not serious, the attack thoroughly alarmed the nation. President Sandro Pertini declared that dangerous remnants of terrorist formations were once more poised to strike at the state. Many pentiti predicted that the Red Brigades would try to disrupt the national elections, scheduled for June 1983; they interpreted the attack on Giugni as the start of that subversive campaign. Their predictions went unrealized, but the fear remained.

Then on 15 February 1984 three young Red Brigadists killed Leamon R. Hunt, an American diplomat responsible for supplying the multinational force in the Sinai. Hunt had taken the utmost security precautions. Armed guards kept his house under constant surveillance, and he rode in a bulletproof car. Despite these measures the terrorists experienced no difficulty in killing him. Diamond-tipped bullets penetrated the armored vehicle as the driver prepared to enter Hunt's garage. Suffering massive head wounds, the victim died in the hospital a short while later.

In taking credit for the Hunt assassination, the Red Brigades boasted that they had struck a blow against the Camp David accords, by means of which the forces of imperialism had subjugated the Arab masses. To some extent, the anti-Zionist stance of the Red Brigades evolved out of their longstanding anti-Americanism. Ever since the kidnapping of General Dozier, in December 1981, the Red Brigades had specifically targeted the United States as the linchpin of world imperialism. They intended the Hunt murder to be a blow against that order.

The novel element in this terrorist attack was the clear shift it marked in the organization's agenda. For nearly fifteen years the Red Brigades had invoked a Marxist-Leninist justification for their actions on behalf of the Italian proletariat. Now they put this same ideology into the service of the Arab revolutionary cause in the Middle East. The Hunt killing had been ordered for its effect not on Italian politics but on Middle Eastern politics. Instead of contracting and hunkering down in a period of evident decline, the Red Brigades had expanded their field of operations and had allied themselves with such Euroterrorist groups as Action Directe in France and the Red Army Faction in Germany. One consequence of Red Brigade factionalism had been a diversification of the organization's terrorist activities. Red Brigadism was both less and more than formerly: less active in the field, but more varied in its approach to revolution. The Red Brigadists had failed to radicalize the masses, but they had not relinquished the quest for revolution.

To hear Moretti talk in December 1984, one might conclude that the Red Brigades were only suffering from a temporary reverse and that they would rebound in 1985. Prime Minister Bettino Craxi, for one, feared that this was no idle boast. Intelligence reports and warnings from the pentiti convinced him that the latest Red Brigade pamphlets meant what they said about a new revolutionary offensive. The atmosphere of the trial was deeply tinged with this impression.

On 14 December the Red Brigades attempted to hold up Metro Security Express in Rome. A terrorist command of three men and one woman shot and gravely wounded two night watchmen. Police foiled the holdup and killed one of the terrorists, Antonio Giustini. His female companion, Maria Trapani, was critically wounded in the shootout. A passerby was also wounded. The other two terrorists escaped.

For Valerio Morucci, the bloodily bungled robbery attempt signaled yet another stage of his former organization's irreversible decline. "These would be the Red Brigades that put a country in crisis [but] today cannot even bring a robbery to a successful conclusion," he sarcastically commented.[10] Nevertheless, at the Moro appeal trial on

17 December hard-line defendants offered this salute: "Honor to comrade Antonio Giustini, militant of the Red Brigades, and to all the militants who have fallen fighting for communism."[11] They interpreted the action as a further sign that the Red Brigades were returning to full strength. While few terrorism experts would concede so much, the 14 December robbery attempt had the Italian authorities deeply worried over what other violence the holiday season might bring.

Only ten days later, on Christmas eve, right-wing terrorists were responsible for a train bombing in the Apennine Tunnel near San Benedetto Val di Sambro. It produced a Christmas of blood for Italy, with fifteen people dead and 117 injured. This slaughter made a pair in the public mind with the violent return of the Red Brigades earlier that month. Italians had suffered fifteen years of antidemocratic assaults from both ideological extremes, and the terrorists still possessed the power to disfigure Italian public life. To one young man the situation appeared so hopeless that life itself could no longer be endured. Despairing of Italy, twenty-nine-year-old Filippo Alberghina, who had helped clear the train wreckage of its human remains, shot himself in the head. In a farewell letter to his father and sisters, he called Italy "a damned society" and refused to go on living "in this absurd way."[12] His suicide quickly became a tragic symbol of Italy's new dark time with terrorism.

The violence continued. On 9 January 1985 Ottavio Conte, twenty-eight, became the first NOCS (Nucleo Operativo Centrale di Sicurezza) agent to be killed by terrorists. The newspapers reported that three members of the Antonio Giustini column of the Red Brigades shot him near Rome. On 11 January, however, the police changed their minds about the Conte slaying. Reacting to information provided by a neofascist pentito, they decided that in all probability the radical right-wing organization, Nuclei Armati Rivoluzionari (NAR) had killed him in revenge for the death of a neofascist terrorist, Giorgio Vale. While both extremes remained in the public eye, the left received the most attention because of the vast publicity engendered by the Moro appeal trial.

The two star witnesses in the trial were Faranda and Morucci. After listening to President De Nictolis state the crimes, including numerous homicides, for which she stood charged, Faranda, garbed in her trademark Peruvian poncho, began to testify on 4 January 1985 and went on for nearly two weeks. The witness received President de Nictolis' permission to read from a "Premessa." In these pages she struck a tone of abject repentance. Moro's death, she began, still weighed heavily on the public, and those responsible for the crime had to lighten the burden as much as possible. Faranda promised to give her full cooperation, "to assume the task of clarifying, according to our conscience, the events that led to the kidnapping and death of Aldo Moro."[13] As a *dissociata*, Faranda would not discuss the actions of other Red Brigadists but swore to divulge all the details of her own role in the Moro kidnapping and murder.

Faranda had been raised in a solidly middle-class home. Her father was the advocate general of the state in Messina. One of his other children became a lawyer, another a journalist. Adriana, however, conceived an invincible disdain for the establishment her family served. She described for the court how the protest movement of 1968 had radicalized her. The young woman then embraced the extraparliamentary religion of revolution that for many thousands of Italians from her generation defined the era. The main outlines of her political biography were now exceedingly familiar to anyone who had been following the Moro trials.

With other like-minded comrades, she joined Potere Operaio, which for some of its members functioned as a halfway house along a path leading to the terrorist underground. After marrying Luigi Rosati, also of Potere Operaio, Faranda gave birth to a daughter, Alessandra, in 1971. The little girl was five when Faranda joined the Red Brigades, a decision that had its origin in high idealism, she averred at the appeal trial. If one began with her premise that the abomination of capitalism threatened the world with slavery and extinction, then the logical path to revolutionary politics lay clear and straight. In order to create a better world for Alessandra and for all the children, anticapitalist violence of the kind ordained by Marx and Lenin was the only possible recourse.

Her beliefs had led to a practical nihilism, Faranda now thought, and she felt a terrible anguish over "the irreparable lacerations caused by the devaluation of fundamental ethical principles."[14] In helping to lead an organization that had made widows and orphans out of blameless men's wives and children, she had ruined her own life and had deprived her daughter of a normal existence. Faranda now knew that she had deluded herself. Under the beguiling spell of revolution's mystique, she had not realized that the victims of the Red Brigades were human beings. To her these defenders of a demonic status quo had been no more deserving of pity than a rabid animal would have been. She could not apologize or ask forgiveness. Her crimes were atrocious, the visibly miserable witness lamented; she could only tell her story and hope that others would learn from it.

As the witness began to talk about via Fani and its aftermath, it began to seem that the long-awaited Godot had come at last. She wasted no time. The motive of the Red Brigades on 16 March 1978 was obvious. Fearing that Christian Democracy would renew itself under Moro, the Red Brigades resolved to attack the party by striking at its head. The fundamental rationale behind the massacre and kidnapping on via Fani was political. Throughout the succeeding fifty-five days the Red Brigades struck numerous other targets, always trying to force the Christian Democrats—the indispensable base of the capitalist order in Italy—into a fatal misstep. With the shamelessly antirevolutionary PCI the Red Brigades had a "highly conflictual rapport," but because of its huge base in the working class, the Communist party was never itself a target.[15] Although a few Communists had been killed or wounded as a result of some particular actions, the policy of the Red Brigades was to leave the PCI alone. Christian Democracy loomed as the immediate enemy, and the paramount Christian Democrat was Moro.

Faranda claimed to have experienced some moral perturbations over the killing of Moro's security guard, "certainly not a thing one undertook lightly," but only during the subsequent negotiations for a prisoner exchange did her conscience begin to trouble her seriously.[16] Part of her problem arose from the Moro interrogation, which went very poorly for the Red Brigades. They had expected vital intelligence from Moro, but at the end of his testimony it began to dawn on them that "they had constructed, let us say, a vision that did not correspond with reality. Because of this we did not understand how much complexity there was . . . in the evolution of the state, in the distribution of power, in the organization of power, in the formulation of political decisions."[17] The Red Brigades had no inkling of any of these things, Faranda observed, "wanting as we did to give everything a directness that was absolutely removed from reality."[18]

On the next day the witness spoke of the efforts she and Morucci had made to save Moro. Faranda's tremulous voice often failed her, and sometimes she broke down completely. The central question on President De Nictolis' mind was the same one that President Santiapichi had raised repeatedly in Moro 1: what chance did Moro have of ever getting out of the People's Prison alive? Faranda responded by commenting sorrowfully on "the two rigidities" that killed Moro: the militarist mentality into which "the Red Brigades fell absolutely" and "the intransigence of the government," which categorically refused to negotiate for the prisoner's life.[19] Moro's only chance to survive was to find a middle ground between the extreme positions of the Red Brigades and the government. Faranda claimed that she and Morucci had worked to promote a compromise solution, but that proved to be a hopeless undertaking.

The court wondered why this pair, with many homicides to answer for, including some that they perpetrated after the 9 May 1978 killing of Moro, had exhibited such an uncharacteristic solicitude for a lackey of the bourgeoisie. Faranda admitted that their primary motivation had been political. They knew from conversations with Lanfranco Pace (of the extraparliamentary left-wing Autonomia organization) that important leaders in the large network of radical groups more or less sympathetic to the revolutionary project were opposed to killing Moro because of the repercussions such an act would surely provoke.[20] Faranda and Morucci thought that if the Red Brigades lost their base in the Movement, as these groups were called, the armed struggle against capitalism would end in an annihilating defeat for communism. Because they themselves had been members of Potere Operaio, Faranda and Morucci had a particular appreciation for the importance of the rapport between Red Brigadism and the Movement, and they did not want to see it destroyed.[21] Hence their moderation was born mainly of practical considerations, although Faranda wanted the court to know that ethical concerns had begun to affect her at this time as well.

Her comment about ethics seemed especially hard to believe. What could that possibly mean in the light of crimes she had gone on to commit after the Moro murder? Faranda explained that to abandon the clandestine life of a terrorist entailed exceptional difficulties. An organization like the Red Brigades becomes the whole world for its members, and "the isolation from reality is total."[22] In such an environment, the group ideology drives out everything not in express conformity with it. To live in the terrorist underground requires that the enemy be demonized. One must assiduously cultivate a heightened sensibility for seeing "the hideousness of things as they are," which alone creates the essential precondition for a violent, revolutionary attack on them.[23] A revolutionary had to be hard and cruel in the present in order to be kind and generous to posterity. Only thus could Faranda explain her continued membership in the Red Brigades following the Moro murder, and even after formally withdrawing from the organization, she continued to believe in the absolute validity of the armed struggle. More time would have to pass before she would abandon that belief in favor of "fundamental ethical values."[24]

Because Faranda refused to name other people involved in the Moro kidnapping, her testimony did not provide a breakthrough in the case. The lawyers cross-examined her in vain. One lawyer pressed her for details about via Fani. He began by observing that Faranda had lived with Morucci, and he had participated in the massacre; it did not seem possible that there could have been any secrets between them. The lawyer would have to talk with Morucci, she said. "He will want to, he will be able to explain it much better than I can."[25] When asked how she, as a member of the Red Brigades' Executive Committee, could be so ignorant of the details of Moro's experiences inside the People's Prison, not even knowing the address, Faranda replied that the organization functioned with "a criterion of the most rigid compartmentalization."[26] True, she had important responsibilities in the organization, but they did not go beyond certain clearly delineated boundaries. In this way the Red Brigades could limit the damage that might result from any single leader's capture.

Under the pressure of continued questioning Faranda evinced a weariness of mind and body, evidently the result of a severe moral crisis. She appeared to be a woman destroyed. When not giving hesitant, fumbling, and contradictory answers to specific questions about the treatment and comportment of Moro during the fifty-five days, Faranda pleaded ignorance. Her assignment during the entire Moro operation was to deliver letters and communications. She did not actually witness any part of the drama.

After seven long sessions in the witness chair Faranda only contributed to the controversy swirling around the questions of motive and objective in the Moro case. Even on the lesser mysteries of how many letters Moro actually wrote and what parts, if any, had been dictated, Faranda could shed no light. She did not remember or she did not know. Was she sincere? Some accepted her confession as genuinely contrite, whereas others viewed it only as a clever defense tactic. At the end, however, everyone agreed that she had not said anything fundamentally new about Moro.

Of the defendants who were prepared to talk, only Morucci had been present at via Fani. He began his testimony on 18 January 1985 by reading a declaration entitled "To Reopen a Dialogue with Society: A Manifesto of Political Detainees," signed by himself and various other former terrorists. "In these years of profound transformation," Morucci intoned, "there have been events that have lacerated, at times tragically, our country."[27] Conceding that no generation could write its own history, the signers wanted to offer an explanation of what had inspired them to strike their blows. They still felt in conflict with society, but no longer actively "belligerent" toward it. Above all, they rejected their violent past, proposing now to go beyond "the culture and ideology . . . of the armed struggle." Theirs would be a search for "a higher quality in human relations [and] an opening to constantly expanding liberty." The age of terrorism had ended; the age of "the human personality's free development and its well-being" had begun. They now welcomed human diversity and no longer chose to indulge their former penchant for "exasperated and sterile antagonisms."

Morucci and the other advocates of dialogue now wanted a "reconciliation" with society. They hoped "to stimulate a new sensibility" in Italy, particularly regarding the prisons. Society's prevailing attitudes toward punishment appeared to be "inspired by unfriendliness [*inimicizia*] toward the accused or the guilty." To become reconciled with the former revolutionaries, society should abandon these attitudes and recognize "the changes" that were taking place in the prisons. "Resocialization" should be the goal of all in order to decrease "social tension" and "reduce . . . violence." In short, they asked for the abolition of "the atrocity of life sentences, an expression of a blind punitive desire that forever excludes the individual from the social context [dal contesto sociale]." Every human being had one "radical and inalienable right: HOPE [LA SPERANZA]."

For three hours Morucci described his ideological itinerary. Like Faranda, he had been a child of 1968 and had moved by what appeared to be the most natural and logical steps from Potere Operaio to the Red Brigades. Their violent actions did not derive from "a particular criminal interest" or "mental derangement," but rather from "a degeneration of ideology."[28] With high ideals about a just society, young people became part of the Movement, that eclectic, amorphous, and contradictory left-wing phenomenon. Part of it began to degenerate very early: "in this restricted segment the conviction grew that only a drastic act, only a violent act could modify the present state of things [and] . . . therefore the armed struggle was necessary."[29] The mirage of a perfect society beckoned, and they believed that their actions as Red Brigadists would create the essential preconditions for a communist utopia. The Red Brigades held to the myth of a communist society of the future, and in the name of another myth, revolution, they tried to smash a capitalist order that appeared to radiate an evil unparalleled in history. Theirs were sincerely held if tragically stupid beliefs, Morucci explained. As a Red Brigadist he was perfectly willing to kill and to risk his life for the communist revolution.

Morucci's monologue, with some tearful pauses, went on for several court sessions. The attention of the entire courtroom was riveted on his description of the via Fani attack. The planning for Operation Fritz, Morucci nervously began, had been meticulous in the extreme. For months Red Brigadists trailed Moro and his security guard, carefully noting their habits and schedules. On the day of the via Fani operation, Morucci and another Red Brigadist he would not name, in keeping with the code of the dissociati, had the assignment of killing the two men accompanying Moro, Oreste Leonardi and Domenico Ricci. Pouring machine-gun fire into the lead Moro vehicle while "two other persons" were killing the three bodyguards in the car behind, Morucci could not help but be impressed by the tenacity of Ricci and the truly heroic reaction of Leonardi. Under heavy fire Ricci, the driver, strove desperately to get out of the trap, maneuvering the vehicle as best he could until struck by a mortal wound. Leonardi's first reaction to the shots was to protect Moro, "that is, he turned around to shove the Honorable Moro down and indeed the Red Brigades found him in this position."[30] "I must say," Morucci continued, "that afterwards this behavior made a deep impression on me."

Morucci downplayed the legend of the Red Brigades' "geometric potency"—the notorious phrase of Franco Piperno, an extraparliamentary left leader. In fact, they dropped any proposed action that presented substantial difficulty and generally attacked only the easiest targets. That Moro's car was not bullet-proof was a major element in their decision to go ahead with the plan. Even so, some things went wrong at via Fani. For example, Morucci's own weapon misfired. The Red Brigades' greatest advantage always had been the element of surprise, and the via Fani attack was no exception.

Morucci's moving performance still failed to dispel the alternative interpretations of what happened during the attack. Heated arguments continued over the size of the terrorist command, and ballistics experts contested his reconstruction of events. As for the events in the People's Prison and the circumstances of Moro's murder, Morucci prefaced virtually all his statements with some variation of "I can only make suppositions." He did not know where Moro had been kept prisoner or how the Red Brigades had killed him. Lawyers cross-examined him, but on some questions Morucci, as a dissociato, refused to name names; on others he professed ignorance.

To complicate matters even further, on 5 February 1985 Antonio Savasta contradicted some of Morucci's testimony, although this pentito readily conceded that his own version of events was based on what others had told him. And after all these years it was no longer possible for him to keep the story straight: "I could be mixing up some of these things," Savasta plaintively noted.[31] Many of the onlookers in the Foro Italico courtroom could sympathize with that.

In a 14 February letter to the court, Enrico Fenzi inadvertently commented on what had been lacking in Morucci's testimony. Pentito Fenzi, who had made such a favorable impression on President Santiapichi in Moro 1, wrote to President De Nictolis in praise of Morucci. He wished to dispute one lawyer's claim that Morucci and Fenzi were in contention on key issues in the case: "I have always found [Morucci's] declarations convincing and coherent from what I have been able to know and understand about the Red Brigades."[32] Following several expressions of solidarity with Morucci, and preceding others in the same vein, the inadvertent note was struck: "I personally deem absolutely necessary a different attitude of full and open collaboration with justice."[33] Such had not been Morucci's attitude. He had imposed limits on his collaboration with justice, and for many in Italy the essentially reticent character of his testimony, despite nine courtroom sessions and fifty hours in the witness chair, was its most notable feature.

The lawyers on both sides of the case had already begun to give their summations. Procuratore Generale Carlo De Gregorio summed up the prosecution's argument. Only the pentiti should receive the court's mercy, he claimed. The life sentences of Morucci and Faranda should be confirmed because they had not fully and unreservedly disclosed what they knew about the Moro case. De Gregorio disparaged Faranda's testimony in particular. The woman wants us to believe that she desperately tried to save Moro's life, but after his murder she nonetheless participated in murderous terrorist assaults against Judge Giuliano Tartaglione and the bodyguards of Christian Democratic leader Giovanni Galloni. Faranda was part of a criminal conspiracy that had resulted in the death and maiming of some of Italy's finest men, and she still had not repented of these acts in the only way the law could accept, by cooperating with the court fully and without reservations. Anything short of unconditional repentance implied an element of resistance to the law, which the court, in homage to terrorism's victims, was obliged to punish with the utmost severity.[34]

It took ten days for the dozen defense lawyers to have their say. Tommaso Mancini, the lawyer for Morucci and Faranda, predictably requested lesser sentences for his clients, but even some of the other lawyers backed his request. For example, Giuseppe Dante, who represented the sister of Judge Tartaglione, expressed his belief in the couple's sincerity and invited the court to act with mercy toward them. The court took Dante's recommendation under advisement and on 6 March 1985, after fifty-two court sessions in the Moro appeal trial, withdrew to the council chamber to consider the evidence.

Nine days later President De Nictolis handed down the judgment of the court. Relatives of the defendants, photographers, newspapermen, and lawyers crowded into the courtroom to hear the pronouncement. A hush fell over the courtroom as President De Nictolis began to read, sonorously intoning the phrase, "In the name of the Italian people."[35] Many, but not all, of the defendants also listened attentively.

President De Nictolis substantially modified the sentences of the first trial. He did confirm twenty-two of the life sentences, but this number was down by ten from President Santiapichi's earlier ruling. Among the beneficiaries of his revision were Morucci and Faranda: instead of life in prison they received thirty-year sentences. In the "Motivi della Decisione" Judge Caso and President De Nictolis explained why Faranda and Morucci had earned a reduction in their sentences. They had admitted their guilt and had cooperated significantly with the law. Together they had provided a "reconstruction of the facts and . . . the ideology, the political program, and the *modus operandi* of the Red Brigades."[36]

Morucci in particular had given vital information about the via Fani massacre and kidnapping. The judges did not want to claim too much for his testimony: "Still lacking were precise corroborative elements that would render his declarations true or false."[37] Yet his testimony before the court contained many positive elements: "the reconstruction of the action [on via Fani] given by the defendant does not contrast with [eyewitness testimony], and it explains the operation better than theirs does."[38]

The judges had to admit that lacunae still existed. For example, the number of terrorists who participated in the massacre remained in dispute, and the court had not been able to learn the names of everyone involved in it. Moreover, they found it difficult to believe that Morucci and Faranda did not know more about developments inside the People's Prison than they had divulged. The witnesses claimed to have been excluded from contact with Moro during the entire fifty-five days of the kidnapping. The judges doubted their claim: "if true . . . it would mean that the leaders of the Red Brigades excluded the two from any possibility of involvement in the kidnapping."[39] Such an exclusion did not make sense. Why would Morucci, at the very center of things in the via Fani assault, be reduced to a marginal role thereafter? This question had never been answered to the satisfaction of the court.

Yet in the main Faranda and Morucci had been helpful witnesses. It was this kind of cooperation that the special legislation on terrorism had been designed to encourage: "to prevent the phenomenon of terrorism's armed subversion from generating further tragic consequences."[40] In extending relative leniency to these two, President De Nictolis was simply applying the principle wisely invoked by President Santiapichi in Moro 1 regarding other former terrorists who had cooperated with the law. Numerous defendants in that earlier trial had criticized President Santiapichi for accepting "uncritically" pentito testimony, which should have been viewed with "extreme caution and diffidence."[41] This "censure is baseless," President De Nictolis and Judge Caso declared.[42] President Santiapichi's court had been extremely careful about cross-checking the testimony of all witnesses against "the results of vast and extensive *istruttoria* investigations."[43] The appeal court sought to emulate Santiapichi's practice and to apply it to defendants, notably Faranda and Morucci, who deserved the special treatment that the laws on terrorism allowed. President De Nictolis reduced many other sentences as well, one by twenty-two years. In total, the appeal court lopped off 786 years of prison time.

The entire sentencing session was over in forty-five minutes, and immediately afterwards the court erupted in a cacophony of derisive hoots and excited hurrahs. The defense lawyers celebrated the decision as an overall victory for their clients. Other lawyers in the case complained about the court's leniency. Attorney General Carlo De Gregorio castigated the sentence as a travesty of justice. Most of the prosecuting attorneys thought that the sentence was less a reflection of the case's merits than of the comparatively tranquil times Italy then enjoyed. Terrorism, while not completely eliminated, had been largely contained, and the public perceived Red Brigadism as a decidedly lesser peril now than during the dreadful years 1978–1982, when the Moro and Dozier kidnappings had created panic in Italy. During that five-year period the Red Brigades had the country's undivided attention. They were feared as no other subversive organization had been during the history of the Italian Republic, but by 1985 people understood that the tide had turned against the terrorists. More than a year had passed since the Hunt murder. Immediately following the appeal trial, many interpreted the moderate sentence as an official declaration that the terrorist era had ended. The state was stronger now and therefore could be more indulgent.

Instead of winding down, terrorist violence erupted anew. On 25 March 1985, with the recent sentences in the Moro case continuing to spark angry polemics, a gun battle in Alessandria ended with two young men dead. Two of their companions and a police officer were wounded in the fray. Killed were Diego Macciò, twenty-three, and Enrico Ferrer, nineteen. The wounded were Andrea Cosso, twenty-three, and Raffaella Furiozzi, nineteen, the fiancée of Macciò. Police had stopped them as part of a normal security procedure for a nearby antinuclear demonstration, and Cosso jumped out of the car firing a weapon. After the carnage, investigating authorities discovered that all four belonged to the Nuclei Armati Rivoluzionari (NAR), a right-wing terrorist organization.

Two days later, terrorists from the opposite ideological extreme assassinated Ezio Tarantelli, a forty-four-year old economist and a voice of reason and moderation in the country's tense labor negotiations. He had just given a lecture on political economy at the University of Rome. Just as Tarantelli was leaving the building that housed the faculty of economy and commerce, someone was heard to say, "Professor, excuse me."[44] Before dozens of witnesses, two men fired twenty rounds of machine gun fire into his face and head. He fell dead against the windshield of his car.

In a seventy-one-page document left next to Tarantelli's corpse, the Red Brigades explained the objectives of their new spring campaign. "With revolutionary love" they dedicated this strategic resolution "No. 20" to Antonio Giustini, who had been killed in Rome a few months earlier.[45] Tarantelli's name was not mentioned in the resolution, but he was viewed by the Red Brigades as a symbol of Craxi's neocorporativist policies. The Red Brigades despised Craxi, a Socialist who imagined that socialism could be achieved by betraying the proletariat to the corporate leaders of Confindustria. The Red Brigades were obliged to defend the proletariat against him and his cronies with the revolutionary violence prescribed by Marx and Lenin.

The Red Brigades viewed Craxi as the real heir of Moro in Italian politics. With the elimination of the DC's "supreme strategist," the bourgeoisie required a new powerbroker in order to maintain the democratic appearance of the capitalist order.[46] Craxi, strategically positioned between a DC that without Moro could no longer even pretend to be a united party and a PCI ravaged by the disease of reformism but still penalized politically for its very distant revolutionary past, opportunistically offered his services. By making the status quo more stable with his infamous "neocorporativist social pact," Craxi, in effect, proposed to eliminate once and for all the "Italian anomaly, . . . the presence [in a Western democracy] of a proletarian movement animated by a strong class consciousness."[47] An evil counselor to Craxi, Tarantelli had been at the center of this counterrevolutionary scheme.

An obvious parallel existed between the murder of Tarantelli and the attack on Gino Giugni nearly two years before. Both acts of terrorism were part of the Red Brigade campaign to pit the fighting forces of the left against capitalism in all of its forms, including shameful reformists like Craxi, the most accomplished political prostitute in Italy. Yet even in their greatly reduced state the Red Brigadists quarreled among themselves over how they could best advance the workers' struggle and bring it to a final victory over the class enemy. In 1982 the Red Brigades had split up into three different factions: the Fronte Carcere, known as the *linea movimentista* or the Guerrilla Party; the Executive Committee, known as the *linea militarista* or the Centro; and the Colonna Milanese Walter Alasia, known as the *linea spontaneista.* These groups exchanged such bitter epithets as "frac-tionism," "opportunism," "bureaucratism," "genericism," "econo-mism," and—most wounding of all—"neorevisionism."[48] Some fur-ther splits had occurred within these factions. According to Judge Francesco Amato, who spent years investigating the problem of terror-ism in Italy, factionalism arose in the Red Brigades over "how to evaluate the political situation, how to consider the relationship be-tween the power of the revolution . . . and SIM [the Imperialist State of the Multinationals]."[49]

By 1984 the internal stresses within Red Brigadism had become much more intense, and in the fall of that year the *movimentisti* of Giovanni Senzani announced that the *militaristi* of Barbara Balzerani had been expelled from the organization. Then, in the strategic reso-lution of March 1985, the militaristi condemned the movimentisti as "the most exemplary expression of idealist subjectivism."[50] As for the linea spontaneista, "the teachings of Lenin" expressly condemned "every spontaneous tendency" in the revolutionary movement.[51]

Balzerani's militaristi claimed to represent all sincere revolution-aries who wanted to be guided by "the principles of Marxism and by the historic experience of the international proletariat," from the Paris Commune to the present.[52] Marxist-Leninist revolution might be out of fashion in this dark age of the pentiti who now, with hand on heart, were telling the credulous media that the people should put their trust in the rule of law. But the militaristi would not join this abject capitulation before the money god by people who once called themselves communists. The true Red Brigades would fight on by striking at Italian capitalism, as they had done on the University of Rome campus in March 1985. Claiming to ad-here to the genuine Marxist-Leninist strategy, they also proclaimed their solidarity with revolutionaries all over the world fighting against the common capitalist enemy. There was one revolution and one capitalism. The politically conscious element of the workers fought for the revolution; the bourgeoisie everywhere defended capitalism, and behind the pro-capitalist forces in any given country American military power always loomed. The ultimate enemy of every revo-lutionary movement was the United States. Both the Dozier kidnap-ping in 1981–82 and the Hunt murder in 1984 had to be placed in the context of the international front on which the Red Brigades perforce had to fight.

Although the second Moro trial had ended in an atmosphere of hope and optimism about the collapse of terrorism, the Red Brigades regained the initiative with the Tarantelli killing. The Moro case could not yet be separated from a political backdrop conditioned by sporadic terrorism, as the many violent events of March 1985 made clear. Further clarification of Strategic Resolution No. 20 came soon afterwards.

8

Moro Ter
The First Year

The third trial in the Moro case began in the aftermath of new terrorist violence that seemed to follow the political logic of the Red Brigades' Strategic Resolution No. 20. All revolutionary groups had work to do at home, but in doing it they also furthered the cause of world revolution. The sympathetic relations between the world's revolutionary groups ineluctably made joint action desirable in some circumstances. Therefore, when Palestinian terrorists massacred thirteen people and wounded seventy-seven others at the Fiumicino airport outside Rome on 27 December 1985, the Italian police immediately suspected that the Red Brigades had furnished machine guns and other logistical support to their allies in revolution.

That Middle Eastern objectives could be pursued in perfect harmony with the traditional Red Brigade aim of producing revolution in Italy was demonstrated on 10 February 1986, when two terrorists shot and killed Lando Conti, a few months past his term as mayor of Florence. Here too the assassins left behind an explanation for the murder. To begin with, Conti was guilty of being a close collaborator of Defense Minister Giovanni Spadolini, described by the Red Brigades as a "Zionist pig."[1] Moreover, he had been an Italian agent for General Motors, which produced radar, electronics equipment, and guidance systems for missiles. A frequent target of pacifist demonstrators, Conti had become a symbolic figure in Italian participation in the arms race, especially regarding Star Wars, the U.S. weapons research program begun in 1984 to explore outer space technologies for destroying attacking missiles and warheads. To the Red Brigades he was vital to the "war industry" and deeply involved with Zionists, NATO right-wingers, South Africans, Philippine and other dictators, "to cite only a few."[2] American imperialism "stood at the center of this colossal combination" in the service of which capitalist war production threatened the world.[3] Having struck a blow at "the belly of the beast," the killers of Conti imagined that they had performed a signal service for all mankind.[4]

Through the war industry, which in the nature of things steadily absorbed more and more of society's wealth, Italy was turning into an antiproletarian neocorporativist state. In such a social environment class conflict would give way to the complete subjugation of the working class. To this end Tarantelli had employed his considerable talents, and so the Red Brigades had eliminated him.[5] Such so-called socialists were class enemies by another name, and their antiworker program rendered "even more evident the necessity of a revolutionary political representation of the working class's general interests," a role in which the Red Brigades cast themselves.[6] Their new tactics were adapted to "the base of a Marxist-Leninist analysis."[7] It was in this light that the Red Brigades viewed "the treasure in the experiences of the international communist movement."

American imperialism was still the paramount evil in the world. In other words, the revolution in Italy depended on "the weakening of Western imperialism in the area," something all European revolutionary forces had in common.[8] The rationale for Euroterrorism could not be more bluntly stated. "Western imperialism, with the United States in the lead, is the principal and declared enemy of the international proletariat and of progressive peoples who struggle for their own emancipation," and revolutionaries all over Europe had a duty, amply confirmed in the teachings and historical experiences of Marxist-Leninism, to strike against the upholders and the beneficiaries of this imperialist system.[9] Therefore, the Red Brigades' campaign in defense of the proletariat should be informed by "the principles of proletarian internationalism consistent with militant solidarity and with working for the revolution in one's own country."[10] It followed that the servants in the highest ranks of Italian capitalism, like Tarantelli, and their more internationally connected colleagues, like Conti, would continue to be hunted by the Red Brigades. The terrorists emphasized repeatedly how the Middle East would give revolutionaries their best chance for effective action against the capitalist world order.

The terrorist killings of 1985 and early 1986 lent credence to the warnings of Roberto Sandalo, a repentant former member of the Prima Linea terrorist organization. In a television interview on 14 February, he stated that in Rome alone no fewer than sixty Red Brigadists remained at large. Three hundred more circulated abroad and could return to Italy at any time. "The assassination of Conti," he prophesied, "is not the last gasp of fringe survivors but the signal of a dangerous resurgence."[11] Just three days later Red Brigadists shot and wounded a carabiniere officer in Naples, and on 21 February they attacked Antonio Da Empoli, another one of Craxi's economic counselors. In this atmosphere of continuing alarm about the Red Brigades, preparations for the third Moro trial got underway.

The mysterious death of Michele Sindona on 20 March 1986 further aggravated the nation's sense of consternation. Sindona had vowed to commit suicide if he lost in court, and, following his conviction for the murder of Giorgio Ambrosoli, it was thought that he swallowed a lethal dose of potassium cyanide in his prison cell. His last words, however, were, "They have poisoned me."[12] As in the Roberto Calvi case, the question of Sindona's "suicide" was discussed endlessly. The evidence pointed toward suicide, but not conclusively so. The television cameras in his maximum security cell did not record any suspicious activity; nevertheless, by turning his back at a certain angle, he could have created a blind spot and done the deed himself. The truth could never be known, and therefore even the most fantastic explanations of Sindona's death could not be disproved. The Italian imagination required only the slightest stimulation on such matters, and the Sindona case had stimulated it vigorously.

The Moro ter trial began at Rebibbia with a discussion of procedural matters. The president of the court was Sergio Sorichilli, and Pasquale Perrone acted as the giudice a latere. Nitto Francesco Palma served as the public minister. The trial would be based on a judicial investigation that had been conducted by Judge Rosario Priore and completed on 13 August 1984. In seven volumes and 2,112 pages, Judge Priore recounted the history of the Rome column of the Red Brigades. He included numerous descriptions of the terrorists, wherever possible in their own words. One such figure, Roberto Buzzatti, gave him nearly one hundred pages of testimony.[13] Several others provided nearly that much.

Once again, the confessions of pentiti and dissociati would be central to the state's case against the Red Brigades, although Judge Priore indulged in no illusions about the two most important witnesses, Valerio Morucci and Adriana Faranda. It was important, he thought, to underscore their true motives in voting against the Red Brigades' death sentence for Moro. They definitely were not humanitarians underneath their ski masks or emblematic personalities of Red Brigadism with a human face in the heavily romanticized style employed by some of their apologists. Faranda and Morucci had voted against the death sentence "not with humanitarian intent . . . but only because Moro alive would have been a much more destructive drifting mine [*mina vagante*] for the Italian political system."[14] The best that could be said for them was that their subsequent defection led to a series of internal shocks from which the Red Brigades never recovered.

Judge Priore thought that the major developments in the Moro case had already emerged with sufficient clarity during the first trial.[15] Moro ter would shed more light principally on three points that were not clear in 1982–83. First, there was the long-vexing point of whether there had been a foreigner in the terrorist command on via Fani. Judge Priore explained that Cristoforo Piancone, born in France, had probably shouted some words in French that were misheard as German.[16] Second, Judge Priore professed to be "reasonably certain" that a via Montalcini apartment was the place where Moro had been held prisoner for fifty-five days.[17] Finally, many details about other terrorist attacks during the Moro kidnapping operation, as well as its immediate aftermath, had come to light since the end of the first trial.

One hundred and seventy-three defendants accused of taking part in terrorist acts committed from 1977 to 1982 went on trial amidst now habitually stringent security measures. Prominent in this list of crimes was the Moro case. Some of the lawyers attempted to prevent the trial from taking place at all, and indeed many in Italy doubted that anything new was likely to emerge from the costly proceedings. Although they did manage to delay the trial for a while, the lawyers failed to stop it. The confessions of new pentiti and dissociati would be added to the court record on the Moro case.

As lawyers debated in court, the leading celebrities of Italian terrorism looked on: Barbara Balzerani, captured in June of the previous year and accused of killing Ezio Tarantelli; Prospero Gallinari, the reputed murderer of Moro; Renato Curcio, the founder of the Red Brigades and now, at forty-five, getting paunchy and almost completely white-haired; Mario Moretti, the mastermind of the Moro kidnapping; and Giovanni Senzani, who played the same role in the 1981 Ciro Cirillo kidnapping. They behaved in the spirit of a school reunion, one journalist noted.[18]

Before Moro ter got started in the fall of 1986, Moro's name came up repeatedly in the Milan and Turin oil scandal trials because of his decades-long relationship with Sereno Freato, his office manager. The government charged that Freato had betrayed his position of trust and influence by joining forces with Bruno Musselli, an oil magnate, in a scheme to avoid $225,000,000 in taxes on oil sales. Musselli, arrested on 2 July 1983, testified that he had given the Moro office monthly checks of up to $11,000 as payment for Freato's silent partnership in these fraudulent transactions. Freato rejoined that the checks were part of a scheme to move Moro's emergency account in Switzerland back to Italy. He further disclosed that Moro had earlier established this account, totaling $300,000 because of fears that a right-wing coup would drive him into exile.[19]

When Mrs. Moro corroborated Freato's almost universally disbelieved story, the political fallout threatened to contaminate her husband's reputation, but the threat soon passed. Although a public minister demanded that Mrs. Moro be imprisoned for lying to the court, that was not about to happen. As for the tarnish on Moro's image, his critics could only prove that he had been guilty of bad judgment in his choice of associates. No evidence could be found that he personally had profited from any of the dealings between Freato and Musselli. Moro had led a life conspicuously lacking in consumption, and his family continued to live modestly. Like all politicians, he had to raise money from supporters who could be expected to want something in return. The 1985–86 testimony in the oil scandal trials made it clear that Moro was not unschooled in matters of campaign finance, but nothing excessively incriminating could be attributed to him directly. His defenders claimed that if there had been wrongdoing, Moro remained ignorant of it, and no counterclaim could be proved decisively.

If anything, the oil scandals generated a new mood of sympathy for Moro. Paolo Cabras, the editor of the Christian Democratic newspaper

Il Popolo, and others attempted to explain this pro-Moro phenomenon. When we consider Moro's end, Cabras wrote, perhaps it is not so very surprising that the Christian Democratic leader always feared the worst. The story of his secret Swiss bank account was not yet clear, but in the light of what happened it would be wrong to ridicule his fears.[20] Moro had been afraid for his own safety and that of his family long before 1978. The vivid and terrifying testimony of his family dramatically reinforced the image of Moro as the prey of fanatics both right and left, at home and abroad. Since the late 1960s Moro repeatedly had confided to his wife that "anything can happen" in Italy, and his fears grew as time passed.[21] Toward the end he told the *Corriere della Sera*'s editor, Franco Di Bella, "We are living in terrible moments . . . it is as though we are in the catacombs."[22]

A few days before via Fani, his daughter, Maria Fida, asked him directly about the danger that he might be kidnapped. "In life," Moro replied, "one never knows," which she took to mean that he estimated his danger to be very great.[23] Afterwards the family continued to receive threatening letters, but now these referred to a highly publicized act of forgiveness toward Moro's murderers. Maria Fida even went to Mass and had dinner with Valerio Morucci and Adriana Faranda, which many found excessively magnanimous. One anonymous letter warned: "He who pardons assassins is an assassin, and assassins must die."[24]

The Moro ter court began to hear the testimony of witnesses in the fall of 1986. One of the witnesses who most deeply affected the outcome of these lengthy Rebibbia proceedings was Roberto Buzzatti. The court listened to him for several days in October. During the fase istruttoria of the trial, he had given Judge Priore an immense amount of information about his background and activities as a terrorist. In a book-length analysis of his short but eventful stint in the Red Brigades, Buzzatti provided an adept's view of the Movement, that is, "the collectives in school and the various neighborhood committees involved in the social issues that agitated the students and that would then lead almost inevitably, almost necessarily, into membership in the Red Brigades."[25]

In 1975 Buzzatti was seventeen, a *liceo* student and a member of the school's political collective known as the Lenin Section. He described this membership in the matter-of-fact way that an American high school student might mention his participation on the yearbook staff or in the drama club. At eighteen he found himself *(mi ritrovai)* in the Comitato Comunista Centocelle, a neighborhood revolutionary group from whose ranks several Red Brigade notables would emerge: Antonio Savasta, later a leader and executioner of some of the organization's most famous victims; Bruno Seghetti, a participant in the massacre and kidnapping on via Fani; Emilia Libèra, the inseparable companion of Savasta and described in the "Sentenza" of Moro 1 and bis as "guilty of a series of shocking crimes"; and Norma Andriani, the University of Rome philosophy student who received a seventeen-year sentence in the same trial for various acts of terrorism.[26] These were Buzzatti's role models, and they gave revolution a tangible meaning. To be in their presence was exhilarating and instructive in the same way that a freshman athlete would be affected by his team's senior stars.

The rich and varied revolutionary culture that thrived in Buzzatti's neighborhood of Centocelle comprised many basically like-minded organizations, though some were more openly violent than others. To read Buzzatti's account, one could liken them to American student fraternities, each with its own special characteristics but functioning within a general system of usages and values recognized by all. Like American fraternities, too, Italian revolutionary groups engaged in a fierce competition for members. They did not want just anybody, but recruits who would bring luster and continuity to the group's efforts. Buzzatti and his friends would discuss for hours on end the position of this or that group and who was guilty of "subjectivism" or "militarism" or "organizationalism." These youths naturally had their lighter moments, but they became ultra-serious on the subject of correct revolutionary behavior, on how best to advance the class interests of the metropolitan proletariat. Buzzatti passed his entire youth in the company of like-minded fanatics, and from his school alone some seventy to eighty individuals ended up charged with acts of subversion against the state.[27] His close friends in high school who did not become political subversives became drug addicts, he told Judge Priore.[28]

After 16 March 1978 the Red Brigades acquired an absolute primacy over all competing revolutionary groups. For some time before this, Buzzatti had been "openly philobrigadist," but the Moro operation sharply accelerated his evolution as a terrorist.[29] There was a distinctly paradoxical element in this process. Although he and his friends enthusiastically supported the kidnapping of Moro, Buzzatti personally disagreed with the decision to kill him. News of the execution perturbed him, although, with the moral values Buzzatti had acquired in the Lenin Section, he could not even begin to specify why. For about a year he remained confused and uncertain about what political direction he should take.

Buzzatti returned to the fold sometime in 1979. He simply could not think of any alternative to the revolutionary overthrow of the evil capitalist establishment. The moral reservations that had oppressed him about the Moro killing had to be wiped out. He could only end the intolerable confusion in his thinking by focusing solely on the beautiful simplicity of Lenin's principle: that which advances the revolution is moral, that which does not is "profoundly immoral."[30] Death was fundamentally not a moral problem but a political one, because politics thoroughly conditioned every aspect of morality. Therefore, to kill a bourgeois was "as Mao says, as light as a feather."[31] Thus enlightened, he could get over the necessary evil of killing people in order to create the classless society promised by Marx and realized by Lenin before the apostasies of Stalin had ruined the revolution in Russia. The Marxist-Leninist cause remained undefiled and worthy of any effort necessary to bring about its realization.

Such was the theory that the fledgling terrorist worked out in his mind in order to be a Red Brigadist, but the reality of life in the Red Brigades rudely mocked the theory. A person can spill just so much blood before he is nothing but a murderer, no matter what his principles are, Buzzatti in effect told Judge Priore. Buzzatti had never liked killing people, and he knew no one in the Red Brigades who did. They all thought it was a "disagreeable but unfortunately necessary duty . . . almost a social duty imposed by the laws of class warfare."[32] In the end, however, "a profound nausea . . . for exasperated hatred, for bloodshed" overwhelmed him.[33] Buzzatti did not want to cave in to hypocrisy by pretending that he had become a pacifist, like some truly shameless pentiti. The world had always been filled with violence and still was violent. No, it was not just the fact of violence that alienated him; it was the complete, undeniable uselessness of Red Brigade violence that made the deepest impression on him.

Their meticulously detailed analysis of the revolutionary situation in Italy had been logically deduced from Marxist-Leninist principles, the required starting place for a truthful analysis of politics and history. But it was all make-believe. The revolutionary situation, which alone separated the Red Brigades from violent anarchists, existed only in their fantasies. The "cause" rested not on objective social conditions but on the vulgarized dogmas of Marx and Lenin. The ideas of his youth had betrayed him, Buzzatti lamented to Judge Priore. The contrast between the myth of revolution and his life as a Marxist-Leninist revolutionary in the Red Brigades could not have been sharper. All they did toward the end was bicker. "If this was an anticipation of the society that we wanted to build, God help us."[34] The history of the Red Brigades could best be summarized as "a tragic chain of errors, irrationality, and idiocy."[35]

On the witness stand in Rebibbia Buzzatti repeated many of the points he had made in his lengthy deposition to Judge Priore, but his most interesting remark concerned the Moro case, with which he had nothing to do directly. After Buzzatti had described his role in the 1980–81 kidnapping of Judge Giovanni D'Urso, Public Minister Nitto Francesco Palma asked him if Moretti ever had said anything about "a kind of rudimentary closed television circuit" in a previous kidnapping.[36] Buzzatti had been in charge of logistics for the D'Urso kidnapping and had arranged for a sliding door with a peep-hole to observe the prisoner. Moretti, upon hearing this, began to laugh: "We are evidently on hard times. . . . For Moro we had a closed circuit television camera."[37] Buzzatti's testimony promptly fueled speculation about the existence of a People's Prison film, and his revelation affected the rest of the trial both directly and indirectly.

Apart from Buzzatti's account of this conversation, Moro ter produced little stir during the fall of 1986. Public interest focused more on the conspiracy-theory film by Giuseppe Ferrara, "Il caso Moro," and the oil scandal trials.[38] Nevertheless, if Moro ter had few moments of drama, it did result in much additional information about the Red Brigades. Moreover, the letters of 29 October that Lauro Azzolini and Giorgio Semeria wrote to President Sorichilli, which were read in court and entered into the trial records on 4 November, encouraged the hope that hitherto silent or reticent Red Brigadists might be on the point of telling all they knew.

Neither Azzolini nor Semeria would testify at Moro ter, but their refusal stemmed from personal and family considerations, not from the irriducibile code. Both of these "fathers" of the Red Brigades had disassociated themselves from the organization and expressed complete willingness to be interrogated personally by President Sorichilli

"if he would find that opportune."[39] They had become disillusioned
with the Red Brigades because "in fact, our initiative [Red Brigadism]
distanced us from solutions instead of bringing us closer to them."[40]
According to Red Brigade ideology, people were either good or bad,
revolutionaries or counterrevolutionaries, but with such crude ideas
Azzolini and Semeria confessed to have made the world a worse place
than it was before. As Azzolini and Semeria got older, they began to
realize that life with its myriad details, complex circumstances, and
human ambiguities cannot be made to conform to a few dialectical
generalizations. For the horrors that these "phantasms" had produced
and were still producing, the two felt shame and guilt, the genuine
idealism of the original Red Brigades notwithstanding. Their statements encouraged hopes for a breakthrough in the Moro case.

Some familiar people testified in November and early December of
1986. Antonio Savasta and Emilia Libèra provided new versions of
testimony that had been heard before. On 12 December Walter Di Cera
began to illuminate some important details about the via Fani attack.
Born in 1958 of a middle-class Roman family, Di Cera had a typical
Red Brigadist ideological background and came from the same neighborhood of Centocelle as Buzzatti. Di Cera gave Judge Priore a long
deposition in the fase istruttoria of the trial. As a student, he had
undertaken a systematic study of "the classics of Marxist-Leninism,"
especially "the theories about the party of Lenin, Mao, Luxemburg,
Stalin, and Castro."[41] Thus did Di Cera prepare himself for a life of
action in the Movement, beginning with his participation in a Potere
Operaio-dominated political collective at the Liceo Francesco di Assisi.
In the layered revolutionary culture of Italy such a collective might
seem insignificant simply because there were so many of them in the
school system and the neighborhoods, but they were the basic institutions for young revolutionaries who aspired to reach the top, which for
that generation meant the Red Brigades. Men like Antonio Savasta
always had an eye out for promising recruits, and the best place to find
them was in the motley world of Lenin collectives, revolutionary
nuclei, and resistance committees. Di Cera met Savasta this way and
in January 1978 joined the Red Brigades.

At the time of the Moro operation Di Cera was still in training, as a
member of the Centocelle brigade "network" (la rete), to become a
full-fledged Red Brigadist.[42] In this Red Brigade boot camp recruits
learned the rules and techniques of the organization before moving to

a regular column. Because of his lowly status at the time, Di Cera had no information to give the court about any of the decisions that had led to Moro's kidnapping and death. He only learned about the attack on via Fani the day it occurred, from a radio report. This news instantly illuminated the purpose of the activities of his training group. Saying only that "the organization was preparing a big operation," Savasta had ordered Di Cera and his fellow trainees to steal "as many automobiles as possible."[43]

The court wanted to know what Di Cera had learned at Brigade meetings after 16 March. He replied that in fact no one had very much to say about via Fani or its aftermath. The members of the training group did meet with Bruno Seghetti some days after the kidnapping, and on that occasion they had been informed in the most general terms how the organization thought of the Moro operation as a necessary "high level" action that would intensify armed resistance in Italy. This explanation thrilled Di Cera and the others, who then complained about their virtual exclusion from the event that might prove to be the revolution's turning point, but Seghetti would only allow them to distribute propaganda. He told them nothing at all about matters "regarding the development of the operation."[44] Moreover, neither Seghetti nor Savasta ever asked for their opinions about whether Moro should be killed or freed. Di Cera in fact would have agreed to the death sentence because membership in the group required total psychological and political allegiance. He would have been incapable of offering anything but his fervent assent to whatever the leaders decided during those fifty-five days.

The next two witnesses, Emilio Manna and Antonio Marocco, testified that they had joined the Red Brigades only after the Moro murder. But Marcello Basili declared on 16 January 1987 that he had been a member of the group since 1977. Basili, born in Rome on 26 January 1959, had become a Red Brigadist after an extended period of militancy in various "communist committees" which took their ideological direction from *Senza tregua*, one of the many journals of the day calling for the immediate and bloody revenge of the proletariat.[45] Sandro Padula was his sponsor and tutor in the Red Brigades, as Savasta would be for Di Cera. Padula, an exacting taskmaster, gave Basili reading assignments from the major doctrinal statements of Red Brigadism. The two young men then engaged in lengthy discussions about the theoretical meaning and political practicability of these texts. Basili, a successful student then working on a degree in banking economics at the University of Siena, easily mastered the lessons imparted by Padula and moved into a training group in 1977. The bright and ambitious young man, perhaps thinking ahead to the new economic order that would arise after the revolution, continued his studies at the university, and not until 1979 did he attain full membership *(a pieno titolo)* in the Red Brigades.[46] He could only comment in the most general way about the Moro case.

Giovanni Maria Marceddu, also born in Rome and just a few months older than Basili, was likewise just a would-be revolutionary at the time of the Moro operation, but his testimony contained some fascinating comments about the Red Brigades and the revolutionary culture on which they depended for their vitality and long life. Marceddu, the son of a construction worker and himself a carpenter, explained that the Red Brigades had long remained for him beyond the realm of legitimate aspiration, despite his years of radical militancy and devotion to revolutionary literature. It may have been his working-class background that inhibited him. To be sure it was an honor to be named the political head of a neighborhood "nucleus," but it only had five members. He and his comrades thought that in time, if they proved worthy, the nucleus might become part of the Movimento Proletario di Resistenza Offensiva. The Red Brigades themselves had described the MPRO in the first communication from the People's Prison of Moro as working-class forces committed to the revolutionary destruction of "the imperialist project"[47]; the Red Brigades would be the "point of unification for the MPRO."[48] The Red Brigadists did not say that they functioned as an elite force, for the party and the other revolutionary nuclei had a dialectical and even a symbiotic relationship with each other.[49] On the Rebibbia witness stand, however, Marceddu spoke of the Red Brigades in worshipful terms. For him, the difference in quality between the Red Brigades and the generic revolutionary movement seemed enormous and intimidating.

Although Marceddu prized the Red Brigades as the premier revolutionary group in Italy, the Moro operation had an immediately debilitating effect on his neighborhood organization. During the spring of 1978 they stopped meeting because of all the police activity in the Moro manhunt. Later, after the regular meetings resumed, splits occurred over the way the Moro kidnapping had ended. There was not much of an organization left when in January 1980 Marceddu met

Bruno Seghetti. Nonetheless the revolutionary hero of via Fani wanted to know all about the group, as did later the ubiquitous Antonio Savasta. Initial contacts with the Red Brigades did not result in anything definite, but the group members sensed growing Red Brigade interest in their activities. Still, doubts assailed them, and Marceddu recalled for the court how he and the others recognized that "our entrance into the organization [was] a little premature."[50] After all, they had not done anything except hide a few weapons. As late as the fall of 1980 they continued to agonize over their lack of practical experience as revolutionaries. But then in November 1980 the Red Brigades gave them the long-awaited call, and they joined the Brigata Aureliana. That the organization was already in decline and desperate for members did not diminish the consummation of Marceddu's hopes and dreams as a revolutionary.

Marceddu's tiny band testified during the rest of January and the first week of February 1987. On 11 February Giuseppe Palamà took the stand and described how he had entered the Red Brigades in 1978 "more or less the regular way for [my] generation . . . through the Collectives inside the schools."[51] He only joined the organization after the summer of that year and could not comment on the Moro case. Between Palamà's first and second court appearances eight Red Brigadists attacked a postal truck on via dei Prati dei Papa in Rome. This occurred on 14 February. Using machine guns and pistols, they killed two guards, critically wounded a third, and then fled with more than US $1,500,000 in lire. The holdup renewed fears of large-scale terrorist activity. Terrorism in the streets of Rome was grave enough; now the authorities looked nervously ahead to the even more ambitious operations that such a vast sum of money could finance. Minister of Interior Oscar Scalfaro warned the nation that the problem of terrorism could get dramatically worse. Incredibly, more than five years after their supposedly decisive defeat and following hundreds of defections, the "fighting communist party" continued to live up to its name.

On 17 February President Sorichilli called the Moro ter courtroom to order, but the Red Brigadist prisoner Cecilia Massara cried from her cage that she wanted to make a statement regarding "the expropriation" of via dei Prati dei Papa: "We claim the action in the name of the Red Brigades for the fighting communist party."[52] She then offered to have a document entered into the court records. President Sorichilli replied that nothing she had to say about the recent murders and holdup in Rome could be judged relevant to the Moro ter proceedings, but one of the lawyers, Attilio Baccioli, demanded to know the document's contents in order to ascertain for himself whether it was relevant. Public Minister Nitto Francesco Palma exploded: "It refers to a homicide that occurred two days ago, counsel!"[53] Did the court want to give these terrorists the publicity they craved? In the midst of these heated exchanges another prisoner, Stefano Petralla, called out from his cage, "I wanted to say something very briefly. As a revolutionary communist I declare my support for the action of proletarian expropriation."[54] When President Sorichilli cut him off, Barbara Balzerani and nine other prisoners requested permission to leave the courtroom. Immediately afterwards another cage-full of prisoners, "in solidarity with the comrades," demanded to go. The President then suspended the session for five minutes "as a sign of mourning" for the men killed in the via dei Prati dei Papa terrorist attack.

The weekly magazine *L'Espresso* acquired a copy of the terrorist document and published long excerpts from it on 1 March 1987. It declared that the Red Brigades had not given up the armed struggle: "To maintain today the level of conflict, to work and to fight for the renewal of the revolutionary offensive against the State and the imperialist bourgeoisie's projects of war are the tasks the Red Brigade fighting communist party has assumed in this difficult phase."[55] For Barbara Balzerani, the alleged author, and the other nine Red Brigadist cosigners, the via dei Prati dei Papa attack demonstrated that "the revolutionary conflict is not at all ended; that the armed struggle and the Red Brigades are not defeated." The attack gave the lie to the heavily publicized bromides of those tired middle-aged founders of the Red Brigades, Renato Curcio and Mario Moretti, who claimed that a momentous phase in Italy's class struggle had drawn to a close. These two wanted to justify their actions as revolutionaries while simultaneously requesting release from prison on the grounds that the Red Brigadists, guilty of no crime, had fought honorably if unsuccessfully in a war made inevitable by the tensions and conditions of society. Balzerani wanted to hear nothing about a lost war; for her there could be neither peace nor truce, only a relentless and constantly expanding attack on the oppressors of the proletariat. She thought that no other position was worthy of the name "communist."

L'Espresso also received another communication from the Red Brigades and published excerpts from it along with Balzerani's statement.

Essentially, the Red Brigades repeated what they had written in the 10 February 1986 declaration on the occasion of Lando Conti's murder: the goal of the "fighting communist party" had not changed, but its strategy had become more complex. The centerpiece of that strategy remained "the attack on the heart of the State," which still meant "destroying the political equilibrium" of Italy and "giving impetus to a class war of long duration for the conquest of political power and the installation of the dictatorship of the proletariat."[56] In more specific detail than they had provided before, the Red Brigades also proclaimed their solidarity with all anti-American peoples, notably the Lebanese, Iranians, Palestinians, and Libyans united in an anti-imperialist fighting front (Fronte Combattente Antimperialista). The vanguard of the Italian workers, as the Red Brigades continued to describe themselves, saw in the United States the fundamental cause of what was wrong with the world.

Less than three weeks later, on 20 March 1987, two Red Brigadists riding a motorcycle shot and killed General Licio Giorgieri in Rome. The sixty-two-year-old military officer had been the director of Costarm Aereo, which made aeronautical and space armaments. His assailants killed him with .38 caliber pistol fire on his way home from work at the end of the day. Giorgieri never had suspected that he was in danger and had taken no security precautions.

Because Giorgieri belonged to the highest echelon of the military, authorities surmised that the murder formed part of anti-NATO Euro-terrorist violence. Since 1985 the Euroterrorist alliance of diverse left-wing revolutionary groups had claimed the lives of five victims involved directly or indirectly with the production of armaments. First, René Audran, the vice-director of the international affairs section in the French Ministry of Defense, had been shot to death by Action Directe. Also in 1985 the Red Army Faction killed Ernst Zimmerman, the president of a factory that produced motors for military aircraft in Munich. The RAF struck again on 9 July 1986, this time using a radio-controlled bomb device to kill Karl Heinz Beckurts, a high-ranking official in the Siemens company. On 10 October of that year they also murdered Gerold von Braumuehl, a foreign affairs official in the Federal Republic of Germany. Giorgieri was thought to be the fifth victim in this series of killings, although he might have been the sixth, for Lando Conti had connections with the military-industrial complex as well. Giorgieri's death came as yet another reminder that the terrorist emergency had not ended in Italy. Tense and nervous, Italy's foremost political and military leaders met to formulate their response to this latest manifestation of Red Brigade terror. The Giorgieri murder gave new urgency to the Moro ter proceedings.

On 23 March the Red Brigades produced a fourteen-page single-spaced typed document in which they elucidated their motive for shooting Giorgieri: "the General has been struck *exclusively* because of his responsibility for Italy's participation in the Star Wars project."[57] With this act of revolutionary justice, the Red Brigades intended to express their opposition to the reactionary course of Italian foreign policy in general, but to them the plan to involve Italy in Star Wars loomed as the clearest example of what the country could expect from the ruling five-party clique—the *pentapartito*—that took its orders from Washington. Through NATO, the United States long had ruled Italy, but the Reagan administration was now formalizing procedures of control that previously had been followed informally: *"the political and military primacy of American imperialism in the world"* more than ever had become the basis of Italian politics.[58] In other words, to understand contemporary Italy one had to understand Washington.

Condemning the entire Italian political system as a front for the American war machine, the Red Brigadists concluded that they alone offered effective opposition to the militarization of space and the enslavement of the world. They were an authentic revolutionary alternative to the capitalist order that was running amok. Marx and Lenin provided the theoretical means to escape from the inhuman conditions created by capitalism. These masters had declared that a violent revolution would be necessary to accomplish the destruction of capitalism; the Red Brigades, and no one else in Italy, remained true to their word. Revolution necessitated exactly the kind of political violence they had undertaken in the Giorgieri assassination. They would continue the struggle by "impeding, retarding, rendering more difficult the coordination of the bourgeois parties."[59]

Meanwhile, in Rebibbia, the Moro case appeared to be completely stalled. A succession of witnesses in February, March, and April 1987 produced not a single new piece of information or lead. By April disappointment over the results of Moro ter prompted some Italians to respond positively when Curcio and Moretti, along with two Red Brigadists of lesser fame, Piero Bertolazzi and Maurizio Ianelli, proposed a dialogue with the country's political leaders. Writing in *Il Manifesto*, these men emphasized that their proposal did not suggest in any way "a denial or repudiation" of their past.[60] They could think of nothing more "regressive" than the path of "dissociation," the conduct of the pentiti being too base even to require comment. The class war in which Curcio, Moretti, and the others had been protagonists could not be criminalized, and therefore they declared themselves innocent of all criminal charges, especially of terrorism. The Italy of Piazza Fontana and P2 deserved to be attacked, and the four Red Brigadists expressed no regrets about what they had done. Students, workers, prisoners, and others by the many thousands had participated in the movement of revolutionary protest to which the Red Brigades belonged. It served the purposes of many people to forget that fact today. These individuals wanted to give the Red Brigades "another history, a 'separate' history," but in reality the organization had been "entirely within 'the critical practice' of that state of things [*quello stato di cose*] that vast and varied class strata had developed in a thousand forms." The Red Brigadists defended their violent actions by placing them in the political and historical context of the period, which had been one of revolution.

That period was now over; the time was beginning when a dialogue about the past could take place. The Red Brigadists continued to interpret the class war in standard Marxist-Leninist terms. That war had not ended, nor would it ever end until the final triumph of communism. The class struggle, however, had entered a new phase. Because history never repeated itself, the dialecticians who authored this open letter declared that the Red Brigade experience had drawn to a close. In other words, the dynamics of class struggle had changed since the inception of Red Brigadism, resulting in a "discontinuity" between that particular phase of the historical process, "rich and multifaceted" though it had been, and the present. Their intentions had been honest and even admirable within the Marxist-Leninist limits of how they understood society. The state should abandon its misplaced intransigence toward them and welcome the opportunity for dialogue.

In the same issue of *Il Manifesto* Rossana Rossanda declared that the Red Brigadists' offer should be accepted by their "political interlocutors."[61] That doyenne of the extraparliamentary left noted that only the DC's Flaminio Piccoli had shown the slightest interest in a dialogue with the four prisoners. In fact, Piccoli, from 1980 to 1982 the party secretary and currently the president of Christian Democrats International, soon became identified in the press as the leading political spokesman for such an initiative. Between them Curcio and Moretti could resolve the Moro mystery once and for all; therefore, talks with these men should be pursued, Piccoli counseled. The so-called *perdonismo* movement found many adherents in April and May, but within the faction-ridden DC party a predictable free-for-all erupted. Giulio Andreotti and Virginio Rognoni took the lead in opposing any kind of special understanding with the terrorists. Apply the law in all its rigor to the men who tried to destroy democracy and to kill its upholders, was their unyielding response to doves like Piccoli. The Andreotti-Rognoni faction showed no willingness to forgive Curcio even though, as the other side pointed out, he had never killed anyone. The argument for pardon looked exceptionally feeble to people who actually had been at mortal risk during the years of terror. For one thing, they could not forget Curcio's exultant public approval of Moro's murder. He had plenty to be guilty about, even if no bullet of his had left anyone dead.

Indeed, Curcio himself already had rejected the notion that the Red Brigades could be divided into the "good" who had not shed blood and the "evil" who had.[62] All the Red Brigadists shared "political and collective . . . responsibility." With equal emphasis, Lauro Azzolini even earlier had used the same phrase, "collective responsibility," in underlining the "fortuitous" distinction between those Red Brigadists who were guilty of violent crimes and those who were not.[63] As one of the "fathers" of the organization, he felt responsible for the entire Red Brigade experience, including the acts of terrorism now occurring after his own dissociation: "if it had not been for the Red Brigades of which we were a part fifteen, ten, five years ago there would not be *these* people carrying out *this* stage [of terrorism]."

Not surprisingly, many other people denounced the idea of pardon. Relatives of those killed by the terrorists added their voices to the loud chorus of dissent that greeted the Curcio-Moretti initiative. If people felt the desire to be compassionate, they should direct their sympathy to the children of murdered fathers, the mothers and fathers of murdered sons, the wives of murdered husbands. In that large and unhappy quarter all the compassion possible or imaginable would find an outlet.

All the same, perdonismo continued to attract support, in part at least for the reason Piccoli implied: the judicial system appeared to be incapable of getting at the truth about Moro. In Rebibbia, paralysis afflicted the Moro ter trial. On 5 May Public Minister Nitto Francesco Palma complained about the repeated failure of defense attorneys to appear in court on time or at all, forcing numerous costly postponements of the proceedings. Twenty of these attorneys were charged with abandoning defendants in the trial. The lawyers retorted that the country's terrorism trials, involving many of the same defendants, were taking place in courtrooms separated by great distances. "We do not have the gift of ubiquity," one of them declared.[64] All of this wrangling created the impression that Moro ter had become a counter-example of Cesare Beccaria's injunction about justice swift and sure.

On 7 May Valerio Morucci took the witness stand, declaring that the dissociato code would continue to guide him as a witness. "I am willing to make my contribution to the court in order to clarify all the aspects . . . of my responsibility," Morucci began, but he would not comment on the actions of other Red Brigadists except for those already cooperating with the law.[65] When asked to be more specific about his reconstruction of events, Morucci repeatedly said, "I cannot respond." This response in itself might have been frustrating enough for President Sorichilli, but he found Morucci's reticence on some crucial matters puzzling and on still others totally implausible.

For example, he could not believe Morucci when the witness claimed that the organization's passion for secrecy and compartmentalization accounted for his own lack of detailed knowledge about Moro's fifty-five days in the People's Prison. Morucci continued to claim that he never knew the address of the People's Prison. According to him, among the via Fani terrorists only Moretti and Gallinari knew that address. President Sorichilli asked: "what if Moretti and Gallinari had been killed during the massacre and kidnapping?" As members of the shooting force they were "the most exposed" in an action of extreme danger. Did Morucci and the other Red Brigadist leaders not consider such a possibility in planning the 16 March 1978 attack?

Morucci said that they had not. It was impossible as a practical matter, he continued, to consider every eventuality, particularly in an action as complex as the via Fani attack. In any gun battle there would always be "an infinity of variables . . . anything could happen"; one could only fashion a plan and then concentrate all of one's energy on its execution.[66] President Sorichilli was exasperated. "Do you mean to say that if Moretti and Gallinari had fallen [the rest of you] would have found yourselves with Moro in the [getaway] car without knowing where to go?"[67] Morucci only repeated: "It was too complicated to calculate all the variables, it was an impossible task."[68] This explanation did not enhance his credibility as a witness, and it was exactly the sort of evasive and excised testimony that the people most inclined toward perdonismo had come to expect from the whole crowd of dissociati and pentiti.

Morucci continued to testify without illuminating the Moro tragedy, while the most exciting developments in the case were taking place outside the courtroom. In mid May Flaminio Piccoli electrified the country again, as he had done the previous month on the issue of perdonismo. In an interview he gave to La Famiglia Cristiana, he claimed to have information about a People's Prison film of Moro.[69] In fact, he linked the perdonismo issue to this film and to other materials, such as unmailed letters from the People's Prison.[70] He specifically stated that a closed circuit television camera had recorded "every second of the days of the kidnapping." As a Christian, Piccoli could not in any case judge the Red Brigadists "eternally guilty," but in exchange for clemency on a case-by-case basis they would have to produce whatever physical evidence the organization still had. He wanted the country to avail itself of the Curcio-Moretti appeal as an opportunity to shed light "on the splendid figure of Aldo Moro."

Piccoli's declarations set off a chain reaction of polemics in the country. On 14 May l'Unità spoke for Piccoli's critics by asking two questions: what did the DC politician really know about a People's Prison film, and how did he learn about it. Piccoli obviously had conducted some "personal diplomacy" with the Red Brigadists, and instead of leaking sensational information to the media he should have been telling all he knew to the proper judicial authorities.[71] In a public letter published that same day in Il Giornale, Piccoli tried to clarify his remarks about the film. On the basis of his statement, it appeared that he had no new information at all. Piccoli's comments in La Famiglia Cristiana only had been a probe for the truth beyond "the partial accounts" of the "absurd" Moro crime.[72]

The newspaper war spilled over into the Moro ter courtroom the next day, 15 May. As Piccoli retreated, Giuseppe De Gori, a lawyer for the DC, advanced. De Gori was outraged by the double standard employed against Piccoli. He proceeded to read a long passage from another article by Piccoli that also had appeared in print the day before, in *Il Popolo*, the DC newspaper:

> I denounce . . . the fact that everybody—political forces, the mass media, and the men of culture—can expatiate on the Moro drama, expressing evaluations and judgments, in some cases using slanderous expressions, but when a Christian Democrat asks that full light be shed on these interminable fifty-four days, in a more profound analysis . . . a tempest erupts as if one had touched something that belongs only to others and not also and above all to us, the party friends of Aldo Moro.[73]

President Sorichilli then interrupted with the dry query, "you're not going to read the whole thing?" A prolonged exchange followed between some of the lawyers, who wanted the court to acquire all possible information about this latest development, and the public minister who held that it was "irrelevant" to the Moro ter proceedings.

Piccoli's declaration shifted the public's attention away from the courtroom at Rebibbia toward the many failures of the police investigation of the Moro case. When, after Moro's death, they had raided the Red Brigade archive in Milan on via Monte Nevoso, no film had been found. A number of critics now reminded the public about documents captured in that raid that had disappeared under obscure circumstances. General Carlo Alberto Dalla Chiesa, the hero in the war against the Red Brigades, had supervised the via Monte Nevoso raid, and some of his papers, possibly including materials dealing with the Moro case, also had vanished. The missing film fit perfectly into this loudly lamented pattern of police negligence.

The public image of the authorities, never very bright in Italy, seemed to darken daily in the clamorous month of May. The Italian judicial system appeared sluggish when not completely immobile. But then something moved. On May 16 a trial ended that had paralleled the proceedings at Rebibbia, often intersecting with them topically and finally combining with them in that some of its testimony was entered into the court record of Moro ter. This was the *Metropoli* trial, which in large part had dealt with the Moro case. During the summer recess people eagerly turned to the *Metropoli* trial sentence in the hope of finding more clarification there than had been produced in the Rebibbia courtroom.

9

The *Metropoli* Trial

The *Metropoli* trial essentially was about the state's charge that connections existed between two leaders of the extraparliamentary left, Franco Piperno and Lanfranco Pace, and the Red Brigades. The close relationship between Red Brigadism and Italy's multifarious left-wing Movement had been established firmly long before the 26 June 1986 opening of the *Metropoli* trial, and if additional documentation confirming that link had been the only result of these proceedings we would not be long detained by them. That trial, however, also dealt directly and dramatically with the Moro case.

Judge Francesco Amato had taken charge of the fase istruttoria, and on 31 March 1981 submitted his 1,018-page-long *sentenza-ordinanza*. Basing his findings on the testimony of numerous pentiti, he set out to explain the substantial rapport between such revolutionary groups as Potere Operaio, Autonomia, and the Red Brigades. Their differences regarding tactics could not obscure their fundamental agreement on the need for a Marxist-Leninist revolution in Italy. Judge Amato's explanation of these points was cogent but not surprising to anyone who had been following the state's case against the leaders of Potere Operaio and Autonomia in other terrorism trials. The judge went on to remind the court, however, that two leaders of the revolutionary groups, Piperno and Pace, had played an important role in the Moro case by acting as go-betweens for the Red Brigadists and the Socialist exponents of the humanitarian line. Their link to the Red

Brigades was neither casual nor superficial, according to Judge Amato, and he insisted that the two men stood guilty of trying to subvert the state. The journals they edited and wrote for plainly called for the creation of a "fighting party," and the judge had no doubt that their call was for something very much like the Red Brigades.[1] Piperno and Pace admired the Red Brigades and would have admired them still more had the organization accepted the leadership of Autonomia. The noncompliance of the Red Brigades was the cause of Autonomia's most serious disagreement with them. Otherwise, Red Brigadism corresponded almost exactly to their specifications for revolution in Italy.

Judge Amato based much of his argument on "Dal terrorismo alla guerriglia," an article Piperno wrote in May 1978 and published that December in *Pre-print*. "Things being what they are," Piperno began, "armed violence [is] almost like . . . a natural phenomenon," and if it were not occurring, that would be a cause for amazement in contemporary Italy.[2] Dysfunctional societies inevitably produce revolutions, and the "coherent" and "efficacious" use of terrorist violence by the Red Brigades had to be understood as such a consequence. He did not shrink from the word "terrorism" and understood it to mean a necessary form of revolutionary violence, which, in conjunction with a wide range of violent cultural and political activities, would destroy the capitalist order. Piperno perfectly understood and frankly admitted the "nexus" between Red Brigadism and the Movement, what he chose to call "the interfunctionality between the two phenomena." The Movement was a motley array of communist and other leftist workers, students, and intellectuals struggling against capitalism and its institutions; the Red Brigades gave this struggle its genuinely revolutionary character, and Piperno pronounced their work good.

He cited the Moro kidnapping and murder as prime examples of why Red Brigadism should be welcomed and supported by all true communists. The "facts of via Fani" fit logically into the quite proper revolutionary plans of the Red Brigades: "It is not difficult to understand that with the Moro kidnapping the brigadists wanted to show how the high priests who preside over the rites of the modern corporate State are not untouchable nor do they enjoy any impunity." Moreover, this bloody event had given the Movement a new spontaneity by raising the revolutionary consciousness of the masses. In other words, Red Brigadism functioned as a catalyst of the radical left. In a prerevolutionary phase of history, terrorism alone could intimidate the capitalist establishment, forcing a realignment of antiproletarian forces and thereby creating "an objective possibility of growth for the movement." The attack on via Fani provided just such a growth opportunity.

Even the massacre of Moro's security guard had to be judged as "an obligatory move." The murder of Moro was "another obligatory move," arising from the need of the Red Brigades to maintain their credibility. Defending the 1871 decision of the Communards to kill dozens of their hostages—including Archbishop of Paris Georges Darboy—Marx had made the same kind of argument in *The Civil War in France:* "Was even this last check upon the unscrupulous ferocity of bourgeois governments—the taking of hostages—to be made a mere sham of?"[3] From Marx, Piperno would have learned that the authentic revolutionary justice of the people is above reproach.

From the same source, he also would have learned that oppression by the state warrants violence by the proletariat, always provided that the cause of revolution is advanced thereby. Indeed, this Marxist rule became the basis of Piperno's argument when he ventured a criticism of the Red Brigades' conduct of the Moro operation. Although in principle there was nothing wrong with the kidnapping or murder of Moro, the operation had resulted in a palpable strengthening of the state. Wherein lay the error of the Red Brigades? Piperno thought that they had failed to understand what the strategic goal of their tactically brilliant plan should have been. To have used "an action of such potence on a minimal, almost private and at the same time unrealistic objective" made no political sense at all. They had exhibited the mentality of mere blackmailers, content with a politically obtuse request for a prisoner exchange. Even their closing gesture, of leaving Moro's corpse on via Caetani, was "contrived, mocking," and symbolic of the operation's real political failure. In short, the Red Brigades went their own way without consulting anyone in the Movement to which they belonged. Nevertheless, they could still resume their proper role in the revolutionary project, as the Movement's terrible swift sword. The "geometric potency displayed on via Fani" should be married to the widespread spontaneous anticapitalist violence that the Movement generated. The success of the revolution depended on this marriage.

Piperno and Pace had authored many such articles for *Metropoli* and *Pre-print*, but this one was the most explicit in its exaltation of terrorism. Judge Amato quoted from it at length in his sentenza-ordinanza, concluding that pro-terrorist sentiments reflected not only

Piperno's general state of mind but also his specific criminal actions during the Moro kidnapping. Through Morucci and Faranda, well known to him since Potere Operaio days, he had involved himself in the Moro operation, Judge Amato charged. His involvement had been made possible by the world-view Piperno shared with the Red Brigadists: "It is certain that the 'armed struggle,' the 'red terror,' the 'armed party,' the 'war of anti-imperialist liberation,' 'insurrection' [and] 'civil war' are not only the menacing glossary from the Red Brigade archive and of other terrorist groups, but [also] preachments, programs and facts that characterize the life and activities of 'organized Autonomia operaia.'"[4] Through *Metropoli* Piperno had attempted to unify all the Movement's elements, including the Red Brigades, and Morucci and Faranda were the foremost Red Brigadists involved in his project. They all had a "complicit" relationship with each other. Their complicity extended to criminal activities in the Moro case, although Judge Amato found no evidence of Piperno or Pace's direct involvement in the kidnapping and murder. The judge could only declare that, as highly sympathetic interlocutors of Faranda and Morucci, both defendants should be made to stand trial in order to determine what they had done during the fifty-five days.

On 9 February 1984 Judge Ferdinando Imposimato completed a second judicial investigation in the *Metropoli* case. He, too, had sought to ascertain the "probatory connection" between *Metropoli* and the Moro affair.[5] Since Judge Amato's decision three years earlier, new evidence in the case had been presented by diverse *dissociati* and *pentiti*. On the basis of their testimony, Judge Imposimato found that Piperno and Pace had played a double game: ostensibly working as consultants for Craxi and Signorile, they actually used the Moro crisis for their own Progetto *Metropoli*, or the establishment of a "hegemony of all the armed formations of Marxist inspiration."[6] During the negotiations for Moro's life their aim was not to save him, but to sow confusion and "to bring about the surrender of the state through a recognition of the Red Brigades."[7]

On the crucial matter of indictable behavior in the Moro case, Judge Imposimato went much farther than Judge Amato in accusing Pace and Piperno. He claimed to have "an imposing mass of univocal and uncontradictory evidence,"[8] which proved conclusively that "Piperno and Pace were among the promoters of the Moro operation and that they worked constantly to force the State . . . to yield to terrorist blackmail."[9] Pace even had been a member of the Rome column, and through him, as well as through Faranda and Morucci, Piperno had influenced Red Brigade actions, including the Moro kidnapping. Judge Imposimato portrayed Piperno, a physics professor and a man widely admired for his accomplishments in science, as the dominant personality in his dealings with Pace. Together they bore a heavy responsibility for the crimes in the Moro case, as the *Metropoli* trial would show irrefutably, Judge Imposimato predicted.

The trial opened in the Foro Italico courtroom in the early summer of 1986, with President Severino Santiapichi presiding, but only in October of that year did witnesses begin to appear. Calling into question President Santiapichi's objectivity, Piperno's lawyers tried to forestall the proceedings. In a 12 September 1986 letter to the President of the court, written in Edmonton, Canada, where Piperno was teaching at the University of Alberta, the defendant himself addressed the issue of objectivity. He recalled that at the first Moro trial President Santiapichi had proclaimed Piperno's guilt: "Consequently, I maintain that the composition of the court does not respect my natural rights as a defendant since the President of the court has already pre-judged me."[10] He requested that President Santiapichi recuse himself from the trial, but on 30 September the court of appeal judges denied the request.

Valerio Morucci, one of the most important witnesses, began to testify on 13 October. From him the court learned how the *Metropoli* project had been conceived in 1977, at a time of widespread rebellion and rioting in Italy, as a means of organizing the Movement into a coherent revolutionary force. Morucci had shared Piperno's vision and had proposed to the other Red Brigade leaders that they all participate in the *Metropoli* project, as a way of helping the Movement overcome its regrettably "spontaneous" character and to recruit new members.[11] Initially, the organization showed some interest in Morucci's proposal, but the campaign to launch *Metropoli* became bogged down over the usual disputes about the meaning of revolution. Later on, the Moro operation completely changed the character of revolutionary politics in Italy, defining and crystallizing the essence of the Red Brigades' strategy, but frightening the Movement as a whole and confusing it more than ever about how its goals should be accomplished or even what they were. When *Metropoli* did finally appear, in June 1979, it counted for far less on the revolutionary left than its editors had hoped it would. For their part, the Red Brigades contemptuously dismissed the journal for its theoretical jargon and intellectual pussyfooting around all the hard practical questions pertaining to revolutionary violence here and now.

President Santiapichi asked Morucci about Pace's membership in the Red Brigades, to which Judge Imposimato had attached the highest significance in explaining the connection between the Moro and *Metropoli* cases. Morucci thought that the istruttoria judge had misrepresented Pace's role in the organization. In fact, Pace never went beyond basic training, which he began in October or November 1977. He proved to be a bad recruit, failing repeatedly to keep appointments with other members and showing more interest in all-night card games than in learning the revolutionary's trade. By January 1978 the Red Brigades had seen enough and discontinued his candidacy. To indict Pace as an important go-between in the Moro case was to give him undue credit: Morucci insisted that neither Pace nor Piperno had anything to do with the Moro kidnapping. They had tried to use the Red Brigades, but nothing had come of it.

As proof of their failure, Morucci pointed to Moro's death sentence, which they had opposed by arguing that it would have been better for "the Movement's goal" if the Red Brigades had left him alive.[12] To kill him, they had argued, "would have been an act—how to say it—too great, too enormous, abnormal."[13] But the Red Brigades treated Piperno and Pace with studied indifference. Even Morucci and Faranda, who had spoken with Pace during the fifty-five days, never told him anything about Moro's circumstances. Such caution was a "mental habit" with them, the result of long years in the revolutionary underground.[14]

One of the lawyers who cross-examined Morucci brought the discussion back to Piperno's notorious article, "Dal terrorismo alla guerriglia." If Piperno had opposed the Moro death sentence, why did he write—in the very month of May 1978—that the execution had been an "obligatory move"? This appeared to be an especially gross contradiction in Morucci's testimony. After some hesitation and meandering, the witness hit upon the explanation that all the Italian revolutionaries of his generation, inside and outside the Red Brigades, had more or less Marxist-Leninist ideas about the nature of right and wrong.[15] To understand the revolutionary mentality "we must not talk about ethics," at least not in the normal sense.[16] Thus men like Piperno thought of the good as that which advanced the cause of revolution, of the bad as that which impeded it. Morucci could only surmise the details of Piperno's thinking about Moro, but he knew that the editor of *Metropoli* had strenuously opposed the execution as an act of political folly. After 9 May 1978, however, it became a fact. Piperno had to factor it in and to interpret it in a light that would enhance the revolutionary project. Thus the seeming contradiction in Piperno's logic had resulted from a permutation of the revolutionary dialectic. In keeping with a typical Marxist attitude toward politics, every event had to be interpreted as ultimately part of the irresistible onward course of communism.

President Santiapichi, who earlier had urged the witness "to keep his feet on solid ground," brought up another apparent contradiction regarding the Red Brigades' plans for Moro inside the People's Prison.[17] Morucci had testified before the Moro Commission that the prisoner's death had been decided from the beginning. In this trial, however, he had talked as though something actually might have come from the proposal of the Red Brigades for a prisoner exchange. "Was Moro's fate sealed" or not, President Santiapichi wanted to know.[18] Morucci answered: as late as 5 May he continued to hope for "something"; until then "nothing was closed off."[19] This response threw the court into some confusion over his earlier and fundamentally contradictory testimony. President Santiapichi's pejorative description of him as "someone of selective repentance" seemed to be confirmed.[20]

For the rest of the session Morucci continued to falter as a witness. In an interview with Giorgio Bocca for his book *Noi terroristi*, Mario Moretti had singled out Morucci as the person responsible for suggesting that Moro's corpse be left on via Caetani. President Santiapichi wanted to know if this was true or not. Morucci stammered that he could not remember for sure. President Santiapichi then interjected sharply, "Excuse me a minute, [but] we are not talking about an unimportant thing . . . we are not discussing the sex of angels."[21] It was unlikely that anyone would forget such a detail, least of all a revolutionary leader like Morucci, superbly conditioned as he was by years of experience in the underground to maintain alertness and vigilance.

During the next two months the *Metropoli* trial produced no new evidence in the Moro case, but then on 15 December 1986, Alberto Franceschini, one of the founders of the Red Brigades, appeared as a witness in the courtroom. In prison since 1974, Franceschini began by saying, "my memories are very old."[22] He had been out of circulation for so long that he doubted his capacity to shed any light on the major issues before the court, though he spoke with an authority rivaled only by that of Curcio about the prehistory and the early history of the Red Brigades. Franceschini had nothing firsthand to say about Piperno or Pace, but he did know that the Red Brigades historically had a polemical relationship with their ideological confreres. The key difference between them arose over the issue of violence: while every Marxist had to believe in the necessity of violent revolution, the Red Brigades distinguished themselves among Marxists by emphasizing the armed struggle to the virtual exclusion of all other revolutionary tactics. Within revolutionary Marxism there were "very many positions" *(tantissime posizioni)*, and the Red Brigades stood on the far left of this spectrum of radical entities as the acutely self-conscious heirs of Lenin and the Italian partisans.[23]

Despite Franceschini's protestations of ignorance about most post-1974 developments, President Santiapichi invited him to consider the court's principal business, the Moro-*Metropoli* connection: "We seek to be clear on this point of the motive for the Moro action, of the way it was concluded, of how it could and could not have concluded; they are the fundamental points of this trial."[24] Franceschini responded that about Moro there were "very many truths," but at the heart of his tragedy lay a truth "of enormous simplicity, to further the armed struggle."[25] Obviously, the Red Brigades kidnapped him in order to strike a crippling blow against the hated Christian Democratic regime, "the principal enemy" of the Italian proletariat. In addition, they hoped that Moro would reveal incriminating details about the right-wing plots that Franceschini called "il progetto Neo-Golpista." President Santiapichi interrupted him at this point to say that only yesterday he had seen Giuseppe Ferrara's conspiracy theory film, "Il caso Moro." He wondered if the Red Brigades had any connections or contacts with secret service organizations or right-wing plotters eager to exploit terrorist violence for antidemocratic ends. Franceschini completely dismissed the idea that the Red Brigades had had any kind of formal understanding with such groups or individuals, but it did not require very much insight into Italian politics to see how various reactionary elements would have welcomed left-wing terrorism as a golden opportunity to smash democracy.

Franceschini commented authoritatively on the role of the imprisoned Red Brigade leaders in helping to decide Moro's fate. At that time everyone in the Red Brigades and in the Movement as a whole regarded Curcio and Franceschini as "charismatic" revolutionary leaders: "Therefore, it seemed quite obvious to us that if we had spoken positively about something in a certain manner those outside probably would have had to take [it] into account."[26] To President Santiapichi's question about their role in the death sentence, Franceschini replied that they were not involved: "It was technically impossible; that is, we were in a maximum-security cell block in Torino [under] complete surveillance."[27] When they talked with visitors it was through a glass partition, and unsupervised telephone calls were out of the question. Even their discussions with the lawyer Giannino Guiso, who had hoped to arrive at "a painless solution," were subject to these conditions.[28] They simply did not have any way of contributing to the Red Brigade debate about what to do with Moro, any more than they could have participated in planning the attack on via Fani. Throughout the fifty-five days the imprisoned leaders could only play a supporting role.

Their most dramatic moment came on the day of Moro's murder, an event that Franceschini likened to the sudden and violent fall of an emperor. On trial then in Turin, the terrorists quoted to a horrified court Lenin's pronouncement about the elimination of class enemies as the highest act of humanity possible in a class society. Their gesture reflected "the psychological climate" in which the Red Brigadists lived and acted at that time.[29]

Franceschini continued to testify in the *Metropoli* trial the next day, 16 December. He spoke about his decision to break with the Red Brigades and to become a dissociato. By the early 1980s Franceschini had realized that Red Brigadism was finished, although the real end had come in 1978 with Moro's murder, he thought. Their choice of terrorism had been "totally unproductive"; not only had it failed to bring about the revolution, but it had actually strengthened the status quo.[30] A greater political folly than Red Brigadism Franceschini could not now imagine, and he felt like an idiot with blood on his hands.[31]

In trying to sum up Franceschini's testimony, President Santiapichi began by observing that, according to the witness, the kidnapping could have ended without bloodshed, "apart from the great bloodshed . . . on via Fani."[32] Franceschini had referred repeatedly to the blood-less outcome of the 1974 Sossi kidnapping as a precedent. President Santiapichi then asked: if the Moro kidnapping could have ended bloodlessly, why didn't it? Franceschini himself had testified to the immense prestige the imprisoned Red Brigade leaders enjoyed within the organization. "You were people . . . whose opinion could have tipped the scales," the President declared.[33] They could have stated their position through the ever-attentive media, and they had two incentives for doing so. First, they genuinely thought that Moro should not be killed. Second, Franceschini had admitted to his and Curcio's strong fear that they might be "suicided," as several Baader-Meinhof gang members had been a few years earlier in Germany, should Moro die. Political and personal considerations should have prompted them to hold Moretti back.

Franceschini acknowledged that they had been afraid and had wanted "to find a way to avoid a bloody solution of the situation," variously described by the witness as a "swamp" and a "cesspool."[34] The President continued to press him: if they viewed the death sentence as "a gross error," why "during the critical phase of the Moro kidnapping did you, Franceschini and Curcio, who embodied the charisma [of the Red Brigades], who had the charisma [of being] the founding fathers, fail to give up or invite others to give up the logic of negotiations" in which the Andreotti government would never participate?[35] For Franceschini, however, the essence of the Moro tragedy lay in the refusal of the government to negotiate. No Red Brigadist, in or out of prison, could contemplate Moro's release without government concessions. But the Red Brigades had freed Judge Sossi without concessions, President Santiapichi rejoined. A similar act of clemency in the Moro case would have been in the personal interest of the imprisoned Red Brigade leaders and would have reflected their true political judgment as well. Franceschini could only say that the event had overwhelmed them all; at no time during the fifty-five days did the imprisoned Red Brigadists ever feel in control of the situation. It was always Moretti's operation. "Our intervention was an external one," Franceschini concluded.[36]

On 17 December 1986 Lauro Azzolini, another founding father of the Red Brigades, sat in the witness chair. Two months earlier he had written to President Sorichilli in the Moro ter trial about his willingness to enter into a dialogue with the authorities. Although he had not appeared in the Moro ter courtroom, he agreed to follow Franceschini in the *Metropoli* trial. Captured on 2 October 1978, Azzolini had been among the Red Brigade high command during the Moro kidnapping, and his testimony promised to be even more valuable than that of

Franceschini. The witness began by setting some limits: he wanted only to answer questions regarding Pace and Piperno. Nevertheless, he exceeded these limits almost immediately.

Azzolini declared that the Moro kidnapping was "the central part" of the Red Brigades' spring campaign to attack the state.[37] The public minister wanted to know whether it was true that the Red Brigades originally had intended to hold Moro for many months. Azzolini replied that this was one possible outcome of the kidnapping, since nothing about it had been determined in advance. The Red Brigades simply planned to exploit the situation as shifting circumstances dictated.

When the decision was made to kill the prisoner, Azzolini thought that nearly everyone in the organization supported it. Before 9 May 1978, a serious discussion took place in every column and in the prisons, "because every life that is wasted *(sprecata)* . . . also had to be weighed politically."[38] Azzolini had been informed of some "minor dissent," but he did not then know the identity of the dissenters. Only later did he learn of the Morucci-Faranda initiative to spare Moro. Azzolini told the court that those opposed to the death sentence could have requested a high-level meeting to discuss their concerns, but they did not. Therefore, he had concluded that the opposition only concerned "a political interpretation of some things" in the Moro operation.[39] Azzolini had not viewed the matter as a cause for worry, and he thought that Morucci and Faranda were now exaggerating their former solicitude for Moro.

Azzolini certainly had no inkling in 1978 that within the organization Morucci and Faranda might be representing Piperno and Pace. Here the witness touched on the heart of the state's case in the *Metropoli* trial, and he could not imagine how it might be true. Piperno probably had tried to control the Movement and the Red Brigades, but all left-wing extremists in those days had such aspirations to the extent that all of them wanted the revolutionary project to be conceived and executed according to their specifications. Within the context of Italian radicalism, there was nothing at all peculiar about Piperno's "designs." To argue, however, that Piperno somehow participated in the Red Brigades and even helped to determine the outcome of the Moro kidnapping was to distort the facts completely. Azzolini and his confederates had dismissed the intellectuals of Autonomia as fake revolutionaries, with no capacity to organize anything except seminars and conferences, where they talked endlessly about matters that plainly required not talk but the revolutionary action supplied by the Red Brigades. Piperno, Pace, Scalzone, and Negri held forth as the Movement's chatterboxes who occasionally would come up with a moderately interesting idea, but most of what they said moved the Red Brigadists to amused or bemused contempt. These self-styled leaders of the proletariat never actually did anything, as they all frantically had sought to prove in the various trials where they had appeared as principals.

The Moro case was really quite simple, Azzolini observed. All or nearly all of the mysteries in the case had been manufactured for political purposes. "Those who want mysteries will have mysteries," but the central facts in the case were obvious: a communist culture existed in Italy, and extremist elements could be found within it; among these the Red Brigades were the most extreme; they had kidnapped Moro to advance the cause of revolution and possibly to topple the state there and then; they had killed him in the end because they felt that problems were multiplying for the organization and that they were running out of time.[40] After listening to this summation, President Santiapichi asked if Azzolini thought there were any mysteries at all in the Moro case. "But what mysteries," he answered.[41] None of the alleged mysteries and plots and occult powers mattered even if a few existed, which Azzolini very much doubted. Too real in the spring of 1978 were the passion for communist revolution and the will of the Red Brigades to carry it out or to die trying. The Moro case could only be understood as a tragic consequence of their passion and will.

Following the Christmas recess, Carlo Fioroni took the stand. Nicknamed the *professorino* (little professor), Fioroni had the distinction of being the first pentito. Much of the state's case against *Metropoli* reflected Fioroni's interpretation of the extraparliamentary left in Italy, and he began by summarizing his experiences. Entering the Movement from the Catholic left, Fioroni moved through the ranks of Potere Operaio to a position just below that of the organization's principal leaders: Toni Negri, Oreste Scalzone, and Piperno. Fioroni remembered the late 1960s and early 1970s as a prolonged stay in an insane asylum. He lived on tranquilizers. As the Movement became more radical and violent, Fioroni felt the need to be as "hard" as possible to withstand "the assault of doubt."[42]

Always in these years under the domination of more forceful personalities—particularly Negri, whom he now despised—Fioroni finally cracked up after the 14 April 1975 kidnapping and accidental murder of his close friend, Carlo Saronio, also a member of Potere Operaio. According to Fioroni, Negri had hoped that the wealthy Saronio family would pay a ransom for their son. Carlo Casirati, a politicized criminal of Negri's acquaintance, carried out the kidnapping, with Fioroni as one of his accomplices. It was supposed to be all playacting, but Saronio died when a chloroform-soaked cloth was held on his face too long. His death broke Fioroni. In severe moral crisis, he went to the authorities and told them about the criminal activities of Potere Operaio and Autonomia. After some years in jail for his role in the Saronio kidnapping, Fioroni fled to Morocco and eventually to Lille, France, where he worked as a teacher of Italian. His greatest desire now, apart from wishing that Saronio could be brought back to life, was to lead a quiet, anonymous life and to forget as much of the past as he could.

In the witness chair on 12 January 1987, Fioroni spoke in rambling detail about the terrorist agenda of the *potopisti* in the Fronte Armato Rivoluzionario Operaio (FARO), "a political-military structure constituted by militants of Potere Operaio" and in Lavoro Illegale, which was "nothing other than the armed wing of Potere Operaio."[43] Fioroni claimed that under the *nom de guerre* of Saetta, Piperno had directed FARO, while Morucci had been in charge of its military operations. The potopisti leaders had many contacts with Curcio during the early days of the Red Brigades, for they considered each other as allies against Italian capitalism. They did not then segregate themselves according to meticulously delineated points of revolutionary theory, as they would do later. Though composed of disparate elements, the Movement remained strongly united on the central point: armed struggle for communist revolution. For a period of years this core of agreement permitted an ongoing dialogue between the Red Brigadists and the potopisti.

Fioroni had known Piperno even before the creation of Potere Operaio, but within the organization he had been much closer to Negri. In the factional disputes between Negri and Piperno, he took the part of the University of Padua professor. Piperno had wanted to promote armed struggle through FARO, whereas Negri downplayed the importance of a clandestine organization in favor of a much more generalized resistance to capitalism. As Negri's acolyte, Fioroni participated in meetings between his chief and Curcio, but he knew nothing about any dealings of Piperno or Pace with the Red Brigades. Following the dissolution of Potere Operaio, Fioroni completely lost track of the two. A prisoner during the spring of 1978, he could tell the court nothing at all about the *Metropoli*-Moro connection. At one point laughing out loud, at other times tense and nervous, Fioroni made a poor witness for the prosecution.[44]

Patrizio Peci and Norma Andriani followed Fioroni as witnesses, but the court learned nothing new about Moro from them and nothing whatsoever about Piperno or Pace. In contrast, Giorgio Bocca's court appearance on 27 January was more consequential. This sixty-six-year old journalist and political commentator had been asked to testify because of a book that he had written two years earlier, *Noi terroristi: 12 anni di lotta armata ricostruiti e discussi con i protagonisti*, essentially a compilation of his well-informed views regarding the rise and fall of left-wing terrorism in Italy and liberally sprinkled with the thoughts of the protagonists in their own words. The court attached enormous significance to his book and regarded Bocca as an extremely important witness because, according to the public minister, he had been "a privileged interlocutor of persons we have cited but have been unable to hear in this trial."[45] The public minister and diverse lawyers in the courtroom wanted to hear about how he came to write this book, the ground rules that had been set up and followed, his general estimate of the prisoners' reliability—in short, the entire background of *Noi terroristi*.

Bocca commenced by explaining that his book was never intended to be a complete history of the Red Brigades, only an attempt to understand them from their own point of view. He began by sending questionnaires to imprisoned terrorists. Some responded right away. Others, like Moretti, said they would not cooperate, but then unexpectedly changed their minds. Personal interviews followed with participating prisoners. At that point Bocca dispensed with questionnaires and simply followed his instincts as a reporter in leading the conversations.

One of the lawyers interrupted, noting that a journalist of "his stature" had professional obligations to cross-check the statements in these interviews with the courtroom documents from the various terrorism trials, all of which were available to the public.[46] Why had Bocca not done so? First, said the journalist, it was impossible for him to consult all the court records: "I could not do [all that] research," he protested.[47] Second, and more to the point, direct interviews gave him the key to writing the book he wanted to produce, a kind of oral history. Bocca had not satisfied all of his Red Brigadist interlocutors either; Lauro Azzolini and Alberto Franceschini, for example, criticized him earlier in the trial for not getting their stories straight. Nevertheless, for the views of the irriducibili terrorists, *Noi terroristi* was the only source available to the court. Accordingly, the book was entered into the court records of the trial.

For his thesis, Bocca relied heavily on an insight provided by Franco Bonisoli:

> Often I ask myself how a small group like our own with little political culture, slight union experience, and modest military attainments could have endured for ten years and upset national life. I am convinced that the answer is this: impulsively, we made our existential and political choices in an exceptional social and political situation, the big bang of the years 1969 and 1970. By ourselves we could have gained little ground, but toward us gravitated consensuses, demands, coincidences, usages, expectations, diverse rancors, all of which contributed to the attrition of the system. There were old communist comrades who felt we were doing what they should have done in 1945. There was the restless and violent youth that lived its desires for adventure through us. There were labor unions that constantly felt backed against the ropes because of restructuralization. There was also the limbo of ongoing change, the sense of not knowing what was there at the end of the tunnel. I believe that we held on for over ten years because, if only involuntarily, we put something into that void, a sign at least of drama.[48]

Bocca interpreted Bonisoli's words to mean that "the rapid, chaotic mutation" of Italian society during the late 1960s resulted in a crisis in the country's political culture that extremists sought to exploit for revolutionary ends.[49] In a country filled with half-baked intellectuals "intoxicated by revolutionism" and always on the prowl for "worker initiatives," the social disruption offered unlimited opportunities for subversive activity.[50]

Red Brigadism, like all forms of long-lasting political violence, could not have flourished without sympathy and support from substantial elements in society at large. Azzolini noted that "one cannot understand the history and the function of the Red Brigades if one does not take into account the rapport between the handful of regulars with the many sympathizers."[51] For example, from 1976 to 1980 the

Turin column numbered at most only ten regulars and thirty irregulars, and yet this small group of terrorists made the Piedmontese capital "a city of fear."[52] Bocca explained that the organization succeeded in posing the threat it did because of "the diffuse terrorism that expressed itself in a hundred ways," including absenteeism and industrial sabotage.[53] Although numerically weak, the terrorists enjoyed the support of a vigorous and long-lived extremist culture in Italy. Even Red Brigade assassinations met with approval beyond the ranks of declared terrorists. The response to the 29 April 1976 murder of Neofascist party member Enrico Pedenovi is a case in point. Near the site of the attack, 5,000 youths appeared, shouting: "Ten, one hundred, one thousand Pedenovis."[54] Had not Resistance fighters killed Fascists this way in 1944–45? What had been highly moral then could not be called evil now, least of all by anyone professing to be a communist, or so large numbers of angry, revolutionary-minded Italians sympathetic to the aims of the Red Brigades continued to believe.

Alberto Franceschini, too, described the Red Brigadists as young Marxists who saw themselves as the heirs of Italy's unfinished Resistance, bent on striking their blows before it was too late and all hope of revolution was lost. It was "now or never," they believed.[55] To Franceschini and to many other terrorists in Bocca's book, the Red Brigades appeared when the PCI's betrayal of the revolutionary faith became impossible to ignore any longer. Berlinguer completed the apostasy begun by Togliatti, while Red Brigadism became the supreme incarnation of that faith for the lost generation of 1968. A pure communism, uncorrupted by the concessions and compromises that had ruined the PCI, was their goal, and, for the most extreme fanatics in their midst, revolution as Marx and Lenin had thrillingly described it became the only worthwhile political activity. Throughout their history the Red Brigades sought to fight capitalism in the Marxist-inspired manner prescribed by Lenin in *State and Revolution*.[56] They lacked the subtlety of the typical Marxist intellectual found on university faculties, who could reconcile a practical conformity to the status quo with a metaphysical commitment to communist revolution; least of all did they like talking tough while doing nothing, another emblematic activity of the leftists who severely overpopulated the groves of academe. They had nothing but contempt, Bocca wrote, for these academic communist theoreticians.

Bocca devoted seven chapters in *Noi terroristi* to the Moro case. Above all, he wanted to know why Moro had been killed. All the terrorists interviewed more or less agreed with Moretti, who explained that the Red Brigades had singled out Moro because for twenty years the Christian Democratic leader had been the supreme exponent of bourgeois power in Italy, always "present in the decisive deliberations and choices."[57] By kidnapping the preeminent figure in Italian politics, the Red Brigades intended to signal to the forces of revolution that their time had come. There was thus no mystery about the political logic of the kidnapping.

In the immediate aftermath of the attack on via Fani, while many Italians suffered disorientation and shock as a wave of hysteria swept the country, "for large minorities of communists [the kidnapping] was an excellent piece of long-awaited news."[58] In many places champagne bottles were opened in celebration of the event.[59] For Bocca such a festive reaction made an odd but historically illuminating pair with the rush to embrace fermezza by the PCI. Both reactions could only be understood as a consequence of the active schizophrenia endemic to Italian Marxism. It was a movement historically at war with itself over the issues of reformism and revolution. The PCI of Enrico Berlinguer had made its choice for reformism, but to the left of the official party position, where many thousands of Italian radicals found themselves, Red Brigadism became the last best hope for revolutionary action.

Bocca agreed with the terrorists who said that not Red Brigadism alone, but Red Brigadism tolerated and even supported for a long time by various extraparliamentary left groups, is what made the armed struggle the terrible ordeal it was for Italy. By standing fast during the Moro crisis, the government inflicted a decisive defeat on the Red Brigades precisely because many of their longtime sympathizers broke ranks and ran for cover immediately after 9 May 1978.[60] Paradoxically, the Red Brigades themselves grew in strength during the year after Moro's death, and the incidence of terrorist violence rose. Without the support of mediating elements in the extraparliamentary left, however, the faction-ridden Red Brigades became increasingly isolated, desperate, and hopeless. The Moro operation catapulted the Red Brigades to worldwide fame as the paramount symbol of left-wing terrorism in the Western world, but they ended up drowning in their victim's blood.

Bocca persistently questioned the terrorists about what had happened in the People's Prison, and some interesting details about the case came to light. Moretti spoke volubly with the journalist he most wanted to see dead when the armed struggle was in full cry. He told Bocca that the first question Moro asked him inside the People's Prison was: "But why have you kidnapped me of all people? for I am a gentle person, and I have always been a mediator between the right and the left."[61] Moro did not comprehend or affected not to comprehend that he had been kidnapped because of his pivotal role in Christian Democratic Italy. As Moretti explained to Bocca, "for you of the middle class this is difficult to understand, but for the communists the Moro action has been the realization of the dream of a lifetime: to put the Christian Democrats on trial, to put this monstrous and elusive party in shackles; after forty years, to strike at the enemy."[62]

In his talks with Bocca, Moretti denied that any other organization had been involved with the Red Brigades in the Moro operation: "One thing that I will never succeed in making the Italian bourgeoisie believe is that the Moro kidnapping was exclusively ours, organized by about twenty mere workers. The Italian bourgeoisie will never acknowledge this truth; it will always search for the hidden instigator or the foreign agency that never existed."[63] Moretti laughingly dismissed the conspiracy theories. He derided the notion that Licio Gelli, the grotesque caricature from Italy's right-wing underworld, was the secret manipulator of the Red Brigades. He doubted that P2 counted for much or that Gelli was half as frightening and destructive as the upholders of Italy's legal order. It was they who had manufactured and then exploited the notoriety of the "Venerable Master" for their own political purposes. The truth about the Moro case was so simple and straightforward that it could not be believed by the excessively subtle Italians. Moretti and his fellow conspirators in the Red Brigades should know the truth, for they had conceived and executed the entire operation. With a craftsman's pride in a task well done, Moretti boasted of via Fani as his masterpiece. Under his direction the Red Brigades had plunged the Italian capitalist order into the deepest crisis of its postwar history.

The terrorist leader was right about one thing: many people in Italy found little merit in his version of the Moro case, and in the *Metropoli* trial the quest for a more complex explanation continued as before.

Antonio Savasta testified on 16 February that he knew of a meeting between Faranda and Morucci with Pace during the Moro kidnapping, but the couple had talked with him as "a person external to the organization."[64] In his testimony Morucci already had spoken about this meeting, but Faranda, who testified in February and March, furnished additional details. She had known both Piperno and Pace since the days when they were comrades in Potere Operaio. Afterwards they had remained friends, going out to dinner together occasionally, but without further "organizational ties" except for the very brief period in 1977, when Pace was a Red Brigade recruit.[65] Faranda then confirmed Morucci's characterization of Pace as a recruit of "slight seriousness." Because of his highly intellectual nature, he lacked the temperament, discipline, and ordinary know-how to function effectively in a revolutionary organization.[66]

Morucci and Faranda did meet with Pace in a Trastevere restaurant, at his request, during the Moro kidnapping. Pace explained to them that a representative of the PSI had contacted him as an expert on the "humus" in which both *Metropoli* and the Red Brigades had germinated, but, independently of Craxi's humanitarian initiative, he was "extremely worried about the evolution of the Moro kidnapping."[67] He wanted to make them fully aware of the repercussions that would adversely affect the Movement if Moro were to be killed. Morucci and Faranda, who shared these fears, had arrived at their assessment independently. Within the organization, they denounced the death sentence, but Moretti curtly announced that the vote had gone against them. From that point on, the couple began to think about leaving the Red Brigades.

When they finally did abandon the organization, Piperno helped them to find an apartment, but he had participated neither in their new terrorist organization nor in their post-Red Brigade terrorist actions. He had an inveterate interest in the Movement, but joined no particular group. When Faranda noted in passing that Piperno had asked them to stay in the Red Brigades, President Santiapichi commented that he must have wanted to retain some influence over the organization. She dismissed the President's comment as completely erroneous. Whatever his ambitions may have been, Piperno never had any influence, much less control, over them. For people to agree on some general political matters did not necessarily imply the kind of complicitous relationship that the state, with no solid evidence at all, was trying to establish here.

Nearly two months before President Sorichilli would ask Morucci in *Moro ter* what the Red Brigades would have done had Moretti and

Gallinari been killed or incapacitated on via Fani, Public Minister Antonio Marini put the same question to Faranda in the *Metropoli* trial. The terrorists could not have known that the five armed professional policemen protecting Moro would fall without offering effective resistance. A serious gun battle could have taken place there, with casualties on the Red Brigade side. They had no backup plan, Faranda responded. The public minister could not believe her, any more than President Sorichilli in Moro ter would believe Morucci's similar answer to the same question. Relentlessly, he pressed Faranda and repeated his question: "What would you have done if Moretti and Gallinari had fallen?" "Oh God," she stammered, "if these two had been killed it would have been completely disastrous."[68]

Under further questioning, Faranda surmised that the surviving members probably would have continued with the next stage of the plan and would have been met by "another person who knew the house," a dissociato-style reference to Anna Laura Braghetti, one of Moro's jailers in the via Montalcini prison. Faranda did not know for sure if the details of the Moro kidnapping had been arranged in the way she was now hypothesizing or if they had been arranged at all. The public minister had no interest in these hypotheses; he only wanted to find out whether other people in the terrorist command besides Moretti and Gallinari knew what the plan was. "But I don't know," Faranda began hesitantly before concluding, "No, it was not decided."[69] As for Faranda's conjecture about Braghetti, the public minister scoffed, would a lone female terrorist be expected to carry out the interrogation of Moro and the rest of the kidnapping by herself? Perhaps someone else knew the plan, Faranda conceded: "It is possible. I don't know what to tell you."[70] The public minister commented sarcastically that, according to Faranda, the Red Brigades—otherwise famous for their meticulously planned actions, he parenthetically noted—based their do-or-die Moro operation on how things "probably" should be done. In his opinion, she was obviously holding back vital information.

Morucci testified a second time in the *Metropoli* trial, beginning on 9 March. He repeated many of his speculations about Moro's kidnapping and murder, but Public Minister Marini now wanted him to comment again and in greater detail on the timing and meaning of the Moro death sentence, which still made no sense at all to him. He could not understand why the Red Brigades refused even to wait for the DC's reaction to Fanfani's plea on Moro's behalf. Moreover, if the most important purpose of the action had been, in Morucci's words, "to demonstrate that in Italy there existed an organization capable of kidnapping Moro, capable of attacking the state at that level," then why was it necessary to kill him at all?[71] Morucci replied that the Red Brigades did not want to be perceived as though they had been "bridled" *(imbrigliati)* by the situation; they wanted to appear to be in charge of everything, and the 9 May 1978 scene at via Caetani created the desired impression, if only ephemerally. Moretti was not "a criminal madman."[72] He did not want to kill Moro but could see no alternative that made political sense. The need for the Red Brigades to behave publicly as hard and virile revolutionaries was the determining factor in the tragic climax of the kidnapping. The intransigence of the state dictated Moretti's final response, which came as much from his fear of Fanfani's initiative as from the growing sense within the Red Brigades, totally unfounded though it proved to be, that the police might be closing in on the People's Prison. Fanfani's intervention troubled Moretti more than any other development during the fifty-five days, because it opened the way to the small symbolic concession that would have put the Red Brigades on the defensive with the Movement, instead of inflaming it with their own passion for armed struggle against the state. Indeed, Pace had issued a warning about just such a confrontation when he conferred with Morucci and Faranda.

When the pair told Moretti about Pace's urgent appeal, the Red Brigade leader reacted angrily, fearing that the organization's security could have been compromised by such an encounter. They assured him that Pace had sought them out after the Red Brigades had pronounced Moro's death sentence in Communication no. 7, and Moretti was mollified. He showed no concern and little interest, however, in what the leaders of Autonomia thought about the kidnapping. Moretti had an even lower opinion of the PSI's humanitarian initiative. The only party that mattered to him was Moro's, the DC. Moretti declared that there would be no behind-the-scenes negotiations with any other leaders, which Morucci explained this way: "The Red Brigades are not like the White House staff, that is, they are serious fanatics, not fanatics like the collaborators of Reagan who . . . make compromises under the table. That is, serious fanaticism, true fanaticism . . . there is a moral rigor in this most rigid fanaticism."[73]

In summing up his opinion of the role that Piperno and Pace had played in Italian terrorism, Morucci once again and more vividly than before minimized their importance. During the great epidemic of Marxist-Leninist subversion to which Italy fell victim in the late 1960s and the 1970s, "all the militants and leaders . . . knew each other."[74] These inhabitants of an ideological archipelago engaged in much island-hopping during the Movement's early years, and at any one time radicals eager for action, such as Curcio and Franceschini, easily commingled with men only apparently inclined that way, such as Piperno and Negri. The real differences of temperament between them would only begin to emerge clearly after the first wave of murderous violence by the Red Brigades, in 1974, although, until Moro's death, they all saw themselves more or less as allies in the war against capitalism. In the "infinity" of small and large revolutionary groups, Piperno aspired to occupy a position of leadership that he never came close to filling.[75] The Red Brigades in particular dismissively lumped him in with the other talkative intellectuals of Autonomia "not directly involved in combat activity."[76] At one time, certainly, Piperno would have liked to think of himself as a revolutionary deserving of the state's indictment in the *Metropoli* trial, but he was merely representative of the madness, not its author or director.

One of the last important witnesses to testify was Franco Bonisoli, a Red Brigadist who had been arrested in October 1978 along with Lauro Azzolini. On 13 April 1987 he told the court that as a member of the executive committee he knew nothing "of attempts to infiltrate or to manipulate [the Red Brigades] by these persons [on trial]."[77] In his subsequent testimony Bonisoli repeated many of the major points, particularly about the Moro case, that he had made in a sensational *Corriere della Sera* interview published on 6 October 1985, and indeed this article was included in the court records for both the *Metropoli* and the Moro ter trials. He had "said and resaid" all of these things before, but that interview contained the fullest expression of his thinking about Moro in particular and about the general history of Italian terrorism.[78]

To the reporter interviewing him, the convicted murderer serving four life sentences seemed to be a simple, good-natured, and earnest young man. Bonisoli had been nineteen in 1974 when he left family and work in Reggio Emilia to join his *reggiani* friends in the Red Brigades: Fabrizio Pella, Lauro Azzolini, Alberto Franceschini, Prospero Gallinari, Tonino Paroli, and Roberto Ognibene. Growing up in "the shadow of the partisan tradition" that was especially prominent in Reggio, he had joined the PCI and become a union activist.[79] But his reading of Mao, Lenin, and Che Guevara convinced him that in a capitalist society Marxist-Leninist revolution remained the only moral choice for a communist. As reformism and neocorporativism completely overtook the PCI and the union movement, Bonisoli joined the Red Brigades to become a working revolutionary in the historic tradition that connected the most politically conscious radicals with the Bolsheviks.

When the reporter brought up the Moro case, Bonisoli remembered that after the Sossi kidnapping in 1974 the Red Brigadists began to discuss another such action, this time against "a highly representative figure in order to strike at the heart of the state." The stunning arrests of Curcio and Franceschini that same year forced the remaining leaders to shelve this plan for the next two years. Then in 1976 the imprisoned Red Brigade chiefs went on trial in Turin. Their comrades on the outside began to think once again about a high-level kidnapping that would lead to a "countertrial" embodying proletarian justice. At this time, however, the Red Brigades had so few regular members in the field that nothing concrete could be accomplished.

Nevertheless, the organization did create the Front in the Struggle against Counterrevolution, which had the specific task in Rome "of studying the centers of state power and picking out the man to be kidnapped for the countertrial." This group chose Andreotti instead of Moro as their top candidate. Andreotti had long held the reputation of party reactionary, and he also happened to be the Prime Minister, which substantially increased his symbolic value for the Red Brigades. Bonisoli explained that in 1976 and 1977, as plans for the kidnapping steadily took shape, "Moro did not appear to be in the front rank as Andreotti [did]," but everybody knew what his real power was and always had been *(da sempre)*. The more the Red Brigades examined the situation, the more tempting Moro became, particularly in view of his relatively lax security arrangements.

In the fall of 1977 the operational phase of the plan went into effect. Reinforced by a number of recruits that spring and summer, the Rome column now had sufficient manpower for its mission. Moreover, in that year of extraordinary turmoil in Italy revolution seemed to be in the offing, and hopes rose in the organization that one carefully aimed spark might set the whole country ablaze. Bonisoli remembered that "we were surrounded by sympathetic well-wishers who filled us with optimism." Without such a hospitable environment for terrorism, the Moro tragedy never could have occurred.

They trained rigorously for the via Fani operation, and by then many members already had acquired considerable experience in armed attacks. Even with these advantages, to say nothing of the always decisive element of surprise, the via Fani action did not unfold according to plan. They experienced numerous difficulties and failures. For example, only half an hour before the Moro entourage was expected to pass through the fatal intersection, the terrorists had to push a disabled vehicle out of the way. More critically, at different times four of their machine guns misfired. Far from being a textbook example of guerrilla warfare, the assault on via Fani glaringly exposed the organization's persistent ordnance problems.

Bonisoli attempted to dispel some of the myths and popular fetishes about the Moro kidnapping. Much had been written about the number of terrorists present at via Fani, but did it really matter if there were nine or eleven of them? In fact, eleven people originally had been assigned to the strike force. Then the number dropped, although Bonisoli declined to say exactly how many, insisting that one or two more or less made no difference. People had become similarly exercised over Moro's missing briefcases, but Bonisoli knew categorically that nothing of importance had been found in them: one had contained his medicine, the other some student papers. As for the excited public interest in the address of the People's Prison, Bonisoli shook his head in bewilderment. All the Red Brigadists had been trained to keep quiet about organizational business that did not concern them directly; therefore, people should not be shocked about their "silence" on the People's Prison. Bonisoli could say nothing at firsthand about Moro's time there, except that the prisoner had given the Red Brigades no worthwhile information about SIM or any of the other capitalist conspiracies in which his captors devoutly believed.

If Red Brigade conspiracy theories had been childish and the result of his generation's pernicious left-wing "cultural baggage," conspiracy theories about the Red Brigades were no better, Bonisoli affirmed. The ex-terrorist vehemently denied the existence of any conspiracy in the Moro case "on the part of the secret services, P2, and the Mafia." Speculations along such lines "are improbable stupidities that have never found even the smallest support in reality . . . they can only be classified as a form of gossip." Bonisoli conceded that some government people might have wanted Moro dead, but this was a separate matter, having nothing to do with the fiercely independent Red Brigades, which acted alone in kidnapping and killing their victim. They had conceived and executed the entire operation in order "to catalyze existing tensions in the various movements and armed groups." Red Brigade guilt in the Moro case was the fundamental truth for which piles of evidence existed. Why people would want to give up this clearly established certainty for a cloudy realm of undocumented conspiracies could only be explained as an expression of certain political needs in Italy.

The *fase dibattimentale* of the *Metropoli* trial ended shortly after Bonisoli's testimony. But early in May newspaper revelations about secret DC negotiations with Red Brigade leaders caused Public Minister Marini to request a reopening of the courtroom proceedings. President Santiapichi complied. On 12 May the assistant director of the Christian Democrats' paper *Il Popolo*, Remigio Cavedon, testified. He raised the same issue that in the days ahead would dominate the contemporaneous Moro ter trial, Flaminio Piccoli's claim about a film of Moro in the People's Prison. Reports of the film had raised new hopes in Italy about a real breakthrough in the Moro case. Cavedon's name had been linked in the press with Piccoli's in an independent DC initiative to obtain information from imprisoned Red Brigade leaders about Moro's fate. As a result of their initiative, it had been reported, the existence of a People's Prison film had come to light.

When President Santiapichi urged Cavedon to summarize his jailhouse discussions, the DC editor replied, "I have no new truths to reveal regarding the Moro case."[80] He had spoken many times with Moretti and "other personages" of the Red Brigades, but always on condition that no aspect of the Moro case be raised. "Do you mean that you have nothing to tell us," President Santiapichi exclaimed, expressing the disappointment of many. "Absolutely nothing," Cavedon said.[81] He had merely engaged the Red Brigadists in a general dialogue with no particular aim other than understanding them. The newspaper reports about a People's Prison film were all made up, he insisted.[82]

A little more than two months later, on 21 July 1987, President Santiapichi and Judge Ferdinando Attolico handed down their decision in the *Metropoli* trial. It was important to remember the charges against Piperno and Pace: legal responsibility for the deaths of Moro's security guards, for the kidnapping itself, for providing weapons to the

Red Brigadists, and for some three dozen additional terrorist acts. The prosecution had claimed that before and during the fifty-five days a strong bond existed between the defendants and the Red Brigades. Moreover, according to the indictment, Piperno and Pace had played a traitorous part during the PSI-inspired negotiations for Moro's life, using trattativa initiatives not to save the kidnap victim but to advance their own timetable for revolution. The prosecution had described Morucci and Faranda as nothing but pawns in the hands of Pace and Piperno, literally as their agents in the Red Brigades.

The judges began by summarizing the indictment and then criticized it for its exaggerations and deficiencies. To be sure, Piperno and Pace were products of the revolutionary culture that also produced the Red Brigades. Nevertheless, the law had an obligation to ascertain the personal responsibility of defendants for specific acts, not for their role as intellectuals in fostering ideas that had a disruptive effect on society. A clear line separated acts from ideas; the former concerned the court, the latter did not. The so-called *Metropoli* Project, to unite all the country's revolutionary forces, had been a conspicuous fiasco, and therefore Piperno and Pace could not be found guilty for something that had failed to happen, however much they had wished its consummation. The paper trail that they had left behind in *Metropoli* and *Pre-print* convinced the court that these men were clearly part of "the Italian subversive panorama," but their ambition—and the state's indictment against them—vastly exceeded their actual crimes.[83]

The court agreed with the prosecution's characterization of Piperno's "Dal terrorismo alla guerriglia" as a blatantly pro-terroristic diatribe, but at the same time, Judge Attolico wrote, the piece revealed important differences between the author and the Red Brigades. Courtroom testimony in the trial substantiated these differences. Between the *Metropoli* group and the Red Brigades the court could only see an ideological contiguity of positions, not an actual alliance in specific crimes. All the evidence showed that the Red Brigades consistently had resisted and rejected Piperno. The prosecution could only show that the defendants had attempted to influence and manipulate the Red Brigades, but no evidence existed to prove that their attempt had any effect on Moro's fate. Moreover, the prosecution had overstated its case in characterizing Morucci and Faranda as Piperno's pawns. Courtroom testimony led the judges to take a considerably different view of this complex relationship: namely, that the four of them had been friends, and the prosecution had not proved that the two Red Brigadists had been maneuvered by their supposed masters. The convergence of opinions regarding Moro's execution did not necessarily imply a subaltern position on the part of Morucci and Faranda before Piperno and Pace.

That Piperno and Pace should be found guilty of subversive activity in promoting armed struggle, insurrection, and civil war the court did not doubt. Accordingly, both men received ten-year prison sentences and fines, but the judges exonerated them of any wrongdoing in the Moro case. Even Pace's membership in the Red Brigades had been shown to be of no consequence in the Moro kidnapping. The two deserved to be punished, but in "terms of juridical applicability," not for the crimes with which the state had charged them regarding via Fani.[84] Despite all the new and important testimony that had been presented, the *Metropoli* trial turned out to be a dead end in the Moro case.[85]

10

Moro Ter

The Second Year

Following a summer recess the Moro ter trial resumed on 22 September 1987. Flaminio Piccoli, who in May of that year had caused a sensation with his public statements about a Red Brigade film of Moro in the People's Prison, testified on 8 October. Under questioning from President Sorichilli, the DC leader sought to explain the background and the real meaning of those statements. "I belong," he began, "to that group of five or six persons who had the unhappy responsibility of taking the hard line during those fifty-four days for the DC."[1] These men felt they were under relentless bombardment in that period. Every day they repeated to themselves and to the public that no negotiations should be undertaken with the terrorists responsible for the massacre on via Fani. Even the DC leaders close to Moro—and Piccoli described himself as one of the closest *(vicinissimo)*—gave their vigorous assent to fermezza.

After Moro's death and with the passing years, Piccoli had changed his mind about the state's intransigent reaction to the kidnappers' demands, and his interview in *La Famiglia Cristiana* earlier that year had to be interpreted as an expression of the "anguish" that continued to trouble him. "Even today," he continued, "I think that at bottom perhaps it would have been better to negotiate; at least [that way] we still would have had this statesman with us."[2] Above all, Piccoli now wanted to know the full truth about Moro. To find this out, he was prepared to offer clemency and pardon, when deserved, in exchange for a definitive reconstruction of what had happened to his colleague and friend.

Piccoli's comment about a film of Moro in the People's Prison had not been based on a revelation from the terrorists but was the result of his own reading, he testified. Piccoli cited two articles that had appeared in the January and February 1985 issues of *Il Borghese*, a right-wing publication. The first was only a brief mention of a report that "video-cassettes of the Moro interrogation" had disappeared after being impounded by the police in an antiterrorist raid.[3] In a follow-up article three weeks later, Francesco D. Caridi wrote that Tommaso Mitrotti, an MSI senator, had asked the head of the government and the interior minister about this report. The senator had received no reply. Caridi then conjectured that such a film probably existed and that the secret services retained possession of it. So much secrecy and silence had to mean that it contained material damaging to the state, perhaps to its case in the various Moro trials, which had been based essentially on the depositions of pentiti and dissociati. If Caridi had guessed right, the film would undermine the credibility of the state's witnesses and destroy the basis of its legal arguments in the Moro case, which, in any event, the parties now desperately wanted to forget.[4] These articles made a deep impression on Piccoli, as did the 9 October 1986 testimony of Roberto Buzzatti in Moro ter.

Then Piccoli came to the main point in his own testimony: he had no information of his own to add to what had been published. The Christian Democratic leader wanted merely to draw attention to the many mysteries in the Moro case, one of which had to do with the diverse reports about a film of the People's Prison. Piccoli had no idea that the interview would cause such an uproar: "I have nothing, I know nothing. . . . I have not had contacts with anyone on this matter."[5] He disavowed media reports about his secret negotiations with Curcio, a man known to him only by sight. As for similar stories about what Moretti supposedly told him, Piccoli allowed that he had met once with the Red Brigade chief, but their dialogue had nothing whatsoever to do with Moro. They only spoke about general religious questions ("sul piano cristiano, sul piano cattolico").[6] Piccoli long had maintained that a way should be found to bring former terrorists back into society, and this had been his sole motive in meeting with Moretti.

Later that same month, Remigio Cavedon restated and amplified the testimony he had given in the *Metropoli* trial. The assistant director of the DC party newspaper had spoken with Moretti four times, but from the beginning they had agreed not to mention issues dealing with trials in progress, which Cavedon understood to mean the Moro case above all. President Sorichilli wanted to know what the *Corriere della Sera*'s Paolo Graldi meant by headlining his article as follows: "From the Red Brigadist Moretti I have learned secrets about the Moro crime."[7] Cavedon, a veteran newspaperman, stated bluntly that newspapers were not always to be believed. Graldi had misreported his remarks, Cavedon told the court. Although he had repeatedly challenged the accuracy of Graldi's article, nothing had come of his efforts to obtain a retraction.

Unlike Piccoli, Cavedon had spent many hours talking with terrorists in prisons all over Italy. On the basis of these talks, he had formed a general impression of what the truth was in the Moro case, even though the dead statesman's name had never come up explicitly. Reading between the lines of their voluminous testimony, Cavedon sensed very strongly that "there is no longer any big secret to reveal regarding the Moro matter."[8] Some details of the case remained to be explained, but its general outlines had become clear. What were mere details for Cavedon were the heart of the case for one lawyer in the courtroom. He pressed the witness for more information, but Cavedon had nothing more to say. In a closing comment which the reporters present must have found odd and unnatural, the assistant director of *Il Popolo* said that he had not visited the prisons "in search of a scoop."[9]

Ever since Flaminio Piccoli had cited the two *Borghese* articles about a People's Prison film, the court had wanted to learn more about them. Accordingly, the magazine's head, Mario Tedeschi, was summoned to testify on 3 November. When President Sorichilli asked him what the factual basis of these articles had been, the witness demurred. First, he would have to provide a little background. It all began when one of his writers, Francesco Caridi, informed him that he had heard of such a film: "He told me he had the clear impression that the person who told him these things was a member of the police—on account of a number of particular details, the way he spoke, [and] how he described the operation."[10] Caridi, an experienced investigative journalist who had written articles about the Mafia and about organized crime in general, had used information provided by anonymous police sources before, and they had always proved reliable. Tedeschi had been a right-wing senator in 1978, and he knew at firsthand about the sloppy police work in the Moro case. Therefore, he felt strongly inclined to accept Caridi's initial report about a Moro film. The existence and disappearance of such a document would not have surprised him at all, for it would have fit into a well-established pattern of police negligence, omissions, and uncooperativeness in handling the investigation.

In the 27 January 1985 issue of *Il Borghese* Tedeschi decided to carry just a brief reference to the film. He thought of this piece as a probe, to see how the authorities would react. Tedeschi, director of *Il Borghese* for more than thirty years, explained that he often published trial balloons designed to confirm or to invalidate his hunches. Usually they would have their desired effect, and within forty-eight hours at the latest some high government official would call with a revealing comment one way or the other. The reaction this time, though, was "absolute silence."[11] When Senator Mitrotti's subsequent appeals to the government proved unavailing, Tedeschi concluded that Caridi's information had been accurate. He then asked the reporter to write the second article. Once again, the government issued no clarifications or denials. Tedeschi still thought that the government's silence eloquently proclaimed the truth of Caridi's story.

The fall testimony in Moro ter renewed the hoary debate over fermezza. As the trial continued into 1988, the government itself had to undergo a public scrutiny unprecedented in its rigor for the way it had investigated the Moro crime. After the last witnesses had appeared, Public Minister Nitto Francesco Palma asked on 4 February for twenty-nine life sentences and long prison terms for the 173 defendants. Many months of lawyers' summations would pass before sentencing, but Moro ter was already being judged a disappointment. The public did not feel it had the whole truth and nothing but the truth in the emotionally charged Moro case. The trial closed amidst a pitched rhetorical battle between extreme advocates of the two positions: to have negotiated or not to have negotiated. Each side held that everything now known about the kidnapping reaffirmed the validity of its cause. Each side pointed to itself as a repository of final truth in the Moro case. As the judges of Moro ter listened to the lawyers and then slowly conducted their own deliberations for most of the rest of 1988, the case was thrown fully once again into the public arena from which, of course, it had never been entirely absent. The remarkable feature of the public debate now was how little views had changed after four trials and two parliamentary investigations.

On the eve of the tenth anniversary of via Fani, Andreotti and Craxi summed up their positions in a series of newspaper interviews. Andreotti continued to denounce the trattativa initiative of the PSI as nothing but "acts of agitation."[12] He had not changed his mind about Craxi's independent efforts in 1978: they lacked seriousness and realism; the Socialists had never produced an effective alternative to the government's policies. While repeating his old criticisms, Andreotti added that the one credible alternative had been formulated by the Vatican, which secretly had offered a ransom of 100 billion lire for Moro.[13] The Red Brigades, however, did not want money. They wanted to force the government to take a false step, and Andreotti refused to fall for it.[14] His guiding principle throughout the ordeal had been that "we did not have the right to release any terrorists from prison to save the life of one of our own. If the law enforcement officials had seen us liberate the assassins of their colleagues in exchange for a politician's life, there would have been the risk of a revolt or at least a 'folded arms' policy on their part. We would have been heading toward the dissolution of the state."[15]

To have given the Red Brigades what they wanted—political recognition and a prisoner exchange—was the exact opposite of what the situation demanded, Andreotti continued. The thing the terrorists desired most had to be denied them on principle at whatever the cost, which turned out to be dreadful. It was a disaster to have lost Moro, Andreotti mourned. His prestige and moral authority were enormous and still growing when the Red Brigades cut him down. No one had begun to replace him in Italian politics. Christian Democracy had paid a fearful price in 1978, but the government had demonstrated that it knew how to defend the Republic. The DC leader was more convinced than ever that he had made the right decision in the Moro crisis.

Andreotti viewed the perdonismo movement as a latter-day expression of the erroneous logic in the trattativa argument. In a swipe at Piccoli, he flatly condemned the DC advocates of appeasement in his own party for their misguided sentiment. The Christian Democrats had the responsibility of power and justice; these ends could never be achieved by forgetting the government's paramount obligation to the via Fani victims. It would be politically asinine and morally offensive to give the impression that "after a little time has passed all is forgiven, that he who is alive is alive and so much the worse for him who is dead."[16]

For Craxi the prison letters of the martyred Christian Democratic leader contained an unanswerable refutation of Andreotti's hard-line refusal to negotiate with the Red Brigades. The very principles of democratic policy required that every attempt be made to preserve human life. These letters should be studied by Italian school children; to its shame the Andreotti government appeared not to have read them at all. Deaf to Moro's repeated calls for help, that government did nothing. Craxi conceded that Andreotti personally wanted to save Moro, but an efficacious concern was clearly lacking in the centers of power.[17] Moro himself hauntingly rebuked his colleagues for this. Nothing was tried: "not negotiations . . . ., not a unilateral gesture by the state . . . ., not serious [police] investigations."[18]

Craxi's severest criticism was directed at the failure of the police in their search for Moro. Was it enough for the advocates of fermezza to say now that the state simply had been "unprepared"? Craxi and the trattativa party continued to think that some people in the government had played a treasonous role during the Moro kidnapping. The fermezza front simply refused to acknowledge that there were unanswered questions in the Moro case.

Lawyers in the Moro ter case continued to present their summations during the spring of 1988. Their statements received little press coverage, for the trial as a whole had faded from the public's consciousness. Interest had waned in part because the entire issue of terrorism looked like yesterday's news. No terrorist killings had happened in more than a year. The last one, in March 1987, had been followed in June and November by the arrest of numerous terrorists belonging to the new Red Brigade formations. Once again the organization appeared to be in ruins.

With the war on terrorism seemingly over, the backers of perdonismo argued that the time had come to bury the past. In victory, magnanimity. Moreover, special considerations should be given to terrorists such as Curcio who had never killed anyone. The postemergency mentality united an unlikely coalition of dissident Christian Democrats—notably Flaminio Piccoli and Maria Fida Moro—the Socialist party, and virtually the entire extraparliamentary left.

In rebuttal, most Christian Democratic leaders and all of their counterparts in the Communist party more or less echoed the arguments of Enrico Fenzi, who declared that a general pardon would be wrong. He could think of no greater obfuscation than the notion of terrorists with clean hands. This former Red Brigadist and professor of literature had never shot anyone, but his "innocence" was strictly technical and only a matter of chance. Fenzi just as easily could have been given military tasks to perform, and he would not have hesitated to obey. He explained, "I do not see much difference between those who shot and killed and those who limited themselves to adhering to the armed struggle. We were all in the same game."[19] The activists and their supporters on the radical left together shared responsibility for the terror. They had complemented each other in their respective roles.

Fenzi had addressed these points in *Armi e bagagli: un diario dalle Brigate Rosse* (1987), a book that deeply affected the debate over perdonismo and terrorism in general as Moro ter unfolded. The book is "a slow patient journey around possible answers" to the question of why he became a terrorist.[20] Fenzi thought that his motives were rationally deduced from self-evident premises. Italy appeared to be on the verge of collapse, and for her systemic crisis Red Brigadism alone offered clear and comprehensive solutions drawn directly from the Marxist-Leninist tradition to which Fenzi long had professed unquestioning allegiance. Each step in his itinerary toward Red Brigadism seemed to follow naturally from the preceding one. By his own account a perverse logic characterized the entire process.

It all began with the idea of revolution. Fenzi had believed in revolution the way a properly catechized Roman Catholic believes in the communion of saints and life everlasting. Unlike his Catholic counterpart, Fenzi did not think that the millennium awaited in the indefinite future. For him the period of general righteousness and happiness when a man could enter his house justified was literally at hand. Capitalism, he thought, was a "dying dinosaur."[21] By putting this creature out of its misery, the Red Brigadists were clearing the way for the communist fulfillment of history. That was how Fenzi and many other communists in Italy understood Marxist-Leninism.

Fenzi had read what he believed to be the seminal revolutionary text for his generation, Jean-Paul Sartre's *Critique of Dialectical Reason*, and had interpreted it as a Marxist-existentialist call to arms: the present could only be changed through revolutionary force; we are alive only as we actively attack the capitalist structure of domination; the revolutionary is the only authentic hero in the world today. The mystique of revolution pervaded the atmosphere in which Red Brigadism had taken hold. Fenzi charged that the Italian left in general wanted to forget its own acceptance of the revolutionary premises from which Red Brigadism had sprung. Therefore, the left was always the first to depict terrorism as a spawn of plots on the right and hallucinations on the left. The truth was different, as Fenzi knew from his own grinding experience.

What distinguished the Red Brigadist from other communists was the coherence of his thinking and acting; he believed in the absolute necessity of unremitting class violence and acted on that belief. Even in his postterrorist period Fenzi thought that there was an element of grandeur in the Red Brigade act of Marxist-Leninist revolutionary faith that was far superior ethically to the elaborate ideological shiftiness of such ingeniously coy radical ideologists as Toni Negri, who now wanted the world to believe that the revolutionary program of Autonomia stood in the sharpest possible contrast to the revolutionary program of the Red Brigades.[22] According to Fenzi, the real difference between them was the unambiguous directness of the Red Brigades about what they were doing. Negri had endeavored, without success, to perform "the bizarre surgical operation" of separating the revolutionary movement of the 1970s, which he had helped to lead, from the armed struggle of the terrorists.[23] Such surgery could have many purposes, but not that of providing a serious understanding of how terrorism arose in Italy.

Fenzi regretted that he could never master the art of verbal evasion in the manner of Negri. He had the brain for it, but not the stomach. In his mind, revolution loomed as an either/or choice, and when the Red Brigades beckoned to him, he abandoned family and career without compunction. He would have done anything the Red Brigades asked him to do, even murder, for revolution meant total war against capitalism. The Red Brigades understood and accepted the Marxist-Leninist concept of ideologically sanctioned homicide. Terrorist deaths and maimings were offered as human sacrifices to the god of history. Fenzi, an internationally acclaimed Dante scholar, at the time could see nothing wrong with this slaughter. It was as though Hegel's Absolute Spirit had revealed itself to the Red Brigades and to them alone. Their presumption of omniscience was complete. "I and the Red Brigades knew everything, we understood everything"; all the others, even on the left, "were shit, traitors, the corrupted."[24]

A minute quantity of self-doubt did seep into their thinking after the Guido Rossa assassination. A highly skilled factory worker and a member of the PCI, killed by the Red Brigades in January 1979 for exposing their attempts to infiltrate the workplace, Rossa commanded the respect of his fellow workers. At his funeral they wept while cursing the Red Brigades. Fenzi described the Rossa murder as a colossal blunder, leading directly to the quite sudden collapse of the sympathy that vast numbers of people hitherto had felt for the Red Brigades' revolutionary project. The shooting of a Communist worker ended the hesitations in left-wing factory politics about the rules governing dissent. Thereafter the Red Brigadists became pariahs in the factories, but it took the Rossa murder to effect this change of attitude. The Moro murder and all the others before January 1979 had not sufficed. Fenzi's analysis provided the opponents of perdonismo with some of their most powerful arguments.

The February 1988 publication of Alberto Franceschini's book, *Mara, Renato e io: storia dei fondatori delle br*, occasioned more discussion on the subject of perdonismo, which dominated public discussion as Moro ter drew fitfully to a close. Unlike *Armi e bagagli*, this most recent Red Brigadist memoir contained some specific references to the Moro case. Franceschini began by describing the circumstances in which he, Curcio, and Cagol had created the Red Brigades. His own ideological itinerary began in the Franceschini family home. Born on 26 October 1947 into a staunchly communist clan in Reggio Emilia, the boy never heard or read any fairy tales; instead, at his grandfather's knee, he learned about the legendary exploits of Togliatti, Lenin, Stalin, and Gramsci. His grandfather had been one of the first in Reggio to join the PCI, and he fought as a Partisan in World War II. The mention of Khrushchev never failed to provoke a fiercely polemical reaction: he hated the Soviet premier for having de-Stalinized the Communist party. Grandfather Franceschini's son, a political moderate by the family's standards, supported the PCI without taking the party to task for its strictly legalistic approach to all political questions.

Alberto identified completely with his unreconstructed grandfather. Steeped in the Franceschini family lore about the Resistance and its betrayal after 1945, young Alberto acquired a political viewpoint to which he remained faithful while moving from the ranks of the Communist party to the outer fringes of the extraparliamentary left. The

PCI's growing moderation during the 1960s tormented him, and he complained bitterly about the party's unwillingness to work for revolution. It was the complaint of a generation of Marxist radicals that came of age in 1968. They thought of themselves as the conscience of communism, a generation that meant to keep the faith; "a red thread . . . tied us to the Partisans," Franceschini wrote.[25]

The young man went to Milan, ostensibly to study at a technical institute, but soon the city's radical politics absorbed all of his time. An encounter with Curcio and Cagol became the turning point in his life. These three fueled each other's belief in a Marxist-Leninist revolution as the only remedy for the country's ills. In creating the Red Brigades, they hoped to precipitate such a revolution. The organization would lead a new Resistance and finish the work of regenerating Italy left undone in 1945. In the beginning, the creators of Red Brigadism— the very name an echo of the Resistance—wanted it to be an instrument to avenge the partisans. These connections possessed more than a symbolic significance. For example, the trio of Red Brigade founders lacked expertise in the use of arms, and they all took military instruction from an old partisan of Franceschini's acquaintance. He also gave them their first weapons, a pair of World War II-vintage machine guns, with which they practiced in isolated mountain locations preparing to be guerrilla fighters. Small acts of sabotage were followed by "expropriations" that financed increasingly ambitious terrorist operations. By 1972 the Red Brigades had begun to kidnap industrialists and to make arms purchases abroad, in Switzerland and Liechtenstein.

In those early years, the PCI reacted to the Red Brigades with a mixture of indulgence and feigned incomprehension. But Franceschini claimed the party "knew very well who we were . . . that the majority of us were from its ranks and that some of us, with membership cards in our pockets, still frequented party headquarters."[26] The PCI could never be honest with itself about the Red Brigades because to do so would entail recognizing "people that came from its ranks, from its culture."[27] Therefore, on the subject of terrorism the party could always be counted on to favor the "obscure international plot" interpretation. The obvious connections between historic Marxist culture and Red Brigadism had to be downplayed at all costs. The Red Brigades sought to recall the party to its revolutionary origins, but the exact opposite happened. As the Red Brigades became increasingly violent and destructive in the name of Marx and Lenin, the PCI wrapped itself in the flag of the Italian Republic and on all law and order issues took care to have no one on its right.

People also read *Mara, Renato e io* for the light it could shed on the Moro case. In a chapter entitled "Sequestrare Andreotti," Franceschini gave his version of the Red Brigade plot to kidnap this Christian Democratic leader. Sometime in 1974 Franceschini began to follow Andreotti around Rome to learn the details of his daily routine. What he learned confirmed Andreotti's later claims before the Moro Commission that prior to 1978 no politician enjoyed the degree of security that critics argued should have been given to Moro. Andreotti himself, who only by chance avoided the fate of Moro in 1974, received no police protection at all. The Red Brigades thought of him as "the pivot of the neo-Gaullist project" in Italy and "the very incarnation of Power," but he actually walked the streets of Rome without an escort of any kind.[28] It would have been a simple matter to kidnap him, Franceschini reported, but just before Operation Andreotti was to be implemented, the police captured the two male founders of the Red Brigades. Franceschini also noted that while walking in the neighborhood of Montecitorio he quite casually crossed paths with Emilio Colombo and Mariano Rumor, two other leading Christian Democratic politicians, also with no police protection whatsoever. For a terrorist hunter it was open season on the big game of Rome. The terrorist leader's book vindicated Andreotti on a very important issue in the Moro case.

In his memoir Franceschini repeated much of his *Metropoli* trial testimony about the severely circumscribed role of the imprisoned Red Brigade leaders in deciding the outcome of the Moro kidnapping. Neither he nor Curcio had any idea that such a "clamorous action" had been planned against "one of the most potent and protected men in Italy."[29] At first the prisoners did not know whether to be happy or to be frightened for their lives. They deeply admired their comrades who had dared to aim so high, but at the same time feared reprisals from the state. They thought about what had happened to the Baader Meinhof convicts in Stammheim Prison—it was an article of faith among the Red Brigadists that their German counterparts had been "suicided."

On trial in Turin at the time of the kidnapping and massacre, Curcio and Franceschini became frustrated by the amateurish leadership of Mario Moretti, a "tenacious" man but lacking "the political capacity necessary to lead an organization like ours."[30] According to Franceschini, Moretti fumbled away all the advantages that the Red Brigades derived from the Moro kidnapping. The fundamental goal of the operation should have been the smashing of "the hard-line front" of the Christian Democrats and the Communists, which then constituted "the real heart of the State."[31] Unfortunately, Moretti never understood the actual situation in Italy, and he foolishly clung to the mystical belief that the kidnapping by itself would detonate a revolutionary explosion in the country. By systematically acting on his misguided belief, Moretti reduced the Red Brigades to a mere military organization. Despite the increased pace of terrorism during the following year, any chance of ultimate victory vanished. Franceschini himself did not understand this clearly at the time, but, in retrospect, he viewed the Moro operation as a decisive defeat for the Red Brigades.

Franceschini's comments on the *fermezza-trattativa* debate in the Moro case were quite detailed. He still thought that the state had made a tragic mistake in refusing to negotiate. Nevertheless, his observations did not strengthen the position of Craxi and the other prominent doves. On the contrary, Franceschini painted a brutally unflattering portrait of Craxi and his colleagues in the humanitarian front. They pretended to want negotiations, but their real objective was political, "to open maneuvering room between the DC and the PCI."[32] Through the Socialist lawyer Giannino Guiso, Craxi had begged the terrorists "not to attach too much significance to my public declarations about you, for I cannot do less. Know that I consider you very bright and politically intelligent people."[33] It was all a show for public consumption; had serious negotiations been undertaken, Moro would have gone free. The closing of Asinara and the other special prisons or the release of some foreign revolutionary convicts would have been enough to induce the historic leaders of the Red Brigades to call for Moro's release. Moretti would not have dared to flout such a declaration, and the matter would have been settled without further tragedy. While Franceschini did not rule out a "Machiavellian design" by the state and the Communist party in this period of almost unlimited treachery, he also castigated the leaders of the humanitarian front for their part in Moro's tragic plight.

It took several more years for Franceschini to abandon his dream of the perfect Marxist-Leninist revolution. In the end, he recognized that the Red Brigades had been completely wrong in their analysis of Italian society. The revolutionary project was now something for antiquarians, he admitted. It became increasingly difficult for him even to have conversations with the hard-line Red Brigadists who still talked about the "metropolitan proletariat" as though it were a real force in politics on the verge of realizing Marx's historic prophecies. How could any reasonably alert person continue to believe in political ideas that obviously lacked the slightest connection with social reality? He had been the truest of these believers, but the real truth could no longer be evaded. All of us in the Red Brigades, Franceschini wrote, were "drug addicts of a particular type, of ideology. A murderous drug, worse than heroin."[34] Such sentiments did not endear him to Curcio or the other remaining hard-liners, and to lose their comradeship pained him grievously. They had been his world, and he was giving them up in order to establish a new "rapport" with the prison warden and chaplain. He proclaimed himself acutely aware of the ludicrousness of this outcome.

Although Franceschini had helped to create a murderous organization and had expressed a willingness to kill, legally speaking he had no blood on his hands. He had been captured soon after the Red Brigade reign of terror became murderous. By chance, Franceschini did not have to answer for murder, but, like Fenzi in *Armi e bagagli*, he acknowledged responsibility for all of Red Brigadism's grim legacy. *Mara, Renato e io* further illustrated Fenzi's argument about the fatuity inherent in the concept of terrorists with clean hands.

The cause of perdonismo went into an almost complete eclipse a little more than a month later, when the Red Brigades murdered Senator Roberto Ruffili of the Christian Democratic party. Ruffili had been made to kneel before his executioners who then shot him at point-blank range in his Forlì home. A respected historian with a distinguished record of academic publications, he had become a principal adviser to Ciriaco De Mita, Italy's recently installed Prime Minister, on the question of institutional reforms. The Red Brigades singled him out for revolutionary justice because of his ties with De Mita. They later explained: "We have executed Roberto Ruffili in Forlì [as part of] the attack on the heart of the state."[35] In other words, Ruffili's death served the same purpose Ezio Tarantelli's had: the Red Brigade's proposed to undermine the state by killing the proponents of neocorporativist strategies to make capitalism stronger.

The murder of this mild and gentle scholar caught the nation by surprise. People had come to believe that the age of terrorism had ended. It had been more than a year since the Giorgieri assassination, and since then the terrorists had been quiescent. Moreover, in the late 1980s Italy appeared to be entering a new and dramatically advanced stage of its history, due in large part to a surge in the economy and to the computer and robotics revolutions. Richer and technologically more sophisticated, Italy now had her hands full of intractable first-world problems: pollution, drugs, crime, overcrowding, and alienation. English-language television advertisements in the highly distinctive manner of Madison Avenue, with Italian subtitles or sometimes with none at all, indicated plainly enough Italy's ineluctable consumerist destiny, now largely realized. The Italian passion for American television programs, movies, music, and the English language itself were the surface signs of the country's virtually complete cultural transformation. The decline of the sacred, in sociologist Sabino Acquaviva's phrase, had been followed by the modernist and postmodernist babel characteristic of contemporary mass culture.[36] In such an environment a rise in the crime rates was no surprise, but terrorists in ski masks shooting at the pillars of society now looked like a preposterous anomaly.

Oreste Scalzone, the extraparliamentary left-wing exile in Paris, feared that the party of fermezza (or vendetta, to cite his term) would use the Ruffili murder as a club with which to smash the *perdonismo* movement. This in fact did happen, although the fermezza party had many other weapons in its arsenal for this purpose. The savage execution of a universally respected teacher and writer guaranteed public support in the campaign for continued vigilance against terrorism. Now more than ever the public accepted the main fermezza argument, that the only terrorists deserving of mercy were those pentiti who had surrendered to the state unconditionally and had cooperated fully with investigating magistrates. All the other defendants deserved nothing but strict justice under the law.

The killing of Ruffili conveyed the impression that Italy's problems with terrorism remained endemic and unfathomable. Ruffili, a fresh sacrifice on the altar of revolutionary ideology, seemed to prove that the Red Brigades held a continuing fascination for an inexhaustible reservoir of the country's malcontents. The threat of terrorism continued to be taken seriously; as Secretary of the Interior Antonio Gava pointed out, in April 1988 nearly 3,000 officers were providing escort service for people believed to be terrorist targets, including 151 politicians, 279 magistrates, and 139 economists.[37] He thought it premature to talk about a general pardon for "defeated revolutionaries."

A few months later the Moro ter trial—with its unanswered questions, ambiguities, enigmas, and controversies—ended in a national orgy of recrimination. Sentencing occurred nearly two-and-one-half years after the trial had begun and five years after magistrates had launched the Moro ter investigation. President Sorichilli read the sentence. "In the name of the Italian people" he condemned the defendants to more than 1,800 years of prison time. Twenty-six people received life sentences. Sorichilli gave Curcio one of the lighter sentences, only sixteen years and ten months. "So little?" the Red Brigade leader queried afterwards.[38]

In the 12 October 1988 *motivazione* of the sentence, Judge Pasquale Perrone, the *estensore*, and President Sorichilli provided a historical overview of the Red Brigades, emphasizing the importance of the Rome column, which had planned and carried out the Moro operation. They summarized all that had been learned about the organizational structure of the Red Brigades. The central national governing unit, "the highest organ," was the Direzione Strategica, which met twice a year or at the request of at least one column.[39] The Comitato Esecutivo implemented the initiatives handed down by the Direzione Strategica, directing and coordinating the actions of all the Red Brigade columns. The major columns were territorially based and made up of diverse brigades. These columns had their own command structures and cooperated with each other on various "fronts," such as the Fronte Carceri (Prison Front) and the Fronte Contro-Rivoluzione (Counterrevolution Front) in order to be "terroristically" *(terroristicamente)* more productive.[40] Each brigade also had its own command structure and was made up of "regulars" who had gone underground and "irregulars" who continued to lead seemingly ordinary lives while working for the organization.[41] Brigade regulars organized themselves into cells *(cellule)*. Although irregulars did not have command responsibilities, they could represent their columns in the Direzione Strategica. The brigade *rete* functioned as the training structure through which all recruits had to pass. Weekly meetings to discuss ideology, tactics, and individual assignments were "the soul of the Red Brigades" and reinforced the group mentality.[42]

Testimony in Moro ter had resulted in much additional information about the Movimento Proletario di Resistenza Offensiva (MPRO), "that area of antagonism to the State and to [its] institutions."[43] An unknown but certainly large number of revolutionary groups had taken hold in the schools and factories, and the Red Brigades, according to their own Risoluzione Strategica of February 1978, had sought to inspire the MPRO with an authentic Marxist-Leninist vision of revolution. Ultimately, the Red Brigades hoped "to unify and to organize these groups of 'armed spontaneity'" under the aegis of the five-pointed star. The judges expressed their dismay about the high level of support for the Red Brigades in Italy's large extremist left-wing culture. The sheer number of sympathizers invalidated the thesis of those who argued that, despite media reports and government claims, the Red Brigades posed no serious threat to Italy's democracy. (Those who minimized the problem pointed out that only a few hundred terrorists at most ever had taken up arms against the state, and consequently the entire episode of Red Brigadism should be understood as a minor development that had been blown out of all proportion by the state for its own sinister purposes.)

According to the judges, such logic had clouded the nation's understanding of its problems with terrorism. True, the Red Brigades had been a small organization, but only because the leaders did not want it to become too big, reasoning after Lenin that the worth of a revolutionary organization has nothing to do with its size but rather with its discipline, its sense of purpose, and its understanding of the political situation in which the class enemy must be destroyed. Membership statistics thus revealed very little about the disruptive power of the Red Brigades. In the first place, to inflict serious damage a terrorist organization did not need many members; a handful of fanatics could create chaos, particularly in an open democratic society. Even more important in the case of Italy's left-wing terrorism, the generally agreed-upon number of 300 Red Brigadists was accurate only in the most technical sense. In fact, through the MPRO the Red Brigades had ready access to a large reservoir of manpower and support. At the zenith of the terror, applicants outnumbered the places available in the organization, and for the judges these were the numbers that really mattered in understanding the menace of Red Brigadism.

While Judge Perrone and President Sorichilli could only claim a few advances in the Moro case itself, these were "important."[44] Morucci's testimony, though "reticent and tortuous" on many matters, seemed "fully reliable" on the unfolding of events at via Fani.[45] He had convinced them that nine terrorists—not seven, as found in Moro 1—had participated directly in the massacre "without excluding the presence of other terrorists, engaged in flanking and covering actions, elsewhere along the escape route."[46] Morucci's testimony, too, permitted the judges to reject Judge Rosario Priore's hypothesis in the fase istruttoria regarding the presence of a foreigner in the terrorist command. Only Italians were involved, and they were Alvaro Loiacono, Alessio Casimirri, Mario Moretti, Prospero Gallinari, Raffaele Fiore, Valerio Morucci, Bruno Seghetti, Barbara Balzerani, and Franco Bonisoli.

The judges were nearly certain that the address of the People's Prison was via Montalcini 8 in Rome. This conclusion, they thought, had the deductive and logical force of a "syllogism," but the only people who could confirm it as an absolutely secure historical fact—Moretti, Gallinari, and Anna Laura Braghetti—had refused to talk.[47] Evidence about the location of the People's Prison had been provided by Savasta, Emilia Libèra, Morucci, and others; enough to persuade the judges that their syllogism held. They reasoned as follows: Braghetti and Gallinari, identified as the jailers of Moro, had lived together since 1977; Braghetti had an apartment on via Montalcini 8; therefore the place where Moro had been kept prisoner was this apartment. Once again, Morucci's testimony had been extremely helpful because he had described for the court exactly what kind of base Moretti always preferred: a ground level apartment with a nearby garage and a connecting passage between the garage and the apartment building. This description fit via Montalcini 8 perfectly.

The judges did not always accept Morucci's testimony on other matters connected with the Moro case. For example, he had claimed along with Faranda that the Italian secret service had fabricated the 18 April 1978 note about Moro's supposed suicide, "to prepare the population for an event that seemed inevitable."[48] In this communication, which the Red Brigades immediately denied having sent, it was said that Moro's corpse could be found at the bottom of Lake Duchessa, some fifty miles northeast of Rome. The document did indeed turn out to be a fake. Moro was then still alive, but what had been the motive of whoever had sent it? President Sorichilli and Judge Perrone vehemently rejected Morucci's hypothesis, as an "underhanded, miserable attempt to transfer the moral responsibility of the homicide to others."[49] Morucci had declared that the Lago di Duchessa forgery had been a death sentence for Moro, "accelerating the time of execution."[50] Sorichilli and Perrone retorted, "Morucci and the other brigadists know that they assassinated Moro, not because of that communication, but because by this time the idealists had been transformed into jackals" capable of any enormity in the service of their fanatically held abstractions.[51]

The judges thought that the evidence produced in Moro ter favored only one of the hypotheses advanced to explain the counterfeit communication: "that of a serious attempt to save the life of Moro with a false document that, in its intentions, aimed at smashing the diabolical strategy of moral and political tension created by the Red Brigades in the country."[52] The authors of this forgery, who remained anonymous, must have hoped that the public reaction to an announcement of Moro's death would convince the Red Brigades to let their victim go. The kidnappers would have to see that an act as "pitiless and insane" as the murder of Moro would only produce "a sense of disgust and moral condemnation" among the public.[53] Even individuals as cut off from the everyday world as were the Red Brigadists would be forced to take note of the nation's indignation; this last and not the "destabilization" they pathetically envisaged would be the result of Moro's murder. The strategy failed, but the judges could think of no other reasonable explanation. Naturally, such a conjecture did not end public debate on the episode.

The judges' analysis of the court's sentence also lacked specifying detail on a subject much discussed inside and outside the Moro ter courtroom: the putative Red Brigade film of Moro in the People's Prison. According to Roberto Buzzatti, Moretti had told him about a closed circuit television monitor in the apartment where Moro had been kept prisoner. No one else had any knowledge about the matter. Morucci testified that he had never heard anything about it.[54] "Certainly, Morucci could be lying," President Sorichilli and Judge Perrone acknowledged, but Buzzatti's hearsay evidence did not give credence to the claims concerning such a film.[55]

Finally, the trial had revealed more details about the purpose of the Moro kidnapping. The Red Brigades "aimed at achieving the goals of the band—civil war and the subversion of democratic and constitutional institutions—through the masses who had to be educated about taking up arms and recruited after a consciousness-raising and proselytizing campaign."[56] Via Fani would inflame the nation, according to the Red Brigade plan, and during the fifty-five days they assigned the highest priority to the dissemination of propaganda. Lawyers and court officials had often asked why many of the most important figures in the Rome column of the Red Brigades, to say nothing of those in other columns, had not been directly involved in the kidnapping of Moro or in some related logistical activity. The answer had to do with two decisions made at the highest level of the organization: first, to saturate key sectors of Italian society with Red Brigade propaganda and second, to mount other terrorist operations in order to increase pressure on the state.

The propaganda campaign made relentless demands on Red Brigade manpower. The judges observed that "all of their communications were scattered in every Italian city. Hundreds and hundreds of copies were left in every part of the country."[57] In answering questions about their activities during the Moro kidnapping, many defendants had said that they did nothing but distribute leaflets *(il compito di volantinag- gio)*. Savasta, for example, had been sent to Milan with "packages of communications."[58] Rome was "inundated" by these volantini, espe- cially the university and the working-class quarters.

Their sentence in Moro ter reflected the seriousness with which they viewed the Red Brigade publicity campaign: "Those individuals who distributed these communications are guilty of being accessories in the kidnapping and murder of the Honorable Moro."[59] Leafleting might appear to be a relatively innocuous activity, but not while Moro was a kidnap victim, "who could be killed" at any time.[60] The judges found it difficult to draw clear lines between categories of guilt in this case. All the terrorists involved bore a grave moral responsibility for what happened to Moro, even those who merely slinked around university campuses with literature proclaiming the good news of revolution. The judges thought it worth noting that all the Red Brigade columns had declared themselves in favor of Moro's execution. Notwithstanding private reservations, the same pitiless verdict had been echoed in public by the imprisoned Curcio and Franceschini, still popularly referred to as terrorists with no blood on their hands.

Following the sentencing and the promulgation of the motivazione in Moro ter, a pervasive sense of disquiet about the case remained. People felt that despite all the trials and parliamentary investigations the truth was still not known. Instead, there was a Pirandellian suc- cession of truths, each packed with a political charge, competing in the arena of public opinion. There was still no consensus in the case, no sense that full justice had been done. The responsibility of the Red Brigades for the actual commission of the crime had been established irrefutably, but even before the end of Moro ter the publication of a sensational book about the Moro case had deepened the impression that P2 conspiracies were the real heart of the matter.

Sergio Flamigni's *Tela del ragno: il delitto Moro* was published in May 1988. Flamigni, a former PCI deputy and senator, had served on both the Moro and the P2 parliamentary commissions and had read thousands of pages of documents in the case. Not only had Flamigni heard witnesses testify before the two commissions; he also had the opportunity to participate in the cross-examination process. The veteran politician became consumed by the Moro case and zealously followed all of its developments. His book was enriched by privileged access to all the available sources as well as by lengthy private discussions with imprisoned terrorists.

Flamigni lambasted the government for its myriad failures in the Moro case, from via Fani and the manhunt to all the trials and parliamentary investigations. He scathingly rebuked the police for not following up the 18 March lead about a Red Brigade hideout on via Gradoli. The entire Moro case might have been cracked there and then, but a competent—let alone an exhaustive—investigation had not been undertaken. In explaining their conduct the police blamed bad luck. They offered the same explanation when questioned about some missing photographs of the via Fani attack. Gherardo Nucci, the husband of a journalist, shot a roll of film minutes after the ambush. He turned the film over to the authorities on 18 March, but it was immediately misplaced and never recovered.[61] This same fate befell numerous other documents in the case, including tapes of vitally important telephone conversations. Chance alone could not explain a pattern of negligence so complete that it appeared to follow a law of physics.

The author mocked the police for relying on mediums and clairvoyants during the Moro search. Valuable time and manpower were wasted this way. Seriously understaffed antiterrorist forces chased will-o-the-wisps while ignoring solid leads and misplacing the physical evidence on which a professional police investigation might have been based. All the paranormal information proved useless except, of course, to the men of P2, who controlled the police and the intelligence services. The pursuit of phantoms was more conducive to their covert end than serious police work would have been. For example, Morucci and Faranda long had been under suspicion but had not been placed under surveillance. Instead, the police put themselves under the guidance of spirit rappers and other experts in the arts of divination. Meanwhile, the two known subversives entrusted with the task of delivering Red Brigade communications during the Moro operation walked about Rome undisturbed and unnoticed by the police, while leads from another plane of existence claimed the undivided attention of the manhunt's organizers, Flamigni acidly observed.[62] According to him, Moro probably thought that by writing numerous letters he would give the police plenty of opportunities to detect the terrorist couriers. He could not have remained deluded for long. His bitterness at the end must have resulted from the demoralizing feeling that the effort to find him had been perfunctory—if not worse. Flamigni shared Moro's bitterness.

According to Flamigni, it was P2, with its far-flung network of support in official Rome and Washington, that sent the police down one blind alley after another. They wanted Moro to die and, at the same time, to use his kidnapping as a pretext for going beyond the constitutionally ordained order to the authoritarian state they desired. That the United States government, especially in the person of Henry Kissinger, contributed to both the prehistory and the history of the Moro case, Flamigni did not doubt. Key points of convergence existed between the political design of P2 and American policy in Italy. Both Gelli and Kissinger would have agreed that Moro served as the advance man for communism and might have led the Italians out of NATO and into the neutral camp. Alive, Moro would always be the man of risky initiatives; dead, he would take his opening to the Communists with him. There could be no doubt about which of these two outcomes Washington preferred.

La tela del ragno appealed to a wide reading public because of its sensational conjectures about the complicity of deviant elements in the state with the Red Brigades. Flamigni held that the former used the latter as a battering ram against Italy's democratic order. His thesis was not conceptually new, but Flamigni succeeded brilliantly at both summing up the case for fermezza and showing how that policy had been undermined by the very men in charge of its execution.[63] Fermezza was the only chance that Moro had, but it turned out to be a poor chance because of the P2 conspiracy. Flamigni hoped that the magistrates in charge of the Moro quater trial would undertake a serious investigation of all the lies, omissions, and transgressions recounted in *La tela del ragno*.

11

Moro Quater

To Tangentopoli

On 20 August 1990, when Judge Rosario Priore submitted his findings in the judicial inquiry for Moro quater, he had *La tela del ragno* very much in mind.[1] Flamigni's book had drawn attention to the uncertainties in the Moro case, but Priore wanted to make the opposite point. He emphatically stated that with the assistance of Morucci and Faranda it was now possible to explain virtually every detail of the Moro kidnapping and slaying. No further doubts could be entertained about the main sequence of events. All "those empty spaces" left over from previous judicial inquiries were now filled.[2]

Judge Priore dealt first with the via Fani attack. The judge confidently asserted that he had exhaustive answers to the questions of who had been present and what had been done by whom. Mario Moretti had driven the blue Fiat 126 that blocked the Moro entourage, and he had remained in his vehicle until the shooting was nearly over. In their white Fiat 128, Alvaro Loiacono and Alessio Casimirri had come in behind the Moro escort vehicle to close the trap. Barbara Balzerani had got out of Moretti's car and had taken up a position at the point where via Fani intersects via Stresa to block traffic there. Bruno Seghetti had driven the escape vehicle, a Fiat 132. The killers, who had been hiding behind the hedge of a nearby bar, were Valerio Morucci, Raffaele Fiore, Franco Bonisoli, and Prospero Gallinari. Armed with machine guns and pistols—some of which misfired—the Red Brigadists had held the decisive advantage of complete surprise.

Morucci and Fiore had killed Oreste Leonardi and Domenico Ricci in the Moro vehicle; immediately behind them, Bonisoli and Gallinari had wiped out Giulio Rivera, Raffaele Iozzino, and Francesco Zizzi. All four killers had worn bulletproof vests underneath their raincoats. There had been no Mafia "hit men," no superkillers or foreigners as various rumors had it. Moretti, Fiore, and Gallinari moved Moro to the escape vehicle; Moretti and Fiore made a second transfer of the kidnap victim to yet another vehicle, a little way from the scene of the kidnapping, and then Moretti drove it away.

Inside the People's Prison, at via Montalcini 8, Moretti had taken complete charge. Gallinari had been the jailer, but Moretti had interrogated the prisoner and had made all the decisions. He had chosen which letters would be sent through Morucci and Faranda and which would be kept in the Red Brigade archive. Moro quater had produced little new information, but in his "Sentenza" for the fase istruttoria of the trial Judge Priore wanted to reconstruct the entire story of the fifty-five days, to demonstrate just how much of it was beyond serious dispute. One of the few factual revelations to come out of Priore's investigation concerned the roles of Loiacono and Casimirri in the via Fani attack. Shortly after Morucci's testimony about them, Casimirri gave an interview to *La Famiglia Cristiana* in which he confirmed the accuracy of the new information.[3]

Certainty in the Moro case extended to the time he was killed, shortly before 8:30 A.M. on 9 May 1978, and to the exact route taken by Moretti and Gallinari in the famous red Renault. Staying on side streets wherever possible, they had arrived at Piazza Monte Savello, near the synagogue in the old Jewish Ghetto, where they parked the car. They walked a little ways and met Morucci and Seghetti, with whom they talked about the final part of the trip. In their Simca 1300 Morucci and Seghetti drove ahead of the Renault. The two cars had moved slowly through the dark narrow streets of the Ghetto. But for their gruesome cargo they could have been typical sightseers, appreciating Taddeo Landini's exquisite sixteenth-century Fountain of the Turtles in the Piazzetta Mattei before reaching the main thoroughfare of the via delle Botteghe Oscure. From this one-way street they turned right onto via Caetani. Morucci and Seghetti had to go almost to the end of via Caetani, practically to the door of the Biblioteca di Storia Moderna e Contemporanea at the end of the street, before they could find a parking space for the Renault behind them. The Simca 1300 quickly drove off, leaving three of the terrorists to walk across Piazza Lovatelli and then along via S. Angelo in Pescheria, eventually return-ing to Piazza Monte Savello where they separated.

On several crucial points Judge Priore openly criticized Flamigni's conspiracy thesis in the Moro case.[4] For six years, since the conclusion of the fase istruttoria for Moro ter, it should have been clear that via Montalcini 8 was the site of the People's Prison, but "notwithstanding the evidence" polemics had continued and become even more heated.[5] Flamigni had also claimed that another unnamed person had actually killed Moro, but Priore countered that with no evidence to support such a claim, the court would accept the reports of pentiti and disso-ciati alike on Prospero Gallinari's responsibility for the crime.[6] The police investigation did not give rise to a single serious legal concern in Judge Priore's ruling.

Flamigni's celebrated list of missing or misplaced or mutilated items of evidence shrank in significance, too, the more it became subjected to critical scrutiny. The famous roll of film shot in the immediate aftermath of via Fani and which had then disappeared had been examined by a magistrate attached to the investigation, who found it "useless."[7] Flamigni had imagined that only a conspiracy could ex-plain the disappearance of this evidence, but the photographs, taken from far away after everything was over, revealed nothing at all. Their very lack of importance led to an almost immediate loss of interest in them by the authorities, who might be forgiven their negligence amidst the thousands of pieces of evidence that came flooding into their midst.

What about Flamigni's claim that some telephone conversations the police had taped during the kidnapping had been tampered with? Judge Priore downplayed these allegations. Other explanations for the mishap, which had been suggested by experts in the field, could not be ruled out. Something as basic as faulty equipment might have been responsible for some of those gaps and garbled sections that had so stimulated Flamigni's imagination. Operator errors, too, occurred all the time in criminal investigations, and the Moro case was no excep-tion. In short, the causes of these particular problems could not be pinned down. Moreover, it was not reasonable to presume foul play on the part of the police just because a few tapes, out of the many thousands in their custody, were damaged. The judge added that, in any event, the Red Brigadists knew full well that their conversations were being taped and were smart enough not to reveal anything of importance. "Not a single intercepted [telephone] message ever furnished any useful information about the kidnappers, the location of the kidnapping, or any of the activities of the armed band."[8] The judge doubted very seriously that the damaged tapes contained any information worth the fuss Flamigni had raised.

On two other points prominently featured in *La tela del ragno*, Judge Priore sought to exert a calming influence. First, he praised the Comitato Esecutivo per i Servizi di Informazione e di Sicurezza for their cooperation in furnishing copious material upon his request and in facilitating the court's investigation. These documents proved that the Red Brigades had no connection with terrorist groups from other countries until after the Moro operation, when they "deprovincialized themselves."[9] Flamigni had maligned Italy's secret services by saying they had played an obstructionist role in the Moro manhunt and in the subsequent investigation of the case; Judge Priore could find no evidence for such a view.

Second, Judge Priore refused to express any alarm about P2. Much had been made about the presence of piduisti on the special crisis committee that met every day and sometimes twice a day at the Viminale, but the judge had found no proof of any irregularity. He did not exonerate P2, the exact character of which remained to be determined fully, but no substantiated instances of wrongdoing had come to light, either in previous investigations of the case or in the one just completed. In some of the more fantastic versions of the P2 connection in the Moro case Licio Gelli himself had been in attendance at the committee's meetings, but Judge Priore stated flatly that such visits had never occurred. On the basis of the evidence, he concluded that the committee members had gone about their task, consulting among themselves and with numerous experts in various fields as well as advising Minister of the Interior Cossiga, in strict accordance with their public charge. He could see no P2 conspiracy in the Moro case.[10]

Priore's was a well-reasoned decision, but hardly had it been published when the spectacular 9 October 1990 discovery of a cache of Moro letters and testimony from the People's Prison dramatically shifted perceptions of the case. Routine alterations in a Milan apartment on via Monte Nevoso, where the Red Brigades had kept their archive, resulted in this windfall of documents. While knocking down a wall, a workman found a box filled with 418 photocopied sheets of paper. In the same hiding place were some thirty detonators, numerous cartridges, a machine gun, a pistol, and sixty million lire. Thus ended one of the longest controversies in the Moro case, which had erupted after the via Monte Nevoso raid of October 1978. In its aftermath, the captured terrorists accused the carabinieri of stealing an undisclosed sum of money and documents without a word to the public. The discovery started a series of complicated overlapping and interlocking controversies over why these materials had not been discovered twelve years earlier and, of course, over what their true meaning was.

Judge Priore's summary of the case in Moro quater, a product of more than five years' work, suddenly seemed quite obsolete, and there was a feeling in the country that the investigation would have to start from zero again. A journalist put the matter this way: "With a rap on a plaster wall in the former hideout of the Red Brigades on via Monte Nevoso, a workman named Gennaro has at a stroke rendered ridiculous, incomplete, and insufficient four judicial inquests, three trials, and a parliamentary investigation."[11] All the doubts of the past, beginning with those of Leonardo Sciascia in *L'affaire Moro*, came bubbling to the surface of Italian public life.

To the end of his own life, in November of 1989, Sciascia had remained skeptical about the official explanations of Moro's murder. A little more than a year before his death he observed, "If I were still a parliamentary deputy I would return to investigate the Moro case, and whatever turned up would not amaze me."[12] Sciascia's thesis in *L'affaire Moro* and in his minority report for the Moro Commission in Parliament was that a full explanation of Italian terrorism would have to go beyond a mere analysis of the terrorists themselves. The Red Brigades were certainly sincere about their revolutionary project, but anyone who knew anything about Italian life realized that these "terrorists with weak minds" would not produce the "definitive chaos" that the country had experienced in the 1970s.[13] In other words, Sciascia believed that the Red Brigades had been manipulated from the start by forces inside and outside Italy interested in maintaining there a state of tension, of "confusion and insecurity."[14] The discovery on via Monte Nevoso seemed to strengthen this interpretation. Certainly, the conspiracy theory of which Sciascia had been a pioneering formulator commanded new respect after 9 October 1990.

In a widely quoted interview Alberto Franceschini asserted that the new Moro materials deepened his long-held suspicion about how the Red Brigades had been manipulated by the carabinieri and by secret service agents at home and abroad.[15] Among these last, the Israelis were high on his list of official establishment forces that welcomed the destabilizing activities of the Red Brigades. On the basis of his discussions with Mossad agents in the early 1970s, this founding father of Red Brigadism thought that Israel's actual foreign policy in the Mediterranean, as opposed to its declared policy there, was to promote as much instability as possible. The Israelis' purpose was to convince the United States that Israel was its one true ally in the region and therefore deserved unlimited financial and military support. Franceschini claimed to see a pattern of encouragement to the Red Brigades not only in the form of assistance actually proffered by the Israelis, presumably with the tacit approval of the CIA, but also in the reluctance of the carabinieri to wipe out the terrorists when they could have done so easily, especially during the early years. It was almost as though counterrevolutionary forces in Italy and abroad needed the Red Brigades to crush the entire left, which, incidentally, was pro-Arab as a rule on the Middle Eastern question—another reason the Israelis took a special interest in the Italian situation. "We were just a bunch of kids," Franceschini reminisced, and in retrospect he thought that such a crew of amateurs could not have inflicted the damage it did over a ten-year period without some discreet contributions from vastly more powerful forces whose interests the Red Brigades objectively furthered.[16]

Franceschini reflected on the Moro operation in the light of the recent revelations from Milan. Could we of the Red Brigades, he speculated, have carried out this operation from via Fani to via Caetani without some assistance, if only in the form of a wink and a nod at crucial moments by the investigating authorities? The organization was not all that efficient; indeed, "the myth of Red Brigade power had been created artificially" by the media in the service of the political establishment.[17] He had to believe—and perhaps a larger segment of the population than ever before agreed with him—that "they" let the Red Brigades get away with the crime because it was in their political interest to do so. Reticence on the part of terrorist-hating officialdom had been a characteristic feature of all the trials and parliamentary inquiries, because from the beginning "there was the desire not to get to the bottom of these matters."[18]

At the other extreme in Italian politics, Giulio Andreotti also joined the renewed speculations about plots. He had always resisted that temptation in the past, but on national television the Prime Minister said it was impossible for him to imagine that the recently discovered papers could have been in the via Monte Nevoso apartment since 1978. A *manona* ("big hand") had in all probability placed them there at a moment when their discovery would do the most harm.[19] Moreover, Andreotti could not free himself of the suspicion that someone was still holding the original Moro materials until the moment was propitious for another shock to the Italian political system. Andreotti's image of a "big hand" was a completely transparent reference to Bettino Craxi, who earlier had speculated about a *manina*, or "little hand,"—referring to Andreotti without mentioning him by name—meddling in this latest development in the Moro case.[20] It would be difficult to recall a more vapid or demeaning exchange than theirs in the entire tragic history of the Moro case.[21]

For some two weeks after the initial burst of publicity, daily bomb-shells went off in the media about the contents of the Moro *carteggio*, as these papers came to be called. On the receiving end of the flak was the Christian Democratic party. Especially hard-hit was Francesco Cossiga, now President of the Republic, once again, as in the 1977 student demonstrations, called "Kossiga," enemy of the People. Things eventually got so bad that Arnaldo Forlani, the party secretary, pub-licly complained about a plot against Christian Democracy—a charge he quickly withdrew when members of his own party criticized him for abusing the term.[22] Even in retreat Forlani contended that there was at least an "orchestration" against his party.

On 24 October 1990 the Italian people could read for themselves what Moro had written about his plight and his party, because on that day *l'Unità* published virtually the entire carteggio. Only a few private letters to the family were left out. That issue of the Communist party's newspaper had a seismic effect on the country's political landscape.

L'Unità published the Moro letters and testimony in the same "strange disorder in which the material had been found."[23] It was impossible to say how complete these papers were and what omissions or manipulations might have been involved, but here the reader would find, in writing "at times clear and orderly, at times tormented and incomprehensible," Moro's last tender farewells to his family and friends as well as his angry leave-taking of the Christian Democratic party and of "a regime that is corrupting and exhausting itself."[24] These had been the basic themes of previously published Moro letters and testimony, but the new details and expressions of agony, bitterness, and feelings of betrayal weighed heavily on the public consciousness.

Coming under a steadily mounting barrage of invective from the very first page of the carteggio were Andreotti, Cossiga, Fanfani, Zaccagnini, Piccoli, and Galloni—the foremost chiefs of the party. Moro castigated them all. He condemned Andreotti—"to our misfortune and the misfortune of the country . . . the head of the government"—as a corrupt, cynical protector of Sindona and a spirit sympathetic to all the most disgusting elements in Italian political life.[25] A man of "no human fervor" or "goodness, wisdom [and] flexibility," Andreotti was the embodiment of DC collusion with the Mafia.[26]

One by one, Moro slashed away at the other pillars of Christian Democracy. Despite his experience in politics, Cossiga had shown himself to be lacking the necessary independence of mind and spirit required in a truly effective leader. Moro ranked him far below Andreotti and Berlinguer, even accusing him of having become "hypnotized" by the latter, a fellow Sardinian.[27] According to Moro, Cossiga was one of those talented but essentially weak men who needed the guidance of a stronger personality to get anything done. Fanfani, too, had great gifts as a leader, but over the decades the intellectual basis of his political ideas had become so obscure that it might be said not to exist any longer, its place taken by naked ambition.[28] For Zaccagnini, Piccoli, and Galloni the prisoner saved some of his harshest condemnations. Zaccagnini had been his disciple and friend, but he was also "the worst secretary" the DC ever had.[29] Having begged Moro to take the party presidency at a time when he wanted to retire from public life, Zaccagnini bore a crushing burden of guilt for doing nothing to save his chief. In a letter to "Zac," Moro wondered if it were "possible that you are all agreed in wanting my death for a presumed reason of state . . . almost as a solution for all the problems in the country."[30] Piccoli he dismissed as one who "always errs and always will err because he is by nature called to error."[31] Galloni's reputation took this blast from Moro: he has "a Jesuitical face that knows everything but in knowing everything he knows nothing of life and of love."[32]

Moro despised these false friends and treacherous colleagues now: "I have an immense pleasure in having lost you, and I hope that you lose yourselves with the same joy with which I have lost you."[33] Because of his "complete incompatibility with the Christian Democratic party" he formally resigned from the organization. It was the death speech of Mercutio in *Romeo and Juliet*, with all that character's spite concentrated on one house. Moro thought that his blood, which they had chosen to shed, would fall on all of them now. To his wife he wrote that these partisans of the hard line were the real villains in his tragedy, for they led him "to certain death."[34]

Not content to condemn only contemporary Christian Democratic leaders, Moro went on to berate the party's dead heroes as well. He charged that the greatest leader of them all, Alcide De Gasperi, had handed over Italy to American-controlled NATO during the post-World War II period. Moro had shared the fears of his left-wing friends within the DC about Italy's effective loss of independence on all serious foreign policy matters in exchange for the investment capital the country needed to recover from the lost war as well as a steady flow of money from Washington into party coffers.

Only when Moro himself took power, however, did he discover what Italy's relationship with the United States actually entailed. The crucial issue was always the Middle East no matter what else might be going on in the world. For Moro it was plain enough: the United States expected and demanded that Italy support Israel with no questions asked. Moro found it increasingly difficult to do what the United States asked, not only for practical political and economic reasons, but for moral reasons as well. That the Palestinian people wanted their own country was neither "shocking" nor "criminal"; these words might better be used to describe America's demands concerning Italian attitudes about the Middle East. After Italy's policy toward the Middle East became more "calibrated" to the realities of the region, the United States lost patience with its ally; this was especially true when American foreign policy lay under the control of Henry Kissinger, "who cultivated an animosity for the Italian role and for me personally."[35] The relationship between these two men deteriorated completely when Moro embraced the "historic compromise" opening to the Communist party.

The behavior of American ambassadors to Italy was indicative of the true nature of the relationship between the two countries. Moro had minimal dealings with Graham Martin, whose interference in Italian political life, as reported by the Pike Commission, included financial support of the Neofascists. He knew John Volpe ("a crude anticommunist") much better, although it became obvious to him that the ambassador had received directions from Kissinger to freeze out Moro as much as possible and to work instead with more pliant DC leaders, eager to do Washington's bidding on all key questions.[36] Moro could always tell what his standing in Washington was by the number of invitations he received to the embassy on via Veneto.

With Richard Gardner, though, the most cultivated and refined of all the American ambassadors Moro knew, Washington found a highly able interpreter of its Italian policy of "non-interference and non-indifference."[37] Gardner's very reticence on exactly what "non-indifference" meant was an eloquent commentary on how power politics American style worked. In general, Gardner gave him the impression of being interested in Italy's politics only as a detail in a wider strategy. For Washington, evidently, Italy was a part of the world they thought was theirs to control on all matters to which they were not "indifferent," such as the Middle East and the opening to the Communists. Moro's fall from grace in Washington came as a consequence of the temerity he showed in challenging the imperialist assumptions of America's policy in Italy.

The Red Brigades had questioned Moro specifically about the country's right-wing terror bombings, especially the Piazza Fontana massacre in December 1969, and an entire section of the carteggio was entitled "All I know about the mysteries of the massacres."[38] The argument here was particularly hard to follow because he began the section with a long, rambling disclaimer about how his power in the DC was actually much smaller than the media made it out to be. As the editors of *l'Unità* had warned, there were problems with pagination and continuity of the papers.

When he got to the point, Moro vividly described the sensation of horror he experienced at the moment when "the terrible news" of Piazza Fontana reached him.[39] He immediately grasped the full seriousness and the distinctive political character of that hideous crime. Not for a moment did he accept the first official explanation of Piazza Fontana, that it was the work of anarchists. Moro had an intuitive understanding of the bombing as a radical right-wing attack on Italy's democracy, and in the carteggio he used the phrase *le trame nere*, or "the black plots."[40] He did not doubt that the Piazza Fontana attack had been supported by foreign elements eager to destabilize Italy. Moro surmised that foreign right-wingers had more to gain from such an outcome in Italy than their Italian counterparts, but in all probability, he wrote, some kind of alliance between Italian and outside intelligence agencies had produced Piazza Fontana. The world of espionage and counterespionage, which with astounding euphemism went by the name of "intelligence," produced monsters of inhumanity from whom any enormity might be expected.

Moro wanted to clear the DC of direct responsibility for Piazza Fontana, but at the same time there were "sections, areas, organs" of the party that did not face this tragedy "with the necessary clarity and firmness."[41] Here he obviously had Andreotti chiefly in mind, for in the preceding paragraph Moro described him as the eternal guiding spirit of Italy's secret services who moved easily in an environment dominated by the CIA. Andreotti was the man "always in power."[42]

Andreotti reflected the mainline DC reaction to the carteggio when he professed to be unmoved and even unconcerned by those attacks, which came from Moro while terrorists had a gun to his head.[43] He claimed that nothing fundamentally new had emerged from the via Monte Nevoso cache of papers. Yes, now all the world could hear once again what a viper Andreotti was, but could someone please explain why, if he was the incarnation of everything detestable in Italian political life, Moro personally had chosen him to be the leader of the national unity government in March 1978? Here was one of those obdurate facts that stood in the way of the facile conspiracy theories offered by credulous or prejudiced souls foolishly hoping to destroy him with the mostly vague accusations of an obviously terrorized man, whose forty years of public life contradicted the "testament" of via Monte Nevoso.

Of course Christian Democracy's enemies relished the latest "scandal," but Andreotti very much doubted that the repetition of old canards, here and there embellished with a novel phrase or image, would produce any lasting damage. He could see nothing of importance in the carteggio except for the opportunity it gave to the malcontents to rehearse their grievances against the DC. Nearly half a century in Italian political life had taught him the virtue of patience. The via Monte Nevoso scandal would pass, and people would realize how perfectly ludicrous it was to take at face value Moro's annihilating criticism of the DC from the People's Prison. Moro *was* the DC, and it was impossible to think of the party as it had developed through thirty years of history without placing him at the very center of it. His sweeping condemnation of everyone in the DC and everything done by the DC had to be dismissed by any honest person as a grotesque caricature in which Moro himself could never have believed, although the party's congenital enemies naturally would take it for gospel.

Mario Moretti also found himself on the defensive following *l'Unità*'s publication of the via Monte Nevoso letters and testament. In a 15 December 1990 interview for the magazine *Sabato*, Alberto Franceschini professed to be shocked that such important disclosures about the sinister workings of the Christian Democratic regime had not been made public by the Red Brigades.[44] Moretti had told everyone that the trial in the People's Prison had not resulted in anything worth printing, but now Franceschini had to wonder what the interrogator's true motive had been in May 1978. The journalist interviewing him, Rocco Tolfa, then observed that for a long time there had been suspicions that Moretti was a "spy"; this might explain why Moro's extremely damaging revelations about the CIA's activities in Italy as well as covert operations by NATO there had remained a secret.[45]

Tolfa's speculations seemed to be the romance of Italian terrorism rather than its history. Indeed, Moretti already had answered these charges, in a December 1984 interview with Giorgio Bocca, when he said that the Red Brigades had not organized the Moro operation to discover the scandals of the Christian Democratic party: "those [the scandals] did not have to be discovered [for] all Italy knows them; they are, so to speak, routine, ordinary."[46] In taking Moro, the Red Brigades had a completely different objective: to call the revolutionary left in Italy to arms. For such an audience to have heard more incriminating details about DC corruption and treason would have been an exercise in redundancy, and therefore Moretti found nothing new or damaging in Moro's testimony.

Moretti's interpretation of the carteggio did not prevent the PCI's Achille Occhetto from publicly expressing his belief that the Moro operation was orchestrated by "users" *(utilizzatori)* and performed by the "used" *(utilizzati)*.[47] Thus, he concurred with Franceschini that the Red Brigades had been "piloted" by an ensemble of conspiratorial forces, including secret service agencies both domestic and foreign: "that occult system on which those who govern us do not want to shed light."[48]

What struck Franceschini so forcefully were Moro's specific references to "parallel" military forces, connected with NATO, but out of the public eye. Before long, all Italy was making connections between the via Monte Nevoso papers and an alarming government scandal over Operation Gladio, which for some months had been the subject of an investigation by Felice Casson, a Venetian judge. He made public the existence of a secret military operation, ostensibly conceived in the late 1950s to give the country another element of protection against Soviet invasion. In the Cold War context of the 1950s and 1960s, Gladio could have been a normal part of Italy's defense establishment. Indeed, Gladio-like operations had been in place all over NATO-controlled Europe. Some commentators, such as Bettino Craxi, wondered how serious it was: "I've tried to imagine Italy occupied [by the Red Army] and how the five hundred men of 'Gladio' would have liberated the country."[49] His imagination could not quite take in such a prospect: Gladio was a "little thing," certainly not an issue over which a government should fall. Nevertheless, against the long-ago sponsors of the *gladiatori* a chorus of faultfinders vehemently demanded justice.

Prime Minister Andreotti quickly censured those who wanted to use Gladio as a club against his government. He insisted that this organization had been completely legal, and given the threat that communism posed at the time, it was an understandable answer to quite legitimate fears.[50] Andreotti cited the present outcry as another example of *dietrologia*, or reading the past in the light of present knowledge and opinions. As usual, the proponents of conspiracy claimed too much. To argue that Gladio proved how for forty years Italy had been a fictitious democracy dominated by antidemocratic forces at home and in Washington was hardly more than a warmed-over helping of the standard fare fed to the Italian people by the left. Individuals who had somehow subsisted without proper mental nourishment would inevitably begin to drool over Gladio, but it was a confection that could only reinforce their disorder.

To *Il Popolo*, the official newspaper of the DC, the attack on the party over Gladio proceeded from the mentality of dishonesty and distortion the PCI had always displayed in its dealings with the Christian Democrats. Paolo Cabras, a former editor of the newspaper, commented that to hear certain people on the left talk—whether about Gladio or any other "mystery" of the day including the Moro case—one might conclude that Christian Democratic-run Italy was a vast concentration camp or at the very least a place where no real freedom existed.[51] According to such critics, who for so long and with such baleful results had exerted an influence on Italian cultural and political life out of all proportion to their real worth and reliability, the DC amounted to little more than a front concealing the Mafia and deviant secret service operatives, propped up by police and military forces crawling with traitors. The left-wing fairy tale of these critics was the first principle of politics for a large clan of opinion makers in Italy, relentlessly waging a vendetta against the DC. The stated issue of their attacks, such as Gladio or the Moro case, was only a pretext; the real issue always remained Christian Democracy itself.

Cabras wanted the world to remember that under the Christian Democrats Italy had become one of the most advanced and richest societies in the world. The party's real achievements, for which it never received adequate credit, had resulted not from plots and the machinations of occult powers, as left-wing intellectuals fervently believed with a kind of touching piety, but from a four-decade-long mandate from the Italian people themselves. One could only wonder what opportunity the people, not to mention opposition intellectuals, would have had to express themselves in a state run by Italian Communists, who long after World War II were still taking their cue from Stalin. Communism had proved to be one of the sorriest legacies of the twentieth century, but in the amazing world of Italian politics it was Christian Democracy that aroused the dire suspicion of intellectuals.

Despite reassuring press releases from the government and its supporters that Gladio was nothing more than an administrative detail of the Cold War, the feeling grew that this secret operation typified the "hidden government" (sottogoverno) of a Christian Democratic regime suffering once again from a visitation by Moro's ghost. Indeed, in the rancorous debate over Gladio, the via Monte Nevoso papers of Moro were frequently cited as a source of high historical value. Throughout the fall of 1990 and the early winter of 1991, the DC "nomenklatura," as the party establishment was disparagingly referred to, took one punishing blow after another. Further dismaying revelations about Gladio continued to appear in the press. This hidden parallel structure of the military secret services, it was learned, had operated without the knowledge of Parliament and of various defense ministers and prime ministers. While Andreotti, Cossiga, Cabras, and other notables were right to insist that their party could not be equated with Gladio (Moro had made the same kind of argument during the Lockheed scandal of the 1970s), the issue appeared to many in Italy to be a serious matter.

The existence of this secret formation raised deeply disturbing questions about the real character of Italian democracy.

Early in December, protest demonstrators commemorated the twenty-first anniversary of the still unsolved Piazza Fontana massacre, which they denounced as the archetypal *strage di stato*, or "massacre by the state." The thousands of people demonstrating in Rome, Bologna, Milan, and Florence believed there had been secret service and police involvement in the Milan crime. Higher powers in the Mafia, P2, and the CIA no doubt had made their wishes known to "Kossiga" and Andreotti, who then had set their "intelligence" operatives to work. Graffiti on a wall in Rome summed up the feelings of these contentious spirits: "DC = forty years of terrorism." In other words, the country's real terrorists could be found in the Quirinale and Palazzo Chigi. For these protestors, Gladio had laid bare the fundamentals of democracy Italian style.

When Senator Libero Gualtieri, the president of Parliament's commission on terrorist massacres, revealed that Operation Gladio had been part of "Piano Solo"—the notorious right-wing coup plot by General De Lorenzo in 1964—antigovernment forces increased their attack. Here was more proof, they proclaimed, that an illegal and treasonous coalition of right-wing elements, including government agencies and P2, had long been at work trying to undermine the Republic. The most recent reports from Montecitorio confirmed and dramatically darkened the image of an irredeemably corrupt and godforsaken DC. Now even the Moro case itself, along with the Piazza Fontana bombing, the Bologna train station massacre, and all the other unsolved crimes of the era might turn out to be interconnected plots of right-wing subversives and their protectors in the government.

No wonder Arnaldo Forlani, the DC secretary, exasperatedly railed against a "plot" that he saw forming against his party. Everyone else in Italian politics could escape life's complicated realities by taking refuge in a beautifully simple and emotionally satisfying world of melodramatic conspiracies. Expressing the siege mentality of his party, Forlani sought the same asylum. In other words, Gladio might reveal some disagreeable truths about Cold War Italy, but to see in this squalid little affair the paramount symbol of Christian Democracy was simply characteristic of the vehement prejudice that the party's many enemies, at home and abroad, brought to every discussion of Italian politics.

About the Moro case, the certainties of 20 August 1990, as expressed in Judge Priore's sentence for Moro quater, had dissolved. By the usual standards of the Moro case, each legal stage of which had generated vast quantities of documentation, Judge Priore had composed a masterpiece of succinct judicial reasoning about what could be taken for fact in the tragic events of 16 March to 9 May 1978. In 174 pages he advanced an argument that contested the conspiracy theory of Sergio Flamigni and others. Lacunae existed and shadows remained here and there, but whereas Flamigni saw only shadow, Judge Priore saw mainly light.

After the sensational discoveries of via Monte Nevoso Priore's sober findings could hardly compete with newspaper headlines about "piloted" Red Brigadists or what the imprisoned Moro had to say about Gladio, the secret services, and the knaves in his own party. The trial phase of Moro quater might yet fully justify the judge's conclusions in his sentence, but on 18 December 1990 he expressed some frustration about trying to keep up with this case. "Things keep coming out of the blue," he lamented.[52] "Will this case never end," he was asked. Taking a long meditative puff on his cigar, this elegant, soft-spoken yet intense man looked around his enormous Tribunale di Roma office and answered, "Perhaps never."[53]

Almost exactly one year later, President Severino Santiapichi called the court to order in Moro quater. This time no one sat in the public gallery. Apart from those who had to be present at the Foro Italico courtroom, not a single person came to watch the trial. "Evidently," President Santiapichi wrote in a letter the next day, "for different and well-founded reasons, interest [in the case] has been diminishing."[54] Actually, people continued to be interested in the case, if not in this particular trial. For example, on 16 January 1992 the newspapers carried reports about the progress of a new judicial investigation headed by Judge Luigi de Ficchy and based on testimony given by criminals in other trials as well as by witnesses before Parliament's commission on massacres. Once again some "clamorous revelations" were promised, but the reporter who used this phrase later narrowed it down to new information possibly forthcoming about the number of Red Brigadists in the People's Prison.[55] There might have been a fourth person in addition to the three whose identity had been established. "We know 90 percent of what happened to Moro, and we are only talking now about the remaining 10 percent," this long-time observer

of the case explained.[56] Judge De Ficchy would not talk about percent-
ages, but he did say that a few points in the case required further
clarification, including the possibility of a fourth terrorist in the People's Prison. His own investigation remained at a preliminary stage.
He could not say where it might lead, but certainly there were no
revelations, sensational or otherwise, to report as yet.[57]

On 23 January 1992, Moro quater resumed after the long holiday
recess. It was cold and almost completely overcast in Rome. A policeman outside the Foro Italico courtroom directed visitors to the public
entrance on one side of the building. He still worried about the possibility of an attack by the Red Brigades on the Foro Italico building
itself. "There is always a danger with them," he said. At the public
entrance, another policeman opened the door for the small group of
onlookers that included this historian.

The lawyers—nearly half of them women—began to arrive soon
afterwards. Microphones had been set up only on the first three of ten
tables in the lawyers' section, and that was more than sufficient. Only
three people sat in the public gallery. A radio reporter and a newspaperman sat next to the technician in the section reserved for the media.
The so-called trial-of-the-century in Italy had left this city of nearly
four million people completely cold by now.

Two defendants, preceded and followed by carabinieri, entered the
second prisoner cage closest to the bench. Antonio Fosso and Sandro
Padula, short, slight, and unkempt-looking, had committed murder
and robbery in the 14 February 1987 postal truck attack on via dei
Prati dei Papa in Rome. They had nothing to do with the Moro case,
but the court was considering their crimes along with others by the Red
Brigades.

President Santiapichi and a train of people, including popular
judges and court officials, entered the courtroom at 10:40 A.M., about
an hour and a half after the announced starting time of the session. A
lawyer rose to lodge a complaint about procedure, and President
Santiapichi immediately announced that the court would recess temporarily while the matter was discussed in an adjoining chamber. Ten
or fifteen minutes later President Santiapichi and the others returned,
but another lawyer also raised procedural objections. For the next five
minutes the President read something from a book in a low inaudible
voice, a performance that evidently satisfied all concerned sufficiently
to permit the trial to continue.

Annunziata Francola, a dark petite woman who appeared to be in her mid thirties, was called to the witness chair. A University of Rome architecture student and an alumna of Unità Comuniste Combattenti before joining the Red Brigades and becoming an active recruiter in the MPRO as well as a murderess, Francola was now cooperating with the law as a dissociata. Public Minister Antonio Marini did most of the questioning. She could tell him nothing at firsthand about the Moro kidnapping and murder because her membership in the Red Brigades did not commence until after the summer of 1978. Marini wanted to know about her background, but Francola hardly had begun to respond when one of the female lawyers objected to any further questioning because this witness was not connected in any way to the Moro case. Her objection provoked a loud blast of verbal abuse from Marini. President Santiapichi later smilingly explained that shouting of this kind is routine and not taken seriously by anybody.[58]

Francola, speaking in a halting manner that almost made her sound like a foreigner, described the standard Red Brigadist ideological itinerary. Revolutionary groups had been her world. One of them she talked about in detail. This was the Unità Comuniste Combattenti that for her had served as a passageway to the Red Brigades. Francola's memory failed her, however, on the one question that most interested Marini: when did she leave the UCC? Francola could not remember, but it was before the Moro kidnapping. During the Moro operation she had been between groups. The public minister had no further questions. President Santiapichi summed up her testimony: "Well, you did not know anything, then." "No," she agreed.

After Francola's departure from the witness chair, President Santiapichi announced that because of other more pressing cases the next session in Moro quater would be postponed until 11 March 1992.[59] He and the other judges rose and walked out. The lawyers gathered their papers and singly or in small groups followed. The entire session, including all the interruptions, had lasted little more than an hour. The trial phase of Moro quater appeared to have reached an early dead end, scarcely of concern even to the people immediately involved in these proceedings, but, as so often in the past, interest in the case quickened as a result of developments taking place outside the courtroom.

12

Moro Quater, Tangentopoli, and Giulio Andreotti

The Moro quater trial virtually disappeared from public notice. To infer from the newspaper accounts, it was as though President Santiapichi and the other judges had gone on an extended holiday. Prolonged by many delays and postponements, the trial did not end until December 1994. The historian who had visited the Moro quater courtroom on 23 January 1992 revisited it on 10 January 1994. The scene was even more desolate than before with fewer lawyers, no prisoners, and a completely empty public gallery. And yet, in the interval, momentous historical events had occurred in the Moro murder case, against a backdrop of revolutionary change in Italy.

The change, which is of fundamental importance in understanding the events, came about partly because of a political and economic scandal known as Tangentopoli. In February 1992 judicial authorities began to unearth a gigantic network of bribe-giving businessmen and bribe-taking politicians. Over the next two years more than 4,000 individuals would be indicted. Nearly all of the top politicians in the major governing parties went down in the scandal, including Bettino Craxi of the PSI and Arnaldo Forlani of the DC. Numerous leaders of the smaller parties in the long-standing *pentapartito* coalition, most notably the well-respected secretary of the Republican party, Giorgio La Malfa, saw their careers founder. One hundred and thirty members of Parliament would be implicated in Tangentopoli, and the investigation is still far from complete.

The judicial investigators accused these politicians of receiving illegal campaign subsidies, kickbacks *(tangenti)*, and other favors from construction magnates, chairmen of the state-run corporations, and executives in the private sector. No public works project could be undertaken without tangenti being paid all along the line. Turin's Einaudi Institute estimated that corruption had cost the Italian economy 6.1 trillion lire (4.1 billion dollars) annually for the past decade.[1] The corruption had added as much as 15 percent to the nation's debt, which in 1993 totaled 105 percent of Italy's gross national product. State-run companies, which controlled half of the Italian economy, reeked of these practices. Bogus jobs and inefficient companies had been created and were kept in existence for political reasons alone. The indictment of chief officers of major companies such as Fiat and Olivetti demonstrated that Tangentopoli had corrupted the entire economy.

Tangentopoli was neither new in Italy nor unique to Italy. Political corruption did not begin with the Christian Democrats. Italian history from unification to the present is full of episodes that illuminate the dark side of representative political institutions, where money talks louder than principles. In the 1870s the poet Giosué Carducci thundered against "this Italy whose history is the daily chronicle of thefts, this Italy that believes in nothing but gold."[2] The notorious Banca Romana scandals of the 1890s bear a close resemblance to today's Tangentopoli. Over time, *bustarelle*—money-filled envelopes—have been replaced by suitcases filled with money, but corruption in Rome is a very old theme. The only truly novel aspect of the present situation, apart from the scale of things, is the unprecedented publicity available through the modern media, and this factor ineluctably becomes a leavening element of any story they emphasize.

The problem is not limited to Italy; many democratic governments today are facing a crisis of credibility. The degradation of the democratic governing process is the greatest remaining threat to the idea of democracy, and corruption takes endless forms. To cite an example close at hand, it would be very surprising if US leaders had accumulated the country's four-trillion-dollar national debt by entirely honest means or with eyes sharply focused on the common good of the American people. Corruption in the military-industrial complex and the ignoble practices of foreign and domestic lobbyists have also contributed to our acute insolvency and widespread cynicism about politics. Scandals of a similar nature are rife in Japan, France, Germany, and other advanced nations. At worst, the Italian situation is only an extreme case of a quite common problem: how to insulate democratically elected leaders from the relentless and corrupting pressures of fundraising and related political activities.

By themselves the scandals would not have destroyed the Italian political establishment, but their timing was fatal. They occurred during the immediate aftermath of communism's nearly absolute destruction in Europe and the end of the Cold War. For more than fifty years after World War II, Italian political life had been thoroughly conditioned by the Cold War. American power in the synchronized forms of money, military protection, and advice had helped to shape this system along the anticommunist line that it took. From the strategic viewpoint of Washington, Moro's moderate policies regarding the Communist party seemed either stupidly or wickedly perverse. In retrospect, though, it is clear that Moro, and not the government in Washington, understood and cared about the long-term problems of his people.

Moro could see something like the Tangentopoli crash coming. He divined its inevitability from his understanding of human nature and history. The interviews and speeches he gave in his last years are filled with warnings about just this kind of catastrophe awaiting the Christian Democrats. At the same time, he always stoutly defended his party against the critics of the left and the right, who charged that Christian Democracy represented and was representative of the most squalid practices in Italian political life. Its political adversaries habitually denounced the DC for corruption, for having ties to the Mafia, and for generally maintaining a low moral tone in Italian civic life. In repelling these attacks as coarse and politically motivated oversimplifications of Italy's complex Cold War history, Moro hotly argued that Christian Democracy was more than the sum of its failings. Its solid and even heroic achievements could not be denied by any fair-minded person.

Nevertheless, Moro knew that many of the charges against his party were true. How could it be otherwise in a de facto single party state? Corruption did become a way of life in Italian politics, the influence of the Mafia in Rome did grow, and the moral tone in civic life did inspire the widespread cynicism that, eventually, would turn into the national revulsion inspired by Tangentopoli. Moro was trying to head off this debacle by creating an effective democracy in Italy: a bi-polar system of majority and opposition groups that would follow each other in power and help to keep each other honest. There is a grandeur in his failure because, almost alone in the political establishment, he understood its fundamentally abnormal nature and was prepared to lead a campaign to normalize it within the limits of Italy's political realities. After Moro's death the logic of Cold War anticommunism was triumphantly reasserted in Italy, the Communists were frozen out, and the system's worst defects became magnified. Nobody, not even Moro, thought that the historic compromise would be a panacea, but it is difficult to see how things could have turned out worse for the badly battered and now renamed Christian Democratic party (Partito Popolare Italiano) if his ideas had been given a thorough testing.

With the collapse of communism and the end of the Cold War, symbolized in Italy by the breakup of the Italian Communist party and its re-emergence as the Democratic Party of the Left, the purpose of Italy's one-party system vanished. All that remained were that system's expensive and outrageous defects. Nearly every day for more than two years front-page articles broadcast the story of Tangentopoli, with its thousands of instances of illegality and dishonesty, high and low. It was a national drama heightened by televised courtroom scenes, celebrity suicides, and showdowns at the polls ending in defeat for the mainstream traditional parties. A referendum vote in April 1993 resulted in a fundamental alteration of the way the Italians elected their political representatives, giving more power to the people while taking it away from the party secretaries, by then designated by the public as the number one evildoers of Tangentopoli. A mood reminiscent of the antifascist fury of 1945 gripped the Italians, and at the polls the Christian Democrats and the Socialists suffered a symbolic version of Mussolini's fate.

During 1992 and the early months of 1993 the list of marked Christian Democratic leaders—individuals who had been notified through an *avviso di garanzia* that they were under investigation by the Tangentopoli judges—included some of the party's most illustrious names. One name was conspicuous by its absence: Giulio Andreotti, who in 1992 became the sixth longest-serving Prime Minister in Italian history. Precisely because of his unsavory reputation, many observers thought that he would be among the first to be implicated, but after more than a year of Tangentopoli investigations he continued his political activities undisturbed. A Senator for Life in Rome, Andreotti lived up to the name the media had given him: *divo* Giulio, which could mean Giulio the star or the divine Giulio, and his public image contained elements of both meanings. He remained the most popular politician in Italy, the author of best-selling books of political commentary and reminiscences, and a much sought-after television guest and subject for newspaper and magazine interviews. Asked how he had come through the Tangentopoli storm while his colleagues all around him had been lost, he replied with typical Andreottian jauntiness that by good fortune he had never been secretary of the DC and had not been assigned fund-raising responsibilities. Andreotti smiled when he said this and seemed to be enjoying himself as he toyed with reporters. One of the very few Christian Democrats in an expansive frame of mind, he liked to tell interviewers that God had been kind to him.

Repeatedly accused of wrongdoing over the years, Andreotti always had slipped off the hook. In the Tangentopoli scandal he did not even have to go through the motions of wriggling. Of course people continued to suspect him, but Andreotti liked to say that he was the eternal Italian scapegoat. "They would have blamed me for the Punic Wars but for the inconvenient date of my birth," was a familiar Andreotti line. In the spring of 1993 Tangentopoli appeared to be like all the previous political crises in his life: a fire through which he would pass unharmed.

Appearances deceived him, and Andreotti's political career ended with shocking swiftness in 1993. Overnight he went from being the godlike Giulio to being just another politician with his avviso di garanzia. He did not fall because of Tangentopoli, although without the shock of that scandal to the Italian political system as a whole, it is doubtful that Andreotti would have been as vulnerable as he was to the blows that crushed his reputation in the spring and summer of 1993. His nemesis was Moro.

In April of that year judicial authorities in Palermo and Rome announced that eight Mafia pentiti had accused Andreotti of collusion with organized crime, and their testimony included crucial references to the Moro case. The story of his links to the Mafia was not new. He had been accused of having criminal associations many times before. For example, Nando Dalla Chiesa, the son of the slain carabiniere general, pilloried Andreotti in *Delitto imperfetto: il generale, la mafia, la società italiana* (1984). The Andreotti faction in the DC drew most of its strength from Sicily, and Dalla Chiesa quoted his father in describing them as "the most polluted political family of the place."[3] The *andreottiani* of Sicily were in with the Mafia up to their necks, according to General Dalla Chiesa. Shortly before his departure for Sicily as the prefect of Palermo, General Dalla Chiesa told Andreotti that his Sicilian associates were corrupt and warned that he would attack them. In his diary the general wrote that upon hearing this Andreotti "went white."[4] Later he told his son that Andreotti was "too compromised" and that in the state's war against the Mafia he played a "double game."[5] Nando Dalla Chiesa believed that this "letter of intent" most probably had brought about his father's death. He encouraged readers of *Delitto imperfetto* to conclude that Andreotti had made nefarious use of the information imprudently and ingenuously provided by the general. Nando Dalla Chiesa did not know the details of what happened next or the content of any communications between Rome and Palermo, but the motive for his father's murder seemed obvious to him: as the political godfather for the Mafia, Andreotti had let the general's intentions be known, whereupon a hit-team of gangsters killed him, his young wife, and their security guard on the streets of Palermo in 1982.

In response, with a smile and a quip at the ready, Andreotti struck his trademark pose and softly asked what real evidence there was for any of these charges. He and the general had been close associates during the war on terrorism and had become friends. They admired each other. The historical record would bear him out on this, should it ever come to a matter of furnishing documents. As usual, all that his adversaries had were inspired but unsupported guesses. Politically motivated individuals such as Nando Dalla Chiesa could yammer all they liked, but they were not going to bring him down with vehemence alone, he coolly affirmed.[6] And so it was. The divo Giulio years at their gaudiest lay ahead as he formed his sixth and seventh governments, remaining for the rest of the 1980s and into the 1990s Italy's most important political figure.

Nando Dalla Chiesa's severe judgment of Andreotti's role in Italian politics had long been and would continue to be an undercurrent of left-wing thinking, but anti-Andreotti feeling rose to the surface after Tangentopoli. That he embodied the DC cosmos, which after Tangentopoli had lost its order and harmony, was part of his dilemma. He stood out as the symbol of the suddenly bygone order, all the more so because, nearly alone among DC leaders, he continued to stand at all.

His alleged Mafia connections attracted increased notice and comment. Leoluca Orlando, a reform politician in Palermo, led the campaign against him, and Andreotti was forced to fight back in a serious way. The quips and smiles no longer sufficed in the Tangentopoli era. In the fall of 1992 newspapers began to publish reports about new evidence linking Andreotti to the Mafia. A 31 December 1992 article in the *New York Times* acquainted American readers with the reported charges against Andreotti.[7] He was furious at these "insinuations." Used as he was to taking low blows from the Italian press, he found it outrageous that his enemies—armed with nothing but rumor and innuendo—would mount an international campaign against him.[8] Andreotti doggedly maintained that the only relationship he ever had with the Mafia was one of implacable opposition.

For months before March 1993, when the judges of Palermo presented him with an avviso di garanzia, Andreotti knew that he was in the worst trouble of his long and checkered career. Twenty-seven times before he had been under investigation for corruption to no avail, but this time it was different. Even with this knowledge, Andreotti was not prepared for the avalanche of brutal publicity that struck him in the spring of 1993. Headlines about the fallen *Belzebú*—Craxi's name for Andreotti as the Great Satan of Italian politics—were soon followed in the newspapers by verbatim transcripts of the judges' case against him. Procuratore Gian Carlo Caselli and his colleagues divided their analysis into eight parts, corresponding to the testimony of the eight pentiti: Leonardo Messina, Gaspare Mutolo, Vincenzo Marsala, Antonio Calderone, Francesco Marino Mannoia, Giuseppe Marchese, Baldassare Di Maggio, and Tommaso Buscetta. Even Andreotti's most merciless detractors were shocked by the details of the story that emerged from this testimony. According to the pentiti, he was guilty not only of the political corruption for which he had long been under suspicion, but of murder as well.

Each testifying independently of the other, the pentiti agreed that Andreotti had profited politically from Mafia support. His principal associate in Palermo was Salvo Lima, who served the Mafia as their channel to Andreotti. When the Mafia needed favors, such as the adjustment of sentences in trials against *mafiosi*, Lima was the man they contacted—and he, in turn, communicated their desires to Andreotti. Among themselves the mafiosi called Andreotti *zio*, their uncle in Rome, who could be trusted to do their bidding in exchange for support at the polls. Antonio Calderone vividly explained what Mafia support at the polls meant: between his friends, relatives, and dependents every *uomo d'onore* directly controlled forty to fifty votes at election time; the Mafia network thus produced tens of thousands of votes for DC candidates who thereafter remained securely within the Mafia's orbit on all issues vital to the organization.

The Rome-Palermo axis had worked well for both the Mafia and the andreottiani over many years, but increased public concern about organized crime led to difficulties. Beginning in the late 1980s Andreotti had to be more circumspect and outwardly critical of the Mafia. Trials, for example, could no longer be adjusted as in the past. The Mafia felt betrayed by him and, as a sign of its displeasure, killed Lima on 13 March 1992. Rumors about the motive for the murder soon began to engulf Andreotti. The pentiti confirmed the rumors and added what for many was a very believable explanation of the relationship between Andreotti and the Mafia.

The two most important pentiti were Francesco Marino Mannoia and Tommaso Buscetta, both of whom tied Andreotti to the Moro affair. Mannoia had enjoyed a close relationship with one of the highest Mafia chieftains, Stefano Bontate, and from this source had learned that "Cosa Nostra had been urged by influential representatives of the DC to intervene and try to save [Moro]."[9] Bontate personally sponsored a pro-Moro initiative within the Mafia. At a meeting of Mafia leaders, he made his case for Moro, but failed. One of the bosses who opposed him on the matter, Pepe Calò, observed, "Stefano, you still don't understand, top leaders of his own party do not want him free."[10] In other words, if some DC leaders had expressed a desire to free Moro, the party's real godfathers wanted him to stay where he was. This was a concrete example of how the Mafia and selected political figures in Rome and Sicily communicated with each other. That such negotiations had taken place and that such a scheme was in the offing revealed the true nature of politics Italian style. At the same time, what Mannoia had to say about the DC powerfully reinforced the conspiracy theory in the Moro murder case.

Tommaso Buscetta added further details to the story of Andreotti's involvement with the Mafia. Of the eight Mafia pentiti, he was by far the best known to the public. Buscetta had lost two sons and other family members as a result of murderous Mafia feuds, and in 1984 he turned against the organization that had been his world. Judge

Giovanni Falcone, killed by the Mafia in May 1992, had used Buscetta's testimony as the basis of a successful case against them.[11] Procuratore Caselli also found him of great assistance. According to Buscetta, the recent transformation of Italian political life had created an unprecedented opportunity to deal a mortal blow to the Mafia. For years the Mafia had battened on the Italian political system, but with its collapse under Tangentopoli all the country's structures of organized crime suddenly lay exposed. The stunning murders of Falcone and, in July 1992, of his successor Paolo Borsellino, also had helped to create an atmosphere supremely unfavorable to the Mafia. Buscetta deemed the moment right to tell all he knew about the *intreccio*, the intertwining between the criminal underworld and the state.

Buscetta had known Lima since the early 1960s, and their relationship illustrated the uses of the intreccio for the Mafia: he was the politician "to whom I turned when I needed favors."[12] Buscetta viewed all the politicians in Andreotti's faction as flunkies who would do exactly as they were told while putting the best face on the recurrent failures of the government to get any serious police work done against the Mafia. Under orders, in effect, from the Mafia, the andreottiani conspired to keep Italy in a perennial state of semi-anarchy, a good climate for furthering the criminal ends of the country's drug dealers, extortionists, and money launderers. The minute that a politician like Lima lost his usefulness or, worse in his case, became offensive, the Mafia thought nothing of eliminating him.

The judges thought Buscetta's testimony against Andreotti was entirely credible, especially in view of the confirming statements made by the other pentiti. In asking the Senate in April 1993 for permission to proceed with their investigation—a request made necessary because of parliamentary immunity—they relied heavily on Buscetta's testimony. The judges acknowledged that they did not have enough evidence to go to court, but the testimony of these eight pentiti could not be ignored. More investigations would be necessary.

Andreotti contemptuously dismissed the charges against him. He would continue to defend Lima's reputation, asking not to be told what everybody "knew" about him, but what the evidence was. He had heard these charges about Lima years earlier, had investigated them personally, and had found absolutely nothing to confirm them. As for the charges that he personally faced, Andreotti declared (on 7 April 1993) that they were too absurd to be believed and, besides, they rested exclusively on what someone had told someone else many years before about a third party.[13] Andreotti wanted to know what specific criminal acts he allegedly had committed, and he wanted to see the evidence of his accusers. He felt entirely confident that the moment these individuals started talking about particulars their accusations would lose all credibility. His lawyer, Odoardo Ascari, added that the investigation itself was deeply flawed. Andreotti's guilt was a given, a "Kantian category," and the unquestioned point of departure for the judges' labors, not, as it should have been, the conclusion of a dispassionately conducted judicial inquiry.[14] Moreover, well-timed leaks to the press, amounting to a smear campaign of "unimaginable proportions," had destroyed the very possibility of justice for Andreotti.[15]

Just a few days later, appendices based on new testimony by Mannoia and Buscetta were added to the Andreotti dossier, and hints and asides about the Moro case in the earlier documentation now became heavily detailed allegations. Mannoia described meetings that supposedly took place between Andreotti and Mafia chiefs in Sicily, but it was Buscetta's testimony that delivered the heavier blows. First, Buscetta personally had been involved in the Mafia's stillborn plan to save Moro. While serving prison time in Cuneo, the mafioso had been asked by the organization to contact Red Brigade prisoners about securing Moro's release. He agreed to do this, but first had to gain a transfer to Turin where the Red Brigade chiefs were standing trial. The transfer never came through. It was blocked by politicians who did "not want to liberate Moro," he later learned.[16]

Then, with his biggest bombshell, Buscetta zeroed in on Andreotti directly, and the ensuing explosion was to what had gone off before as a thermonuclear device is to a Molotov cocktail. To the utter stupefaction of the Italian people, Buscetta accused Andreotti of personally ordering two murders that were connected with the Moro case. According to him, Andreotti had asked the Mafia to kill the newspaper editor Mino Pecorelli, as well as General Carlo Alberto Dalla Chiesa, whose assassin was also responsible for the incidental deaths of the general's wife and security guard. Buscetta told Procuratore Caselli that the motive was the same in both crimes: to keep potentially damaging Moro papers out of the public eye. Andreotti would have known how to keep himself far removed from the actual violence, but on the basis of what Stefano Bontate and other Mafia bosses had told him, Buscetta had no doubt about the true author of the Pecorelli and Dalla Chiesa murders. From his sources Buscetta learned that "Giulio Andreotti was worried that these secrets, connected with the kidnapping of the Honorable Moro, secrets that General Dalla Chiesa also knew, might get out. Pecorelli and Dalla Chiesa are in fact 'things that are connected with each other.'"[17] And the connection was Moro.

As with the Mafia's abortive Moro rescue plan, Buscetta knew about the Dalla Chiesa murder from his own direct experience. In 1979 Buscetta, still in prison, was once again asked to contact Red Brigade prisoners, this time about the possibility of having their organization take responsibility for killing Dalla Chiesa. Andreotti wanted him dead, but the Mafia did not have a plausible public motive in 1979 for such a deed. Dalla Chiesa was then in charge of the state's war on terrorism and had nothing to do with the Mafia, which in the 1970s took advantage of soaring drug profits and the distractions created by the Red Brigades to spread in a rank growth all over the country and into other parts of Europe as well.[18] Buscetta's instructions were to explain that the Mafia would do the killing if the Red Brigades, which had the best of motives for the crime, would publicly take credit for it. In this way the Mafia would avoid any inquiries that might lead to the discovery of the intreccio, on which the crime syndicate depended for political protection.

Buscetta attempted to strike just such a deal, but the Red Brigades would not even consider it without some participation of their own on the hit team. Andreotti could not act on his desire to have Dalla Chiesa killed until 1982. By then, with the general in Sicily on an expressly anti-Mafia mission, a cover of the kind contemplated in 1979 was no longer needed. Buscetta insisted, however, that it was Andreotti who wanted Dalla Chiesa killed, to end his fears about what the general would do with certain Moro papers.

After learning of the latest Mannoia-Buscetta allegations, Andreotti claimed that he found these completely made-up tales highly comic, but with a long prison term as one possible outcome of his present tribulations it did not take him long to get serious. He angrily dismissed Mannoia's testimony about clandestine meetings with Mafia dons as a stupid lie. How could such meetings take place when he was always under heavy police escort? If people would only stop to think, which was difficult to do under the relentless media appeals to emotion, they quickly would realize how implausible Mannoia's story was.

As for the testimony about Moro, Pecorelli, and Dalla Chiesa, no writer of science fiction could have felt more liberated from a concern for historical accuracy than Buscetta. Andreotti professed absolute perplexity about Buscetta's motive for these charges, but passionately insisted that his government had done everything possible within the law to save Moro. The dark allusions to his role as Moro's nemesis infuriated him, but he had been forced to deal with that story for years. To be accused of outright murder was new, however, and "the culminating point" of the absurd and insulting investigation to which he had been subjected.[19]

A second appendix, based on the testimony of pentito Baldassare Di Maggio, became public soon after the Mannoia-Buscetta appendix to the Andreotti dossier. According to Di Maggio's latest testimony, Andreotti, along with Salvo Lima, had met with the boss of bosses Totò Riina in the home of Ignazio Salvo, another one of the intermediaries between the Mafia and Rome. The meeting had been arranged to address Riina's concerns about judicial proceedings against the Mafia. It was a very friendly meeting, and Riina had given each man a kiss of greeting. The day after this testimony became public, headlines proclaimed, "Andreotti kissed Riina." The newspapers also made much of twenty-six photographs showing Andreotti at a religious ceremony in the presence of a known mafioso's relatives, which were included along with the Di Maggio appendix.[20]

Although he was reportedly badly shaken by these latest accusations, Andreotti showed no sign, in his published responses, of exhaustion or defeat. In a rejoinder to the second appendix, Andreotti dismissed the photographs as meaningless. Politicians were photographed often with people they did not know. For the judges to use these particular photographs of Andreotti at a church consecration ceremony in the company of some unknown mafioso's relatives was one sign among many that their case had no foundation.

Andreotti turned on Di Maggio in a fit of violent resentment. To take seriously a single word of his was the end of history and the end of logic. As for history, even the false history of the pentiti, gross contradictions leapt off every page. For example, in the Mannoia-Buscetta appendix, Andreotti was said to have broken with the Mafia in 1987, but now Di Maggio was describing a 1988 meeting, including kisses, in Palermo's broad daylight. Such a glaring inconsistency indicated desperate confusion in the case against him. Moreover, to be present at such a meeting, in the company of numerous witnesses, would have been an act of appalling stupidity even for a very stupid man, but the one thing that his critics had granted him was a legendary shrewdness in politics. As a point of logic, the clumsily stupid kiss in Palermo was incompatible with the shadowy mastermind of Italian politics. The story of the kiss belonged in the same category of tales as an earlier report in the dossier about his rite of initiation as a mafioso: both were preposterous. Andreotti and his lawyers unwaveringly held to this line of defense.[21]

On the issues pertaining to Moro Andreotti received support from an unexpected source. Franco Bonisoli, who had participated in the via Fani ambush and had been arrested during the October 1978 raid on via Monte Nevoso, denied that there ever had been any kind of relationship between the Red Brigades and the Mafia. Moreover, the thirty-seven-year old ex-terrorist insisted that the motive ascribed to Andreotti in the Dalla Chiesa and Pecorelli killings was completely fictitious. There were no missing Moro papers, no dreadful secrets for which a terrified Andreotti would have had to transform Palazzo Chigi into an annex of Murder Incorporated. "All the interrogation transcripts of the Honorable Moro have been found and published," Bonisoli assured a newspaper interviewer.[22] Neither Pecorelli nor Dalla Chiesa had anything on Andreotti that was outside of the public domain. During the raid on via Monte Nevoso the carabinieri had overlooked the apartment's hidden panel, and therefore the public had seen only a fragment of Moro's memoriale, but this was all anyone, other than the Red Brigadists themselves, knew about that document in 1978. The error of the carabinieri was natural; so many papers were found lying about in the via Monte Nevoso hideout that even veteran police officers could be excused for thinking that no further search for documents was required. In 1990 all the rest of the memoriale was found and immediately published. "I assure you that there are no mysteries," Bonisoli concluded.

A key element in this part of the story was the public's reaction, in 1990, to the publication of the entire Moro memoriale. Andreotti continued to be divo Giulio for a long time after the release of those papers. There was nothing in them to alarm him even if he had known about their existence, which, according to Bonisoli, he could not have. This interview helped to rally those who held the Christian Democratic leader to be innocent. However, even as the *innocentisti* disputed with their antagonists, the *colpevolisti*, over the merits of the dossier compiled by the Palermo judges, another group of judges, in Rome, issued a second indictment against Andreotti. Once again, the Moro case lay at the heart of the matter.

Andreotti's problems unfolded as Italian politics continued to undergo historic changes as a result of Tangentopoli. With the appointment of Prime Minister Carlo Azeglio Ciampi (former governor of the Central Bank), that political office was for the first time filled by a man from outside Parliament. Ciampi's nomination by President Oscar Luigi Scalfaro symbolized the hope for a new day in Italian politics just as the Andreotti investigations symbolized, at an even deeper level than Tangentopoli did, the complete collapse of Parliament's prestige. Also forming part of the backdrop in the Andreotti case at this time was a mysterious and still unsolved explosion in Rome on 14 May, the first of several that would occur in Italy during the spring and summer of 1993. These explosions, which would cause a shocking loss of life and incalculable damage to the nation's art treasures at the Uffizi Gallery in Florence and at Rome's San Giovanni in Laterano and San Giorgio in Velabro, added immensely to fears that the country was returning to the terrible days of terrorism.[23]

The publication of Andreotti's second indictment in June 1993 was also preceded by a barrage of media stories. Buscetta's revelation about Andreotti's involvement in the 20 March 1979 Pecorelli killing had forced Rome's Procuratore della Repubblica Vittorio Mele to reopen the case. The original investigation had led to a dead end, but now the magistrates had new leads to explore. While this second investigation proceeded, newspapers headlined the charges against Andreotti while he angrily protested that he was the victim of a wicked plot. We are in "the times of the Borgia," he lamented.[24]

Mele relied heavily on the testimony Buscetta had given Caselli, but the Procuratore della Repubblica di Roma had acquired additional information from the pentito and other witnesses during the course of his own investigation. At the very outset of this second request to lift Andreotti's parliamentary immunity, Mele conceded that he had no evidence against the senator. In fact, the Procuratore repeatedly stressed how tentative the case against Andreotti was. They were in "the earliest" *(primissima)* stage of the investigation, and there was need for great caution in interpreting and evaluating the testimony of Buscetta and others in the case.[25] For now, Mele needed to ascertain if the charges were true and if they could be proved in a court of law. He expressly stated that his office had no grounds for a legal action against Andreotti.

Few adult Italians would have to be reminded of who Mino Pecorelli was. A journalist linked to P2 and the secret services, Pecorelli had been the director of *Osservatore Politico (Op)*, a scandal sheet of the 1970s. His murder had been front-page news. Pecorelli had made a living by peddling inside information on politics, and a typical example of his style—namely, blackmail—was included in Mele's dossier on Andreotti. Shortly before his death, Pecorelli had claimed to have evidence of Andreotti's crooked dealings; to keep this story out of *Op* the Senator was said to have paid thirty million lire, a considerable sum for those days. Pecorelli received this money the day before he was murdered. Andreotti later denied any knowledge of this blackmail scheme, but the story told by Mele was highly representative of Pecorelli's reputation. Many in Italy had a motive to kill him.

Mele was interested in the Andreotti connection with this murder. Buscetta had said that Andreotti wanted to silence Pecorelli because of "political things" having to do with Moro, that is, the unpublished papers of Moro had to be kept hidden at all costs. This part of Buscetta's story was not new, and because it still rested on what he had been told by other mafiosi, it could not be construed as evidence. Nevertheless, the story possessed an undeniable coherence. The political things mentioned by the witness were not made up. For instance, many *Op* articles on the Moro case mentioned "Pecorelli's knowledge of facts of particular gravity."[26] Pecorelli's style was allusive and cryptic, and he made obscure references that only adepts in the intelligence field would grasp. The journalist mixed fact with fiction, but one eerily prophetic article about the Moro case made a deep impression on Mele. Writing shortly after the October 1978 raid on via Monte Nevoso, Pecorelli insisted that the full Moro memoriale had not been made public. Pecorelli gave his readers to understand not only that there was much more in the memoriale than the public knew, but that he personally was familiar with all of its shocking contents. Mele wanted to be cautious, but he had to admit that with this article Pecorelli had scored a direct hit. How had he come by such knowledge?

One possible answer was that this had been a lucky shot by a professional scandalmonger who by the law of averages would guess right now and then, but Mele concluded instead that Pecorelli could have had inside information from General Dalla Chiesa. The two men knew each other, and one witness reported that Dalla Chiesa had sought out Pecorelli as someone who might be a useful conduit of information to a select public. The general in this dossier did not emerge as a shining national hero. As one who might have held back vital documents in the Moro case, he was seen to be conforming to the low ethical standards that prevailed in Italian public life. His link with the repellent Pecorelli cast a dark shadow on this new and lesser image.

The general did not lack for defenders. His mother-in-law, Maria Antonietta Setti Carraro, acknowledged that he had not given Andreotti all of the documents turned up in the via Monte Nevoso raid, but that was a necessary precaution on his part. General Dalla Chiesa felt that he had to have some hold over Rome's treacherous leaders. She recalled hearing her daughter say: "I know some terrible things, but I can't tell them to you. If I were to tell you, you would not be able to believe it. Carlo made me swear not to tell them to anyone."[27] After his murder, these documents, which he kept in a chest, mysteriously vanished. Signora Setti Carraro insisted that their disappearance was part of a plot.

In the course of investigating Buscetta's allegations Mele heard disconcerting testimony from other witnesses as well. Franco Evangelisti, a DC senator and Andreotti's long-time close colleague, surprised everyone with his account. Very ill at the time, but lucid, Evangelisti testified that he often served as the go-between for Andreotti and Dalla Chiesa. He described one 2 A.M. visit when Dalla Chiesa presented him with a typed manuscript said to have come from Moro's prison. Mele concluded that this document "could have to do with the so-called memoriale."[28] Another witness was Ezio Radaelli, a businessman, who claimed that a representative of Andreotti had tried to pressure him into changing his testimony regarding the Senator's financial affairs. To determine the full truth about such a "complex intertwining of facts and persons" would require the deeper and more systematic investigation that Mele was now requesting permission to launch.[29] Although Andreotti had rejected every charge against him as either false or the result of a misunderstanding, the very substantial testimony against him could not be ignored.

Certainly the Italian people were not ignoring it, and for many weeks the case dominated the news. Day after day Andreotti was shown on the evening news programs. Half-blinded in the glare of television lights, jostled by throngs of reporters, and hemmed in by their equipment—he looked like the man who repeats over and over again that he does not beat his wife. Although he claimed to be confident about the final outcome of these proceedings, the mere repetition of such a defense aroused suspicion. He was in the exceptionally difficult position of having to deny accounts put forward by former aides and colleagues, as well as the testimony of the pentiti and the interpretations of the judges.

With great plausibility for many well-informed observers of Italian politics, Andreotti denied any involvement in the Pecorelli and Dalla Chiesa murders or any knowledge of the Moro memoriale, but the mass of accusations and judgments against him, in combination with the general breakdown of the Italian political system occasioned by Tangentopoli, flattened his career and eliminated him as a major power in Christian Democratic politics.[30] Andreotti played no role in the restructuring of his party that took place in 1993 and 1994, and in the vaunted "revolution" of Italian politics his name appeared only as a totemic figure of the old regime. Even his popular *Europeo* column "Bloc Notes" was no longer wanted, and he suffered the indignity of receiving a pink slip from the editor, who claimed that the journal had to change with the times. Andreotti later remarked that he always had led a charmed life. Success had come easily to him. Having risen to the top early, he had commanded power and influence for nearly fifty years. Now the wheel of fortune had turned.

While the Andreotti investigations were proceeding through the Italian judicial system, the Moro quater trial began to spark renewed public interest. As Antonio Marini, the pubblico ministero in the trial, put it: "At this moment there are three concentric actions, that of the Procura di Palermo on the murder of General Dalla Chiesa, that [of the Procura di Roma] . . . on the murder of Mino Pecorelli, and our fourth trial in the Moro case."[31] He hoped that these three judicial proceedings would clarify once and for all "the black holes, these mysteries" in the Moro murder case. Marini called upon the irriducibili to testify in the Foro Italico courtroom. Only in this way, by closing at last the terrible Moro case, could Italy ever hope to make good her claims for national renewal. Marini thought that the dramatic changes unfolding in Italian public life had created a unique opportunity for the truth finally to emerge.

Ballistics and medical experts, rather than irriducibili, put Moro quater back in the news. In October 1993, three experts provided the court with a 100-page report on their findings regarding the via Fani ambush and kidnapping. In it they repeatedly criticized Valerio Morucci, whose testimony about via Fani had been adopted uncritically by investigating magistrates. According to the experts, he had misrepresented some important facts about that historic day, such as the number of terrorists involved and the number of weapons fired. Ten Red Brigadists were on hand, not nine, and seven weapons had been fired, not six, as Morucci had testified in Moro ter. The experts also contradicted him on the positions taken up by the terrorists and the direction from which most of the fire had come. The next day's newspapers predictably announced "New Mysteries in the Moro Case."

In court, Morucci played down the contradictions between his account of via Fani and that of the experts. The numbers nine or ten and six or seven, as well as the precise angles from which the Brigadists fired their weapons, meant very little. He did concede that a tenth person had been present at the ambush site, but this individual had departed before the shooting began. As for the seven weapons mentioned in the experts' report, Morucci explained this discrepancy by noting that backup arms had been available and were used. He strongly questioned the significance of these "contradictions" and denied that they seriously detracted from the reliability of his testimony about via Fani.

By the time that Morucci testified in the Foro Italico courtroom, on 25 October 1993, the Moro case was in the headlines again because of two developments earlier that month, and in an interview with *Il Manifesto* he commented on both of them. First, a pentito from the criminal underworld, Saverio Morabito, declared that a crime boss from the 'ndrangheta underworld organization, Antonio Nirta, had been present at the via Fani ambush. Second, Adriana Faranda told magistrates that four people, not three as previously reported, had been inside the People's Prison with Moro and that it was the fourth man, Germano Maccari, not Prospero Gallinari, who had done the killing. These revelations created a sensation in Italy.

On the first point, Morucci echoed the opinion of all the Red Brigadists: it was simply absurd to think that they had been infiltrated by the hoodlums of 'ndrangheta. Compelling logic, based on history, clinched Morucci's argument. The telling point was made that if

Israel's Mossad had tried to infiltrate the Red Brigades without success, was it plausible to think that the notoriously uncouth criminals of the Calabrian 'ndrangheta could have succeeded where the most resourceful and effective intelligence agency in the world had failed? Morucci and his colleagues unanimously ridiculed the Nirta story as an unusually inept canard. There were no underworld infiltrators in the Red Brigade nucleus at via Fani, and anyone speaking to the contrary would have to present some credible evidence. Morabito had no evidence at all for any of his assertions about via Fani.

Morucci, still describing himself as a dissociato, would not comment directly on his former lover's accusations against Maccari. Like Morucci and Faranda, Maccari had been a member of Potere Operaio, but this carpenter, unemployed at the time of his arrest, had never joined the Red Brigades. In October 1993 and for months afterwards Maccari remained the subject of conflicting reports and testimony, with many in the Red Brigades declaring Faranda completely mistaken in her charges. About the Maccari story, Morucci would only say, "I neither confirm nor deny it."[32]

Morucci did point out that the revelation about Maccari, even if true, was not an essential element of the Moro story. Did it really matter whether three or four people had stood guard over Moro in the People's Prison? Once again, Morucci disputed the significance of the numbers game with which his countrymen were obsessed. The report about Maccari, like the one about Nirta, served mainly to distract people from the real truth about the Moro case. And that had more to do with *Manifesto*'s self-description as a "communist daily," he provocatively continued to the journalist interviewing him. The Moro case from the beginning was "a story of communists." The reports about plots, infiltrators, and manipulators were all deeply misleading because even if some evidence could be found for them, they would still be only of marginal significance. Italy's revolutionary left-wing culture was the source of the plot that had resulted in Moro's murder. Everyone involved in that culture, to the extent that he or she had supported the Marxist-Leninist revolutionary cause of its most fanatical exponents, the Red Brigades, bore some degree of responsibility for this crime, Morucci insisted. There were tens of thousands of such people in Italy, and they all had a desperate psychological need to avert their gaze from that brutal fact. It was no wonder to Morucci, who had an empathic understanding of the culture he was describing, that an insatiable market for conspiracy theories and obfuscatory reports existed in Italy.

That same day *Il Manifesto* also published passages from a prison interview of Mario Moretti by Carla Mosca and Rossana Rossanda. Here and in another interview that Moretti gave to the *Corriere della Sera*, he anticipated many of Morucci's statements. The two men echoed each other in their insistence that the Red Brigades alone had conceived and engineered the entire operation.[33] Moretti had always insisted on the complete independence of the Red Brigades, but in this latest interview for *Il Manifesto* he added some new information. After admitting that indeed four people were involved in the task of guarding Moro, Moretti turned to his own role on the last day of the kidnapping. Moretti did not tell Moro that he was going to die: "That cruelty was spared him."[34] But once they were inside the garage Moretti, not Gallinari or the fourth man, shot him, using two weapons. "I would never have allowed someone else to do it," Moretti said. Lamenting that the interview was opening up "a terrible wound" for him, Moretti swore that this was how Moro had met his end.

There were more headlines and front-page photographs at the end of the month about another development in the Moro case. On 28 October it was reported that new photographic evidence proved that the Red Brigades had not taken Moro's briefcases at via Fani, and that they remained in one of the bullet-riddled vehicles for some time after the ambush. The most extreme theories were advanced in the papers to account for the missing briefcases, including the assertion that someone in the P2-dominated police and secret services later gave them to the Red Brigades. Important secret documents had fallen into the terrorists' hands this way, newspaper readers learned. The Red Brigades themselves scoffed at this revelation. There had been no clandestine meetings between the police and the Red Brigades; furthermore, the briefcases contained no secret documents or even anything of particular interest. When President Santiapichi looked into this matter, he decided that it was a "foolishness" *(fesseria)* based on a misunderstanding and certainly not part of any plot.[35]

The most important testimony of Moro quater was given in late November, when Anna Laura Braghetti and Barbara Balzerani took turns in the witness chair. These two irriducibili never had testified in court, and their appearance generated great public interest. Braghetti began with a short statement about the secret of Red Brigadism's strength, which alone explained why the organization never had been infiltrated and why it had maintained an imposing presence in the country for so long: it was because they all found unity in "their political project."[36] She had believed completely in that ideal, having been prepared for the Red Brigadist life by long militancy in Lotta Continua. Braghetti's life, had been shaped decisively by the Movement, which in the Red Brigades had found its most straightforward expression. Now that the revolutionary project was over, she wanted to clarify the historical record. Although willing to pay for her mistakes, she insisted that the Red Brigades should be given credit for their idealism. Without understanding their Marxist-Leninist beliefs, nothing about the Red Brigades, including the Moro case, could be understood. The conspiracy theorists who portrayed the Red Brigadists as lackeys or allies of the 'ndrangheta or the secret services, "poor simpletons *(beoti)* under the control of someone or other," would always distort the true sense of the situation.[37] Braghetti now proposed to shed what light she could on the Moro case.

In 1977 Braghetti received instructions from her superiors in the Red Brigades to acquire an apartment. The instructions came with precise guidelines for the kind of apartment that the Red Brigades had in mind. She was told that the apartment would be used in "a very important . . . action."[38] The long search took her at last to via Montalcini 8, where preparations for the People's Prison got underway. President Santiapichi asked her to describe the apartment's furnishings and where she had purchased them. Much of her testimony that first day took the form of an inventory.

At one point Braghetti described a large wicker basket. President Santiapichi wanted to know what the purpose of the basket was. She replied that she had already told the court about it. For the first time that morning President Santiapichi put an edge on his words: "Don't tell me where you had described it because I don't know. You are here before a court that is a tabula rasa."[39] He wanted the confusion and controversy over via Montalcini 8 to be settled definitively, and this witness could help him to do it. "The basket," she said, "was used on 9 May to transport Moro into the garage."[40] Detailed knowledge of this kind about the People's Prison had never been presented in court before.

Braghetti had much to say about the small enclosure that held Moro inside the apartment. The Red Brigadists themselves had built it, and she described its materials, tiny dimensions, and special features. They set up an air conditioning system for it and a toilet facility, but Moro had no access to a shower or a bathtub during his imprisonment. He was given only a small basin of water for sponge baths. He slept and did all of his writing on a very narrow cot. They neither taped their conversations with him nor used a television camera.

Moro was always a model prisoner, Braghetti told the court. Once inside the cell, he had never cried out or tried to free himself; he was always composed and never uttered a cross word or showed any sign of impatience. Moro did what he was told and even read the Marxist-Leninist texts the Brigadists gave him. They wanted him to understand their "belief system" (credologia).[41] Touched by his long ordeal, Braghetti opposed the death sentence for Moro. When President Santiapichi observed, however, that to deny the sacrament of confession to a practicing Catholic was "like denying a Muslim the right of turning toward Mecca to offer up the final prayer to Allah," she allowed that none of the Red Brigadists had been concerned about Moro's soul.

Because she was stationed at the via Montalcini apartment on the morning of 16 March 1978, Braghetti could not respond to President Santiapichi's questions about via Fani. Barbara Balzerani could; she had direct experience in the attack. Known as the "pasionaria" of Red Brigadism, Balzerani, now forty-four, had been one of the most violent, cruel, and fanatical of the terrorist leaders. She had the distinction of being the only woman directly involved in the via Fani attack, but in view of her proficiency as a killer it was surprising to learn that she had performed the relatively minor task of helping to prevent traffic from coming through the fatal intersection. This meant, Balzerani told the court, that she never fired a round and that during the action her back was to the scene of the crime. She did not see a thing. Balzerani only heard the shots behind her and therefore could offer no corroborating testimony, whether for Morucci's version or that of the ballistics and medical experts who earlier that fall had presented rival versions of the attack.[42]

Balzerani's testimony was useful for other aspects of the Moro case, however. She talked volubly about the Moro inchiesta, or inquiry, which the Red Brigades had undertaken several months before the attack on via Fani. Balzerani had been given an important role in this intelligence-gathering operation, and she confirmed earlier reports about the thoroughness with which the Red Brigades had prepared for the kidnapping. They had been inspired by the 1977 Red Army Faction kidnapping of German industrialist Hans Martin Schleyer.[43] She discussed the strong bonds of sympathy and support that existed between the RAF and the Red Brigades. The Schleyer kidnapping had a bedazzling effect on Balzerani and her confederates. Although it had ended in failure, the Red Brigadists reasoned that an operation of this type stood a good chance of succeeding in Italy, a more vulnerable country than Germany was. To the Red Brigades, Italy at the time appeared to be in a uniquely promising revolutionary situation. Their actions from 16 March to 9 May could only be understood in that context.

Likewise, their interrogations of Moro and the use they made of the information he gave them turned on one consideration only: what would activate the revolutionary potential of the "very vast" stratum of left-wingers in Italy who thought of the revolution as the main organizing political concept of their lives?[44] These people did not have to be told how corrupt, reactionary, and CIA-dominated the Italian government was. Balzerani described this information, which was the bulk of what they got from Moro, as part of the "public domain" in Italy.[45] Much had been written about why the Red Brigades had not used Moro's memoriale, but Balzerani thought these were the speculations of people unmindful of the kidnap operation's sole purpose: the revolutionary overthrow of capitalism and the creation of a Marxist-Leninist dictatorship of the proletariat then and there, not in the indefinite future. The Red Brigades made many mistakes, Balzerani acknowledged, but their actions during the Moro kidnapping possessed a consistency derived from a scrupulous adherence to Marxist-Leninist ideas about what a revolution required.

At the same time that Braghetti and Balzerani were giving their dramatic testimony in Moro quater, other developments in the case made page one news. In late November Francesco Cossiga gave an interview to German television in which he disclosed that had Moro returned alive from the People's Prison, the government would have implemented its so-called Plan Moro-Victor: Moro would have gone straight to a psychiatric clinic and been kept in isolation for an indefinite period, until "calm."[46]

Even more unsettling to many in Italy was Cossiga's disclosure about another plan called Moro-Mike. This was to be implemented upon Moro's death, and it called for a mass arrest of all those suspected of Red Brigade sympathies. The plan was criticized for its violation of civil liberties; that it remained inoperative did not soothe these critics. The mere existence of such a plan reinforced the image of an Italian government that lacked the understanding, capacity, and integrity to be a true democracy.

Long delays held up the proceedings of Moro quater, and only on 1 December 1994 did the judges hand down their sentence. In a "serial" trial such as this, they began, in which the same fact or group of facts are "revisited" after many other trials, clarifications and rectifications can be expected.[47] So it had gone in Moro quater, and the judges interspersed their sentence with numerous references, including some long quotations, to previous sentences and to other trial documents in the case. What was new in Moro quater was not negligible though. Further details had emerged regarding Alvaro Loiacono's culpability in diverse acts of terrorism, including via Fani. He had been one of only two Red Brigadists at via Fani who were not members of the Rome Column (the other was Alessio Casimirri). Loiacono had been one of the attackers responsible for traffic control, had escorted the escape vehicle in which Moro was taken prisoner, and had assisted in the task of disposing of the bulletproof vests, weapons, and other equipment used in the ambush.

Also in connection with via Fani, the judges had relied mainly on the testimony of Barbara Balzerani and Mario Moretti (through his interviews with Carla Mosca who on 11 February 1994 had testified at Moro quater) in determining that a tenth terrorist had been present, a woman stationed about one hundred and fifty meters from the spot of the ambush, on the lookout for the Moro vehicles. Balzerani also had furnished another piece of information that according to the judges was "dense with significance."[48] She had explained in detail how each member of the Red Brigades, not only those directly involved in the operation, had been consulted about Moro's death sentence. According to her, Morucci's opposition to that sentence was one of the principal reasons for the dissension that soon afterwards tore the group apart. Another member of the Red Brigades who had opposed the death sentence and had made a contribution to Moro quater of "exceptional depth" was Anna Laura Braghetti.[49] Her detailed description of Moro's life and death in the People's Prison was one of the major gains of the trial.

Such noteworthy advances in the quest for justice notwithstanding, the judges left no doubt about their opinion that the core findings in the previous trials were still the essence of the Moro murder case. Moro quater indeed had resulted in some clarifications and rectifications, but President Santiapichi and Judge Attolico repeatedly referred to Moro 1 and ter as the fundamental historical sources for the case. Moro quater had added some magnification to our view of the general picture provided by the previous trials; it had made even plainer than the previous trials that the Red Brigades bore sole responsibility for Moro's kidnapping and murder, and that from their first People's Prison communications they had intended to kill the prisoner if their political demands were not met. Moro's guilt was assumed, and his death sentence was automatic absent a capitulation by the state: "In this scheme of things, from via Fani on, the death of the kidnap victim was in prospect."[50] The judges felt no need to appeal to conspiracy theories in explaining these "mournful events."

This is certainly not the last that we will hear about the Moro murder case. Additional details and facts will continue to emerge for years to come. The identity of the fourth man will be revealed one day. More will be learned about the kidnapping and shooting at via Fani and much more about the horrors inside the People's Prison. The government's failures in the case will continue to be scrutinized, and from this process new facts and conjectures will doubtless emerge. On the level of chronicle the Moro case may well be, as Judge Priore said, without end. Nonetheless, the chronicle that has been compiled after sixteen years of investigation permits and demands a historical interpretation.

Conclusion

Four trials and two parliamentary investigations have produced much crucial information about the Aldo Moro murder case. It is certain that the Red Brigades kidnapped and killed him. His murderers have been caught, tried, and convicted. The purpose of the crime was to trigger a Marxist-Leninist revolution in Italy. By abducting the Republic's most prominent leader, the Red Brigades hoped to plunge the political establishment into a crisis that would lead to its collapse. The destruction of the Christian Democratic-run state was their goal from the beginning, and they never veered from it. The trials and the parliamentary investigations have established these points beyond any reasonable doubt.

Former Minister of the Interior Virginio Rognoni was right to say in 1988 that the points of certainty in the Moro case should not be ignored or undervalued. Some people in Italy wanted the world to think that the Moro murder had never been solved, he complained. This simply was not true. The case had been solved and in a manner that reflected the highest credit on the Italian government and judicial system. The quest for justice in Italy's crime of the century had resulted in a completely satisfying triumph against his murderers, Rognoni concluded.[1]

The continuing controversy in the Moro case, however, does not hinge on the direct responsibility of the Red Brigades or on actions and motives that have been securely documented. The problem is the government's role in opposing the terrorists. Even the authors of the Moro Commission's majority report pointed out how hard it was to believe that the police genuinely made so many mistakes in their fifty-five-day manhunt. Still in question, long after the prison doors have slammed shut on the perpetrators of the kidnapping and murder, are the real motives of the government's *fermezza* policy and the integrity of its effort to find him alive.

The performance of the police and the carabinieri, as well as the alleged machinations of the politicians in Rome, have been agonizing issues in the Moro case almost from the beginning. Many in Italy have claimed that an honest effort was not made to find Moro. The most ambitious of the conspiracy theories is proposed in *La tela del ragno* by Sergio Flamigni. His thesis is that dishonest and disloyal officials subverted the Moro manhunt and sought to turn the kidnapping into a political windfall for P2.

In an updated edition of the book (October 1993) Flamigni added new material on P2, on the Andreotti-Pecorelli-Moro connection, and on the Moro carteggio found in October 1990. These recent developments and revelations allegedly reinforced his earlier assertions about official wrongdoing in the case. Flamigni insisted that the judicial inquiries in the case always had stopped short of investigating the activities of the P2-contaminated police forces and secret services. The trials were a whitewash and a sham because the authorities did not want the truth. In the conclusion of the book, Flamigni wrote that after all these years the Moro case is still encumbered with many "questions, doubts, real and true mysteries."[2] He called for a magistrate who would have the courage to clarify the issues once and for all.

Indeed, the Moro murder case remains contested, and for years to come it will continue to cause partisans of different camps to draw battle lines. The time for final historical judgments has not yet arrived, and a foreign historian in particular has to exercise great caution on such a sensitive topic. Yet a foreigner might have an advantage in not being directly linked to historical material rigged with this sort of explosive political and emotional charge. Open though many questions in the Moro case may be, a historical analysis of the available evidence does not permit us to accept the conspiracy theory. Given the treacherous political conditions in Italy at the time of Moro's death, however, it is no wonder that such a theory found many avid supporters. Conservatives in his own party despised him for the historic opening to the Communists. Parties to the right of the Christian Democrats were even more incensed. As for the United States, Henry Kissinger gave biting expression to the conventional view in Washington that Moro's willingness to compromise with the Communists endangered American interests.[3] American leaders always opposed Moro's historic compromise, and he believed that efforts to implicate him in the Lockheed scandal originated in the United States. If radical left-wing groups such as the Red Brigades viewed Moro as the embodiment of the corrupt Christian Democratic establishment, conservatives feared him as the man of dangerous initiatives.

Enemies of the Italian Republic found in Moro the embodiment of its institutions and power. The left and the right, both conceivably with help from abroad, sought to destroy him politically. Although the Red Brigades murdered him, Moro's enemies on the right—starting with P2 and continuing all along the anticommunist spectrum—had every reason to take delight in the sudden liquidation of a man they despised as a rank Communist sympathizer. I cannot have witnessed the only toast in Italy by right-wingers to the killers of Aldo Moro who, it was said in the summer of 1983, had rid the country of a truly dangerous man. We can safely presume that on both sides of the Atlantic the killing of Moro produced relief rather than sorrow in some quarters.

The logic of the conspiracy theory as applied to P2 possesses considerable force, but the problem of evidence thus far has remained insuperable. To say, as Tina Anselmi did in the majority report of Parliament on P2, that Licio Gelli probably attempted to derail the 1978 manhunt is not the same thing as saying that his attempt explains the Moro case. As all the judges in the Moro trials have insisted, there is no proof of any kind that such attempts had a bearing on the victim's fate or that they occurred at all. Mistakes, however numerous and astonishing they may have been, cannot be redefined as crimes without a more solid basis of fact than has ever been unearthed.

Moreover, even on the level of logic the conspiracy theory runs into some serious difficulties, for it assumes an efficiency, an astuteness, and a knowledge on the part of the police, the secret services, and the compromised politicians that are not characteristic of Italian institutions generally. Criticizing the conspiracy theory for its fanciful elements, President Santiapichi noted in the sentence for the first Moro trial that an efficient police search conducted with a high degree of professionalism would have been a much more surprising development in the case. The actual search was quite in keeping with the government's performance in most of its endeavors, and he could find no basis in fact for a conspiracy theory that with manifest improbability assumed the potential for efficiency had the desire been present.[4]

Two explanations account for the staying power of the conspiracy theory despite the failure of its exponents to arrive at anything more persuasive than a recitation of conjectures about why the unrelieved pattern of incompetence by the police must have been the work of P2 or deviant elements in the secret services. The first one is political, the second psychological. In *Armi e bagagli*, Enrico Fenzi, elaborating on a point also made by Valerio Morucci, put an important part of the political explanation in an admirably compressed form. He noted that consciously or unconsciously the Italian left feels an urgent need to repress the memory of its own involvement in the larger revolutionary culture from which Red Brigadism sprang.[5] For more than thirty years after World War II, Italian Marxism had two faces: a benign populist face and a fierce revolutionary one. Out of one mouth it spoke soothing phrases about democracy while out of the other it screamed for the necessarily violent end of the capitalist order. The Communist party advertised itself as the champion of humane Marxism, but numerous extraparliamentary left formations kept faith with the hard Marx of *The Civil War in France* and the even harder Lenin of *State and Revolution*, as did some extremists within the PCI itself. From the highly varied world of revolutionary communism emerged the Red Brigades. While certainly not synonymous with the radical left, the Red Brigadists were a part of it, or as Toni Negri once explained, "a variable of the movement gone crazy."[6]

To the Red Brigadists, their "back to Marx and Lenin" revolutionary fervor seemed to be sanity itself. What could be more natural than a proletarian revolution against a dysfunctional capitalist order? Marxist-Leninists were supposed to be revolutionaries. Acting on what they perceived to be pristine Marxist-Leninist principles, the Red Brigades called upon the revolutionary faithful to desert a corrupt and dying PCI church in favor of the old-time communist religion. The Red Brigades believed that they and they alone in Italy continued to represent a pure and undefiled Marxist-Leninist faith. They appropriated the central ideological tradition on which the Italian left was based, and with highly intelligent, superbly trained radical intellectuals like Renato Curcio, Giovanni Senzani, and Enrico Fenzi on their side it was not easy to dispute their claims on Marx and Lenin. More than a mortification for the Italian left, Red Brigadism appeared as its moment of truth after all the many equivocations about revolutionary violence. Having established themselves as the authentic voice of Marxist-Leninist revolution, the Red Brigades discredited that tradition along with themselves and brought on a severe moral and intellectual crisis for the entire left. The result has been a widespread abandonment of the cultural tradition in Italy that revered the cause of revolution as the one bright certitude in a sordid capitalist society. The capitalist society remains stronger, if more sordid, than ever, but the certitude vanished with Moro and the other victims of the Red Brigade reign of terror. Red Brigade authors proved so adept in justifying their cause by citing chapter and verse in Marx and Lenin that the rest of the left found itself vulnerable to the charge of guilt by association. For the left to extricate itself from its predicament required footwork not seen since Peter walked on water.

The clear inference of Fenzi's critique in *Armi e bagagli* is that the Italian left has sought to protect itself by obscuring the Marxist-Leninist origin of Red Brigadism. Marxist-Leninism was the central creed of the Italian left, and only now, with the historic transformation of the PCI into the as yet undefined Partito Democratico della Sinistra, has that dogma been rejected, although the process of rejection has occasioned resistance and schisms within the party. The full consequences of that momentous political development remain to be seen.

Writing on the eve of the PCI's demise, Fenzi asserted that the communist left could never be intellectually honest about what had produced the great terror in Italian civic life. The left could not face its own responsibility for having engendered utopian expectations and for having celebrated the myth of revolution, both of which the Red Brigades used to justify their terrorist campaign. These terrorists did not come out of nowhere. They emerged from the cultural background of the Italian left in which a Marx and Lenin cult had long been fomented. It was easier for the left to think of terrorism simply as the unfortunate aberration of a few misguided radical fanatics, on the one hand, and a terror network run by P2 and Washington, on the other, than to undergo the painful self-examination Fenzi recommended. For this still large and important segment of public opinion, now adrift ideologically but tied through personal involvement to the historical experience of communism, there is a natural preference for conspiracy theories, which acknowledge the hallucinations of a few violent mad-men, but really feature the plots of occult powers. Fenzi's argument boils down to a claim that if Licio Gelli had not existed the left would have had to create him. Conspiracy theories about the Moro case in particular and terrorism in general thrive because the truth hurts. Fenzi, a Marxist intellectual who chose Red Brigadism as the most suitable vehicle for revolutionary politics in Italy, knew something about these matters.

In *Brigate rosse: una storia italiana*, Mario Moretti makes the same argument. To two communist journalists interviewing him and assert-ing that he and his fellow Red Brigadists were really not Marxist-Len-inists at all, Moretti replied that in fact they did think of themselves in those terms, as part of the tradition of "communist revolutions."[7] They were not given to "theoretical rigidities," any more than Lenin was in 1917 with his use of Marxist theories, but the Red Brigadists had a very clear idea about where they came from and who they were. According to Moretti, one could say anything one liked about the Red Brigades, except that they were something other than what they always claimed to be and showed themselves to be in all of their actions. They were communist revolutionaries, and like many tens of thousands of Italians who shared their violent hatred of the Christian Democratic establishment, the Red Brigadists thought about politics and revolu-tion in essentially Marxist-Leninist terms.

Moretti described the Red Brigades as the most radical expression of a vast movement in Italy. It was the intention of the Red Brigades to remain small, "a nucleus," but for years their campaign against the Christian Democrats met with widespread approval on the communist left.[8] Without the broad support that the Red Brigades received from an immense network of backers, whose demonstrations and slogans confirmed the organization's belief in the imminence of revolution, terrorism would have faded quickly. "Coco, Coco, Coco è ancora troppo poco" (Coco, Coco, Coco is still not enough) had a mantric appeal for radical left-wing demonstrators.[9] This was a reference to Judge Francesco Coco, slain by the Red Brigades in 1976, and the kind of moral support that Moretti had in mind. The support of sympathiz-ers could and often did take more tangible forms during terrorist operations, and Moretti observed that the Red Brigades could always count on being warned by their friends whenever the police were getting close. Things changed drastically with Moro's death. Thereafter, many erstwhile sympathizers and well-wishers began to reinterpret their ideas about revolution and to invent a more acceptable past for themselves. It is this invention that the books of Fenzi and Moretti systematically deconstruct.

Not only the left, however, believes in or suspects the existence of a conspiracy against Moro. While in the People's Prison, Moro himself alluded to the probability of a government intrigue against him. Others—beginning with Leonardo Sciascia and culminating with Sergio Flamigni—repeated Moro's accusation and added refinements to it. Moro's family members have continued to remind the world of their own doubts regarding the government's efforts to find Moro alive. These doubts are shared by many whose thinking cannot be called leftist in the ideological sense that Fenzi had in mind. A deep public skepticism about the government's real agenda during the search for Moro cuts across party lines. Fenzi's explanation of the appeal of the conspiracy theory to the politicized left does not fully account for its vitality.

The deeper reason for the public's inclination toward a conspiracy theory has to do with human psychology. For human symbols of power to be cut down by nonentities violates our sense of the order of things. Such a grotesque outcome seems impossible without some greater power secretly at work. It is a natural reflex to deny the nonentity his triumph and attribute it to a greater power. The conspiracy theory in the Moro case derives more support from this reflexive response, which is stimulated and given a virtually unlimited outlet by endless conjectures in the media, than from any solid evidence.

Americans went through a similar rite of denial thirty years ago, when John F. Kennedy was killed in Dallas. Young, strong, and charismatic, Kennedy died at the hand of an individual who appeared to have crawled out of the depths plumbed by Dostoevsky. The marginal personality of Lee Harvey Oswald made the sharpest possible contrast with that of his glamorous victim. It did not seem plausible or even possible that this desperately alienated nullity could destroy the incarnation of presidential power. There had to be another explanation for the assassination of President Kennedy. The Warren Commission Report, which upheld the view that Oswald acted alone in the crime, has never been disproved by any of the claimants to the various conspiracy theories in the Kennedy murder case, but lack of proof has failed to still the controversy. The remarkable success of the 1991 film

"JFK" demonstrates this failure and, at the same time, makes clear, as did Giuseppe Ferrara's celebration of the conspiracy theory in "Il caso Moro," that one does not go to the movies to learn history.

Moro's death provoked the same kind of reaction in Italy. He lacked Kennedy's glamour, but he had come to epitomize the political establishment in Christian Democratic Italy. Given their invincibly low opinion of politicians, the Italian people did not exalt Moro in life. He was the human symbol of a status quo more tolerated than admired, but the circumstances of his death guaranteed the Italian Republic's holiest saint and foremost martyr.

The name of Moro now stands for an entire period in Italian history, which was ended by terrorists who came to be regarded by the public as a collective Lee Harvey Oswald. Alberto Franceschini's arresting image of Red Brigadism as a narcotic worse than heroin could be applied to them all. The Red Brigadists who testified in court exhibited a shallow view of the world and human nature. In the main, they appeared to be sociopaths whose intellectual pride would have been comical but for the death and destruction they caused. When Adriana Faranda described how she had begun to appreciate the humanity of all men by watching a class enemy eating a sandwich, people wondered what rubbish had been put into her mind that delayed for so long and at such cost the recognition of an elementary prerequisite of democratic life. The comments to journalists of nontestifying terrorists such as Mario Moretti and Prospero Gallinari revealed a universe of hatred, violence, and inhumanity—all in the name of a revolutionary project so obviously misconceived for contemporary Italy that the projectors seemed to lack ordinary intelligence. Journalists took special notice of how small and nervous Moretti was. It hardly seemed credible that such an unremarkable little fellow could have come up out of the sewer to strike so high.

Along with the conspiracy theory in the Moro case the policy of fermezza—itself connected in the minds of many to plots and intrigue—must also be rejected. Because of some important reservations, however, this second "no" is more difficult to explain than the first one. Even the most heavily qualified comments on the subject of fermezza invite misunderstanding and recrimination because, as President Santiapichi observed, to say anything at all about it is to descend into the nether world of Italian politics, "and, my dear professor, you don't want to do that."[10] Stick to the facts, he advised. Unfortunately, historians have to produce an interpretation of the facts, and to interpret the material under consideration here means making a judgment about the most salient political question in the Moro case: the fermezza-trattativa debate.

To negotiate or not to negotiate? Both positions had much to recommend them in the agonizing days of late winter and spring 1978, but the confusion and anguish of one Christian Democrat, Vittorio Cervone, suggest an answer to this question. A year younger than Moro and a fellow southerner, Cervone was a Christian Democratic deputy from 1953 to 1976 and then became a senator. In 1979 this leading figure in Moro's inner circle wrote a poignant memoir, *Ho fatto di tutto per salvare Moro*. He began by promising to set the record straight about his dead friend. Moro was not the pessimist and introvert of popular legend, but rather the most serene and open man Cervone had ever known. Moro's strong religious faith gave his personality a buoyancy that lifted all who knew him well. The public never really understood him, perhaps because of the rapid "dechristianization" of contemporary Italy.[11] It was an irony of history that such a fervently religious individual could have achieved what he did during an era so deeply inimical in spirit to his fundamental outlook on life.

Cervone correctly sensed on 16 March 1978 that Moro would not survive his ordeal. Despite this presentiment, which continued to haunt him over the next fifty-five days, Cervone resolved to do everything in his power to save Moro. He could not do very much, and the memoir contains a frank admission of his impotence. Cervone and the rest of Moro's friends in the party simply did not know what to do: "The sudden clash that each of us, all prepared in theory, had with hard, impenetrable reality undid us."[12] As the terrible days of March, April, and early May passed, they all wanted to be reassured that the government was doing everything possible to rescue Moro. Yet they never pressed their concerns too far for fear of making things worse, of making the government's difficult job harder still. Indeed, "Moro's teaching of not being a bother, of not being petulant, of not going beyond the rules often blocked us."[13] Cervone had too much respect for the seriousness of the general situation in Italy to break with the fermezza front. Despite his growing misgivings about the government's policies, he did not dare speak out in public.

Cervone's memoir reveals that within the DC people had been desperately concerned about Moro. It was not true that the party simply had forsaken him. Cervone and his friends spoke often with Benigno Zaccagnini, the party secretary, about their anxieties. In April a number of them wrote a letter about the need for an initiative to ascertain Moro's condition. There seemed to be nothing more that they could do without wrecking the unity of the fermezza front. If they did that, Cervone thought, they would necessarily tear apart the Christian Democratic party: "we, at least we friends, [were] lost in doubt between friendship and political justification."[14]

An immense sadness afflicted Cervone on the day of Moro's death, and a strong sense of guilt continued to trouble him at the time that he was writing *Ho fatto di tutto per salvare Moro*. The image of Moro's outstretched hand, waiting for someone to save him, would not fade from Cervone's memory. To make matters worse, Moro specifically had called upon him by name for help.[15] He knew in his soul that they had all failed their friend, and by so doing had gravely damaged themselves, for no other Christian Democratic leader could replace Moro. His death had left a huge void in the party and in Italian politics generally. Cervone felt that his own personal responsibility was not the less because so many other people had let Moro down.

Fermezza, understandable at the time, had been a tragic mistake, Cervone now thought. The government should have had the courage and the wisdom to resist the reflex policy of fermezza, or at least to supplement it with much more compassion and imagination. As early as 1979, Cervone doubted that Italy had been spared anything as a result of the sacrifice of Moro, but he strongly emphasized that he had not thought this the previous year, when events hurtled past him.

In 1978 the situation had been dreadfully uncertain, Cervone acknowledged. He certainly would have agreed with President Santiapichi's characterization of terrorism in Italy as a "devastating" problem. Indeed, to minimize it today, as some left-wing apologists seek to do, cannot be justified by anyone familiar with or interested in the historical record. In a speech commemorating the tenth anniversary of journalist Walter Tobagi's murder by left-wing terrorists, Bettino Craxi reminded his audience about the true nature of "those terrible years . . . those years of the 1970s."[16] It was a decade remembered chiefly for its kidnappings, murders, and massacres. The nearly 8,000 terrorist attacks during those years were intended to destabilize the state and had produced "conditions of emergency" in the country's civic life. Craxi's statements are not exaggerations, and they enable us to understand the historical context of the Moro case in all of its physical brutality and psychological trauma. Andreotti did not simply invent the "menace" of Red Brigadism as a means of shoring up the Christian Democratic regime. All those autopsy reports—"this continuity of blood and tragedies," as Benigno Zaccagnini described Italian terrorism—were real enough.[17]

Yet the fate of the Republic was never at stake during these years. Despite all the terrorist violence, Italian democracy remained deeply rooted. Red Brigadism never made the slightest difference to the relationship between the Italian people and their democratic institutions. Indeed, one of the major reasons many pentiti abandoned terrorism had to do with the increasingly obvious refusal of the Italians to pay any attention to Red Brigade calls for revolution. The appeals of the Red Brigades had a statistically insignificant effect on the proletariat, which in any case was shrinking as Italy entered the postindustrial age. Revolution, Red Brigade style, failed to find an effective constituency, and eventually most of the organization's members came to see that their cause had only succeeded in strengthening the establishment.

Cervone lamented in 1979 that Moro's outstretched hand should have been clasped, and we now know that this could have happened without jeopardizing the Republic. The people who urged negotiations in 1978 acted from varied motives. Their choice was no more informed by an intelligent appreciation of what Red Brigadism represented and what lay behind the Moro operation than was the choice of their antagonists on the fermezza front. The humanitarian line was said to be based mainly on ethical concepts about the sacredness of human life, not on a secure knowledge that the Red Brigades posed a negligible threat to Italian democracy. No one could claim that knowledge in 1978.

An understanding of Red Brigadism did not come in time to save Moro. Red Brigadism turned out to be the death rattle of a revolutionary culture. The story of the Red Brigades ended in repentance and dissociation for some members, in impotent obduracy for others, and in defeat for all. The age of terrorism was a national tragedy born of a mortal duel between a capitalist concept of society, peculiarly represented by Christian Democracy, and a Marxist-Leninist concept of revolution, fanatically represented by the Red Brigades. To the Red Brigades, Moro embodied the ills of the age as the leader of the DC; by seizing him they sought recognition from the working class as its vanguard in the revolution to create a Marxist state. Moro died because of these ideas.

In the long hours and many days of interrogation by Moretti, the truth of Red Brigadism, as the hopelessly quixotic undertaking of communist maniacs, must have become clear to Moro. What the general public grasped about these Red Brigade chiefs during the Moro trials could not have escaped a man of his vast experience. What did having a leader like Moretti indicate about the organization as a whole? His handling of the Moro interrogation was so bizarre that the former Red Brigade chief Alberto Franceschini speculated that Moretti must have been a spy for the secret services. Moretti dismissed this as the weird raving of a pitiable human wreck who had lost all sense of himself and of reality. Nevertheless, even if he were right in so depicting Franceschini, Moretti's role in the People's Prison was, by his own admission, characterized by a gross ignorance of the underlying political realities of the situation with which he was dealing, and by a nearly total failure to understand what Moro was trying to tell him.[18]

Hence, to negotiate with the Red Brigades did not entail the kind of risk that the fermezza front agonized over. This assessment of the situation appears to have been the real message of the prison letters.[19] It fits Moro's character and what reasonably can be expected of human nature when faced with violent death. People can usually put the prospect of death at a safe distance, but Moro was denied this consolation. In his terror he sought to save himself from what Leonardo Sciascia called "that vile death," but could not convince the Christian Democrats, including Cervone at the time, that negotiations could be undertaken at no risk to the state.

It ill becomes a historian to condemn leaders on the basis of knowledge they did not have. That would be the worst form of history conceivable, to say nothing of the insolence that would characterize such an endeavor. Italy's leaders responded to the Moro crisis in a manner that inspires more compassion than condemnation. They took a stand on the basis of the available facts, the context of which was the general emergency they perceived in the country. Moro himself had helped to define their viewpoint, and it almost goes without saying that he personally believed such an emergency existed. We have to remind people of Moro's deeply held and repeatedly stated conviction about how alarming the situation in Italy was, because of the marked tendency nowadays, in some quarters, to pretend that the government of Andreotti, in collusion with the mass media, created a panic out of whole cloth in order to cover its shameful misconduct. Such an elaborate pretense, with its transparently ideological motivation, is not why fermezza, in retrospect, was wrong.

The real reason is that with or without negotiations Red Brigadism, the twilight phenomenon of an epoch now formally ended with the convulsion and radical reduction of communist culture in Italy, had no future. One could argue, as Andreotti continues to do, that the ultimate failure of Red Brigadism was directly related to the fermezza policy of his government, that without firmness at the crucial moment the situation could have disintegrated. Moretti admitted in *Brigate rosse* that fermezza doubly took the Red Brigades by surprise: first, they did not expect such a policy, and then, when it was announced, they felt certain that it could not last. The confounding of their expectations about fermezza and about the immediate demise of the historic compromise came as a "sledge hammer blow" to the Red Brigades.[20] Moretti's admission is a leading example of why the debate over fermezza will never end in a completely clear-cut victory for one side or the other. Nevertheless, in view of everything that has happened in Italy and in Europe as a whole it is doubtful that the Red Brigades' rendezvous with history would have been postponed or in any way altered if the government had talked with the terrorists about getting Moro back. This is easy to write in 1995, but Andreotti had to make his decisions without knowing how the story would end. Only with our added knowledge are we able to second-guess him successfully. Even then he does not begin to resemble the malevolent caricature that some of his opponents have fashioned for him.

The virtue of the man known as the Beelzebub of Italian politics cannot be absolutely guaranteed. Andreotti flourished in that dark arena for fifty years. The notoriety of his associates in the Sicilian DC has become his own, on a larger scale. It would be most surprising if such a career did not result in a high degree of moral failure. Andreotti may have much to answer for once the investigating judges have completed the involved process of sorting out the real evidence against him, but in the Moro case nothing has stuck to him so far.[21] The extent of our present knowledge does not permit us to find in Andreotti the cause or the means of the Moro tragedy. The only possible historical explanation, based on secure documentation and following the rules of evidence, leads us in a different direction.

Men gripped by a fear of the unpredictable could not decipher Moro's situation in the People's Prison. Cervone's memoir is a document of high historical importance because it shows that even the statesman's dearest friends and allies in the party suffered from the confusion that caused a petrified government to proclaim fermezza as a clear rallying cry for nearly everyone in Italian political life. It was the only policy for a disoriented government unsure of itself and its adversary or adversaries. Moro tried to give his colleagues a direction, which from our vantage point makes sense or at least more sense than the government then allowed, but not even the *morotei*, the very men of Moro, knew what to do or whom to believe. Cervone, who came to have his own suspicions about the integrity of the government's efforts to find Moro, himself admits that at the time he did not know how to interpret the prison letters. If those closest to Moro were confused, it is reasonable to assume that the government shared in the general disorientation of the country. Speculation about the government's conduct is inevitable, but the point beyond which the historical record in the Moro case does not permit us to go is this: people, even when they do their best, sometimes fail.

In an interview he gave just a few days before his death in 1989, Benigno Zaccagnini talked about the problem of human error.[22] Like Cervone, Zaccagnini was a moroteo who had supported fermezza. To this close friend, who in 1978 occupied the position of DC party secretary, Moro had appealed repeatedly from the People's Prison. The prisoner quite credibly assured him that if their roles were reversed he would never permit Zaccagnini to die such a ghastly death. "Your word is decisive," he had written to him.[23] His responsibility would be personal in the highest degree. The weight of the wrong decision would never fall from him, Moro had prophesied. It had all happened just the way Moro said it would, Zaccagnini lamented. The interviewer then asked him if he had spoken to Mrs. Moro since the tragedy. He had not. The interviewer wanted to know what Zaccagnini might have said to her if given the opportunity: "I believe I would have said to her . . . only this," he responded slowly, after a pause: "if I made a mistake . . . try to forgive me."

Glossary

Notes

Acknowledgments

Index

Glossary

Action Directe: left-wing terrorist group in France.

andreottiani: the faction of Giulio Andreotti in the Christian Democratic party.

aperturismo: the opening to the Socialist left sponsored by Moro in the early 1960s.

autonomi: members of Autonomia Operaia.

Autonomia Operaia (Worker Autonomy): confederation of diverse extraparliamentary left-wing groups.

avviso di garanzia: notice given by judicial authorities to an individual who is under investigation for criminal conduct.

Bologna train station bombing: a terrorist act attributed to right-wing extremists. It occurred on 2 August 1980, killing eighty-five people and wounding two hundred.

brigatisti rossi: members of the Red Brigades.

Camorra: a criminal organization in Naples.

carabinieri: a national police force under the Defense Ministry.

carteggio (correspondence): term used to describe the collection of Moro's prison letters and testimony that was found in Milan on 9 October 1990; published in *l'Unità*.

Chigi: Roman palace that houses the office of the Prime Minister.

Confindustria (Confederazione nazionale degli industriali): the National Confederation of Industrialists.

Cosa Nostra: a criminal organization in Sicily.

Democrazia Cristiana (DC): the Christian Democratic party.

dissociati: defendants who dissociated themselves from terrorism and took responsibility for their actions without divulging information about their former confederates.

dossettiani: left-wing faction in the Christian Democratic party, led by Giuseppe Dossetti.

D'Urso, Giovanni: Italian judge kidnapped by the Red Brigades in December 1980 and released in January 1981.

estensore: the judge who writes the explanation *(motivazione)* of the court's reasoning in its act of sentencing.

extraparliamentary left: the highly varied segment of Italian political life to the left of the PCI, calling for a revolution against the status quo.

extraparliamentary right: the highly varied segment of Italian political life to the right of the MSI, calling for a revolution against the status quo.

Federazione Universitaria Cattolica Italiana (FUCI): the Italian Catholic University Federation.

fermezza (firmness): the hard-line position the Italian government took of refusing to negotiate with Red Brigade terrorists for Moro's life.

Foro Italico: courtroom for several trials in the Moro murder case.

Gioventù Universitaria Fascista (GUF): Fascist University Youth.

Gladio: name of a secret NATO-sponsored military operation. Disclosure of its existence caused a political scandal in Italy in the fall of 1990.

Guelph: a member of the political party in medieval Italy and Germany who defended the sovereignty of the papacy against the Ghibelline supporters of the German emperors; in contemporary Italian politics the term is applied to pro-Catholic figures.

giudice a latere (associate judge): a judge of the robe who assists the President of the Court in criminal trials.

giudice istruttore (investigating judge): the judicial official who conducts the preliminary investigation in a criminal trial.

giudici popolari (popular judges): the six lay people who serve on the court with two judges of the robe in criminal trials.

historic compromise: the understanding reached in the mid-1970s between the Communists and the Christian Democrats on political cooperation.

intreccio (interlacing): the term used to describe the close relationship between the Mafia and some elements of the government.

irriducibili (the irreducible ones): the hard-core terrorists who remained unrepentant after capture.

istruttoria (investigation): the phase of the legal process in which the evidence in a criminal case is obtained by the investigating judge (giudice istruttore).

linea militarista: a faction of the Red Brigades.

linea movimentista: a faction of the Red Brigades.

linea spontaneista: a faction of the Red Brigades.

Lockheed scandal: a criminal scheme of the 1970s in which Moro was accused of bribery and fraud in the selling of American aircraft in Italy.

Lotta Continua (Continuous Struggle): extraparliamentary left-wing organization.

Madama: Roman palace that is the seat of the Senate.

Mafia: originally a Sicilian criminal organization and still used as a synonym for Cosa Nostra, but also now a general term for the Italian underworld; Cosa Nostra in Sicily, the Camorra in Naples, and the 'ndrangheta in Calabria are all Mafia organizations.

Metropoli: an extraparliamentary left-wing journal.

missini: members of the Movimento Sociale Italiano.

Montecitorio: a Roman palace that houses the Italian Parliament's Chamber of Deputies.

morotei: the faction of Aldo Moro in the Christian Democratic party.

Mossad: the Israeli secret service organization.

motivazione: the explanation of the court's reasoning in its act of sentencing.

Movement: the generic term for the anticapitalist, antiestablishment campaign of the extraparliamentary left.

Movimento Proletario di Resistenza Offensiva (MPRO, the Proletarian Movement of Offensive Resistance): the cluster of revolutionary groups of which the Red Brigades claimed to be the leader.

Movimento Sociale Italiano (MSI, the Italian Social Movement): the Neofascist party in Italy.

'ndrangheta: a criminal organization in Calabria.

Nuclei Armati Rivoluzionari (NAR): the right-wing terrorist group Armed Revolutionary Nuclei.

Partito Armato (armed party): the generic term for left-wing terrorists.

Partito Comunista Italiano (PCI): the Italian Communist party.

Partito Liberale Italiano (PLI): the Italian Liberal party.

Partito Socialista Italiano (PSI): the Italian Socialist party.

Partito Socialista di Unità Proletaria (PSIUP): the Socialist Party of Proletarian Unity, a left-wing splinter group of the PSI, created in 1964.

pentiti (the repentant ones): the defendants who repented of their past terrorist actions and cooperated completely with the authorities.

perdonismo: the movement in Italy that called for the pardoning of Red Brigadists if they would reveal the full truth about the Moro case.

Piano Solo: the right-wing plot formulated by General Giovanni De Lorenzo in 1964.

Piazza Fontana bombing: an alleged right-wing terrorist act perpetrated on 12 December 1969 in Milan, killing sixteen people and wounding ninety.

piduisti: the members of the P2 Masonic lodge.

Potere Operaio (Worker Power): an extraparliamentary left-wing group.

potopisti: the members of Potere Operaio.

Pre-print: an extraparliamentary left-wing journal.

Prima Linea (Front Line): a revolutionary left-wing group.

Propaganda 2 (P2): a secret Masonic lodge with a right-wing political agenda for Italy.

pubblico ministero (public minister): the magistrate who exercises the function of public prosecutor in a criminal trial.

Quirinale: a Roman palace that serves as the residence of Italy's presidents.

Rebibbia Prison: the courtroom for some of the judicial proceedings in the Moro murder case.

Red Army Faction (RAF): a left-wing terrorist group in Germany.

requisitoria: the public prosecutor's bill of indictment in a criminal case.

Resistance: the antifascist, anti-German struggle of the Partisans in northern Italy following the 8 September 1943 armistice with the Allies.

sentenza: the sentence in a judicial proceeding.

SID (Servizio Informazioni Difesa): the major branch of the Italian secret service.

SIFAR (Servizio Informazioni Forze Armate): the Italian military secret service.

Sossi, Mario: the Italian judge kidnapped and released by the Red Brigades in 1974.

Stato Imperialista delle Multinazionali (SIM, the Imperialist State of the Multinationals): the Red Brigadist code phrase for American-dominated international capitalism.

Studium: the Catholic periodical edited by Moro (1946–1948).

Tangentopoli: the political and financial scandal in Italy that broke in 1992.

trattativa (negotiation): the dovish position that supported negotiations with the Red Brigades during the Moro kidnapping; its proponents called it the "humanitarian" line.

uomo d'onore (man of honor): the term used to describe members of the Mafia.

via Caetani: the site in Rome where Moro's corpse was found on 9 May 1978.

via Fani: the site in Rome of Moro's abduction on 16 March 1978.

via Montalcini: the site in Rome of the People's Prison during the Moro kidnapping.

via Monte Nevoso: the site of the Red Brigade archive in Milan where a cache of Moro letters and testimony was discovered on 9 October 1990.

Viminale: a Roman palace that houses the office of the Minister of Interior.

Notes

1. Aldo Moro: Symbol for an Age

1. Istituto Centrale di Statistica, *Comuni e loro popolazione ai censimenti dal 1861 al 1951* (Rome: ISTAT, 1960). The population of Maglie in 1911 was 9,484; in 1921 it was 11,047.

2. Renato Moro, "La formazione giovanile di Aldo Moro," *Storia contemporanea*, 4–5 (October 1983), p. 820.

3. For some of the tensions between the Church and the regime, see Richard Drake, "Julius Evola, Radical Fascism, and the Lateran Accords," *The Catholic Historical Review*, 74 (July 1988), pp. 403–419. See also Renato Moro, "Afascismo e anti-fascismo nei movimenti intellettuali di Azione Cattolica dopo il 1931," *Storia contemporanea*, 6 (1975), pp. 733–799.

4. Aldo Moro, *Al di là della politica e altri scritti: Studium 1942–1952*, ed. Giorgio Campanini (Rome: Studium, 1982).

5. Aldo Moro, "Osservatorio," *Studium*, 10 (October 1946).

6. Aldo Loiodice and Pino Pisicchio, *Moro e la Costituente* (Naples: Edizioni Scientifiche, 1984), pt. 1, "I principi fondamentali."

7. See especially his "Osservatorio" column in *Studium* for May and June 1945.

8. Renato Moro, "La formazione giovanile di Aldo Moro," p. 920; see also Roberto Ruffili, "Religione, diritto e politica," in Pasquale Scaramozzino, ed., *Cultura e politica nell'esperienza di Aldo Moro* (Milan: Dott. A. Giuffrè, 1982).

9. Aldo Moro, *Lezioni di filosofia del diritto tenute presso l'università di Bari: il Diritto (1944–45), lo Stato (1946–47)* (Bari: Cacucci, 1978), "Il problema della vita."

10. Ibid., p. 221.

11. For more on this point, see Norberto Bobbio, "Diritto e stato negli scritti giovanili," in Scaramozzino, ed., *Cultura e politica*. See also Leopoldo

Elia, "Moro, lo Stato e la giustizia sociale," in Pietro Scoppola, et al., *Moro, la Democrazia Cristiana e la cultura cattolica* (Rome: Cinque Lune, 1979).

12. Moro's other major scholarly works are *La capacità giuridica penale* (Padua: CEDAM, 1939), *La subiettivazione della norma penale* (Bari: L. Macri, 1942); *Lo stato, corso di lezioni di filosofia del diritto tenute presso la R. Università di Bari nell'anno accademico 1942–43* (Padua: CEDAM, 1943; some changes were made in the 1946–47 edition of this work, and it was the later edition that Cacucci republished in 1978); *L'anti-giuridicità penale* (Palermo: G. Pruilla, 1947); and *Unità e pluralità di reati-principi* (Padua: CEDAM, 1951).

13. For example, in *L'anti-giuridicità penale* Moro wrote that the law is an "intimate spiritual process" (p. 82). Society, properly conceived, is driven by "spiritual energies" (p. 51). A higher moral power governed everything, including the law.

14. Franco Boiardi, *Dossetti e la crisi dei cattolici italiani* (Florence: Parenti, 1956), p. 163.

15. Paolo Pombeni, *Il gruppo dossettiano e la fondazione della democrazia cristiana italiana, 1938–48* (Bologna: Il Mulino, 1979), p. 25.

16. Jacques Maritain, *Integral Humanism: Temporal and Spiritual Problems of a New Christendom*, tr. Joseph W. Evans (New York: Charles Scribner's Sons, 1968), p. 46.

17. Ibid., p. 191.

18. Ibid., p. 94. Maritain further explained that the Christian's "conception of the body politic has within it the aim to adjust the vale of tears so as to secure for the assembled multitude a relative though real earthly happiness, a good and livable structure of existence for the whole, a state of justice, of friendship, and of prosperity making possible for each person the fulfillment of his destiny," p. 137.

19. Ibid., cited on p. 206.

20. Pombeni, *Il gruppo dossettiano*, p. 316.

21. Pombeni, *Le "Cronache Sociali" di Dossetti, 1947–1951: geografia di un movimento di opinione* (Florence: Vallecchi, 1976), p. 117.

22. Pietro Scoppola, *La proposta politica di De Gasperi*, 2nd ed. (Bologna: Il Mulino, 1978), p. 254.

23. Ibid., p. 245.

24. Piero Ottone, *Fanfani* (Milan: Longanesi, 1966), p. 86.

25. Giorgio Galli and Paolo Facchi, *La sinistra democristiana: storia e ideologia* (Milan: Feltrinelli, 1962), p. 92.

26. Gianni Baget-Bozzo, *Il partito cristiano al potere: la DC di De Gasperi e di Dossetti, 1945–1954* (Florence: Vallecchi, 1974), p. 358. In 1984 a journalist described Dossetti as a frail, worn man with heart trouble who spent his days reading sacred books and "engaged in constant dialogue

with the divinity." Valeria Gandus, "Solo con Dio," *Panorama*, 20 August 1984.

27. Maritain, who read this book in its English translation, *Catholicism, Protestantism, and Capitalism* (New York: Sheed & Ward, 1936), cited it approvingly in *Humanisme Intégral*, p. 213.

28. Galli and Facchi, *La sinistra democristiana*, p. 267.

29. Pier Paolo Pasolini, "Gli italiani non sono più quelli," *Corriere della Sera*, 10 June 1974.

30. Paul Ginsborg, *A History of Contemporary Italy: Society and Politics 1943–1988* (London: Penguin, 1990), ch. 7, "The 'Economic Miracle': Rural Exodus and Social Transformation, 1958–1963."

31. Richard Drake, *The Revolutionary Mystique and Terrorism in Contemporary Italy* (Bloomington: Indiana University Press, 1989), pp. 46–54.

32. Aldo Moro, *L'intelligenza e gli avvenimenti: testi 1959–1978* (Milan: Garzanti, 1979), speech of 27 January 1962.

33. Moro praised John XXIII's encyclical *Mater et Magistra* in a 20 July 1961 speech; see *L'intelligenza e gli avvenimenti*.

34. For a thorough analysis of the role of the Kennedy administration in the opening to the left, see Spencer M. Di Scala, *Renewing Italian Socialism: Nenni to Craxi* (New York: Oxford University Press, 1988), chaps. 8, 9, and 10.

35. Ginsborg, *A History of Contemporary Italy*, p. 272.

36. See Baget-Bozzo, "DC, Moro, partito americano," *Argomenti radicali*, 10 (1978), and his book, which he wrote with Giovanni Tassani, *Aldo Moro: il politico nella crisi 1962–1973* (Florence: Sansoni, 1983), especially ch. 6, "Un Sogno Americano," in which Moro's "Americanism" and "Atlanticism" are severely criticized.

37. Pietro Scoppola offers a testy rebuttal to Baget-Bozzo's "gravely distorted" interpretation of Moro's leadership, in "De Gasperi e Moro," the lead article in Scoppola et al., *Moro, la democrazia cristiana e la cultura cattolica*, p. 12.

38. Roberto Ruffili, "Moro e la Costituzione," in ibid., p. 22.

39. Baget-Bozzo and Tassani, *Aldo Moro*, p. 191.

40. Ibid.

41. Italo Pietra, *Moro: fu vera gloria?* (Milan: Garzanti, 1983). See especially "A Palazzo Chigi," in which Moro is described as an incurable temporizer.

42. Pier Paolo Pasolini, *Empirismo eretico* (Milan: Garzanti, 1972), p. 21.

43. Leonardo Sciascia, *Todo Modo* (Turin: Einaudi, 1974), p. 25.

44. Moro, *L'intelligenza e gli avvenimenti*, speech of 29 June 1969.

45. Ibid., speech of 18 July 1971.

46. Ibid., speech of 20 March 1976.

47. See the following articles by Enrico Berlinguer in *Rinascita:* "Imperialismo e consistenza alla luce dei fatti cileni," 28 September 1973; "Riflessioni sull'Italia dopo i fatti di Cile: via democratica o violenza reazionaria," 5 October 1973; "Riflessioni sull'Italia dopo i fatti di Cile: alleanze sociali e schieramenti politici," 12 October 1973. See Peter Lange's "Crisis and Consent, Change and Compromise: Dilemmas of Italian Communism in the 1970s," in Peter Lange and Sidney Tarrow, eds., *Italy in Transition* (London, Frank Cass, 1980), for an analysis of the PCI's "historic compromise" strategy.

48. Moro, *L'intelligenza e gli avvenimenti*, speech of 21 September 1975.

49. Ibid., speech of June 1975.

50. Ginsborg, *A History of Contemporary Italy; passim.*

51. Baget-Bozzo and Tassani, *Aldo Moro*, ch. 14, "Nuovi confini e piccoli cabotaggi."

52. Giulio Andreotti, "Caro Enrico, se tu ci fossi ancora," *Europeo*, 1 January 1985, p. ix.

53. Ibid.

54. Eugenio Scalfari, "L'ultima intervista di Moro," *La Repubblica*, 18 February 1978, republished 14 October 1978.

55. Moro, *L'intelligenza e gli avvenimenti*, speech of 28 February 1978.

56. Processo Abatangelo, Pasquale + 172 (Moro ter), Corte di Assise di Roma, Udienza 8 October 1987, cartella 157, fascicolo 109, p. 12.

57. Gianfranco Piazzesi, "Aldo Moro: il suo ritratto è nei 'Promessi sposi,'" *Corriere della Sera*, 12 March 1978.

58. "I comunicati diffusi dalle Br nei 55 giorni," Foro Italico archive, Moro quater, la fase istruttoria, cartella 13, fascicolo 2, "Comunicato #1 del 16 marzo 1978," p. 220.

59. Ibid., "Comunicato #2 del 25 marzo 1978," pp. 223–224.

60. Ibid., p. 225.

61. "Le lettere di Aldo Moro," ibid., #7: "A Benigno Zaccagnini, segretario politico della Democrazia Cristiana," written between 11 and 24 April 1978, pp. 262–263.

62. Ibid., #11: "Al Partito della Democrazia Cristiana," written between 25 and 30 April 1978, p. 273.

2. The Italian Legal System

1. To reduce the congestion for which the Italian legal system had become notorious, the criminal code of 1989 called for some important changes in the roles of the public prosecutor and the investigating magistrate. Under the new system, an attempt was made to reduce the ambiguity of the public prosecutor's functions. Instead of combining judicial and prosecutorial functions, as in the old system, the second function was now strongly emphasized. As of

1989, this official replaced the investigating magistrate in carrying out the preliminary inquiries in a case. The investigating magistrate was given the responsibility of overseeing the legality of the preliminary inquiries and of deciding, at a preliminary hearing, whether or not the case should go to trial. The American prosecutorial model, which made it possible for judicial authorities to cut down on the number of cases that actually go to trial, has been cited as an incentive for the Italian reformers, but their efforts have culminated in what the same authority describes as "a kind of Italian-style prosecutorial trial, within a framework of laws which is certainly not that of the systems on which the prosecutorial model is based." Vittorio Grevi, "The New Italian Code for Criminal Procedure. A Concise Overview," *Italian Studies in Law: A Review of Legal Problems*, 2 (1992), p. 177.

2. For the history and structure of the Italian legal system, see Mauro Cappelletti, John Henry Merryman, and Joseph M. Perillo, *The Italian Legal System: An Introduction* (Stanford: Stanford University Press, 1967); G. Leroy Certoma, *The Italian Legal System* (London: Butterworths, 1985), John Henry Merryman and David S. Clark, *Comparative Law: Western European and Latin American Legal Systems* (Charlottesville, Va.: Michie, 1978); and Aldo Schiavone, ed., *Stato e cultura giuridica in Italia dall'unità alla repubblica* (Rome-Bari: Laterza, 1990).

3. The First Trial, Phase One

1. Giuliano Gallo, "Si cerca la verità sui giorni dell'orrore," *Il Giorno*, 13 April 1982.

2. Maurizio De Luca, "Guida al processo Moro," *L'Espresso*, 18 April 1982.

3. Tribunale di Roma, Procedimento penale #1482/78 G.I. EN 18/78 Contro Alunni, Corrado ed altri, vol. 1 bis, fascicolo 5, p. 1210.

4. Ibid., pp. 1452–1453 and pp. 1455–1456.

5. Ibid., fascicolo 8.

6. Ibid., vol. 5, fascicolo 14, pp. 185–189.

7. Ibid., fascicolo 15, pp. 43 and ff.

8. Ibid., "Documentazione fotografica," pp. 153–174.

9. Ibid., vol. 21, p. 90.

10. Ibid., p. 93. Guasco also analyzed Negri's writings, pp. 95 and ff.

11. Ibid., p. 154.

12. Sentenza istruttoria di proscioglimento, Moro bis, vol. 2, p. 432.

13. Ibid., vol. 1, pt. 2, "I motivi della decisione," p. 166.

14. Ibid., p. 163.

15. Ibid., p. 231.

16. Ibid., p. 231 and ff.

17. Ibid., p. 934.

18. Ibid., p. 247 and ff.

19. Ibid., p. 250.

20. Interview with the author, Foro Italico court chambers, 2 January 1991.

21. Costanzo Costantini, "Sei non pentiti in abiti alla moda, senza le stigmate psicologiche di chi uccide a freddo," *Il Messaggero*, 16 April 1982.

22. Ulderico Fiernoli, "Subito espulsi alla prima protesta i falchi delle br al processo Moro," *Il Tempo*, 15 April 1982.

23. "Moro 1," Corte di Assise di Roma, Dibattimento, Verbale Udienza, 28 April 1982, bobina 2, p. 17.

24. Ibid., bobina 1, p. 4.

25. Ibid., 4 May 1982, bobina 1, p. 24.

26. Ibid., bobina 2, p. 4.

27. Ibid., 5 May 1982, bobina 1, pp. 16–17.

28. Ibid., 3 May 1982, bobina 1, p. 48.

29. Ibid., 4 May 1982, bobina 1, p. 12.

30. Ibid.

31. Ibid., 29 April 1982, bobina 1, p. 1.

32. Ibid., 4 May 1982, bobina 1, p. 10.

33. Ibid., bobina 2, p. 29.

34. Ibid., 14 May 1982, bobina 5, p. 2.

35. Ibid., 19 May 1982, bobina 1, p. 21.

36. Ibid., 25 May 1982, bobina 1, p. 10.

37. Ibid., 27 May 1982, bobina 1, p. 45.

38. Ibid.

39. Ibid.

40. Ibid., 1 June 1982, bobina 1, p. 2.

41. Ibid., p. 5.

42. Ibid.

43. Ibid., 4 June 1982, bobina 1, p. 7.

44. Ibid., p. 1.

45. Ibid., p. 9.

46. Ibid., p. 3.

47. "Moro 1 e bis," Corte di Assise di Roma, Sentenza, p. 333.

48. Ibid., p. 336.

49. Ibid., p. 360.

50. "Moro 1," Corte di Assise di Roma, Dibattimento, Verbale Udienza, 14 June 1982, bobina 1, p. 2.

51. Ibid., p. 8.

52. Ibid., 28 June 1982, bobina 1, p. 6.

53. Ibid., p. 21.

54. Ibid., p. 22.

55. Ibid.

56. Ibid., 19 July 1982, bobina 2, p. 19.

57. Ibid.

58. Interview with the author, Foro Italico court chambers, 2 January 1991.

59. "Moro 1," Corte di Assise di Roma, Dibattimento, Verbale Udienza, 19 July 1982, bobina 2, p. 14.

60. Ibid., bobina 1, p. 23.

61. Ibid., 20 July 1982, bobina 1, p. 10 and ff.

62. Ibid., p. 58.

63. Flaminio Piccoli, "Caso Moro: la coerenza della DC," *Il Popolo*, 22 July 1982.

64. Leo Valiani, "La democrazia non deve lasciarsi mai disarmare," *Corriere della Sera*, 22 July 1982.

65. Interview with the author, Foro Italico court chambers, 3 January 1991.

4. The First Trial, Phase Two

1. All of this material is contained in "Moro 1," Corte di Assise di Roma, Dibattimento, Allegato, Verbale Udienza, 20 September 1982.

2. This was Pier Paolo Pasolini's description of Moro, cited by Leonardo Sciascia, *L'affaire Moro* (Palermo: Sellerio, 1978), p. 33.

3. For Andreotti's interpretation of the Moro affair, see his *Diari 1976–1979: gli anni della solidarietà* (Milan: Rizzoli, 1981) and *Visti da vicino: terza serie* (Milan: Rizzoli, 1985). His entire deposition before the Parliamentary Commission is in this last. President Santiapichi remembered Andreotti in "Moro 1" as one of the most intelligent and prepared witnesses he had ever examined in his vast courtroom experience. Interview with the author, Foro Italico court chambers, 3 January 1991.

4. Giuseppe Zupo, a lawyer at the Moro trials and the co-author of *Operazione Moro: i fili ancora coperti di una trama politica criminale*, was an especially hostile cross-examiner of Andreotti. President Santiapichi repeatedly had to chastise him for asking the witness political questions: "We are after concrete facts here." "Moro 1," Corte di Assise di Roma, Dibattimento, Verbale Udienza, 27 September 1982, p. 52.

5. Ibid., p. 63.

6. Ibid., p. 12.

7. Ibid., p. 75.

8. Ibid.

9. Ibid., pp. 12 and ff.

10. Andreotti was here referring to many of the papers found in the October 1978 raid on Milan's via Monte Nevoso. Even Mrs. Moro agreed in part with Andreotti on this point. For example, she described the so-called Moro memorial, recovered on this occasion, as a "poorly crafted collage" of her husband's words. Ibid., Verbale Udienza, 19 July 1982, pp. 7 and ff.

11. Ibid., Verbale Udienza, 27 September 1982, p. 19.

12. Ibid., p. 18.

13. Ibid., p. 9.

14. Ibid., p. 23.

15. Robert Katz, *Days of Wrath. The Ordeal of Aldo Moro: The Kidnapping, the Execution, the Aftermath* (Garden City, New York: Doubleday, 1980).

16. "Moro 1," Corte di Assise di Roma, Dibattimento, Verbale Udienza, 27 September 1982, p. 86.

17. Ibid.

18. Ibid.

19. Ibid., p. 104.

20. Interview with the author, Foro Italico court chambers, 3 January 1991.

21. "Moro 1," Corte di Assise di Roma, Dibattimento, Verbale Udienza, 27 September 1982, p. 106.

22. Ibid., pp. 110 and ff. and pp. 168–169.

23. Ibid.

24. The DC also used a "consultant," Daniele Pifano, the head of the Collettivo di via Dei Volsci near the University of Rome. Senator Claudio Vitalone contacted him, but the imprisoned Pifano was unable to take any constructive action. Ibid., Verbale Udienza, 25 October 1982, pp. 13–15. The significance of this particular effort lies in its DC sponsorship. Some Christian Democrats participated in the PSI's humanitarian initiative as well.

25. *Relazione della Commissione Parlamentare d'inchiesta sulla strage di via Fani sul sequestro e l'assassinio di Aldo Moro e sul terrorismo in Italia.* Camera dei deputati, VIII Legislatura della Repubblica Italiana, 1979–1983, Documenti e relazioni, vol. 131, doc. 23, #5, vol. 9, seduta 6 April 1982, pp. 272 and ff.

26. Under cross-examination Craxi insisted that he had become involved in the Moro case for the same reason that motivated him later in the D'Urso kidnapping case: "because the families asked me to do it. Otherwise, probably I would not have done it." "Moro 1," Corte di Assise di Roma, Dibattimento, Verbale Udienza, 28 September 1982, p. 25.

27. Ibid., p. 2.

28. Ibid.

29. Ibid., p. 4.

30. Ibid., p. 5.

31. Ibid.

32. Ibid.

33. Ibid., p. 7.

34. Ibid.

35. Ibid., p. 16.

36. Ibid., pp. 20 and ff.

37. Giannino Guiso, *La condanna di Aldo Moro: la verità dell' avvocato difensore di Renato Curcio* (Milan: Sugarco, 1979), p. 78.

38. Ibid., p. 17.

39. Ibid., p. 124.

40. Ibid., p. 248.

41. Ibid.

42. Ibid., p. 249.

43. *Relazione della Commissione Parlamentare d'inchiesta,* vol. 6, seduta 13 November 1980.

44. "Moro 1," Corte di Assise di Roma, Dibattimento, Verbale Udienza, 28 September 1982, pp. 19 and ff.

45. Andrea Purgatori, "Rischia di saltare il processo Moro," *Corriere della Sera,* 23 July 1984.

46. "Moro 1," Corte di Assise di Roma, Dibattimento, Verbale Udienza, 13 October 1982, p. 10.

47. Ibid., p. 40.

48. Ibid.

49. Ibid., p. 44.

50. Ibid.

51. Ibid., p. 45.

52. Ibid., p. 57.

53. Ibid.

54. Ibid.

55. Interview with the author at Foro Italico, 2 January 1991.

56. "Moro 1," Corte di Assise di Roma, Dibattimento, Verbale Udienza, 3 November 1982, p. 39.

57. Ibid., p. 40.

58. Ibid.

59. Ibid., p. 43.

60. Ibid.

61. Ibid., p. 45.

62. Ibid., pp. 46 and ff.

63. Ibid., Verbale Udienza, 10 November 1982, p. 41.

64. Ibid.

65. Ibid.

66. Luca Villoresi, "Nell'aula del processo Moro spunta il nome di Kissinger," *La Repubblica*, 11 November 1982.

67. Enzo Roggi, "Furono anni di spietata lotta, non di abbaglio," *l'Unità*, 11 November 1982.

68. The *arringhe* (summations) of the lawyers and the *requisitoria* (indictment) of the public minister are not among the court records in the Foro Italico depository. As President Santiapichi explained, "The lawyers talk too much, and we simply could not afford to transcribe everything they said." Interview with the author, Foro Italico court chambers, 4 January 1991. However, President Santiapichi did dictate brief summaries of the arringhe and the requisitoria, which the court secretary wrote down. His handwritten pages are a part of the court record. Moreover, journalists covering the trial summarized this part of the proceedings.

69. Andrea Purgatori, "Processo Moro: 'Il grande vecchio non è mai esistito,'" *La Repubblica*, 7 December 1982.

70. "Sentenza nel procedimento penale, Moro 1 e bis," Corte di Assise di Roma, vol. 19, p. 330.

71. Ibid. The list of terrorist crimes ran from pp. 23–150 and included 122 separate incidents in vol. 1.

72. Ibid., vol. 2, pt. 5, "I motivi della sentenza," p. 659.

73. Ibid., p. 755.

74. Ibid., p. 811.

75. Ibid., p. 834.

76. Ibid., p. 835.

77. Ibid., p. 908.

78. Ibid., p. 914.

79. Luca Villoresi, "Un gran silenzio nelle gabbie, poi il grido contro i pentiti," *La Repubblica*, 25 January 1983.

80. Tribunale di Roma, Procedimento penale #1482/78 G.I. EN 18/78 Contro Alunni, Corrado ed altri, vol. 1, fascicolo 31, pp. 7535–41 and in many other places as well.

5. The Moro Commission Reports

1. Giulio Andreotti, *Visti da vicino: terza serie* (Milan: Rizzoli, 1983). His entire 23 May 1980 deposition is reproduced in "La tragedia Moro."

2. *Relazione della Commissione Parlamentare d'inchiesta sulla strage di via Fani sul sequestro e l'assassinio di Aldo Moro e sul terrorismo in Italia.* Camera dei deputati, VIII Legislatura della Repubblica Italiana, 1979–1983, Documenti e relazioni, vol. 131, doc. 23, #5, vol. 3, seduta 23 May 1980, p. 242.

3. Ibid., vol. 5, seduta 9 October 1980, p. 304.

4. Ibid., seduta 1 August 1980, p. 10.

5. Ibid., p. 3.

6. Ibid., vol. 7, seduta 16 December 1980, p. 4.

7. Ibid.

8. Maria Fida Moro, *La casa dei cento natali* (Milan: Rizzoli, 1982), p. 29.

9. Ibid., pp. 44–45.

10. Ibid., p. 50.

11. Ibid., p. 56.

12. Ibid., p. 92.

13. Ibid., p. 82.

14. Ibid., p. 86.

15. *Relazione della Commissione Parlamentare d'inchiesta*, vol. 5, seduta 30 September 1980, p. 178.

16. Ibid., p. 215.

17. Ibid., vol. 11, seduta 16 February 1983, p. 5.

18. Ibid., vol. 3, seduta 23 May 1980, p. 191.

19. Richard Drake, *The Revolutionary Mystique and Terrorism in Contemporary Italy* (Bloomington: Indiana University Press, 1989), ch. 5, "7 aprile 1979."

20. *Relazione della Commissione Parlamentare d'inchiesta*, vol. 1, Relazione di maggioranza, p. 129.

21. Ibid., p. 87.

22. Ibid.

23. Ibid.

24. Ibid., p. 105.

25. Ibid.

26. Ibid., p. 113.

27. Ibid., vol. 9, seduta 6 April 1982, p. 350.

28. Ibid., p. 352.

29. See Mario Sossi, *Nella prigione delle Br* (Milan: Editoriale Nuova, 1979). Sossi was a 1974 kidnap victim of the Red Brigades.

30. *Relazione della Commissione Parlamentare d'inchiesta*, vol. 5, seduta 9 October 1980, p. 350.

31. Ibid., vol. 6, seduta 9 December 1980, p. 485.

32. Ibid.

33. Ibid., vol. 2, Relazione di minoranza dei deputati Luigi Covatta e Claudio Martelli e dei senatori Paolo Barsacchi e Libero Della Briotta (gruppo parlamentare del PSI), p. 37.

34. Ibid., vol. 7, seduta 10 February 1981, p. 238.

35. Ibid.

36. Ibid., vol. 2, Relazione di minoranza . . . del PSI, p. 50.

37. Ibid., Relazione di minoranza del deputato Franco Franchi e del senatore Michele Marchio (gruppo parlamentare del MSI-DN), p. 86.

38. Ibid.

39. Ibid., p. 72.

40. Ibid.

41. Ibid., Relazione di minoranza del deputato Leonardo Sciascia (gruppo parlamentare radicale), p. 400.

42. See especially Robert Katz, *Days of Wrath. The Ordeal of Aldo Moro* (Garden City: Doubleday, 1980) and Robin Erica Wagner-Pacifici, *The Moro Morality Play: Terrorism as Social Drama* (Chicago: University of Chicago Press, 1986).

43. Leonardo Sciascia, *L'affaire Moro* (Palermo: Sellerio, 1978), p. 33.

44. Ibid., p. 43.

45. Ibid., p. 73.

46. Ibid., p. 63.

47. *Relazione della Commissione Parlamentare d'inchiesta*, vol. 2, Relazione di minoranza del deputato Egidio Sterpa (gruppo parlamentare del PLI), p. 420.

48. Ibid.

6. The P2 Commission Reports

1. "Tina Anselmi, 'C'è ombra della P2 nei 55 giorni del sequestro Moro,'" *La Repubblica*, 29–30 May 1983.

2. "Riesplode la polemica sulle colpe dei partiti," *La Repubblica*, 31 May 1983.

3. Giuseppe Sangiorgi, "I molti interrogativi sull'uccisione di Moro," *Il Popolo*, 21 September 1983.

4. Giorgio Dell'Arti, "C'è la firma del Venerabile in molte storie di terrorismo," *La Repubblica*, 10 May 1984.

5. *Relazione della Commissione Parlamentare d'inchiesta sulla Loggia Massonica P2*, doc. 23, #2 (Rome: 1984), "Introduzione."

6. Ibid., ch. 1, "L'origine e la natura"; pt. 3, "La seconda fase della Loggia P2: dal 1974 al 1981," p. 23.

7. Ibid., ch. 2, "L'organizzazione e la consistenza," p. 51.

8. Ibid., p. 53.

9. Ibid., ch. 4, "Le finalità perseguite," pt. 3, "Il piano di rinascita ed il principio del controllo."

10. Ibid., ch. 3, "I mezzi impiegati e le attività svolte," p. 87.

11. Ibid.

12. Ibid., p. 93.

13. Ibid.

14. Ibid.

15. Ibid., sect. II, "I collegamenti con l'eversione," pt. 3, "L'affare Moro," p. 103.

16. Ibid., p. 104.

17. Sandra Bonsanti, "Teodori mette sotto accusa Andreotti e Tina Anselmi," *La Repubblica*, 20 July 1984.

18. Ibid.

19. *Commissione Parlamentare d'inchiesta sulla Loggia Massonica P2: Relazione di minoranza dell'onorevole Massimo Teodori*, doc. 23, #2-bis/1 (Rome: 1984), pt. 1, "Prassi: la vera azione della P2," ch. 1, "I rapporti con la P2: lo scheletro nell'armadio dei partiti," p. 9.

20. Ibid.

21. Ibid., p. 15.

22. Ibid., p. 13.

23. Ibid., ch. 2, "I rapporti con il Pci," p. 20.

24. Ibid., ch. 3, "Destabilizzare per stabilizzare."

25. Ibid., ch. 4, "Il sistema P2 erede di Sindona."

26. Ibid.

27. Ibid., ch. 5, "Moro-Andreotti-P2," p. 69.

28. Ibid.

29. Ibid.

30. *Commissione Parlamentare d'inchiesta sulla Loggia Massonica P2: Relazione di minoranza del Senatore Giorgio Pisanò*, doc. 23, #2, 2-bis/2 (Rome: 1984).

31. Malachi Martin, *The Final Conclave* (New York: Stein & Day, 1978), p. 24.

32. Richard Hammer, *The Vatican Connection* (New York: Holt, Rinehart & Winston, 1982), pt. 5, "To the Vatican," esp. p. 195.

33. Luigi Di Fonzo, *St. Peter's Banker* (New York: Franklin Watts, 1983), p. 59.

34. Sindona made this claim to Nick Tosches, the author of *Power on Earth: Michele Sindona's Explosive Story* (New York: Arbor House, 1986), p. 165. The portrait of Sindona in this book is, on the whole, flattering.

35. Tosches expressly contradicts Di Fonzo's account of how Mafia drug profits were invested in legitimate businesses, ibid., ch. 7, "A Christian Darkness."

36. Di Fonzo, *St. Peter's Banker*, ch. 4, "The Vatican Connection."

37. *Commissione Parlamentare d'inchiesta sulla Loggia Massonica P2: Relazione di minoranza del Senatore Giorgio Pisanò*. Vatican corruption is a leading theme of the entire Neofascist report.

38. Di Fonzo, *St. Peter's Banker*, ch. 19, "The Collapse of an Empire: Pope Paul VI and His Banker Fall from Power."

39. *CIA. The Pike Report* (Nottingham: Spokesman Books, 1977), p. 193.

40. Di Fonzo, *St. Peter's Banker*, p. 220.

41. Ibid., ch. 23, "Kidnapped."

42. Ibid., "Epilogue."

43. Ibid. Sindona apparently did that on 20 March 1986, two days after receiving a life sentence for the murder of Giorgio Ambrosoli. See Tosches, *Power on Earth*, ch. 12, "The Terminator's Secret." A prolonged public dispute followed, with many experts still holding that he was poisoned in his cell. On 10 February 1989 the television docu-drama show of Corrado Augias, "Telefono giallo," devoted an entire program to this continuing controversy.

44. *Commissione Parlamentare d'inchiesta sulla Loggia Massonica P2 . . . Giorgio Pisanò*, "1974 l'anno determinante."

45. Larry Gurwin, *The Calvi Affair: Death of a Banker* (London: Macmillan, 1983), ch. 2, "The Priests' Bank."

46. Ibid., ch. 7, "Dangerous Plan."

47. Ibid., ch. 16, "The New Fixer."

48. Ibid., ch. 13, "Arrest and Trial."

49. Ibid., ch. 15, "Letters of Comfort."

50. On 26 January 1989 a Milan judge declared that Calvi had been killed. Accordingly, his widow received his life insurance benefits, amounting to ten billion lire.

7. The Second Trial

1. Franco Scottoni, "Morucci ora confessa, 'In via Fani io c'ero,'" *La Repubblica*, 19 September 1984.

2. Giorgio Galli, *Storia del partito armato: 1968–1982* (Milan: Rizzoli, 1986), ch. 8, "Moro."

3. Giorgio Bocca, "Perché le Br uccisero Moro," *L'Espresso*, 30 September 1984.

4. Oreste Scalzone, "La mia verità su Moro," *Panorama*, 1 October 1984.

5. Piero Valentino, "Morucci ha torto, l'operazione Moro non ha segnato la fine delle Br," *La Repubblica*, 6 November 1984.

6. Giorgio Bocca, "Io, Moro e le Br," *L'Espresso*, 2 December 1984.

7. Ibid. See also Moretti's remarks to Bocca in *Noi terroristi: 12 anni di lotta armata ricostruiti e discussi con i protagonisti* (Milan: Garzanti, 1985), passim.

8. Daniele Mastrogiacomo, "Il Vaticano smentisce i contatti per Moro," *La Repubblica*, 8 December 1984.

9. Enzo Forcella, "Dietro le sbarre il grande regista è ancora Moretti," *La Repubblica*, 11 December 1984.

10. Daniele Mastrogiacomo, "Urla e comunicati, tornano le br," *La Repubblica.* 18 December 1984.

11. Ibid.

12. Luciano Pedrelli, "Sconvolto dalle scene d'orrore si uccide uno dei soccoratori," *La Repubblica*, 27 December 1984.

13. La Corte di Assise di Appello di Roma, Udienza, 4 January 1985, p. 5.

14. Ibid., p. 2.

15. Ibid., Udienza, 5 January 1985, bobina 2, p. 6.

16. Ibid., Udienza, 4 January 1985, p. 28.

17. Ibid., p. 44.

18. Ibid.

19. Ibid., Udienza, 5 January 1985, p. 4.

20. Ibid., p. 8.

21. Ibid., p. 12.

22. Ibid., p. 23.

23. Ibid.

24. Ibid., Udienza, 4 January 1985, p. 2.

25. Ibid., Udienza, 10 January 1985, p. 36.

26. Ibid., Udienza, 14 January 1985, p. 11.

27. Ibid., Udienza, 18 January 1985, p. 7769.

28. Ibid., p. 24.

29. Ibid.

30. Ibid., Udienza, 23 January 1985, p. 20.

31. Ibid., Udienza, 5 February 1985, "Confronto Morucci-Savasta," pp. 2–3.

32. Enrico Fenzi to President of the Court De Nictolis, 14 February 1985, p. 9637 in the court file for 21 February 1985.

33. Ibid.

34. Copies of the arringhe by the lawyers and the requisitoria by the pubblico ministero are not in the court record for the reason President Santiapichi gave in Moro 1: lawyers and public ministers talk too much, and it would be too expensive to transcribe their statements. Brief handwritten summaries of some of these statements are to be found in the court record, but I have cross-checked newspaper summaries of the trial.

35. Daniele Mastrogiacomo, "Trent'anni a Morucci e Faranda," *La Repubblica*, 15 March 1985.

36. La Corte di Assise di Appello di Roma, "Sentenza," 14 March 1985, p. 276. Judge Caso was the *estensore*, or author, of this document.

37. Ibid., p. 60.

38. Ibid.

39. Ibid., p. 63.

40. Ibid., p. 127.

41. Ibid. Cited in the "Motivi della decisione," p. 124.

42. Ibid., p. 125.

43. Ibid.

44. Mino Fucillo and Claudio Gerino, "Venti pallottole firmate Brigate Rosse," *La Repubblica*, 28 March 1985.

45. Brigate Rosse, "No. 20," March 1985, dedication page.

46. Ibid., p. 41.

47. Ibid., p. 42.

48. "Insurrezione Armata contro i poteri dello Stato/Guerra Civile nella forma della proporzione," Tribunale di Roma, Ufficio istruzione, Sentenza istruttoria di proscioglimento, il giudice istruttore Francesco Amato, 21 July 1983, ch. 5, "Contrasti nella Organizzazione," pp. 1818 and ff.

49. Ibid.

50. Brigate Rosse, "No. 20," p. 5.

51. Ibid., p. 17.

52. Ibid., p. 19.

8. Moro Ter: The First Year

1. Brigate Rosse, "Rivendicazione," 10 February 1986, p. 1. This document was entered into the court records for Moro quater.

2. Ibid.

3. Ibid., p. 4.

4. Ibid., p. 3.

5. Ibid., p. 8.

6. Ibid., p. 7.

7. Ibid., p. 8.

8. Ibid., pp. 10–11.

9. Ibid., p. 11.

10. Ibid.

11. Claudio Gerino and Paolo Vagheggi, "L'hanno ucciso con la Skorpion che fu usato contro Tarantelli," *La Repubblica*, 13 February 1986.

12. Nick Tosches, *Power on Earth: Michele Sindona's Explosive Story* (New York: Arbor House, 1986), p. 277.

13. Tribunale di Roma, Sentenza istruttoria di proscioglimento, Moro ter, vol. 4, pt. 3, "I singoli imputati," pp. 1210–1307.

14. Ibid., vol. 2, p. 556.

15. Ibid., vol. 3, p. 692.

16. Ibid. In Moro quater, however, Judge Priore acknowledged that Piancone was not involved in the via Fani massacre. On 19 December 1990 I asked him about his earlier claim involving Piancone, and the judge said that the sentenza istruttoria for Moro ter reflected his knowledge at that time. When I

interviewed him he was wholly convinced that no foreigner had participated in the terrorist command at via Fani.

17. Ibid., p. 693.

18. Franco Scottoni, "Si è iniziato a Rebibbia il processo Moro ter," *La Repubblica*, 17 June 1986.

19. Maurizio De Luca, "L'altro Moro: la vera storia del conto svizzero," *L'Espresso*, 9 November 1986.

20. Paolo Cabras, "Perché difendiamo Aldo Moro," *Il Popolo*, 15 November 1985.

21. Roberto Martinelli and Ezio Mauro, "Nessuno volle credere alle paure di Moro," *La Stampa*, 23 October 1986.

22. Franco Di Bella, *Corriere segreto* (Milan: Rizzoli, 1982), p. 410.

23. Martinelli and Mauro, "Nessuno volle credere."

24. Ibid.

25. Tribunale di Roma, Sentenza istruttoria di proscioglimento, Moro ter, vol. 4, pt. 3, "I singoli imputati," p. 1210.

26. Sentenze nel procedimento penale, Moro 1 e bis, Corte di Assise di Roma, vol. 4, p. 1221.

27. Processo c/Abatangelo, Pasquale + 172 (Moro ter), Corte di Assise di Roma, Udienza, 9 October 1986, cartella 147, fascicolo 17, p. 10. In his courtroom testimony at Rebibbia Buzzatti provided some additional information about his ideological background.

28. Sentenza istruttoria, Moro ter, vol. 4, pt. 3, p. 1260.

29. Ibid., p. 1215.

30. Ibid., p. 1276.

31. Ibid.

32. Ibid.

33. Ibid.

34. Ibid., pp. 1290–91.

35. Ibid., p. 1296.

36. Moro ter, Udienza, 9 October 1986, cartella 147, fascicolo 17, p. 74.

37. Ibid., p. 75.

38. The film premiered on 13 November 1986 and starred Gian Maria Volontè as Moro. Earlier he had played Moro, in an entirely different vein, in Elio Petri's screen version of Leonardo Sciascia's *Todo Modo*. Robert Katz wrote the screenplay for Ferrara's film, and, unsurprisingly, "Il caso Moro" presented the conspiracy theory the writer had advanced in *Days of Wrath. The Ordeal of Aldo Moro: The Kidnapping, the Execution, the Aftermath* (New York: Doubleday, 1980). For the screenplay and much of the controversy surrounding the film, see Armenia Balducci, Giuseppe Ferrara, Robert Katz, *Il caso Moro* (Naples: Tullio Pironti, 1987). The DC and the PCI hated the film, but even some PSI critics who had opposed fermezza in 1978 thought

that "Il caso Moro" ignored the complexity of history in favor of partisanship of the most objectionable kind. See Ugo Intini, "Il caso Moro," *Mondo operaio*, 1 (January 1987).

39. Moro ter, letter from Lauro Azzolini to President Sorichilli, 29 October 1986; letter from Giorgio Semeria to President Sorichilli, 29 October 1986, entered into the court record, Udienza, 4 November 1986, cartella 148, fascicolo 27.

40. Ibid., Lauro Azzolini to President Sorichilli.

41. Sentenza istruttoria, Moro ter, vol. 4, pt. 3, "I singoli imputati," p. 1402.

42. Moro ter, Udienza, 12 December 1986, cartella 149, fascicolo 40, p. 48.

43. Ibid., p. 89.

44. Ibid., p. 91.

45. Moro ter, Udienza, 16 January 1987, cartella 150, fascicolo 46, p. 68.

46. Ibid., p. 76.

47. Giorgio Bocca, ed., *Moro, una tragedia italiana: le lettere, i documenti, le polemiche* (Milan: Bompiani, 1978), "Comunicato 1," received 18 March 1978, p. 35.

48. Ibid., "Comunicato 4," received 4 April 1978, p. 48.

49. See also "Proletario metropolitano e movimento di resistenza proletario offensivo," in "Risoluzione della Direzione Strategica" appended to "Comunicato 4," ibid.

50. Moro ter, Udienza, 21 January 1987, cartella 150, fascicolo 47, p. 77.

51. Ibid., Udienza, 11 February 1987, cartella 151, fascicolo 55, p. 2.

52. Ibid., Udienza, 17 February 1987, cartella 151, fascicolo 57, p. A-1.

53. Ibid., p. A-2.

54. Ibid., p. A-3.

55. Sandro Acciari, "Le due anime delle Br," *L'Espresso*, 1 March 1987.

56. Ibid.

57. Unione dei Comunisti Combattenti, "Communication," 23 March 1987, p. 1. This document was entered into the court records for Moro quater, fase istruttoria.

58. Ibid., p. 2.

59. Ibid., p. 11.

60. Piero Bertolazzi, Renato Curcio, Maurizio Ianelli, and Mario Moretti, "Occorre una soluzione politica per tutti," *Il Manifesto*, 5–6 April 1987.

61. Rossana Rossanda, "Parole e silenzio," in ibid.

62. Bertolazzi et al., "Occorre," in ibid.

63. Lauro Azzolini to President Sorichilli, 29 October 1986, Moro ter, Udienza, 4 November 1986, cartella 148, fascicolo 27.

64. Vittorio Mimmi, "Roma, deferiti 20 avvocati per abbandono di difesa," *La Repubblica*, 6 May 1987.

65. Moro ter, Udienza, 7 May 1987, cartella 155, fascicolo 84, p. 7.

66. Ibid., p. 77.

67. Ibid., p. 78.

68. Ibid.

69. Guglielmo Sasinini, "Le prove che Moretti ci deve dare," *La Famiglia Cristiana*, 20 May 1987. The contents of this interview were leaked to the daily press earlier.

70. See also another interview with Piccoli: Antonio Padellaro, "'Si, diamo pure la grazia a Curcio, ma deve dirci la verità su Moro,'" *Corriere della Sera*, 25 April 1987.

71. Giovanni Fasanella, "Caso Moro: il P.M. chiede che Piccoli venga interrogato," *l'Unità*, 14 May 1987. This was a reference to the *Metropoli* trial, not to Moro ter.

72. Flaminio Piccoli, letter to the director of *Il Giornale*, 14 May 1987.

73. Piccoli, "A proposito di una polemica," *Il Popolo*, 14 May 1987. Udienza, 15 May 1987, cartella 155, fascicolo 88, p. 4.

9. The *Metropoli* Trial

1. Tribunale di Roma/Ufficio Istruzione, Sentenza-Ordinanza nel procedimento penale #1067/97 AG I, cartella 20 (fase istruttoria), p. 881.

2. Franco Piperno, "Dal terrorismo alla guerriglia," *Pre-print*, December 1978.

3. Karl Marx, *The Civil War in France: The Paris Commune* (New York: International Publishers, 1968 ed.), p. 69.

4. Tribunale di Roma/Ufficio Istruzione, Sentenza-Ordinanza nel procedimento penale #1067/97 AG I, p. 326.

5. Tribunale di Roma, Sentenza-Ordinanza contro Piperno, Francesco + 4, #1267/81 AG I, cartella 17 (fase istruttoria), ch. 1, p. 34.

6. Ibid., p. 37.

7. Ibid., p. 150.

8. Ibid., p. 261.

9. Ibid., p. 262.

10. Tribunale di Roma, procedimento contro Pace, Lanfranco e Piperno, Francesco, #1267/81A, cartella 14, unnumbered fascicolo for the 1 October 1986 session, p. 81.

11. Ibid., Udienza, 13 October 1986, p. 18.

12. Ibid., p. 139. On this day President Santiapichi convened a rare afternoon session.

13. Ibid., Udienza, 15 October 1986, p. 78.

14. Ibid., p. 77.

15. Morucci later explained that the differences between the various revolutionary groups could be likened to the *correnti* or currents within the DC: "there are [these differences] in all parties, in all movements." Ibid., p. 153.

16. Ibid., p. 90.

17. Ibid., Udienza, 13 October 1986, p. 33.

18. Ibid., Udienza, 15 October 1986, p. 91.

19. Ibid., p. 92.

20. Ibid., Udienza, 13 October 1986, p. 4.

21. Ibid., Udienza, 15 October 1986, p. 116.

22. Ibid., Udienza, 15 December 1986, cartella 16, unnumbered fascicolo, p. 2.

23. Ibid., p. 6.

24. Ibid., pp. 18–19.

25. Ibid., p. 19.

26. Ibid., p. 40.

27. Ibid., p. 45.

28. Ibid., p. 33.

29. Ibid., p. 73.

30. Ibid., Udienza, 16 December 1986, p. 13.

31. See Alberto Franceschini (with Pier Vittorio Buffa and Franco Giustolisi), *Mara, Renato e io: storia dei fondatori delle BR* (Milan: Mondadori, 1988).

32. Tribunale di Roma, procedimento contro Pace, Lanfranco e Piperno, Francesco, Udienza, 16 December 1986, p. 44.

33. Ibid., p. 55.

34. Ibid., p. 61.

35. Ibid., p. 63.

36. Ibid., p. 65.

37. Ibid., Udienza, 17 December 1986, p. 90.

38. Ibid., p. 103.

39. Ibid., p. 131.

40. Ibid., p. 144.

41. Ibid., p. 168.

42. Marcella Andreoli, "'Ora mi tolgo il peso degli anni di piombo,'" *L'Europeo*, 6–7 1987. On 2 February this issue was entered into the court record of the *Metropoli* trial.

43. Tribunale di Roma, procedimento contro Pace, Lanfranco e Piperno, Francesco, Udienza, 12 January 1987, cartella 17, unnumbered fascicolo, p. 21.

44. M. Antonietta Calabro, "Fioroni torna, accusa, mente e ride," *Corriere della Sera*, 13 January 1987.

45. Tribunale di Roma, procedimento contro Pace, Lanfranco e Piperno, Francesco, Udienza, 27 January 1987, p. 80.

46. Ibid., p. 79.

47. Ibid., pp. 79–80.

48. Giorgio Bocca, *Noi terroristi: 12 anni di lotta armata ricostruiti e discussi con i protagonisti* (Milan: Garzanti, 1985), pp. 58–59.

49. Ibid., "Il big bang del '68."

50. Ibid., p. 125.

51. Ibid., p. 60.

52. Ibid., p. 149.

53. Ibid., p. 151.

54. Ibid., pp. 126–127.

55. Ibid., p. 27.

56. Franceschini told Bocca, "Sometimes after an event we said to each other: but this is what we have read in 'What Is To Be Done?'. This we have found in *State and Revolution.*" Ibid., p. 81.

57. Ibid., pp. 206–207.

58. Ibid., p. 211.

59. Ibid.

60. The reaction of Autonomia's *Rosso* illustrates Bocca's point perfectly. See Richard Drake, *The Revolutionary Mystique and Terrorism in Contemporary Italy* (Bloomington: Indiana University Press, 1989), ch. 5, "7 *aprile* 1979," especially pp. 90–96.

61. Bocca, *Noi terroristi*, p. 214.

62. Ibid., p. 215.

63. Ibid., p. 217.

64. Tribunale di Roma, procedimento contro Pace, Lanfranco e Piperno, Francesco, Udienza, 16 February 1987, cartella 18, unnumbered fascicolo, p. 22.

65. Ibid., Udienza, 23 February 1987, p. 2.

66. Ibid., p. 3.

67. Ibid., p. 59.

68. Ibid., Udienza, 3 March 1987. Faranda's testimony for this session was entered into the court record of Moro ter. See cartella 169 ("C"), p. 58, in the Foro Italico archive.

69. Ibid., p. 60.

70. Ibid., p. 63.

71. Ibid., Udienza, 9 March 1987, cartella 19, unnumbered fascicolo, p. 144.

72. Ibid., p. 151.

73. Ibid., p. 159.

74. Ibid., Udienza, 24 March 1987, p. 14.

75. Ibid., p. 16.

76. Ibid.

77. Ibid., Udienza, 13 April 1987, cartella 20, unnumbered fascicolo, p. 30.

78. See Bonisoli's testimony in Moro ter, Udienza, 22 September 1987, cartella 157, fascicolo 101, p. 15.

79. Fabio Cavalera, "Il primo obiettivo fu Andreotti, ma era troppo protetto," *Corriere della Sera*, 6 October 1985.

80. Tribunale di Roma, procedimento contro Pace, Lanfranco e Piperno, Francesco, Udienza, 12 May 1987, cartella 20, unnumbered fascicolo, p. 2.

81. Ibid.

82. See Paolo Graldi, "'Dal br Moretti ho saputo segreti sul delitto Moro,'" *Corriere della Sera*, 28 April 1987.

83. Sentenza nel processo *Metropoli*, la 1° Corte di Assise di Roma, p. 295.

84. Ibid., p. 331.

85. Piperno voluntarily returned to an Italian prison on 17 January 1988 and proclaimed his eagerness to testify in the *Metropoli* appeal trial, scheduled to begin later that year. In the witness chair, Piperno insisted on his innocence in the Moro case and completely rejected the state's indictment. On 19 May 1988, the appeal court reduced his sentence from ten to four years, holding that he was guilty only of subversive association. Lanfranco Pace, still a fugitive, received the same sentence reduction. It was not certain that Piperno would have to serve any more prison time, and he left the courtroom a free man, obliged only to report twice a week to his local police station. On 27 February 1989, however, the Corte della Cassazione ordered him to serve thirty-six months of his four-year sentence.

10. Moro Ter: The Second Year

1. Moro ter, Udienza, 8 October 1987, cartella 157, fascicolo 109, p. 1.

2. Ibid.

3. "Censurati," *Il Borghese*, 49 (27 January 1985).

4. Francesco D. Caridi, "Dov'è il film di Moro?," *Il Borghese*, 7 (17 February 1985).

5. Moro ter, Udienza, 8 October 1987, p. 5.

6. Ibid., p. 6.

7. Ibid., Udienza, 27 October 1987, cartella 158, fascicolo 117, p. 33. Graldi's article, "Dal br Moretti ho saputo segreti sul delitto Moro," appeared in *Corriere della Sera* on 28 April 1987.

8. Ibid., p. 40.

9. Ibid., p. 41.

10. Ibid., Udienza, 3 November 1987, cartella 159, fascicolo 120, p. 42.

11. Ibid., p. 45.

12. Paolo Graldi, "Su Moro, Andreotti e Craxi divisi (come 10 anni fa)," *Corriere della Sera*, 6 March 1988.

13. Alceste Santini, "Il Vaticano era pronto a pagare ogni riscatto," *l'Unità*, 6 March 1988.

14. Alessandro Natta, Berlinguer's successor as PCI secretary, totally supported Andreotti and praised him as a strong, resolute, and consistent leader throughout Moro's ordeal. Chiara Valentini, "Tutto per lo Stato: intervista con Alessandro Natta," *Panorama*, 20 March 1988.

15. Chiara Valentini, "Il Papa era pronto a pagare: intervista con Giulio Andreotti," *Panorama*, 13 March 1988.

16. Ibid.

17. Giovanni Valentini, "Una ferita aperta: intervista con Bettino Craxi," *L'Espresso*, 20 March 1988.

18. Sergio Criscuoli, "Andreotti attacca il Psi," *l'Unità*, 6 March 1986.

19. Silvana Mazzocchi, "Un br pentito alla Camera, 'Tutti noi avremmo ucciso'," *La Repubblica*, 21 January 1988.

20. Enrico Fenzi, *Armi e bagagli: un diario dalle Brigate Rosse* (Genoa: Costa & Nolan, 1987), p. 25.

21. Ibid., p. 78.

22. For Negri, see Richard Drake, *The Revolutionary Mystique and Terrorism in Contemporary Italy* (Bloomington: Indiana University Press, 1989), ch. 5, "7 *aprile* 1979."

23. Fenzi, *Armi e bagagli*, p. 150.

24. Ibid., p. 76.

25. Alberto Franceschini (with Pier Vittorio Buffa and Franco Giustolisi), *Mara, Renato e io: storia dei fondatori delle BR* (Milan: Mondadori, 1988), p. 8.

26. Ibid., p. 80.

27. Ibid., p. 160.

28. Ibid., p. 109.

29. Ibid., p. 149.

30. Ibid., p. 170.

31. Ibid., p. 156.

32. Ibid., p. 157.

33. Ibid., pp. 157–158.

34. Ibid., p. 204.

35. Luciano Pedrelli and Pietro Visconti, "Un sicario e tre colpi alla nuca," *La Repubblica*, 17–18 April 1988.

36. Sabino Acquaviva, *The Decline of the Sacred in Industrial Society* (New York: Harper & Row, 1979).

37. Sandra Bonsanti, "Mille nomi nel mirino del terrore," *La Repubblica*, 27 April 1988.

38. Antonio Cipriani, "La sentenza del processo Moro ter," *l'Unità*, 13 October 1988.

39. Corte di Assise di Roma, "Sentenza," Moro ter, ch. 2, "La Direzione Strategica," p. 264.

40. Ibid., p. 276.

41. Ibid., p. 284. The judges noted a third category, "the legal regular," who still had a life above ground. Lawyers who worked for the organization would fall into this category.

42. Ibid., p. 287.

43. Ibid., p. 298.

44. Ibid., ch. 24, "L'eccidio di via Fani—il sequestro e l'omicidio dell'on. Moro," p. 372.

45. Ibid., p. 373.

46. Ibid., p. 374.

47. Ibid., p. 375.

48. Ibid., p. 379.

49. Ibid., p. 381.

50. Ibid.

51. Ibid.

52. Ibid., p. 380.

53. Ibid., p. 381.

54. Moro ter, Udienza, 7 May 1987, p. 59.

55. "Sentenza," Moro ter, ch. 24, p. 383.

56. Ibid., p. 384.

57. Ibid., p. 386.

58. Ibid.

59. Ibid.

60. Ibid., p. 387.

61. Sergio Flamigni, *La tela del ragno: il delitto Moro* (Rome: Associate, 1988), p. 75.

62. Ibid. See ch. 6, "Tra parapsicologia e polizia scientifica."

63. See Giuseppe Zupo and Vincenzo Marini Recchia, *Operazione Moro: i fili ancora coperti di una trama politica criminale* (Milan: Franco Angeli, 1984).

11. Moro Quater: To Tangentopoli

1. Judge Priore confirmed this point during an interview with me in his Tribunale di Roma office, on 17 December 1990.

2. Sentenza istruttoria di proscioglimento, Moro quater, 20 August 1990, p. 57. The "Memorie difensive di Morucci e Faranda," including the 282-page-long "Memoriale di Morucci," are to be found in the Foro Italico archive,

Moro quater (fase istruttoria), cartella 13, fascicolo 1–2. Morucci's revealing correspondence with "Teresilla," a nun who works in the prisons, is in the same collection of documents.

3. Angelo Montonati and Guglielmo Sasinini, "'Così noi B.R. ci sfasciammo'," *La Famiglia Cristiana*, 45, (16 November 1988).

4. Judge Priore expressed admiration for Senator Flamigni's intelligence and his knowledge about the Moro case, but on balance he found the thesis advanced in *La tela del ragno* "forced" and "exaggerated" (interview, 17 December 1990). It was a "political thesis," not a legal one, and judges, he said, have to make very careful distinctions in these matters.

5. Sentenza istruttoria di proscioglimento, Moro quater, p. 76.

6. Ibid., p. 83.

7. Ibid., p. 128.

8. Ibid., p. 140.

9. Ibid., p. 169.

10. Ibid., p. 108. At the interview Judge Priore strongly reiterated this point. Judge Francesco Amato, an investigating magistrate during the fase istruttoria of Moro 1, expressed the same viewpoint when I interviewed him in the Tribunale di Roma offices on 22 December 1990. Judge Amato had not read Flamigni's book because he could not bear to go over all of that ground again: "I gave the Moro case six years of my life, during which I never took a vacation and read so much that I suffered a detached retina in my right eye; it was a frantic time that I remember with a sense of oppression."

11. Rocco Tolfa, "Caccia ai manovratori," *Il Sabato*, 15 December 1990.

12. "Terrorismo di servizio," ibid.

13. Ibid.

14. Ibid.

15. Rocco Tolfa, "Brigatisti dalle lunghe ombre," ibid.

16. Ibid.

17. Ibid.

18. Ibid.

19. Wladimiro Settimelli, "Andreotti: 'Qualcuno nasconde gli originali'," *l'Unità*, 13 October 1990.

20. Giampaolo Pansa, "Il giorno dei veleni," *La Repubblica*, 19 October 1990.

21. In December 1990 it was established that the Red Brigades themselves had built the hiding place in the wall where the Moro materials were found. Neither a *manona* nor a *manina* was involved.

22. "Forlani avanza la tesi 'complotto'," *La Repubblica*, 14 December 1990.

23. Vincenzo Vasile, "Dodici anni fa aveva scritto, 'Tutto questo ricomparirà'," *l'Unità*, 23 October 1990.

24. Ibid. To add to the confusion, different versions of the same information were to be found in the carteggio.

25. Ibid., pp. 3, 10.

26. Ibid., p. 10.

27. Ibid., p. 3.

28. Ibid., pp. 3–4.

29. Ibid., p. 4.

30. Ibid., p. 12.

31. Ibid., p. 9.

32. Ibid.

33. Ibid., p. 10.

34. Ibid., p. 18.

35. Ibid., pp. 7–8.

36. Ibid., p. 21.

37. Ibid.

38. Ibid., pp. 22–24.

39. Ibid.

40. Ibid., p. 23.

41. Ibid.

42. Ibid., p. 24.

43. Eugenio Scalfari, "Interroghiamo Andreotti a domanda risponde," *La Repubblica*, 19 October 1990.

44. Tolfa, "Brigatisti dalle lunghe ombre."

45. Tolfa, "Caccia ai manovratori."

46. Giorgio Bocca, "Io, Moro, e le Br," *L'Espresso*, 2 December 1984.

47. Concita De Gregorio, "Occhetto: 'Br pilotate nel rapimento Moro'," *La Repubblica*, 15 December 1990.

48. Ibid.

49. Sebastiano Messina, "Craxi: 'Attenti alla credibilità della Repubblica'," *La Repubblica*, 11 December 1990.

50. Carlo Giorgi, "Perché non indagare sui secchiani?," *Il Popolo*, 14 December 1990.

51. Paolo Cabras, "Omissis del Pci," *Il Popolo*, 8 December 1990.

52. Interview with the author, 17 December 1990.

53. On 22 December 1990 I put this same question to Judge Francesco Amato, one of the investigating magistrates in Moro 1. He replied: "It is beginning to take on an eternal aspect, isn't it?"

54. Severino Santiapichi to the author, 13 December 1991.

55. Franco Scottoni, "Moro, la prigione, e la malavita," *La Repubblica*, 15 January 1992.

56. Interview with the author in the offices of *La Repubblica*, 21 January 1992.

57. Telephone conversation with the author, 29 January 1992.

58. Interview with the author in the Sala del Consiglio of the Foro Italico courtroom, 23 January 1992.

59. Meanwhile, the appeal trial in Moro ter, which began on 17 October 1991, ended on 24 February 1992. This trial was also held in the Foro Italico courtroom. The second court substantially upheld the verdict and sentences of the first court.

12. Moro Quater, Tangentopoli, and Giulio Andreotti

1. Craig Forman and Lisa Bannon, "A Corruption Scandal Leaves Italy's Leaders Weakened and Scorned," *Wall Street Journal*, 1 March 1993.

2. Giosué Carducci, "Per la morte di Giuseppe Mazzini," *Confessioni e battaglie*, 3 vols. (Rome: Sommaruga, 1883–84), vol. 2, p. 220.

3. Nando Dalla Chiesa, *Delitto imperfetto: il generale, la mafia, la società italiana* (Milan: Mondadori, 1984), p. 34.

4. Ibid., p. 35.

5. Ibid.

6. Giulio Andreotti, "Malinconico Autunno," *Il Tempo*, 7 October 1984. In this article Andreotti speculated that the attacks on him had been designed to damage the entire DC.

7. John Tagliabue, "Informers in Italy Accusing Ex-Premier of Ties to Mafia," *New York Times*, 31 December 1992.

8. Nostro inviato, "Andreotti: adesso devono smetterla," *Corriere della Sera*, 3 January 1993.

9. *Panorama, Dossier Andreotti: il testo completo delle accuse dei giudici di Palermo* (Milan: Mondadori, 1993), p. 43.

10. Ibid., p. 44.

11. Giovanni Falcone, with Marcelle Padovani, *Cose di Cosa Nostra* (Milan: Rizzoli, 1991), p. 41.

12. *Panorama, Dossier Andreotti*, p. 55.

13. Andrea Marcenaro, "Ma Riina non ci riderà alle spalle?" *Il Giorno*, 7 April 1993. The reference is to Totò Riina, the supreme Mafia boss who was captured by the police in January of that year.

14. *Il Messaggero*/Dossier, "Il caso Andreotti," 25 April 1993, p. 36.

15. Ibid., p. 35.

16. Ibid., p. 48.

17. Ibid., p. 47.

18. Falcone and Padovani, *Cose di Cosa Nostra*, p. 105.

19. *Il Messaggero*/Dossier, "Il caso Andreotti," p. 52.

20. Ibid., "La seconda integrazione della richiesta di autorizzazione a procedere . . . nei confronti del Sen. G. Andreotti," p. 54.

21. Abraham Sofaer, a prominent Washington lawyer and former legal advisor to the State Department, represented Andreotti in America. In a 93-page memorandum he dismissed the charges against Andreotti as a tissue of vague accusations, at once politically motivated and void of any basis in fact or logic. Sofaer strongly criticized the U.S. government for allowing Buscetta and Mannoia, who benefit from the federal witness protection program, to be used in a witch hunt against Andreotti.

22. Fabio Cavalera, "Il covo delle Br e le carte segrete di Moro," *Corriere della Sera*, 10 April 1993.

23. A 10 August 1993 report by the Direzione Investigativa Antimafia (DIA) concluded that the bombings were the work of the Mafia and its political allies; they hoped thereby "to condition the political and institutional renewal" of the country. Giuseppe D'Avanzo, "'Scontro frontale con lo Stato,'" *La Repubblica*, 3 September 1993. The DIA report did not end the controversy about these bombings.

24. Francesco Gregnetti, "'Andreotti il mandante,'" *La Stampa*, 10 June 1993.

25. Dossier: Delitto Pecorelli/la richiesta integrale di autorizzazione a procedere, *Il Messaggero*, 11 June 1993, p. 5.

26. Ibid., p. 1.

27. Ibid., p. 5.

28. Ibid.

29. Ibid., p. 7.

30. The leading newspaper editors of Italy were polled about the Andreotti case, and the views of Indro Montanelli, the widely respected editor of Milan's *Giornale*, summed up the group's consensus: "I tell you frankly that I can see [Andreotti] involved in a thousand censurable things, but not in the order to do away with Pecorelli and Dalla Chiesa." Even the *Indipendente*'s Vittorio Feltri, who thought that Andreotti was the country's worst politician and "the symbol of all that is wrong in Italy," did not believe the charges involving the Moro papers. Christina Mariotti, "'Non lo vedo a tavola coi boss,'" *L'Espresso*, 25 April 1993.

31. "'E' la grande occasione,' dice il pm del caso Moro," *La Repubblica*, 12 June 1993.

32. Andrea Colombo, "'Ora dobbiamo dire, tutti insieme, la nostra verità,'" *Il Manifesto*, 26 October 1993.

33. Fabio Cavalera and Costantino Muscau, "'Eravamo in quattro, ma si sapeva,'" *Corriere della Sera*, 24 October 1993.

34. "Moretti racconta: 'Solo io potevo farlo,'" *Il Manifesto*, 26 October 1993. This article was the transcript of the previous day's television program based on the Mosca-Rossanda interview of Moretti. The tapes were handed over to the Procura di Roma and became part of the Moro quater record. In

the book-length version of this interview, *Brigate rosse: una storia italiana* (Milan: Anabasi, 1994), edited by Rossana Rossanda and Carla Mosca, Moretti claimed that "nearly 100 percent" of the Red Brigade part of the Moro case was absolutely clear and securely documented (p. 125). Regarding the via Fani massacre and kidnapping, Moretti did add one important detail: he had not been responsible, as previously reported, for the collision that brought the Moro vehilces to a stop at the fatal intersection. The security officers had been vulnerable, "insofar as they did not notice anything. And they did not notice anything because until a second before the shooting there was nothing to notice" (p. 127). What happened was this: after the shooting had commenced, the driver of the escort vehicle lost control and slammed into the Fiat 130 of Moro, which in its turn collided with Moretti's car. On the question about the fourth man in the People's Prison Moretti downplayed the significance of the latest revelations: "The name of this comrade will not change a comma of what happened" (p. 134).

35. Interview with the author, Foro Italico court chambers, 10 January 1994.

36. 1° Corte di Assise di Roma, Procedimento penale C/Aldi, Gino + 12, n. ° 41/90 R.G.N. (Moro quater), Udienza, 18 November 1993, p. 50.

37. Ibid., Udienza, 24 November 1993, p. 41.

38. Ibid., Udienza, 18 November 1993, p. 53.

39. Ibid., p. 65.

40. Ibid. In *Brigate rosse: una storia italiana*, Mario Moretti confirmed that the Moro prison was via Montalcini 8. It was the only prison used during the kidnapping (p. 114).

41. Ibid., Udienza, 24 November 1993, p. 24.

42. Ibid., Udienza, 22 November 1993, p. 34.

43. Ibid., p. 56.

44. Ibid., p. 57.

45. Ibid., p. 62.

46. Mino Fucillo, "Feroci guardiani del regime," *La Repubblica*, 30 November 1993.

47. Sentenza nel procedimento penale, Moro quater, 1° Corte di Assise di Roma, p. 26.

48. Ibid., p. 42.

49. Ibid., p. 45.

50. Ibid., p. 56.

Conclusion

1. Virginio Rognoni, "La verità del caso Moro," *La Repubblica*, 29–30 May 1988.

2. Sergio Flamigni, *La tela del ragno: il delitto Moro*, 3rd ed. (Milan: Kaos, 1993), p. 395.

3. Henry Kissinger, *White House Years* (Boston: Little Brown, 1979), pp. 920–921.

4. See also the excellent article by Giorgio Bocca on these points, "Moro, quel tactito accordo fra un terrorismo alla frutta e un sistema che si illudeva," *L'Espresso*, 31 October 1993.

5. Enrico Fenzi, *Armi e bagagli: un diario dalle Brigate Rosse* (Genoa, Costa e Nolan, 1987), p. 251.

6. "Negri's Interrogation" in "Italy: Autonomia (Post-Political Politics)," *Semiotext(e)*, 3, 3 (1980), p. 190.

7. Mario Moretti, *Brigate rosse: una storia italiana* (Milan: Anabasi, 1994), p. 34.

8. Ibid., p. 45.

9. Ibid., p. 101.

10. Interview with the author, Foro Italico court chambers, 2 January 1991.

11. Vittorio Cervone, *Ho fatto di tutto per salvare Moro* (Turin: Marietti, 1979), p. 38.

12. Ibid., pp. 42–43.

13. Ibid., p. 43.

14. Ibid., p. 44.

15. "Le lettere di Aldo Moro," Foro Italico archive, Moro quater (fase istruttoria), cartella 13, fascicolo 2, #8, "Alla moglie Eleonora," written between 11 and 24 April 1978, p. 265.

16. Leonardo Coen, "Tobagi, Craxi riaccende la polemica," *La Repubblica*, 29 May 1990.

17. Sergio Zavoli, "Intervista a Benigno Zaccagnini" in *La notte della Repubblica* (Milan: Mondadori, 1992), p. 344.

18. Moretti, *Brigate rosse*, p. 156.

19. Francesco Biscione correctly declares in his introductory essay to *Il memoriale di Aldo Moro rinvenuto in via Monte Nevoso a Milano* (Rome: Coletti, 1993) that the complex nature and context of this document do not permit a definitive interpretation: the material is still too incandescent "for a completely detached and serene analysis" (p. 10). This also applies to the letters Moro produced in the People's Prison. The fundamentally practical nature of these documents, however, not their intellectual content, would appear to be their chief significance.

20. Moretti, *Brigate rosse*, pp. 144–146. He goes on to speculate about the covert reasons for fermezza and relates how Moro himself engaged in such speculations. Why could the state not have engaged in a dialogue with the Red Brigades, Moretti asked. His answer, based on what he claims Moro told him, is that in fact fermezza was completely out of character for the supreme party

of mediation in Italian politics, the inveterately accommodationist Christian Democrats. According to Moretti's interpretation of Moro's analysis, the DC was "paralyzed by someone or something" (p. 147). Some external force must have intervened in the DC process of politics as usual to impose the fermezza policy of Andreotti's government. Moro alluded to NATO and the Germans as likely culprits. Much has been made of Moretti's ruminations. For example, Robert Katz wrote an op-ed piece for the *New York Times*, "The Education of an Assassin" (23 April 1994), based on Moretti's disclosures about Moro. Restating the argument he has been making for fifteen years, Katz reasoned that Moretti's book lends further support to the conspiracy theory. Indeed, the book does do this, but only in a very speculative way. See also Katz's "I giorni del complotto," *Panorama*, 13 August 1994, in which he comes to the same conclusions. That article is based on the recollections of Steve Pieczenik, the U.S. State Department official who spent a few weeks in Rome during the kidnapping and has long been suspected by conspiracy theorists of being Henry Kissinger's agent, charged with the task of bringing about Moro's demise. After the interview, Pieczenik has a new role to play for conspiracy theorists. Katz reports Pieczenik had been "amazed" to discover that the generals and politicians at the Viminale did not like Moro. There is much more in this article about false and missing documents in the Moro case and about P2 spies in the Viminale—none of it supported by anything more substantial than the recollections and surmises of a witness who, according to Katz, spoke and understood almost no Italian.

21. On 22 January 1995, after twenty-two months of investigation, the judges in Palermo presented their conclusions in the case against Andreotti. They claimed that the evidence against him was overwhelming and that he had lied consistently and shamelessly about his relations with the Mafia. From 1978 to 1992 he indeed had been their political contact in Rome *(il referente romano)*. Although former colleagues also testified against Andreotti, the foundation of the judges' case was the testimony of seventeen pentiti. Andreotti denounced these Mafia turncoats as convicted assassins who by falsely accusing him had added perjury to their long list of crimes. At the same time, the magistrate in Rome who is in charge of investigating the Pecorelli murder and its connections to the Moro case announced that he was not yet ready to present his conclusions. Now formally indicted and preparing to stand trial in Palermo, Andreotti continues to insist on his complete innocence. All future legal proceedings against him are likely to be long-drawn-out. The trial in Palermo is scheduled to begin in September 1995.

22. Sergio Zavoli, "Il mite Benigno," *Epoca*, 31 October 1990. See also Zavoli, *La notte della Repubblica*, pp. 340–344.

23. "Le lettere di Aldo Moro," #9, "A Benigno Zaccagnini, segretario politico della Democrazia Cristiana," written between 11 and 24 April 1978, p. 268.

Acknowledgments

I compiled the research for this book during parts of four winters in Rome. My main problem was to gain access to the judicial archives housing the documents from the various Moro trials. Without the help I received from a number of Italian judges, it would have remained insoluble. Gian Carlo Caselli, a judge in Turin when I met him in March of 1990 and currently the Procuratore della Repubblica di Palermo, generously put himself at my service in this project. Through him I was able to meet many of the principal judicial authorities in the Aldo Moro murder case.

The first of these was Judge Rosario Priore of the Tribunale di Roma. He put some of the most important documents at my disposal: the two *sentenze istruttorie*, or findings in the investigation phase of the first Moro trial; the final sentence in the courtroom phase in these proceedings; and the sentenze istruttorie for the third and fourth trials. Several members of his staff, notably Paolo Musio, the *collaboratore di cancelleria*, and Vito Cina, the *funzionario di cancelleria*, took interest in my work. Bianca Svampa, the *assistente giudiziaria* in Judge Priore's office, helped me in countless ways with unfailing courtesy and efficiency. Through her I met Judge Francesco Amato of the Tribunale di Roma. Both he and Judge Priore took the time to answer my questions and gave me their unstinting cooperation.

For the documents from the courtroom phase *(la fase dibattimentale)* I had to go to the Corte di Assise di Appello. Once again I met with a most helpful response. *Consigliere* Giovanni Silvestri interceded for me with President Carlo Sammarco, from whom I received unrestricted authorization to examine the court records. Giandomenico Tozzi, the direttore di cancelleria della Corte di Appello then implemented this authorization by requesting that Maria Margherita Celsan and Marilena Vecchini of his staff accompany me to the Foro Italico courtroom building where the documents for Moro 1 and the appeal trial were kept. After that first day Dr. Vecchini was my constant companion in the Foro Italico archives. Her deep understanding of the Italian legal system was of invaluable service during this vital phase of my research, and she took a deep personal interest in seeing me through the entire project.

At the Foro Italico courtroom I met a central historical figure in the first Moro trial: Severino Santiapichi, the Presidente della Prima Corte di Assise di Roma. President of the court in some of the most important Italian trials of our time, he was most generous in offering me his full cooperation, patient instruction, and helpful reading suggestions. He read my essay on the Italian legal system and saved me from numerous errors. I am particularly grateful to Antonietta Conte, his administrative assistant, for her cooperation.

For the third Moro trial, President Santiapichi introduced me to Carmelo Napoli in the Cancelleria della Corte di Assise, and he facilitated access to the main court records. Later, Giulio Franco, the Presidente della Terza Corte di Assise di Appello di Roma, and two assistants in the court office—Liliana Chirola and Domenico Angelini—helped me to obtain the remaining Moro ter documents.

I am indebted to the staff of the Biblioteca della Camera dei Deputati for access to the Moro Commission and the P2 Commission reports of Parliament. I also want to thank the many people who helped me in Rome's Biblioteca Nazionale Centrale, the Biblioteca dell'Istituto di Storia Moderna e Contemporanea, and the Biblioteca dell'Istituto Gramsci. Massimo Faraglia, the head archivist of *La Repubblica* in Rome, put the resources of that newspaper's archive at my disposal and permitted me to reproduce the photographs in this book. I am especially grateful to his associate, Massimo Campitelli, who helped me to find dozens of documents and to understand some of the intricacies of contemporary Italian politics. I can never repay the debt of gratitude that I owe him. Franco Cannatà, an independent journalist in Rome and his brother Sergio have similar claims on me. Professor Francesco Guida, a historian at the University of Rome, also rendered extremely valuable assistance. My good friend Joseph Blacker kept me well supplied with Italian newspapers and periodicals and conducted an important interview on my behalf with Bruno Calo of Brindisi.

Numerous individuals and institutions in the United States deserve thanks. Dr. Benjamin F. Brown of Washington, D.C., provided important information about the Moro case. Thomas and Ann Boone of Missoula, Montana, searched Italy for a film I needed; their help is deeply appreciated, as are the advice and friendship that Larry Riley extended.

At the University of Montana I have benefited from the support of two presidents who through the University of Montana Foundation greatly facilitated my work: James V. Koch, now the president of Old Dominion University in Norfolk, Virginia, and the current president, George Dennison. The University of Montana gave me sabbatical leave in 1989 during which I launched this project, subsidized by a grant from the American Philosophical Society. A University of Montana summer research grant and a Barbieri grant from Trinity College in Hartford, Connecticut, further subsidized my writing and travel.

I am indebted to my colleagues in the History Department at the University of Montana for a departmental forum in which my work was discussed, and especially to David Emmons, Kenneth Lockridge, and Michael Mayer for their written criticisms. A similarly rewarding experience was the University of Montana's Philosophy Forum, directed by Albert Borgmann. Thanks also go to Marianne Farr of the University of Montana's Mansfield Library for her assistance in locating research materials.

I am grateful to Ezio Cappadocia of McMaster University in Hamilton, Ontario, Alexander J. De Grand of North Carolina State University at Raleigh, and John Henry Merryman of the Stanford University Law School, who read portions of the manuscript, for their expert help. Charles Delzell of Vanderbilt University read the whole manuscript and gave me penetrating criticism. Laure Pengelly of the University of Rochester performed the same invaluable service and, along with Vicki Pengelly of the University of Montana and Richard Drake, Jr., of Missoula, Montana, provided computer expertise. My editors at Harvard University Press helped me to keep on course.

Index

Abbate, Antonio Germano, 47, 57, 78–80
Acquaviva, Sabino, 197
Action Directe, 121, 150, 265
Acton, Lord, 31
Agca, Ali, 49
Alberghina, Filippo, 122
Allende, Salvador, 29
Amato, Francesco, 43, 134, 157–160; interviews, 295n10, 296n53
Amato, Nicolò, 47, 62, 71, 76–77
Ambrosiano Bank, 106, 112–115
Ambrosoli, Giorgio, 111, 138, 284n43
Anarchists, 215
Andreotti, Giulio, 31, 61, 63, 92, 97, 153, 194, 211–212, 220, 250, 278n10, 297n6, 298n21; in the first Moro trial, 63–67, 69, 71; and the Moro Commission, 83, 85; and the P2 Commission, 105, 112; in the *Metropoli* trial, 166, 179; defends fermezza, 188–189; in the Moro carteggio, 216–217; reaction to Gladio, 218–219; decline and fall, 227–240, 298n30; and the Moro case, 261, 277n3; supported by the PCI, 293n14; cited by Moretti, 300–301n20; proceedings against, 301n21
Andreottiani, 229, 231, 232, 265
Andriani, Norma, 54–55, 56, 142, 170
Anselmi, Tina: and the P2 Commission, 99–106, 251
Anti-Zionism, 121
Aperturismo, 265; *see* "Opening to the left"

Appeal trials, *see* Trials
Arabs, 120–121
Argentina, 102
Ascari, Odoardo, 233
Asinara, 195
Attolico, Ferdinando, 181–183, 247–248
Audran, René, 150
Augias, Corrado, 284n43
Autonomia Operaia, 67–68, 89, 125, 157–158, 160, 167, 169, 177–178, 191, 265, 291n60
Azzolini, Lauro, 144–145, 153, 171, 178; in the *Metropoli* trial, 166–168

Baader-Meinhof Gang, 166, 194
Baccioli, Attilio, 149
Bachelet, Vittorio, 76
Balducci, Armenia, 287n38
Balzerani, Barbara, 134, 139–140, 149, 200, 206, 243, 247; in Moro quater, 245–246
Banca Romana scandals, 225
Barbone, Marco, 89
Barsacchi, Paolo, 93–94
Basili, Marcello, 146–147
Bayle, Pierre, 96
Beccaria, Cesare, 154; *On Crimes and Punishments*, 38
Beckurts, Karl Heinz, 150
Berlinguer, Enrico, 25, 27, 29, 31, 32, 51, 61, 92, 115, 172–173, 213, 274n47, 293n14

Bertolazzi, Piero, 151
Biblioteca di Storia Moderna e Contemporanea, 207
Biscione, Francesco and *Il memoriale di Aldo Moro*, 300n19
Blackfriars Bridge, 114
Bocca, Giorgio, 117–119, 163, 217, 300n4; and *Noi terroristi*, 163, 170–174, 290n56, 291n60
Bologna train station massacre, 103, 220, 265
Bolsheviks, 179
Bonisoli, Franco, 171, 178–181, 200, 206–207, 236
Bontate, Stefano, 231, 233
Bordoni, Carlo, 110
Borghese, Il, 185–187
Borghese, Junio Valerio, Prince, 103
Borsellino, Paolo, 232
Braghetti, Anna Laura, 176, 200, 243, 247; in Moro quater, 243–245, 246
Braumuehl, Gerold von, 150
Brigata Aureliana, 148
Brigata Universitaria, 54, 56
Brogi, Carlo, 54, 55
Buonavita, Alfredo, 71–73
Buscetta, Tommaso, 230–235, 237–239, 298n21
Buzzatti, Roberto, 138, 141–144, 145, 185, 201

Cabras, Paolo, 140–141, 218–219
Cacciotti, Giulio, 56
Cagol, Mara, 192–193
Calderone, Antonio, 230–231
Calò, Pepe, 231
Calvi, Roberto, 102, 106–107, 112–115, 138, 284n50
Camorra, 265, 267
Camp David Accords, 120
Canada, 161
Carabinieri, 64, 99, 101, 138, 210–211, 236, 250, 265
Carboni, Flavio, 113
Carducci, Giosué, 225
Caridi, Francesco, 185–187
Carteggio, *see* Moro carteggio
Carter, Jimmy, 30

Caselli, Gian Carlo, 230, 232–233, 237
Casimirri, Alessio, 200, 206–207, 247
Casirati, Carlo, 169
Caso, Giovanni, 119, 130–131
"Caso Moro, Il" (film), 144, 164, 256, 287–288n38
Caso Moro, Il, 287–288n38
Casson, Felice, 218
Castro, Fidel, 145
Catholic Church, and Moro, 3–4; and Fascism, 4–5; and anticommunism, 4; and De Gasperi, 14; and the P2 Commission, 108–115
Catholic culture, 3
Catholic left, 16
Cavedon, Remigio, 181, 185–186
Centocelle brigade "network" (la rete), 145
Centro, *see* Executive Committee
Cervone, Vittorio, 260; and *Ho fatto di tutto per salvare Moro*, 257–259, 262
Christian Democratic party (DC): and Moro, 1–3, 7, 10, 17, 21, 26, 31–32, 60–61, 174, 226, 251, 256, 260; history of, 12–16; factionalism in, 17, 153; defended by Andreotti, 63–67, 188, 240, 261, 297n6; defends fermezza, 83; and the Red Brigades, 69–71, 124–126, 133, 164, 177, 181, 195, 196, 217, 249, 254, 300–301n20; reaction to Gladio, 218–219; and Tangentopoli, 31–32, 225–226, 229; demise of, 227–228; connections with the Mafia, 230–231; and Vittorio Cervone, 257–259, 260, 262; participation in the trattativa camp, 278n24; reaction to "Il caso Moro," 287n38; *see also* Moro carteggio, Moro Commission of Parliament, P2, and Trials
Christian Democrats International, 153
Christianity, 3, 7, 8
CIA, 43, 106, 117, 211, 216–217, 220, 246
CIA. The Pike Report, 110
Ciampi, Carlo Azeglio, 237
Cianfanelli, Massimo, 54
Ciardulli, Enzo, 76–77

Cicala, Francesco Bernardino, 8
Cirillo, Ciro, 140
Civil Code of 1865, 38
Civitas Humana, 13
Coco, Francesco, 254
Coco, Giovanni, 70–71
Code of Criminal Procedure (1930), 39
Code of Criminal Procedure (1989), 39
Code of Justinian, 36, 39
Code of 1942, 39
Coffey, Joseph J., Jr., 108
Cold War, 2, 13, 14, 23, 31, 105, 218–220, 226–227
College of Cardinals, 108
Collettivo di via dei Volsci, 278n24
Colombo, Emilio, 194
Colonna Milanese Walter Alasia (linea spontaneista), 133–134; See Red Brigades
Colpevolisti, 237
Comitati Comunisti Rivoluzionari (CO.CO.RI.), 89
Comitato Comunista Centocelle, 142
Comitato Esecutivo, see Executive Committee
Comitato Esecutivo per i Servizi di Informazione e Sicurezza, 209
Commentators, 37
Commission on Massacres, 221
Committee of Coordination, 104, 106
Communards, 159
Communication no. 7, 177, 200–201
Communism, 125, 163, 168–169, 172–174, 190–192, 204, 218–219, 226–227, 242, 254, 261
Communist party (PCI), 192, 217, 219, 267; and Moro, 1–2, 7, 12–13, 20, 23, 25–33, 51, 61, 75, 85–86, 88, 214–215, 226–227, 250–251, 266; and the Red Brigades, 27, 51, 124–126, 133, 172, 179, 192–195; and fermezza, 173; opposed to perdonismo, 189–190; in the Moro carteggio, 214–215; demise of, 227; connections with revolutionary culture, 252; transformation into PDS, 253; reaction to "Il caso Moro," 287n38; support for Andreotti, 293n14; see also

Moro Commission of Parliament, Propaganda 2, Trials
Confindustria, 133, 265
Connally, John, 109
Conspiracy theories, 59–60, 61, 70, 76–77, 79–80, 83–85, 90, 93–98, 220–221, 231, 248, 250–256; and P2, 99–115; comments by Sciascia, 95–97, 210; by Franceschini, 164, 210–211; by Bonisoli, 180–181; by Piccoli, 185; by Craxi, 189; by Fenzi, 191; by Flamigni, 203–205, 206–209, 250; by Andreotti, 216; by Occhetto, 217; by Morucci, 242–243; by Braghetti, 244
Conte, Ottavio, 122
Conti, Lando, 136–138, 150
Corporativism, 5
Corriere della Sera, 33, 102, 141, 178, 186, 243
Corrocher, Teresa, 114
Cosa Nostra, 106, 231, 265, 267; see also Mafia
Cossiga, Francesco, 83–84, 85, 89, 97, 209, 212, 219–220, 246; in the Moro carteggio, 213
Cosso, Andrea, 132
Costarm Aereo, 150
Coup attempt of 7–8 December 1970, 103
Covatta, Luigi, 93–94
Craxi, Bettino, 35, 63, 67–69, 71, 73, 92–93, 104, 121, 133, 138, 160, 175, 188–189, 195, 212, 218, 224, 230, 258, 278n26
Crime and Punishment, 48
Cronache sociali, 13, 16, 17
Cudillo, Ernesto, 43
Cuneo prison, 233
Curcio, Renato, 58, 68, 69, 70, 72, 73, 140, 149, 151–153, 155, 164–166, 169, 178–179, 185, 189, 192–193, 194, 196, 198, 202, 252
Czechoslovakia, 26

Da Empoli, Antonio, 138
Dalla Chiesa, Carlo Alberto, General, 156, 228–229, 233–236, 239–240, 298n30

Dalla Chiesa, Nando, and *Delitto imperfetto*, 228–229
D'Angelo, Claudio, 43
Dante Alighieri, 191
Dante, Giuseppe, 130
Darboy, Georges, Archbishop, 159
Darwin, Charles, 39
Das Kapital, 55
Declaration of the Rights of Man and Citizen, 38
De Ficchy, Luigi, 221–222
De Gasperi, Alcide, 13–18, 23, 34, 63, 214
De Gori, Giuseppe, 155
De Gregorio, Carlo, 129, 132
Della Briotta, Libero, 93–94
De Lorenzo, Giovanni, General, 22, 220, 268
De Mita, Ciriaco, 196
Democratic party of the left (PDS), 227, 253
De Nictolis, Giuseppe, 119, 122, 124, 129–131
Di Bella, Franco, 141
Di Cera, Walter, 145–146
Di Fonzo, Luigi, and *St. Peter's Banker*, 107, 109–110
Di Maggio, Baldassare, 230, 235
Direzione Investigativa Antimafia (DIA), 298n23
Direzione Strategica, 198; *see* Red Brigades
Dissociati, 48, 49, 58, 76–77, 116, 123, 128, 129, 139, 155, 160, 165, 208, 242, 265
Dorotei, 18
Dossetti, Giuseppe, 10–17, 19, 24, 29, 272–273n26
Dossettiani, 11, 14–17, 19, 266
Dostoevsky, Fyodor, 255
Dozier, James Lee, General, 79, 121, 132, 134
D'Urso, Giovanni, 119, 144, 266

Einaudi Institute, 225
Elections: of 1948, 16; of 1953, 16; of 1963, 29; of 1968, 29; of 1972, 29; of 1975, 29, 30; of 1976, 29, 30; of 1983, 120

Espresso, L', 118, 149
Europeo, 240
Euroterrorism, 121, 137, 150–151
Evangelisti, Franco, 239
Executive Committee of the Red Brigades, 126, 178, 198; *see* Red Brigades
Executive Committee, 133–134; *see* Red Brigades
Extraparliamentary left, 25, 50, 52, 54, 64, 66, 67, 89, 92, 123, 125, 128, 152, 157, 167–170, 173, 178–179, 189, 192, 197, 199, 252, 266, 267, 268; *see* Red Brigades
Extraparliamentary right, 103, 105, 266

Falcone, Giovanni, 232
Famiglia Cristiana, La, 155, 184, 207
Fanfani, Amintore, 11, 15–19, 31, 71, 176–177, 213
Faranda, Adriana, 45, 80, 116–117, 123, 127, 129–131, 139, 141, 160–162, 167, 174, 177, 182–183, 200, 204, 206–207, 241–242, 256, 294n2; in the appeal trial for Moro 1, 122–126; in the *Metropoli* trial, 175–176, 291n68
Fascism, 4–8, 12, 14, 16, 32, 39, 47, 103, 172
Federal Republic of Germany, 150, 166
Federazione Universitaria Cattolica Italiana (FUCI), 4, 6, 21, 63, 266
Feltri, Vittorio, 298n30
Fenoaltea, Sergio, 75
Fenzi, Enrico, 73–75; in the appeal trial for Moro 1, 129; and *Armi e bagagli*, 190–192, 196, 252–254, 255
Fermezza line, 61, 63–71, 83, 90, 92–94, 97, 106, 115, 118, 119, 173, 187–189, 195, 197, 204–205, 250, 256–262, 266, 287n38, 300–301n20
Ferrara, Giuseppe, and "Il caso Moro" (film), 144, 164, 256, 287n38
Ferrer, Enrico, 132
Fiat, 225
Fiore, Raffaele, 58, 200, 206–207
Fioroni, Carlo, 168–170

Fiumicino airport terrorist attack, 136
Flamigni, Sergio, 93–94, 221; and *La tela del ragno*, 203–205, 206, 208–209, 250, 255, 295n4, 295n10
Forlani, Arnaldo, 99, 113, 212, 220, 224
Forlì, 196
Formica, Rino, 100
Foro Italico courtroom, 47–48, 60, 63, 74, 80, 84, 90, 119–120, 129, 161, 221–222, 224, 240, 241, 266, 294n2, 297n59
Fosso, Antonio, 222
France, 169, 226
Franceschini, Alberto, 58, 69, 72, 171–172, 178–179, 202, 210–211, 217–218, 256, 260, 290n56; and the *Metropoli* trial, 163–166, 167; and *Mara, Renato e io*, 192–196
Franchi, Franco, 94–95
Franco, Francisco, 14
Francola, Annunziata, 223
Franklin National Bank, 109–111
Freato, Sereno, 88, 140
Front in the Struggle against Counter-revolution, 179
Fronte Armato Rivoluzionario Operaio (FARO), 169
Fronte Carcere (linea movimentista-Guerrilla party), 133–134, 198; *see* Red Brigades
Fronte Combattente Antimperialista, 150
Fronte Contro-Rivoluzione, 198
Furiozzi, Raffaella, 132

Gallinari, Prospero, 49, 80, 140, 154–155, 176, 178, 200, 206–208, 241, 243, 256
Galloni, Giovanni, 19, 130; in the Moro carteggio, 213
Gallucci, Achille, 43
Gamberini, Giordano, 101–102
Gardner, Richard, 215
Gava, Antonio, 197
Gazzetta del Mezzogiorno, 85
Gelli, Licio, 99–107, 109–114, 174, 204, 209, 251, 254

General Motors, 136
German legal science, *see* Pandectists
Germany, 39, 226, 300–301n20
Ghetto (in Rome), 207
Giorgieri, Licio, 150–151, 197
Giornale, Il, 155, 298n30
Gioventù Universitaria Fascista (GUF), 5, 266
Giugni, Gino, 120, 133
Giustini, Antonio, 121–122, 133
Gladio, 218–221, 266
Glossators, 36, 39
Graldi, Paolo, 186
Gramsci, Antonio, 6, 192
Grande Oriente d'Italia Masons, 99, 101
Gronchi, Giovanni, 19
Gualtieri, Libero, 220
Guarino, Philip, 106
Guasco, Guido, 44–46
Guerrilla party, *see* Fronte Carcere
Guerzoni, Corrado, 75
Guevara, Che, 72, 179
Guiso, Giannino, 68, 72, 165, 195; and *La condanna di Aldo Moro*, 69–71
Gurwin, Larry, and *The Calvi Affair*, 107, 112–114

Habbash, George, 47
Hammer, Richard, and *The Vatican Connection*, 107–109
Hegel, Georg, 191
"Historic Compromise," 2, 25–33, 51, 61, 75, 85, 88, 214–215, 227, 250, 266
"Humanitarian" line, *see* Trattativa
Hunt, Leamon R., 120–121, 132, 134

Ianelli, Maurizio, 151
Ideology, *see* Marxist-Leninism
Imperialism, 137, 151
Imposimato, Ferdinando, 43, 46–47, 116; in the *Metropoli* trial, 160–161
Indipendente, 298n30
Iniziativa Democratica, 16–19
Innocentisti, 236
International Red Cross, 65
Iozzino, Raffaele, 44, 207
Iran, 150

Irriducibili, 48, 76–77, 171, 240–241, 243, 267
Israel, 30, 47, 90, 211–214, 242, 267
Istituto per le Opere di Religione (IOR), 114
Italicus train bombing, 60

Japan, 226
"JFK" (film), 256
John XXIII, Pope: and *Mater et magistra*, 21, 273n33; and *Pacem in terris*, 21
John Paul II, Pope, 49, 65, 114
Jus commune, 36–37

Katz, Robert, and *The Days of Wrath*, 66, 287n38; and "Il caso Moro," 287n38; and "The Education of an Assassin" and "I giorni del complotto," 300–301n20
Kennedy, David, 109, 111
Kennedy, John F., 255–256; and Italy, 21, 273n34
KGB (Committee for State Security in the Soviet Union), 89
Khrushchev, Nikita, 20, 192
Kissinger, Henry, 30, 75, 88–89, 204, 214–215, 251, 300–301n20

Lake Duchessa, 200–201; *see also* Communication no. 7
La Malfa, Giorgio, 224
La Pira, Giorgio, 11; and *Il valore della persona umana*, 12
Latin America, 102
Lavoro Illegale, 169
Lazzati, Giuseppe, 11
Lebanon, 150
Legal Humanists, 37
Legal system in Italy, compared with the Anglo-American legal system, 36–37, 40; history of, 36–39; phases of judicial process, 39–41, 267, 268; personnel of the court, 40–41, 266, 268, 274–275n1; Corte di Cassazione, 41
Lenin, Vladimir Ilyich, 27, 50, 53, 54, 55, 72, 78, 119, 123, 133, 134, 141, 143–145, 151, 164, 165, 172, 179, 192–193, 199, 253–254; and *State and Revolution*, 172, 252, 290n56
Lenin Collectives, 145
Lenin Section, 141, 143
Leonardi, Ileana, 88
Leonardi, Oreste, 44, 53, 71, 88, 128, 207
Libèra, Emilia, 53–54, 56, 142, 145, 200
Liberal party (PLI), 97–98
Libya, 47, 150
Liceo Francesco di Assisi, 145
Liechtenstein, 193
Lima, Salvo, 230–232, 235
Linea militarista, 267; *see also* Executive Committee
Linea movimentista, 267; *see also* Fronte Carcere
Linea spontaneista, 267; *see also* Colonna Milanese Walter Alasia
Littoriali, 5
Lockheed scandal, 34, 75, 219, 267
Loiacono, Alvaro, 200, 206–207, 247
Lonigro, Carla, 88–89
Lotta Continua, 55, 57, 244, 267
Luxemburg, Rosa, 54, 145

Maccari, Germano, 241–242
Macciò, Diego, 132
Mafia, 30, 41, 64, 94, 180, 186, 207, 213, 219, 220, 226, 266, 267, 269, 297n13, 298n23, 301n21; and the P2 Commission, 107–115; and Andreotti's decline and fall, 228–235
Mafiosi, 230, 238
Maglie, 3, 271n1
Maj, Arnaldo, 58–59
Mancini, Tommaso, 116, 130
Manifesto, Il, 152, 241–243
Manna, Emilio, 146
Mannoia, Francesco Marino, 230–231, 233–235, 298n21
Marceddu, Giovanni Maria, 147–148
Marchese, Giuseppe, 230
Marchio, Michele, 94–95
Marcinkus, Paul, 108–109, 112, 114
Marini, Antonio, 176, 181, 223, 240

Maritain, Jacques, and *Humanisme in-tégral*, 10–12, 272n18; and Fanfani, 273n27

Marocco, Antonio, 146

Marsala, Vincenzo, 230

Marshall Plan, 13, 20

Martelli, Claudio, 93–94

Martin, Graham, 110, 214

Martin, Malachi, and *The Final Con-clave*, 107–108

Marx, Karl, 12, 50, 54, 55, 78, 123, 133, 143–144, 151, 172, 193, 196, 253; and *The Civil War in France*, 159, 252

Marxism, 10–12; and the Red Brigades, 134, 160, 164, 172, 192–193, 254–255, 260; and Franco Piperno, 163; analyzed by Giorgio Bocca, 173; in Italy, 252

Marxist-Existentialism, 190

Marxist-Leninism, ideology of the Red Brigades, 27, 32, 45, 50–55, 67, 72, 78, 121, 125, 133–134, 137, 143–145, 152, 157, 162, 179, 190–192, 193, 195–196, 199, 242, 244–245, 246, 249, 252, 253, 254–255, 259; cult of in Italy, 32, 178

Masonry, 268; and P2 Commission reports, 99–115

Massara, Cecilia, 148

Media, 199, 225, 234, 237; in the Moro case, 59, 134, 166, 211–212, 255, 261

Mele, Vittorio, 237–239

Messina, Leonardo, 230

Metro Security Express holdup, 121

Metropoli, 89

Metropoli, 267

Metropoli trial, *see* Trials

Micaletto, Rocco, 58

Middle East, 30, 120–121, 136, 138, 211, 214–215

Mimmi, Marcello, Archbishop, 4–5

Minervini, Girolamo, 76

Mitrotti, Tommaso, 185, 187

Moneyrex, 109

Montanelli, Indro, 298n30

Montecitorio, *see* Parliament

Montesquieu, Baron de, 96

Morabito, Saverio, 241–242

Moretti, Mario, 58, 72, 74, 80–81, 118–121, 140, 144, 149, 151–155, 163, 166, 170, 173–177, 181, 185–186, 194–195, 200, 201, 206–207, 217, 247, 256, 260; interview, 243, 298n34; and *Brigate rosse: una storia italiana*, 254–255, 261, 298–299n34, 299n40, 300–301n20

Moro, Aldo: biography, 1–35, 86–88; and the Catholic Church, 3–10, 21, 273n33; and the Christian Demo-cratic party, 1–3, 7, 10, 17, 21, 26, 31–32, 60–61, 174, 226, 251, 256, 260; and Fascism, 4–8; and Commu-nism, 7–8; and Dossetti, 10–11, 16, 19, 24; and Maritain, 10–11; and De Gasperi, 15, 18; as DC party secre-tary, 18–22; as prime minister, 22–25, 30; and the "opening to the left," 19–22, 273n34; and the United States, 2, 15, 23, 29, 30, 33, 59, 60, 75, 76–77, 88, 251, 273n36; and the "historic compromise," 2, 25–33, 51, 61, 75, 85, 88, 214–215, 226–227, 250–251, 266; views on terrorism, 27–28, 59–60, 83, 260–261; kidnap-ping, 2, 34, 35, 44–46, 51–58, 61, 116, 269; murder, 35, 43–45, 54–58, 61, 251, 253, 269; prison letters, 35, 52, 60, 65, 84, 87, 90–95, 97, 126, 155, 189, 255, 260, 262, 300n19; People's Prison "film," 144, 155–156, 181, 184–187, 201; compared with President Kennedy, 255–256

Moro, Anna Maria, 85

Moro bis, *see* Trials

Moro carteggio, 209–219, 221, 250, 265, 269, 296n24

Moro Commission of Parliament, 63, 68, 70, 82–98, 100, 163, 194, 203; majority report, 89–93, 94, 250; So-cialist minority report, 93–94; Neofas-cist minority report, 94–95; Radical minority report, 95–97, 210; Liberal minority report, 97–98

Moro, Eleonora (Chiavarelli), 6, 59–60, 62, 65, 84–85, 86, 88, 140, 262, 278n10
Moro, Fida Stinchi, 3
Moro Foundation, 88
Moro, Giovanni, 60, 85
Moro, Maria Agnese, 60, 85, 87
Moro, Maria Fida, 85, 141, 189; and *La casa dei cento natali*, 86–88
Moro quater, *see* Trials
Moro, Renato, 3, 4
Moro ter, *see* Trials
Moro 1, *see* Trials
Moro-Mike (Plan), 246–247
Moro-Victor (Plan), 246
Morocco, 169
Morotei, 262, 267
Morucci, Valerio, 45, 54, 80, 116–119, 121–122, 124–126, 130–131, 139, 141, 160–161, 167, 174, 176, 182–183, 199–201, 204, 206–207, 241, 242–243, 245, 247, 252; in the appeal trial of Moro 1, 127–129; in Moro ter, 154–155; in the *Metropoli* trial, 161–163, 175, 176–178, 290n15; in Moro quater, 241–242, 294–295n2
Mosca, Carla, 243, 247, 298–299n34
Mossad, 47, 90, 211, 242, 267
"Movement," 27, 73, 125, 127, 141, 157–161, 165, 167–169, 175, 177–178, 244, 252, 267
Movimentisti, *see* Fronte Carcere
Movimento Proletario di Resistenza Offensiva (MPRO), 147, 198–199, 267
Movimento Sociale Italiano, *See* Neofascist party
Movimento Sociale Italiano-Destra Nazionale (MSI-DN), 94
Musselli, Bruno, 140
Mussolini, Benito, 4, 5, 6, 39, 100, 101, 227
Mutolo, Gaspare, 230

Napoleonic Codes, 38
NATO, 14, 31, 106, 137, 150–151, 204, 214, 217–218, 266, 300–301n20
Natta, Alessandro, 293n14

Natural law theory, 38
'Ndrangheta, 241–242, 244, 267
Negri, Toni, 45, 54, 55, 168–169, 178, 191, 252, 275n10; and *La fabbrica della strategia: 33 lezioni su Lenin*, 54
Nenni, Pietro, 20, 22, 24, 25
Neocorporativism, 133, 137, 179
Neofascism, 29, 107
Neofascist party (MSI), 107, 172, 185, 214, 267; and the Moro Commission, 94–95; and P2, 100–101, 104, 106–115
Neofascist terrorist groups, 28, 103
New York Times, 230, 300–301n20
Nirta, Antonio, 241–242
Nixon, Richard, 109, 110
Nucci, Gherardo, 203
Nuclei Armati Rivoluzionari (NAR), 122, 132, 267
Nucleo Operativo Centrale di Sicurezza (NOCS), 122

Occhetto, Achille, 217
Ognibene, Roberto, 178
Oil scandal trials, 141
Olivetti, 225
"Opening to the left," 19–22, 273n34
Operation Fritz (Red Brigade code name for the kidnapping of Aldo Moro), 128
Operation Gladio, *see* Gladio
Orlando, Leoluca, 230
Oswald, Lee Harvey, 255–256

P2, *see* Propaganda 2 Masonic Lodge
Pace, Lanfranco, 45, 67, 71, 125, 157–183, 292n85
Padula, Sandro, 146–147, 222
Palamà, Giuseppe, 148
Palazzo Chigi, 220, 236, 265, 273n41
Palazzo San Macuto, 63, 67, 71
Palestine Liberation Organization (PLO), 89
Palestinian terrorists, 136
Palestinians, 30, 47, 150, 214
Palma, Nitto Francesco, 138, 144, 149, 154, 187
Palma, Riccardo, 76

Pandectists, 39
Pannella, Marco, 104
Panorama, 300–301n20
Paris, 159, 197
Paris Commune, 134, 159
Parliament, 2, 15, 31, 210, 219, 221, 224, 237, 251, 267; Moro Commission reports, 82–98; P2 Commission reports, 99–115, 116
Paroli, Tonino, 178
Partisans, 27, 101, 164, 178, 192–193
Partito Comunista Italiano (PCI), *see* Communist party
Partito Liberale Italiano (PLI), 267; *see* Liberal party
Partito Popolare Italiano (as predecessor of the DC), 14; (as successor of the DC), 227
Partito Radicale (PR), *see* Radical party
Partito Repubblicano Italiano (PRI), *see* Republican party (PRI)
Partito Socialista di Unità Proletaria (PSIUP), 22, 268
Partito Socialista Italiano (PSI), 268; *see* Socialist party
Pasolini, Pier Paolo, 20, 24, 96
Paul VI, Pope, 21, 53, 108, 109, 119
Pavese, Cesare, 7
Pazienza, Francesco, 113
Pecchioli, Ugo, 61
Peci, Patrizio, 56–58, 89, 93–94, 98, 170
Peci, Roberto, 57
Pecorelli, Mino, 233–237, 240, 250, 298n30, 301n21; and *Osservatore Politico (Op)*, 238–239
Pedenovi, Enrico, 172
Pella, Fabrizio, 178
Penal Code of 1889, 38
Pentagon, 117
Pentapartito coalition, 151, 224
Pentiti, 46, 48, 49, 53, 76–77, 80, 89, 90, 116, 119, 120, 129, 134, 139, 155, 157, 160, 185, 197, 208, 230–232, 237, 240, 241, 259, 268, 301n21
People's Prison, *see* Via Montalcini 8
People's Prison "film" of Moro, 144, 155–156, 181, 184–187, 201

Perdonismo movement, 153–155, 184, 188–190, 192, 196–198, 268
Peronists, 102
Perrone, Pasquale, 138, 198–203
Pertini, Sandro, 120
Petralla, Stefano, 149
Petri, Elio, and "Todo Modo," 24, 287n38
Petricola, Ave Maria, 55–56
Petrocelli, Biagio, 5
Philippines, 137
Piancone, Cristoforo, 139, 286n16
"Piano Solo," 22, 220, 268
Piazza Fontana bombing, 27, 152, 220, 268; in the Moro carteggio, 215–216
Piazza Lovatelli, 208
Piazza Monte Savello, 208
Piazza Statuto riots, 20
Piazzesi, Gianfranco, 33–34
Piazzetta Mattei, 207
Piccoli, Flaminio, 33, 61, 100, 152–156, 181, 184–186, 188–189; in the Moro carteggio, 213
Piduisti (members of P2), 268; *see also* Propaganda 2
Pieczenik, Steve, 300–301n20
Pietra, Italo, 24
Pifano, Daniele, 278n24
Pike Commission, 214
Piperno, Franco, 45, 67, 71, 128, 157–183, 292n85; and "Dal terrorismo alla guerriglia," 158–159, 162, 182
Pisanò, Giorgio, 106–115
Pius IX, Pope, and *Qui pluribus*, 21
Pius XI, Pope, and *Non abbiamo bisogno*, 4
Pius XII, Pope, 7, 13
Popolo, Il, 61, 141, 156, 181, 186, 218
Potere Operaio, 45, 55, 56, 123, 125, 127, 145, 157, 160, 168–170, 175, 242, 268
Potere operaio, 54
Pre-print, 158–159, 182, 268
Prima Linea, 138, 268
Priore, Rosario, 43, 116, 138–139, 141–145, 200, 206–210, 221, 248, 286n16; interviews, 294n1, 295n4, 295n10, 296n52

Prison letters, *see* Moro
Propaganda 2 Masonic Lodge, 64, 116,
    152, 174, 180, 203, 205, 209, 220,
    238, 243, 250–253, 268, 300–301n20;
    reports on by P2 Commission, 99–115,
    203; majority report, 100–104, 115;
    minority reports, 104–115
Puzo, Mario, and *The Godfather*, 112

Quaderni piacentini, 54
Quaderni rossi, 54
Quirinale, 220, 268

Radaelli, Ezio, 239
Radical party, minority reports, 95–97,
    104–106
Reagan, Ronald, 102, 151, 177
Rebibbia, 138, 141, 144, 147, 151,
    154, 156, 268
Recchia, Vincenzo Marini, and *Operaz-
    ione Moro*, 294n63
Red Army Faction, 89, 121, 150, 246,
    268
Red Brigades, 2, 23, 111, 116, 120–121,
    221–247, 249, 265–269, 295n21; his-
    tory of, 27; terrorist attacks, 48, 120–
    121, 132–135, 136–137, 148–151,
    196–197; on the University of Rome
    campus, 53–56, 120, 132–134, 142; in
    Turin, 57, 172, 179, 194; the Rome
    Column, 72–74, 76, 138, 161, 179,
    198, 202, 247; in Genoa, 73–75; fac-
    tionalism in, 121, 133–134, 173; Stra-
    tegic Resolution No. 20, 133–135; or-
    ganizational structure of, 198; and the
    Mafia, 233–234, 236; and communist
    culture, 252, 259; murder of Coco,
    254; historical significance of, 259; de-
    mise of, 261
Referendum vote of April 1993, 227
Reformism (in the Communist party),
    133, 173, 179; *see* Enrico Berlinguer
Reggio Emilia, 178–179, 192
Regina, Armando, 5
Republic of Salò, 101
Republican Constitution of 1948, 39
Republican party (PRI), 100, 224
Republican party (of USA), 109

Resistance, 12, 13, 172, 192–193, 268
Rerum novarum, 7
Rete (training unit of the Red Brigades),
    145–146, 198
Revolutionary culture, 147, 162, 190–192
Ricci, Domenico, 44, 128, 207
Ricci, Maria, 88
Riina, Totò, 235, 297n13
Rivera, Giulio, 44, 207
Rizzoli Publishing Company, 102, 113
Rognoni, Virginio, 153, 249
Rosati, Luigi, 123
Rossa, Guido, 192
Rossanda, Rossana, 152, 243, 298–
    299n34
Rosso, 291n60
Ruffilli, Roberto, 23, 196–197, 271n8
Rumor, Mariano, 22, 194

Sabato, 217
Saetta (Franco Piperno), 169
Salazar, Antonio de Oliveira, 14
Salvini, Lino, 101–102
Salvo, Ignazio, 235
San Benedetto Val di Sambro bombing,
    122
San Giorgio in Velabro bombing, 237
San Giovanni in Laterano bombing, 237
Sandalo, Roberto, 138
Santiapichi, Severino, in the first Moro
    trial, 47–51, 54, 56–60, 62–63, 67–
    69, 71–75, 77–81, 82, 124, 129–131,
    251, 258, 277n4; in the *Metropoli*
    trial, 161–166, 168, 175, 181–183;
    in Moro quater, 221–223, 224, 243–
    245, 247–248; interviews, 256,
    276n20, 277n58, 277n65, 277n3,
    278n20, 279n55, 280n68, 297n58,
    299n35, 300n10
Santoro, Raimondo, 4–5
Saronio, Carlo, 169
Sartre, Jean-Paul, and *Critique of Dia-
    lectical Reason*, 190
Savasta, Antonio, 49–53, 56, 57, 77,
    79, 89, 91–92, 93–94, 98, 129, 142,
    145–146, 148, 174, 200, 202
Scalfaro, Oscar Luigi, 148, 237
Scalzone, Oreste, 118, 168, 197

Schleyer, Hans Martin, 246
Sciascia, Leonardo, and *Todo Modo*, 24, 287n38; and Moro Commission report, 95–97, 210; and *L'affaire Moro*, 95–97, 210, 255, 260; on Catholic culture, 96
Scottoni, Franco, 296n56
Secret services, foreign, 47, 89–90, 101, 106, 210, 216, 217, 267; Italian, 22, 47, 101, 200, 210, 216, 217, 219, 220–221, 238, 243, 244, 250–251, 260, 268; in the P2 Commission reports, 99–115; Bonisoli on, 180
Seghetti, Bruno, 54, 142, 146, 148, 200, 206–207
Semeria, Giorgio, 144–145
Senate, 232, 267
Senza tregua, 146
Senzani, Giovanni, 134, 140, 252
Setti Carraro, Maria Antonietta, 239
Sforza, Carlo, 15
Siemens Company, 150
Signorile, Claudio, 63, 67–68, 69, 71, 160
Silone, Ignazio, 7
Simpson, Keith, 114–115
Sindona, Michele, 102, 105–114, 138, 213, 283n34, 284n43
Sinistre di Base, 19
Siri, Giuseppe, Cardinal, 21
Social revolution in Italy, 19–20, 23, 171, 197
Socialist party (PSI), 7, 13, 92, 94, 120; and the "opening to the left," 19–22; and the Communists, 20; defeat in 1976, 29; and Craxi, 35; and the Moro kidnapping, 52, 64, 67–68, 69, 72; defends the trattativa ("humanitarian") line, 83, 93–94, 188–189; and the P2 Commission reports, 100; Red Brigades on, 133; and the *Metropoli* trial, 175, 177, 182; demise of, 227; reaction to "Il caso Moro," 287–288n38
Society for the Propagation of Faith, 108
Sofaer, Abraham, 298n21
Sorichilli, Sergio, 138, 144, 148–149, 154–156, 166, 175–176, 184, 186, 198–203
Sossi, Mario, 68, 166, 179, 269, 281n29

South Africa, 137
Soviet Union, 20, 27, 47, 60, 77, 89, 101, 143
Spadaccini, Teodoro, 56
Spadolini, Giovanni, 100, 113, 136
Spanish Civil War, 101
SS *(Schutzstaffel)*, 101
Stalin, Joseph, 20, 26, 27, 143, 145, 192, 219
Stalinism, 32
Stammheim Prison, 194
Star Wars, 136, 151
Statuto dei Lavoratori, 120
Sterpa, Egidio, 97–98
Strategic Resolution No. 20 (Red Brigade document), 133–135, 136
Studium, 6–7, 269
Switzerland, 111, 193
Synagogue (Rome), 207

Taiwan, 111
Taliercio, Giuseppe, 52, 91–92
Tambroni, Fernando, 21
Tangentopoli, 32, 41, 206, 224–230, 232, 237, 240, 269
Tarantelli, Ezio, 132–133, 135, 137, 140, 196
Tartaglione, Giuliano, 76, 130
Tedeschi, Mario, 186–187
Teodori, Massimo, 104–106
"Teresilla," 294–295n2
Terrorism, 132, 157–159, 177, 189–191, 195, 196–197, 199, 202, 210, 215, 229, 234, 237, 253, 258–259, 261, 267, 268; *see* Red Brigades
Tisserant, Eugene, Cardinal, 108
Tobagi, Walter, 258
Togliatti, Palmiro, 7, 27, 172, 192
Tolfa, Rocco, 217
Tosches, Nick, and *Power on Earth: Michele Sindona's Explosive Story*, 283n34 and n35, 284n43
Trapani, Maria, 121
Trastevere, 175
Trattativa line, 63, 67, 68, 69, 70, 71, 73, 83, 90–91, 92–94, 115, 118, 157, 175, 177, 182, 184, 187–188, 195, 257, 259, 269

Trials: Moro 1, 41–42, 43–81, 82, 83, 84, 90, 100, 115c, 131, 142, 200, 248, 251, 295n10, 296n53; Moro bis, 43, 46–47, 142; appeal trial for Moro 1 and bis, 115, 116–135; Moro ter, 63, 136–156, 166, 175—176, 178, 181, 184–187, 192, 198–203, 248, 291n68; appeal trial for Moro ter, 297n59; *Metropoli* trial, 156, 157–183, 185, 194, 289n12, 290n42, 292n85; Moro quater, 205, 206–210, 221–223, 224, 240–248, 288n57, 298n34
Tribonian, 36
Trilateral Commission, 117
Trotsky, Leon, 54

Uffizi Gallery bombing, 237
Unità, l', 75, 155, 212, 215, 217
Unità Comuniste Combattenti (UCC), 223
United Nations, 65
United States, 12–15, 17, 54, 269; and Israel, 47, 90, 211; and P2, 101–103, 105–111, 204, 253; Red Brigades on, 117, 134, 136–137, 149–150, 151; Moro carteggio on, 214–215; and Gladio, 218; compared with Italy, 225–226; influence in Italy, 226; and Andreotti case, 298n21; and the Pieczenik mission, 300–301n20; *see* Moro and the United States
University of Alberta, 161
University of Rome, *see* Red Brigades
University of Siena, 147

Vacarius, 37
Vale, Giorgio, 122
Valiani, Leo, 61
Valiante, Mario, 63, 82
Varisco, Antonio, 76
Vatican, 188; Neofascist party on, 107–115

Vatican Bank, 108, 114
Via Caetani, 207–208, 211, 269; *see also* Moro
Via delle Botteghe Oscure, 207
Via dei Prati dei Papa holdup, 148–149
Via Fani attack, 206–207, 211, 236, 241, 242, 245, 247–248, 269, 286n16, 299n34; *see also* Moro
Via Gradoli controversy, 66, 203
Via Montalcini 8 (People's Prison), 139, 176, 200, 207–208, 244–248, 255, 260, 262, 269, 298–299n34, 299n40, 300n19
Via Monte Nevoso (Red Brigade archive), 156, 236, 238–239, 269, 278n10; *see also* Moro carteggio
Via S. Angelo in Pescheria, 208
Viminale Palace, 104, 209, 269, 300–301n20
Vitalone, Claudio, 278n24
Vittorini, Elio, 7
Volonté, Gian Maria, and "Todo Modo," 24, 287n38; and "Il caso Moro," 287n38
Volpe, John, 214

Warren Commission Report, 255
Warsaw Pact, 31
Watergate, 110
World War II, 6, 101, 105, 107, 192, 193, 214, 219, 226, 252, 268

Zaccagnini, Benigno, 31, 35, 61, 84, 258–259, 262; in the Moro carteggio, 213
Zedong, Mao, 50, 53, 72, 143, 145, 179
Zionism, 136–137
Zimmerman, Ernst, 150
Zizzi, Francesco, 44, 207
Zupo, Giuseppe, 277n4; and *Operazione Moro*, 277n4, 294n63